ANIMAL LAW AND THE COURTS: A READER

By

Taimie L. Bryant
Professor of Law
University of California at Los Angeles School of Law

Rebecca J. Huss
Professor of Law
Valparaiso University School of Law

David N. Cassuto
Professor of Law
Pace University School of Law

AMERICAN CASEBOOK SERIES®

Mat #40707608

American Casebook Series and West Group are trademarks
registered in the U.S. Patent and Trademark Office.

© 2008 Thomson/West—Compilation
        610 Opperman Drive
        St. Paul, MN 55123
        1–800–313–9378

© 2008—Text, individual contributors

Printed in the United States of America

ISBN: 978–0–314–19025–3

TEXT IS PRINTED ON 10% POST
CONSUMER RECYCLED PAPER

For Mr. Bob Barker,
whose generous gifts to law schools
throughout the United States
have laid a strong foundation for
teaching and scholarship about
animal protection law

*

Preface

Interest in the study of animal law is increasing throughout the United States. At least ninety law schools currently offer a course on the subject and more are considering adding a course in animal law to their curricular offerings. Although many of the contributors to this book began teaching animal law long before it became an established field, recent growth in the number of law schools offering courses in animal law is due in large part to the persistence of students interested in studying the subject. Surely some of that interest is borne of increasing general public awareness of the conditions under which animals are commodified and exploited in our society. Exposés of extremely intensive confinement and sordid conditions at factory farms and puppy mills are becoming more common. Legal issues related to the ownership of companion animals are also arising with greater frequency and complexity. In fact, there are more legal challenges of every kind, including legal actions to require the transfer of zoo elephants to sanctuaries, to reform animal shelter practices to save the lives of homeless animals, and to ban the production of cruelly produced food items such as foie gras.

This diversity of legal activism is dynamically connected to scholarship that explores the subject of how laws should be shaped to prevent and address harms inflicted on animals. A sense of urgency permeates animal law scholarship and practice because of the extent and nature of human-inflicted animal suffering, yet there is considerable disagreement about how laws should be structured or enforced and about the role of legal theory in guiding choices of legal advocacy. This book offers a small slice from the rich variety of animal law scholarship and practice to reveal the range of work that exists within the field. Contributing authors approach animal law from a variety of perspectives from the theoretical to the practical, while remaining grounded by judicial opinions about specific disputes.

In order to accomplish these goals with an accessible format and length, the book follows some writing and formatting conventions, including the use of endnotes instead of footnotes to discourage the inclusion of substantive material outside the body of the chapter itself. We also followed uniform stylistic rules for the editing of judicial opinions. In many cases, authors have deleted footnotes without indication of that deletion other than that the remaining footnotes retain their original numbering. Similarly, unless necessary to provide citation for a direct quotation within the judicial opinions, citations have also been deleted without explicit indication of deletion. Where text has been deleted, deletions are indicated with asterisks (* * *). When authors thought it necessary to briefly explain the content of deleted material, editors used italicized text enclosed with brackets. Grammatical and spelling errors in the original judicial opinions were not corrected.

Special problems arise during production of a book to which many authors contribute. Those problems were ably addressed by Vicki Steiner, Assistant Director of the Scholarly Support and Research Assistant Program of the UCLA Law Library. Ms. Steiner personally participated in the editing and formatting of this book, in addition to supervising the work of others in the Library who were involved in manuscript preparation. The book was significantly improved by her conscientious and thoughtful attention to the form and substance of the book and of each chapter. Thanks are due also to Steven Sarno at Pace Law School for his research and editorial assistance with Chapter Six and to Dennis Lyday at UCLA for his editorial assistance with Chapter Three.

This book was made possible by Mr. Bob Barker's generous gift to UCLA Law School for the purpose of teaching and scholarship in the field of animal protection law. Funds from the Barker gift enabled contributors to meet at UCLA Law School for a workshop to discuss the book project as a whole and the authors' individual chapters. Funds from the gift also defrayed costs of preparing the book manuscript for submission. But Mr. Barker's gift has provided more than the financial means to produce this book; Mr. Barker's optimism about law as a means to help animals inspired the very decision to bring together many of the scholars who have labored over the years to develop animal law as a respected field of academic inquiry. All of us appreciate his support and confidence in our field.

TAIMIE L. BRYANT

Introduction

The field of animal law contains diverse subjects and philosophical perspectives about the legal relationship between humans and animals. This book brings together contributions by nine authors who have taught and published in the field for many years. Each chapter begins with one or two judicial opinions to serve as a prism refracting various features of animal law. While each chapter reflects distinctive views, each is infused with hallmark characteristics of animal law: the status of animals as the legal property of animals, the limitations of current state and federal law to provide even minimally meaningful protection to animals, and the relationship of cultural attitudes and practices to legal structures that inhibit attempts to protect animals from human sources of suffering and death.

Chapter One introduces a primary organizing concept of animal law: the status of animals as the legal property of humans. Professors Francione and Charlton discuss the implications of that legal status as well as attempts by legal advocates to work within or eliminate it. They also describe their efforts in the Rutgers Animal Law Clinic to engage students in legal advocacy projects whose ultimate goal is an end to the legal status of animals as the property of humans. Their chapter reveals the deep inscription in our culture and laws of the property status of animals and the difficulty of choosing advocacy projects that resist further entrenching of that status.

All states have anticruelty statutes which criminalize as cruel some human conduct that causes animals to suffer and die. Cities and counties also sometimes enact anticruelty ordinances that purport to reinforce or extend the protective reach of state anticruelty statutes. In Chapter One, Professors Francione and Charlton introduce readers to the limitations of anticruelty statutes operating in the context of animals as the legal property of humans. In Chapter Two, Professor Cassuto analyzes judicial review of anticruelty statutory provisions that a municipality enacted to prohibit ritual animal sacrifice. Although two lower courts upheld those municipal provisions, the United States Supreme Court decided that the specific laws at issue in the litigation impermissibly targeted a particular religious group. Professor Cassuto's analysis of the Supreme Court's opinion considers how anticruelty laws can be framed both by reference to cultural conceptions of animals and by reference to their interplay with other laws, such as the U.S. Constitution. When religious practices harm animals, substantial, non-incidental limitations on those religious practices must be justified as narrowly constructed to serve compelling governmental interests. Among other issues, Professor Cassuto considers the question of whether protection of animals from human-inflicted suffering is or can be a compelling governmental interest—a question that has an impact on many aspects of animal law.

One of the areas that Professor Cassuto discusses with reference to the question of the public's interest in protecting animals is that of animals raised and killed for human consumption as food. His discussion of that complex issue provides an excellent segue to Chapter Three, in which authors Mariann Sullivan and David Wolfson discuss New Jersey legislation requiring that state's Department of Agriculture to promulgate standards of "humane" farming practices. Farmers and producers who use farming practices designated as "humane" would be protected from prosecution under New Jersey's anticruelty statutes. Equally important to their analysis of the law (and what went wrong with its interpretation by the New Jersey Department of Agriculture and then the court) is Sullivan and Wolfson's description of changes in farming practices themselves that have intensified the suffering of animals over time. An increasing number of animals is suffering and suffering in more profound ways. Awareness of this fact motivates activists to seek legal reform, but seeking reform through criminal anticruelty statutory means is problematic. Sullivan and Wolfson argue that a regulatory approach to reform may be preferable in some instances.

Similarly, in Chapter Four, Professor Favre takes issue with the use of criminal anticruelty statutory amendments to create duties on owners of animals to provide veterinary medical care and to criminalize owners' failures to provide such veterinary medical care. Professor Favre notes an apparent trend in such amendments but argues that a civil law approach designed to increase the access of animals to veterinary medical care is preferable to criminalizing the failures of owners to provide such care. Favre mentions many problems with a criminal law approach if the goal is to secure increased veterinary care for animals: an owner's possible financial inability to provide care, owners' ignorance concerning when an animal needs veterinary medical care, and the fact that criminal proceedings take place, if at all, only after an animal has already suffered from lack of care and it is too late to benefit the animal. He proposes a noncriminal legal structure that would educate owners about animals' needs and provide access to veterinary care while animals can still benefit.

Although Professor Favre's proposal is not necessarily limited to the provision of veterinary care to companion animals, it is most likely to be considered in that context. Indeed, much of the actual practice of animal law concerns companion animals. One reason for that is severe limitation on who can sue on behalf of animals (legal standing); owners of companion animals readily meet standing requirements when they sue to protect their animals or to redress harms to their companion animals. Another reason for a focus on companion animals in animal law is that they are the living nonhuman animals with whom most people have the most frequent contact. In Chapter Five, Professor Huss addresses legal problems associated with people's ability to share their homes with companion animals. In an increasingly urban society, serious consequences for humans and companion animals flow from the legal right of homeowners' associations and landlords to prevent occupancy by people with companion animals. In fact, for companion animals, denial of access to housing with their companion humans can be a death sentence in an animal shelter or veterinary clinic. Professor Huss discusses housing discrimination from a number of perspectives that reveal the significant pragmatic difficulties in practicing law to protect both humans' and companion animals' interests in sharing the same household.

Just as Chapter Five introduces readers to the actual nuts and bolts of practicing animal law in the context of companion animals, Chapter Six, authored by Professor Reppy, guides the reader through the practical details of how attorneys may assist their clients to provide for their companion animals after those clients' deaths. Professor Reppy describes advances for animals in the form of judicial invalidation of will directives to kill companion animals upon the deaths of their owners, if a viable adoption alternative exists. But he also describes unnecessary hurdles placed in the path of owners who wish to provide for the care of their companion animals after they, the owners, have died. Professor Reppy argues that misapplication of the arcane Rule Against Perpetuities resulted in unnecessary judicial invalidation of pet trusts. Although state legislatures have enacted laws to permit honorary or express trusts to provide for animals, judicial resistance requires practicing attorneys to navigate complex rules of trust law. Indeed, no other chapter in this book provides as detailed a view of the perseverance and intelligence an attorney must exercise to help animals in a particular context of complex law seemingly designed to thwart such efforts. If this is the kind of difficulty that attends helping the very animals our society claims to care about—companion animals—imagine the difficulty that attends helping the animals our society cares the least about—animals deemed to be "pests."

Chapter Seven begins with contrasting images of kangaroos in Australia. Revered as a national symbol yet mercilessly killed as pests, kangaroos are but one example the chapter considers of animal species subjected to lethal population control methods when humans believe that members of those species have become too numerous. Most often it is humans who have caused the circumstances that lead to apparent population pressure. Then, instead of addressing their own conduct in ways that would restore population stability through nonlethal methods, humans engage in two conceptual moves: they label as "pests" members of the "overabundant" animal species; and they claim that killing those animals is beneficial for the targeted animal species or another animal species. Like other chapters in this book, this chapter considers advocacy strategies that advance or harm the interests of animals while also underscoring how far removed our current society is from providing meaningful protection to animals. Also, like other chapters in this book, this chapter reveals the extent to which courts deal only with narrow legal questions when responding to legal disputes that actually involve much broader questions about humans' conduct that causes severe harm to animals.

TAIMIE L. BRYANT

Summary of Contents

*

Table of Contents

Table of Cases

References are to pages. Cases cited in principal cases
and within other quoted materials are not included.

*

ANIMAL LAW
AND THE COURTS:
A READER

*

Chapter 1

THE ABOLITION OF THE
PROPERTY STATUS
OF ANIMALS

STATE OF MISSOURI v. A.H. BOGARDUS
4 Mo.App. 215 (Mo. Ct. App. 1877).

HAYDEN, J., delivered the opinion of the court.

The complainant in this case charges that the defendant "did unmercifully kill certain living creatures by shooting them with a shotgun, for the purpose of displaying his skill as a marksman, to wit, twenty-five pigeons, contrary to the form of the statute," etc. The defendant was arrested and held to bail on the charge, tried, convicted, and fined $50, and has appealed to this court.

The question in the case involves the construction of the act to be found in the Session Acts of 1874, page 112, entitled, "An act for the prevention of cruelty to animals." It is claimed that an offence was committed under that part of section 1 which provides that "if any person shall needlessly kill any living creature, every such offence shall," etc. The evidence tended to show that at the Abbey Racetrack a man threw up pigeons, two at a time, and that the defendant, in the presence of a number of persons, shot the pigeons in the air, with a gun, to show his skill; that the birds dropped dead when shot; that they were furnished by the owners to be shot at; that pigeons like these are eaten as food, and bought and sold for that purpose; that they were so eaten when shot.

The object of the act is to prevent unnecessary suffering to animals. Human beings are not included under this expression, but with this exception the act, in its terms, is broad enough to cover all creatures. It is not so material, however, to enquire how low in the order of creation the subjects of this act extend, as it is to ask what is needless mutilation

1

or killing, within the meaning of the act. All needs are comparative. The flesh of animals is not necessary for the subsistence of man, at least in this country, and by some people it is not so used. Yet it would not be denied that the killing of oxen for food is lawful. Fish are not necessary to any one, nor are various wild animals which are killed, and sold in market; yet their capture and killing are regulated by law. The words "needlessly" and "unnecessarily" must have a reasonable, not an absolute and literal, meaning attached to them. As it would not be claimed that the angler who catches fish for pastime, and neither sells nor eats them when caught, is within the prohibition of the law, so the marksman who, as an exercise of skill or as a diversion to himself or to others, shoots pigeons, either from a trap or as they fly wild in the woods, does not violate the essential objects of the act. When the prevention of cruelty and suffering is concerned, there is plainly a difference between instantaneous and lingering death. The former is generally, if not always, painless. Yet, in favor of those sports which are considered healthful recreations, and exercises tending to promote strength, bodily agility, and courage, the pain which comes with a lingering death in the lower animals is often disregarded in the customs and laws of humane and highly-civilized peoples. In England an act of Parliament has been passed to restrict vivisection, a practice which has high scientific ends. Yet fox-hunting, which is a cruel pastime, would no doubt be upheld by the common law. It is certainly the policy of every government to encourage those recreations which serve as manly exercises, and yet do not necessarily lead to protracted pain in the lower animals. The efficiency of the services which the citizen is called upon to render to the State, in exigencies, may largely depend on the qualities acquired in manly sports, and from some of the most attractive of these a certain amount of injury to dumb animals seems inseparable.

In the present case there was no mutilation, or any thing approaching to it. The birds were killed in a more humane way than by wringing their necks, which is an ordinary method of destroying life in pigeons, when they are killed merely with a view to their being eaten. Though we think that the 1st section of the act can not properly receive the construction placed upon it by the appellant, by which its operation would be confined to beasts of burden and animals *ejusdem generis*, we are of opinion that in the present case there was no violation of the act, and that the appellant's instruction to the effect that the evidence was insufficient to sustain the charge should have been given. Accordingly, the judgment will be reversed and the complaint dismissed.

All the judges concur.

* * *

LEWIS v. FERMOR
(1887) LR 18 Q.B.D. 532.

CASE stated by justices.

At a court of summary jurisdiction at East Grinstead in Sussex, the appellant prosecuted the respondent under 12 & 13 Vict. c. 92, s. 2, for that the respondent did ill-treat, abuse, and torture five sows.

On behalf of the respondent it was admitted that he had performed the operation of spaying upon the sows in the manner in which that operation is usually performed; and on behalf of the appellant it was admitted that the operation was performed in a reasonably careful and skilful manner; and it was agreed that the only questions were, whether the operation caused pain to the sows; and if it did, whether such pain was necessary or justifiable.

In support of the prosecution it was contended that the operation caused much pain, and was unjustifiable because it was unnecessary, being performed, not for the benefit of the animals themselves, nor for the welfare or safety of the human race generally, but under the pretence only that it saved money to the owner of the sows operated upon, and that this pretence, though unjustifiable if true, had no foundation in fact.

For the prosecution five veterinary surgeons were called as witnesses. They described the operation, which consists in cutting out the uterus and ovaries, and removing them through an incision made in the flank of the sow for the purpose. It was stated that there were many parts of the country in which the operation was not practised. The witnesses said that the operation caused severe pain, and they all concurred in the opinion that it does not benefit the flesh of the animals, but is unnecessary and useless, because the flesh of a sow that is not spayed is deteriorated only during the periods of heat, which come on at regular intervals, and the sow need not be killed at such times, and not until they have passed off, and the flesh has resumed its normal condition.

No evidence was adduced on behalf of the respondent, but it was contended that the evidence adduced by the appellant did not shew that an offence had been committed within the meaning of the statute.

The justices were of opinion that the operation undoubtedly caused pain, but agreed with the contention of the respondent, and dismissed the information.

The question for the opinion of the Court was whether the evidence adduced by the appellant disclosed an offence under 12 & 13 Vict. c. 92, s. 2.

* * *

DAY, J.

This is a prosecution against John Fermor, a veterinary surgeon practising in Sussex, for performing the operation called "spaying" upon five sows. The prosecution was instituted under s. 2 of 12 & 13 Vict. c. 92 (An Act for the more effectual Prevention of Cruelty to Animals), which provides that if any person shall cruelly abuse, ill-treat, or torture any animal, he shall be liable to a penalty. It is contended on behalf of the prosecution that the defendant did cruelly ill-treat, abuse, and torture the sows in question. There can be no doubt that he did inflict pain, and it may be that he inflicted torture, but the question is whether he was guilty of cruelty within the meaning of the statute. The word "cruelly," like many other words, is of uncertain meaning, and is used with different meanings according to circumstances. In the present case we have to ascertain what it means in this section. It is clear that the section does not mean merely inflicting pain, for if that were so the word "cruelly" would be unnecessary. Much pain is often inflicted where the operation is necessary, as for instance in the case of cautery, which is practised on animals, and sometimes on human beings, often with beneficial results. That is torture, and in one sense it may be called cruel; but in my opinion, in this statute the word "cruelly" must refer to something done for no legitimate purpose. Cruelty must be something which cannot be justified, and which the person who practises it knows cannot be justified. It is true that the word "wantonly," which occurred in the earlier Act, is omitted from the Act now in force, but this cannot affect the meaning of the words which are used. Perhaps the word may have been omitted because it was considered somewhat vague. It seems to me that cruelty means the infliction of grievous pain without a legitimate object, either existing in truth or honestly believed in. The defendant here is a veterinary surgeon in Sussex, where it is customary to perform this operation. It is performed upon sows in order to increase their weight and development. It may be an error to suppose that it has such an effect. I do not know how this may be, but that is the reason for the practice. It is believed to be beneficial to owners, and is extensively carried on, though not in all parts of the country. It is possible that one of the witnesses for the prosecution, who describes the operation as unnecessary and barbarous, but states that he himself performs about four thousand such operations a year, might be liable to a penalty; but that is not the case with the defendant, for he must be taken to have performed the operation for the benefit of the owner of the animals.

In my opinion the magistrates have come to a sound conclusion on the evidence before them, and the only conclusion which they could properly arrive at.

WILLS, J.

I am of the same opinion.

No doubt an Act the object of which is to protect animals from cruelty should be fully administered, but on the other hand it is most important, in the interest of the public who are affected by it, that the Act should receive a fair and reasonable construction, so as not to bring within the criminal law people who act honestly and without any evil mind or motive. The difficulty is as to the meaning of the word "cruelly" in the statute. It cannot apply to cases of merely inflicting pain, for many useful and necessary operations cause great pain. I think there must be something of the moral element of cruelty to bring a case within the section. We were referred to *Murphy v. Manning* [2 Ex. D. 307] as an authority in favour of the appellant; but there it was said that there are acts which are cruel in the extreme, in the sense of giving pain, but yet are lawful, because done for a lawful purpose. The question in the present case is whether the act was done for a lawful purpose; and not whether, in point of fact, in the opinion of the tribunal that has to adjudicate, the practice is a good one. For instance, if a man erroneously thinks that a horse has some malady that requires firing, and it turns out after the operation that he has mistaken the malady, and that the real disease from which the horse is suffering is one for which firing would be useless, and that therefore the great suffering which firing must entail has been, in one sense, purposelessly inflicted, can it be said that because he has made an honest mistake he is liable to conviction? If the appellant's contention be correct such a person ought to be convicted, for the operation would be neither necessary nor beneficial to the animal nor beneficial to the owner in making the animal more valuable. I think some meaning must be given to the words which will prevent such an application of the statute. In my opinion the proper view is that if the person who performs the operation entertains an honest belief that what is done will benefit the animal, he is not liable to be convicted. The belief may sometimes be erroneous, but we must be careful that we do not try to teach new, though perhaps improved, views on matters within the area of fair scientific discussion by means of the criminal law. In the present case I think there was ample ground to justify the magistrates in coming to the conclusion that, whether the notion as to the usefulness of the operation is right or not, it is one which may be bonâ fide entertained. When it has become so well known that a practice is wrong that every one must be taken to know it, then no doubt it would be impossible to establish the defence of a bonâ fide belief that it was reasonable; but where there is room for legitimate difference of opinion, the case is otherwise. The distinction was well illustrated by *Penny v. Hanson* [18 Q.B.D. 478], where it was held to be unnecessary to give evidence that the defendant did not believe in the efficacy of fortune-telling in order to justify a conviction for it, for that in the present day it is not possible to suppose that any one can really have such a belief. A century ago it might have been necessary to give evidence upon the point. There was no evidence here to shew that the question whether or not the operation is beneficial is removed from the category of legitimate doubt. The case would have been very different if instead of the present respondent one of the witnesses called for the prosecution had been made the defendant. A gentleman who admits that for payment he performs in the course of a year some thousands of operations which he believes to be at once extremely painful and perfectly useless could have no possible ground of complaint if he were prosecuted, convicted, and severely punished. It is said that the evidence of the appellant's witnesses as to the inutility of the process was uncontradicted. To prove that it is useless, however, is but one step. It sufficiently appeared that there is a very wide-spread belief in its utility, and I feel bound to say that upon the mere question of opinion, the justices were under no obligation to accept or act upon the evidence of persons who admitted that they were in the daily habit of performing for pay an operation in their own judgment both useless and cruel. In the case of the respondent there was no such evidence against him, nor anything to shew that he did not honestly believe the operation to be beneficial.

For these reasons I am of opinion that the justices were right in refusing to convict.

Judgment for the respondent.

ANIMAL ADVOCACY IN THE 21ST CENTURY: THE ABOLITION OF THE PROPERTY STATUS OF NONHUMANS

Gary L. Francione*
Anna E. Charlton**

INTRODUCTION

Nonhuman animals[1] are property. They are things that we own. They are economic commodities. They are, however, a peculiar form of property; unlike cars, stereos, and other things that we own, animals are *sentient*—they, like us, are the sorts of beings who are consciously aware and have sense perception, and who have *interests*. That is, they have preferences, desires, and wants including, and most particularly, an interest in avoiding pain and suffering and in continuing to live.

Protecting animal interests generally requires an expenditure of resources, and because society regards animals as economic commodities, the costs of that protection relative to the economic value of the animal generally provides the limiting principle. Although there are animal welfare laws that supposedly require that we treat animals "humanely" and that we not impose "unnecessary" or "unjustified" suffering on them, these laws do little more than require that we protect animal interests only to the extent that it is economically beneficial for us to do so.

We humans certainly could treat animals better, but generally we do so only when we become convinced that we have been acting inefficiently and that we would derive greater economic benefits if we were to give more protection to animal interests. To go beyond this and to protect animal interests even when we receive no economic benefit would require that we accord some sort of inherent or intrinsic value to animals, which, as property, have only extrinsic or conditional value. The property status of animals presents conceptual and practical difficulties that militate against treating animals as having inherent value and ignores the fundamental issue that our use of animals—however well we may treat them—cannot be justified morally.

In this chapter, we discuss the practical and theoretical problems involved in our characterization of animals as property. We argue that the prevailing practice of "animal law," which does not challenge the property status of animals and instead seeks to integrate animals into traditional property concepts, will only serve to reinforce the status of animals as commodities. We propose that animal advocates should pursue the *abolition* of animal exploitation rather than its *regulation*. We discuss the role that lawyers can play in an abolitionist approach to animal exploitation and we describe the sorts of projects that we pursued at the Rutgers Animal Rights Law Clinic.

ANIMALS AS PROPERTY: EFFICIENT EXPLOITATION

On one hand, we humans treat nonhumans very badly. We impose excruciating pain, prolonged physical and mental suffering, and an often horrible death, on billions of animals every year.[2] On the other hand, we all agree as a moral matter that it is wrong to inflict "unnecessary" suffering on animals, and there are a great many laws that require that we treat animals "humanely" and that explicitly prohibit "unnecessary" or "unjustified" animal suffering.[3] But our moral and legal concerns about animals are limited to our *treatment* of them; we never really question whether our *use* of animals per se can be justified.[4] Animals are things that we own, and both conventional morality and the law assume that our use of animals is legitimate and that the only relevant issue is how we treat them. Most of our animal use cannot be characterized as "necessary" in any morally meaningful sense totally apart from whether our treatment of them is considered as "humane." Indeed, almost *all* of the suffering and death that we impose on animals can be justified only by our pleasure, amusement, convenience, or habit.

For example, we kill over 10 billion land animals every year in the United States for food. No one maintains that it is necessary to eat animals to lead an optimally healthy lifestyle and an increasing number of mainstream health care professionals tell us that animal foods are detrimental to human health. Animal agriculture is a disaster for the environment because it involves a most inefficient use of natural resources and creates water pollution, soil erosion, and greenhouse gasses. The only justification that we have for the pain, suffering, and death that we impose on these billions of animals is that we enjoy eating animal foods, or that it is convenient to do so, or that it is just plain habit. Our use of animals in entertainment and for sport hunting also cannot be considered as necessary. The *only* use of animals that cannot be dismissed as transparently trivial involves biomedical research that will supposedly result in cures for serious human illnesses (many of which are related to our consumption of animal products) and even in this context, which involves a miniscule number of animals relative to our other uses, there are serious questions about the need to use animals.[5]

We focus only on our treatment of animals given uses that are, for the most part, wholly unnecessary. But what does a rule prohibiting "unnecessary" suffering mean when applied to the treatment of property—things that have only extrinsic or conditional value—and where *none* of the suffering is necessary because the uses are themselves trivial and justified only by human amusement, pleasure, or convenience? As a general matter, the law considers as necessary any suffering that is required for animal use; the interests of animals that are protected are those interests—and only those interests—that must be protected in order to use the animal for a particular purpose. We ignore any other interests that the animal may have because protecting those interests will impose costs on our animal use that cannot be economically justified.

Because "necessary" suffering is linked to what is required to facilitate animal use, the standard for "humane" treatment is, not surprisingly, largely determined by what is regarded as customary in the particular industry of exploitation. If we want to know what is needed to use animals for a particular purpose, the best people to consult are those who use them because we assume logically that it would be irrational for them to impose gratuitous harm (and resulting economic damage) on their property. As a result, state anticruelty laws often explicitly exempt the "normal" or "regular" practices of particular institutions of use, such as animal agriculture, and even when these statutes do not contain an explicit exemption, courts have interpreted anticruelty laws to require only normal or customary treatment.[6] Moreover, anticruelty statutes are criminal laws. To the extent that courts, on a case-by-case basis, go beyond the standard that is set by industry, it could be claimed that there was no fair notice as to what actions constitute behavior prohibited by the statute. The industry standard prevents the requirement for "humane" treatment being impermissibly vague.[7]

Consider the two cases that introduce this chapter, which illustrate some of the consequences of treating nonhumans as commodities. In *Bogardus*,[8] the appellant killed pigeons with a shot gun to demonstrate his skill as a marksman and was convicted of violating a statute that made it an offense to "needlessly kill any living creature," which the court interpreted as seeking to "prevent unnecessary suffering to animals." The pigeons were eaten after they were shot, but their use as food was apparently not the primary purpose for killing them.

On appeal, the appellant argued that the statute did not apply to pigeons. The court held that the more relevant question was not the scope of application of the law but the meaning of "needless mutilation or killing." The court considered a number of animal uses—the killing and eating of animals, or catching fish as a pastime but not eating them—that were not necessary but that were unquestionably lawful because "[t]he words 'needlessly' and 'unnecessarily' must have a reasonable, not an absolute and literal, meaning attached to them." The court analogized shooting pigeons "as an exercise of skill or as a diversion to himself or to others" as similar to catching fish that one does eat. The birds were killed when they were shot, and their death was, according to the court, "more humane" than it would have been had their necks been wrung, which was the way they were killed when slaughtered for food.

In dicta, the court distinguished between killing an animal instantaneously, which did not, according to the court, cause suffering (and presumably was not covered by the statute in question) and a lingering death, which, although undesirable, "is often disregarded in the customs and laws of humane and highly-civilized peoples." The court noted that in England, vivisection, "a practice which has high scientific ends," was restricted by statute whereas the common law permitted fox-hunting, "a cruel pastime." The state should encourage activities that involved "manly exercises" that did "not necessarily lead to protracted pain in the lower animals." But "[t]he efficiency of the services which the citizen is called upon to render to the State, in exigencies, may largely depend on the qualities acquired in manly sports," and these may necessarily involve injury to "dumb animals."[9] The court reversed the conviction, holding that there was not enough evidence to sustain the charge.

Bogardus illustrates a number of interesting aspects of our thinking about animals, which, although expressed in 1877, are as relevant today. First, the court clearly drew a distinction between use and treatment. The question of necessity did not apply to use—many of our uses of nonhumans could not be described as "necessary"—but they were not prohibited by a law that seeks to prevent "needlessly" killing animals. Indeed, the court's discussion about English law is fascinating in this respect. The court noted that English statutory law regulated vivisection, a practice that ostensibly cannot be dismissed as trivial, but foxhunting was not prohibited.[10] The court held that we may, by statute, restrict uses that are arguably necessary, but the general interpretation of necessity where animals are concerned did not focus on whether the use itself is necessary. Second, to the extent that the statute applied to treatment, killing that was instantaneous was ostensibly not prohibited by the statute because, according to the court, there was no pain. This reflects the view, discussed below,[11] that animals do not have an interest in continued existence. Third, even in those cases in which death was not instantaneous, the pain and suffering may still be regarded as necessary if the use served some human purpose, including "healthful recreations" that facilitated the development of "strength, bodily agility, and courage." Fourth, the court described nonhumans as "lower animals" and "dumb animals," a view that persists today in the attitudes of those who maintain that humans are cognitively different from humans and that these differences are morally relevant.

In *Fermor*,[12] an English case, the respondent, a veterinarian, spayed five female pigs. The operation, which all five veterinary witnesses testified caused great pain and suffering, involved "cutting out the uterus and ovaries, and removing them through an incision made in the flank of the sow for the purpose." The prosecution argued that the procedure was done only to provide an economic benefit to the owners of the animals by increasing their weight and development and that this was not, in fact, true because the flesh of the sow became deteriorated only during periods of "heat" and thereafter resumed a normal condition. The prosecution also argued that the procedure was cruel even if it did provide an economic benefit to the owners.

Fermor was prosecuted under a statute which, according to Justice Day, "provides that if any person shall cruelly abuse, ill-treat, or torture any animal, he shall be liable to a penalty." Justice Day stated "[t]here can be no doubt that he did inflict pain, and it may be that he inflicted torture, but the question is whether he was guilty of cruelty within the meaning of the statute." An action was "cruel" under the statute only if it involved "the infliction of grievous pain without a legitimate object, either existing in truth or honestly believed in." Fermor practiced in Sussex, where this operation was customarily done to increase the weight and development of the pigs. Justice Day noted that it might be error to think that spaying had this effect, but as the procedure was common in Sussex, it must be assumed that Fermor performed the procedure to benefit the owner of the animals. Therefore, the procedure, although cruel and constituting torture, did not violate the statute because it had a "legitimate object." Justice Day held that the lower court properly dismissed the case against Fermor.

Justice Willis concurred, holding that "there are acts which are cruel in the extreme, in the sense of giving pain" but that are nevertheless "lawful, because done for a lawful purpose." There was no evidence to indicate that Fermor did not believe that the procedure would provide a benefit to the owners. Although the appellant's veterinary witnesses all testified that the procedure had no utility, Justice Willis maintained that there was still a wide-spread belief that the procedure did increase weight and development and there was no evidence that Fermor did not have a good-faith belief that the procedure would benefit the owners of the sows. Therefore, the lower court properly refused to convict Fermor.

Fermor illustrates that we quite explicitly accept that we treat nonhumans in ways that would constitute torture if humans were involved. The issue is not whether the conduct is "cruel" as we would use that term in ordinary discourse, but whether it is "cruel" in that it has no "legitimate object" or "lawful purpose." In this case, the prosecution witnesses testified that the procedure had no utility and was not practiced in all parts of the country. Both Justices accepted that if the practice was common—if it was arguably a "normal" part of animal agriculture—then it served a "legitimate purpose" and provided Fermor with a presumption that he did not act with the intent required for violation of the statute.

ANIMAL WELFARE: RECENT DEVELOPMENTS

There are some animal advocates who, like us, maintain that the property status of nonhumans is not only inherently morally objectionable irrespective of how "humanely" we treat them, but, as a practical matter, means that animal welfare standards will seldom, if ever, exceed that which is necessary to exploit animals in an economically efficient manner. But most animal advocates, and virtually all of the large animal organizations, maintain that despite the property status of animals, we should focus our efforts on improving animal welfare standards. These advocates fall into two broad groups. There are those who do not object to animal use per se but who maintain that we must improve our treatment of animals through better animal welfare laws and standards, and those who claim to regard our use of animals as morally objectionable, but who see improved animal welfare as an incremental means to achieve reduced animal use or even to eliminate animal use in the long term.[13] Organizations such as The Humane Society of the United States ("HSUS") and the Royal Society for the Prevention of Cruelty to Animals ("RSPCA") are in the first group; organizations such as People for the Ethical Treatment of Animals ("PETA") are in the second group. Although these organizations are ostensibly different in terms of their ideologies, they all share the view that it is possible to protect animal interests beyond those necessary in order to exploit animals even if animals remain property, and that supposedly improved animal welfare is a worthy goal.[14] As a result, groups like HSUS and PETA pursue similar campaigns as a practical matter.

It is, of course, possible to achieve protection for animal interests beyond what is necessary to exploit them as economic commodities; it is, however, highly unlikely. Providing a level of protection beyond the standard of efficient exploitation would increase the cost of producing animal products and generate powerful opposition from producers and consumers alike. Producers are happy to address niche markets for "free-range" products and the like, and some affluent consumers are happy to pay higher prices for such products, but any meaningful industry-wide change of standard that would raise prices significantly would be rejected given the prevailing moral ideology that it is acceptable to use animals for human purposes.

A consideration of recent efforts by animal advocates indicates that animal welfare remains firmly rooted in the notion of nonhumans as commodities. For the most part, welfarist campaigns—whether promoted by HSUS or PETA—involve efforts on the part of animal advocates to persuade animal exploiters that by treating animals better, the exploiters will actually benefit economically because the industry standard is not as efficient as it should be. Even a limited review of the animal welfare efforts of the past decade makes clear that there has been no significant shift away from the property paradigm toward recognition that nonhumans have anything other than their extrinsic or conditional value as commodities.[15] If anything, animal advocates have increasingly accepted their role as participants in institutionalized exploitation who, in effect, advise animal exploiters about how to get more value out of their animal property.

For example, Peter Singer, author of *Animal Liberation*[16], cites as an example of a "successful American campaign[]" efforts by animal advocates and organizations, including PETA, that led to agreement by McDonalds to "set and enforce higher standards for the slaughterhouses that supply it with meat" and to provide increased space to hens confined in egg batteries.[17] Singer claims that these actions by McDonalds, which were followed by Wendy's and Burger King, are "a ray of hope" and "the first hopeful signs for American farm animals since the modern animal movement began."[18] PETA claims that "'[t]here's been a real change in consciousness'"[19] concerning the treatment of animals used for food and praises McDonalds as "'leading the way' in reforming the practices of fast-food suppliers, in the treatment and the killing of its beef and poultry."[20]

This supposed "change in consciousness" is, for the most part, no different from the concerns for increasing the efficiency of animal exploitation that motivated the passage in 1958 of the federal Humane Slaughter Act,[21] which was justified primarily by and limited largely to measures that ensured worker safety and reduced carcass damage.[22] The changes praised by Singer and PETA do not reflect any recognition that animals have interests that should be protected even if there is no economic advantage to humans and do not in any way move away from the property paradigm.

The slaughterhouse standards promoted by Singer and PETA were developed by Temple Grandin, designer of "humane" slaughter and handling systems.[23] Grandin's guidelines, which involve techniques for moving animals through the slaughtering process and stunning them, are based explicitly on economic concerns. According to Grandin:

> Once livestock—cattle, pigs and sheep—arrive at packing plants, proper handling procedures are not only important for the animal's well-being, they can also mean the difference between profit and loss. Research clearly demonstrates that many meat quality benefits can be obtained with careful, quiet animal handling.... Properly handled animals are not only an important ethical goal, they also keep the meat industry running safely, efficiently and profitably.[24]

In talking about stunning animals before slaughter, Grandin states that

> [s]tunning an animal correctly will provide better meat quality. Improper electric stunning will cause bloodspots in the meat and bone fractures. Good stunning practices are also required so that a plant will be in compliance with the Humane Slaughter Act and for animal welfare. When stunning is done correctly, the animal feels no pain and it becomes instantly unconscious. An animal that is stunned properly will produce a still carcass that is safe for plant workers to work on.[25]

She maintains that "[g]entle handling in well-designed facilities will minimize stress levels, improve efficiency and maintain good meat quality. Rough handling or poorly designed equipment is detrimental to both animal welfare and meat quality."[26]

In discussing as a general matter the slaughter and battery-cage improvements to which Singer refers, McDonalds states:

> Animal welfare is also an important part of quality assurance. For high-quality food products at the counter, you need high quality coming from the farm. Animals that are well cared for are less prone to illness, injury, and stress, which all have the same negative impact on the condition of livestock as they do on people. Proper animal welfare practices also benefit producers. Complying with our animal welfare guidelines helps ensure efficient production and reduces waste and loss. This enables our suppliers to be highly competitive.[27]

Wendy's also emphasizes the efficiency of its animal welfare program: "Studies have shown that humane animal handling methods not only prevent needless suffering, but can result in a safer working environment for workers involved in the farm and livestock industry."[28] In a report about voluntary reforms in the livestock industry, the *Los*

Angeles Times stated that "[i]n part, the reforms are driven by self-interest. When an animal is bruised, its flesh turns mushy and must be discarded. Even stress, especially right before slaughter, can affect the quality of meat."[29]

This example illustrates how the producers of animal products—working with prominent animal advocates—are becoming better at exploiting animals in an economically efficient manner by adopting measures that may incidentally improve animal welfare but that are intended primarily to improve meat quality and worker safety. This has absolutely nothing to do with any recognition that animals have inherent value or that they have interests that should be respected even when it is not economically beneficial for humans to do so. Any supposed improvements in animal welfare are limited to and justified by economic benefits for producers and consumers. Moreover, large corporate animal exploiters can now point to the fact that animal advocates such as Singer and PETA are praising them for their supposedly "humane" treatment of nonhuman animals. PETA presented its 2005 Visionary of the Year Award to Grandin, who, in PETA's words, "consults with the livestock industry and the American Meat Institute on the design of slaughterhouses!"[30]

There is also serious doubt as to whether these changes actually provide any significant improvement in animal treatment. A slaughterhouse that follows Grandin's guidelines for stunning, prod use, and other aspects of the killing process is still an unspeakably horrible place. Battery hens that supply some of the major fast-food chains may now live in an area that is equivalent to a square of approximately 8.5 inches rather than the industry standard—a square of approximately 7.8 inches—but it would be nonsense to claim that the existence of a battery hen is anything but miserable.

There are other examples of animal welfare as efficient exploitation. For example, HSUS, in conjunction with Farm Sanctuary and other groups, is leading efforts to have conventional gestation crates for pigs banned in favor of larger individual crates or group housing systems employing an electronic sow feeder ("ESF") to reduce aggression at feeding time. HSUS argues that studies indicate that "[s]ow productivity is higher in group housing than in individual crates, as a result of reduced rates of injury and disease, earlier first estrus, faster return to estrus after delivery, lower incidence of stillbirths, and shorter farrowing times. Group systems employing ESF are particularly cost-effective."[31] In addition, "[c]onversion from gestation crates to group housing with ESF marginally reduces production costs and increases productivity."[32] HSUS cites one study showing that "the total cost per piglet sold is 0.6–percent lower in group ESF systems, while the income to the piglet farmer is 8–percent higher, because of increased productivity"[33] and another showing that "compared to gestation crates, group housing with ESF decreased labor time 3 percent and marginally increased income per sow per year."[34] HSUS claims that "[s]avings at the sow farm can be passed onto the fattening farm, where the cost per unit weight decreases 0.3 percent."[35] This will result in a decrease in the retail price of pork and a small increase in demand. HSUS concludes that "[i]t is likely that producers who adopt group housing with ESF could increase demand for their products or earn a market premium."[36] HSUS claims that despite the greater efficiency of alternative production systems, pork producers in the United States are only slowly adopting those economically more desirable systems because of "inertia and producers' lack of familiarity with ESF."[37]

As in the previous example, this animal welfare proposal does not change or in any way adversely affect the status of pigs as commodities; indeed, HSUS and other animal advocates are, like Temple Grandin, arguing that animal exploiters can make more money from their animal property if they make marginal changes in animal welfare. This has absolutely nothing to do with recognizing that animals have value that goes beyond their extrinsic or conditional value as property.

Similarly, HSUS, PETA, United Poultry Concerns, and other organizations, urge that poultry, which are excluded from the federal Humane Slaughter Act,[38] be covered under the Act and killed through "controlled-atmosphere killing" ("CAK"), or gassing the birds with the use of an inert gas or gas mixture, rather than live shackling and electrical stunning. Shackling and stunning, which cause great pain and distress to the birds, "reduce meat quality and yield. Rough handling during shackling and convulsions induced by electrical stunning cause broken bones, bruising, and hemorrhaging."[39] Moreover, "[d]uring electrical stunning, chickens can defecate and inhale water, contaminating carcasses"[40] and "[t]hese factors lead to carcass downgrades and condemnations, decreasing processors' revenue."[41] The economic consequences are significant. "In 2004, 5 million U.S. poultry were condemned, postmortem, due to bruising and contamination, alone."[42]

Although CAK requires a significant capital cost, it "results in cost savings and increased revenues by decreasing carcass downgrades, contamination, and refrigeration costs; increasing meat yields, quality, and shelf life; and improving worker conditions."[43] CAK "results in fewer broken bones and less bruising and hemorrhaging"[44] and "[t]he reduction in carcass defects increases boning yield and deboned meat quality."[45] CAK is so efficient that "[c]onservatively assuming that CAK increases yield only 1 percent, a plant processing 1 million broilers per week with an average dressed carcass weight of 4.5 pounds and wholesale price of $0.80 per pound would increase annual revenue by $1.87 million after adopting CAK."[46] Producers in Britain that have adopted CAK "were able to recoup their capital investment in one year."[47]

Animal advocates claim that although housing egg-laying hens in alternative housing systems "increases total costs due to higher food, labor, and capital costs; less predictable output; and potential losses due to dirty and broken eggs, parasites, and predators. These costs may be partly offset by an increase in production per hen."[48] Moreover, as "[t]here are no close substitutes for eggs ... consumers continue to purchase virtually the same number of eggs, even as prices increase. . . . [P]roducers could, as a group, pass increased costs on to consumers without a loss in profits"[49] and the average annual per capita consumer expenditure would increase $0.65.[50] Again, the considerations are economic. An alternative housing system for egg-laying hens may increase cost but will not decrease profit and consumers will not have to pay much more for eggs. Given increasing claims that non-battery eggs are more healthy, this is not even a situation where it is clear that a willingness to pay more necessarily reflects respect for the inherent value of nonhumans rather than a desire to purchase what is perceived to be a healthier food product. Indeed, most of the supposedly more "humanely" produced animal products are marketed as being "healthier" in that the animals are fed organic grains, not given antibiotics, etc. Therefore, the existence of niche markets for these products may represent nothing more than consumers who believe rightly or wrongly that "natural" animal products are more healthy for humans to consume.

The foregoing represent only a few examples of animal welfare campaigns, but almost all such efforts are based on the economic efficiency of the proposed welfare improvement. It cannot be disputed seriously that animal welfare laws treat animals as economic commodities with only extrinsic or conditional value and, as a result, require that we protect only those animal interests that we must protect in order to exploit animals. It is important, however, not to lose sight of the fact that even if on the rare occasion a particular change goes beyond what is absolutely required for efficient exploitation, the bottom line is that animals will never receive a significant level of protection as long as they are property. Some welfarists claim that despite animals being property, European countries provide a much higher level of animal protection. For example, political theorist and welfare advocate Robert Garner claims that British animal welfare laws are more stringent than in the United States and "[t]he key point is that the explanatory variable cannot be property since in both countries animals are regarded as the property of humans."[51]

To the extent that Garner's claim is true, the practical results are not as great as Garner proposes because animals still suffer horribly in Britain and any differences are marginal at best. Indeed, Garner claims that although there have been "gradual erosions of factory farming," he also acknowledges that "the fundamentals remain."[52] He discusses the regulation of slaughter and claims that although "[i]n theory . . . the suffering of farm animals in the last moments of their lives should be minimal," there are problems that "occur because animal welfare often takes second place to cost-cutting."[53] He acknowledges that the creation of the single market under the European Union "has been detrimental to British animal welfare because animals, or animal products, can be exported to, or imported from, countries whose animal welfare standards are poorer than those in Britain."[54] Although Garner claims that the importance of economic concerns "has begun to wane,"[55] his evidence for this is a relatively short list of claimed animal welfare improvements some of which have not even been enacted and some of which have been enacted but are not enforced.[56] Finally, many of the animal welfare changes that have occurred in Europe have been based on increasing the efficiency of exploitation. For example, the adoption of alternatives to crates for sows and calves in Europe has been based on increased productivity and decreased costs. This may indicate that the Europeans are better at figuring out how to maximize the wealth represented by animal property but it does not mean that Europeans are moving away from the property paradigm or deciding to accord greater value to animal interests.

ANIMALS AS PROPERTY: THE MORAL PROBLEM OF ANIMAL USE[57]

Although animals have had the status of property for thousands of years, our current thinking about animals and our bifurcation of the issues of use and treatment are informed by the central assumption of animal welfare—that nonhumans, unlike humans, are not self-aware and do not care *that* we use them but only care about *how* we use them. That is, animals do not have an interest in continuing to live but only have an interest in being treated well for however long they live until we kill them.

The notion that animals are not self-aware is part of a general doctrine, accepted by many for centuries, that animals do not have cognitive abilities similar to humans and are not rational or self-aware, or capable of abstract thought, moral reciprocity, or language use. Until the 19th century, these supposed differences were used to justify denying that issues of use *or* treatment raised any sort of moral or legal issue apart from the effect of animal treatment on our treatment of other humans or their property rights. For example, 18th century philosopher Immanuel Kant (1724–1804) argued that although we did not have any moral obligations to animals because they were not self-aware or rational, we did have moral obligations to other humans and we should not treat animals unkindly because that may make us more likely to be less kind to other humans. The law did not impose any obligations on humans to treat animals in a "humane" way and was concerned only to protect property interests in animals.

This situation changed in the 19th century with the emergence of animal welfare, which sought to bring animals at least part of the way into the moral and legal community. An illustrative and influential promoter of animal welfare was British lawyer and philosopher Jeremy Bentham (1748–1832), who maintained that whether animals were rational or could use language was irrelevant to their moral significance as far as their treatment was concerned. According to Bentham, "the question is not, Can they *reason*? nor, Can they *talk*? but, Can they *suffer*?"[58] Bentham did, however, agree that the cognitive differences between humans and nonhumans were relevant to our use of animals in that animals did not care about whether we used them, but only about how we treated them:

If the being eaten were all, there is very good reason why we should be suffered to eat such of them as we like to eat: we are the better for it, and they are never the worse. They have none of those long-protracted anticipations of future misery which we have.... [and] are never the worse for being dead.[59]

This approach, which separated animal use from animal treatment, made it unnecessary to ask whether the property status of animals could be justified. Because animal use was not per se problematic, there was no need to challenge property status but only to require that the treatment of animals be better regulated. This bifurcation set the stage for the structure of the animal welfare laws that were enacted in Britain and the United States in the 19th and 20th centuries, which did not challenge animal use per se and, as a result, did not challenge the property status of animals, but concerned only the treatment of animal property.

An important reason why animal welfare laws remain firmly in place and are not challenged in any meaningful way is that most people agree with the bifurcation of use and treatment and regard animal treatment as the primary, or, perhaps the exclusive, moral issue. That is, the conventional moral wisdom at least in many western countries is that nonhumans are different from humans in that the former have qualitatively different minds from humans, and are not the sorts of beings who care one way or the other about how long they live but only about whether they are treated well. It is common for people to remark, for instance, that dogs "live in the present" and do not think about the past or the future. If this is an empirically correct statement of canine cognition, then, so the reasoning goes, dogs must not be self-aware in the same way that we, who have memories of the past and expectations of the future, are, and the end of life is not a harm or the same sort of harm for dogs as it is for humans, whose future plans will be frustrated.

This thinking is so deeply entrenched that it pervades even the views of leading animal advocates. For example, Peter Singer adopts Bentham's bifurcation of use and treatment and argues that although we ought to take animal suffering seriously, it is permissible to continue to use animals because, with the possible exception of great apes and, perhaps, some other species, animals do not have a sense of the future and an interest in their lives.[60] According to Singer, "[a]n animal may struggle against a threat to its life," but that does not mean that the animal can "grasp that it has 'a life' in the sense that requires an understanding of what it is to exist over a period of time."[61] He concludes that "in the absence of some form of mental continuity it is not easy to explain why the loss to the animal killed is not, from an impartial point of view, made good by the creation of a new animal who will lead an equally pleasant life."[62] Singer maintains that we can be "conscientious omnivores"[63] if we consume nonhumans who have been raised and killed in ways that accommodate their interests. Like Bentham, Singer maintains that it is not the use per se of nonhumans that raises a moral issue but the suffering of the animals incidental to the use. He argues that it is possible to apply the principle of equal consideration—that we should treat similar interests similarly—to non-human interests in suffering and that it is not necessary to abolish the property status of nonhumans in order to accord them equal consideration.

Tom Regan, author of *The Case for Animal Rights*,[64] purports to support the abolition of animal exploitation and distances himself from Singer's welfare theory. But Regan maintains that although death is a harm for nonhumans, it is not as great a harm as it is for humans because death forecloses more opportunities for satisfaction in the case of humans than it does in the case of nonhumans.[65] Regan's view that death is a qualitatively different harm for nonhumans is uncomfortably close to Singer's view that death is not a harm for most nonhumans, and serves as a non-arbitrary way of distinguishing between humans and nonhumans for the purposes of using nonhumans, which presents a problem for Regan's theory.

The notion that animal use per se does not raise a moral issue because animals have no interest in continued existence is problematic in a number of respects. The theory of evolution maintains that the differences between the minds of humans and nonhumans are quantitative and not qualitative. But even if the cognitive states of humans are, by virtue of our use of symbolic communication, qualitatively different from those of nonhumans, we cannot conclude that nonhumans who are sentient nevertheless lack an interest in continued existence because they have no sense of self. As biologist Donald Griffin has observed, if animals are conscious of anything, "the animal's own body and its own actions must fall within the scope of its perceptual consciousness."[66] We nevertheless deny animals self-awareness because we maintain that they cannot "think such thoughts as 'It is *I* who am running, or climbing this tree, or chasing that moth.'"[67] Griffin maintains that

> when an animal consciously perceives the running, climbing, or moth-chasing of another animal, it must also be aware of who is doing these things. And if the animal is perceptually conscious of its own body, it is difficult to rule out similar recognition that it, itself, is doing the running, climbing, or chasing.[68]

He concludes that "[i]f animals are capable of perceptual awareness, denying them some level of self-awareness would seem to be an arbitrary and unjustified restriction."[69]

Even if nonhumans do not have a sense of the past or future in the same sense that normal humans do, that does not mean that they do not have an interest in continuing to live. There are, for instance, humans who have transient global amnesia, a condition that results in their having no sense of the past or the future, and a sense of self only in the present. Can we say that such humans do not have an interest in continued existence and are indifferent to whether they are used as nonconsenting subjects in biomedical experiments or forced organ donors? We may not understand what death means to a nonhuman, but that is a matter of our epistemological limitations and does not mean that a sentient nonhuman does not have an interest in continued existence or that humans have greater opportunities for satisfaction that are foreclosed by death.

Moreover, sentience is only a means to the end of continued existence. If an organism is sentient, that organism relies on perceptions of pain to signal a danger to the organism. To maintain that a sentient being has no interest in continued existence is to deny that the being has an interest in what sentience is intended to protect.

There may be differences between human and other animals just as there are differences among humans. These differences may be relevant for some purposes. For example, an extremely intelligent person and a mentally challenged person may not be similarly situated for purposes of a scholarship to university. But for purposes of being enslaved, or used exclusively as a resource for others, these two humans are equal in that as an empirical matter both have an interest in not being deprived of their fundamental interests because it will benefit someone else. As a normative matter, most of us think that we should treat these two humans equally in that we ought to use neither as a resource. Indeed, many of us regard the vulnerability of the differently-abled human as creating an even stronger moral claim for our protection and respect.

We cannot continue to justify our use of animals as human property based on some notion that animal use per se does not raise a moral issue unless, of course, we abandon rational thought altogether and claim that our use of animals is a privilege granted to us by God.[70] Singer and others maintain that it is possible to give equal consideration to animal interests even if animals remain property. If animals have an interest in continued existence, then property status necessarily makes equal consideration impossible because our use of them in situations where we would use no humans necessarily denies them equal consideration. Even if animals do not have an interest in continued existence and animal treatment is the only relevant question, the property status of animals will remain a significant obstacle to *any* level of meaningful consideration of animal interests, let alone equal consideration. In short, a continued focus on animal welfare and the treatment of animals determined by property concerns misses the fundamental moral point, is not going to result in any significant improvement in our treatment of animals, and may very well result in a net increase in animal exploitation and animal suffering from increased consumption by a public more comfortable with ostensibly more "humane" animal treatment.

ANIMAL LAW: REINFORCING PROPERTY STATUS[71]

Animal issues have become more prominent both in the legal academy and in law practice, but it is important to understand that, for the most part, what is meant by "animal law" involves attempts to incorporate nonhumans into traditional property doctrines and not to challenge that property status. Animal lawyers litigate disputes about "pet custody" in the context of divorce, wrongful death (as when an airline negligently kills a companion animal during transit), and the negligent conduct of veterinarians resulting in the injury to or the death of companion animals. They assist clients in setting up "pet trusts" through which people provide in their wills for the care of their companion animals after the humans die, and they encourage and assist in the prosecution of cases involving violations of anticruelty laws. Through pursuit of these kinds of legal issues, which "are slowly reaching a critical mass in lower courts,"[72] animal lawyers claim that they are "laying the legal foundation establishing that pets have intrinsic worth" that will serve eventually to "support a ruling that animals are not property but have rights of their own and thus legal standing."[73]

These sorts of cases and legal issues may, indeed, provide career opportunities for lawyers, but claims that such cases will have any significant impact on the property status of animals are without foundation. Indeed, such cases will only reinforce the property paradigm and not challenge it. For example, the fact that a court enforces a custody agreement involving a nonhuman is no different from the court enforcing an agreement about the shared use of a car. Awards for amounts that exceed fair market value in wrongful death cases or veterinary malpractice cases do nothing more than recognize that market value is not an adequate measure of compensation in cases in which an owner accords greater value to the property for idiosyncratic reasons. Courts have long recognized that market value may not be adequate in the case of certain types of "unique" property, such as heirlooms, and analogizing nonhuman companions to heirlooms certainly does not mean that the nonhuman is any less property than is the heirloom. Given that anticruelty laws apply only to the miniscule portion of animal uses that fall completely outside the considerably broad scope of permissible institutionalized animal exploitation, it is difficult to see how a few more cruelty prosecutions are going to do anything to affect the property status of nonhumans. Finally, the fact that some states now permit trusts for pets is not likely to lead to a change in the legal status of animals or the recognition that nonhumans have inherent value as a general matter. It is certainly desirable to allow the owners of animals to provide for their animals after their deaths, but again, all that amounts to as a legal matter is a recognition that property owners should be able to decide how to devise and bequeath their property as they see fit, including to benefit other property that they own. Allowing pet owners to establish trusts for their pets is no different from allowing humans to establish trusts to maintain a historical building that they own.

In recent years, some animal lawyers have argued that we should accord special legal protection to certain animals based on their similarity to humans.[74] This argument represents what might be called the "similar-minds theory" of the human/nonhuman relationship,[75] which posits that the moral community consists of humans and the animals who are most similar to them in terms of cognition or consciousness. First developed in the context of *The Great Ape Project*,[76] the goal of this enterprise was to recognize moral and legal rights for nonhuman great apes on the basis of their similarity to humans. Subsequent "similar-minds" theories are derivative of that initial effort and are similarly problematic. Any argument that animals who are "like us" should be accorded special treatment begs the question as to why any characteristic other than sentience is relevant for the purpose of having the right not to be treated as a human resource. Removing some animals, such as the nonhuman great apes, from the "thing" side of the person/thing dichotomy on the basis of some arbitrarily chosen "special" human characteristic while leaving the remainder of nonhumans on the "thing" side because they lack that "special" characteristic merely reinforces the speciesist hierarchy that is at the root of the problem.

Finally, there are animal lawyers who maintain that property status can be a *benefit* to animals because that status imposes certain obligations on humans. Some argue that the problem of animal exploitation is not one of legal status but of failure to enforce laws, which, if sufficiently enforced, would adequately protect animals.[77] Another approach maintains that that the legal category of property can itself be manipulated to provide for the protection of animals. For example, if a human holds legal title in an animal but the animal has "equitable title" in herself, then the equitable title can, it is argued, provide a basis in law for protecting the animal and limiting the legal rights of the animal owner.[78]

The problem with this position is that, however it is expressed, it boils down to the view that humans could treat animal property better than they presently do. We have never denied that possibility; we have, however, argued that the commodity status of animals makes such change very difficult and the history of animal welfare "reform" proves our point. The property status of animals benefits animals in the same way that the property status of human slaves benefited them.

SHIFTING THE PARADIGM: THE ABOLITIONIST PERSPECTIVE[79]

The authors maintain that it is the use of animals and not the treatment of animals that ought to be the primary focus of animal advocates and this involves the abolition rather than the regulation of animal exploitation. Just as the abolition of human slavery required that humans no longer be treated as the chattel property of others, the abolition of nonhuman slavery requires that animals no longer be treated as the economic commodities of humans. We maintain that sentient nonhumans, in order to be members of the moral community, must have one right—the right not to be treated as property. That is, their interest in not being treated as a human resource must be respected even if humans would benefit by not doing so. The right not to be treated as a property is a fundamental, pre-legal right.[80] It is a right that can only exist when a critical mass of society rejects *as a moral matter* the notion that nonhumans are economic commodities for human use. The rejection of the property status of animals means, as a practical matter, that we stop bringing domestic nonhumans into existence for human use, including nonhumans brought into existence to serve as human companions, as well as those produced for other human consumption purposes, such as food.

We find unconvincing the three arguments commonly advanced in support of welfare reform. First, welfarists claim that if we do not focus on animal welfare regulation, we, in effect, abandon animals suffering now in favor of concern for the interests of animals not yet in existence. This claim is problematic in a number of respects. As an initial matter, given that animal welfare regulations, whether in the form of legislation or the result of litigation or campaigns to persuade animal exploiters to improve welfare, take a long time (usually years) to obtain, the over-whelming number of nonhumans presently in existence, particularly those who are used for food or food products, will be dead before such improvements come into existence. Therefore, the welfare advocate is, like the abolitionist, working for the future. More importantly, the welfare advocate assumes that welfare regulations actually do decrease animal suffering in significant ways but this is a questionable, and most likely inaccurate, assumption.

Moreover, welfarists ignore the fact that representations by animal organizations that animal exploitation has been made more "humane" will necessarily have the effect of making the public more comfortable about animal use and this militates in favor of continued, and perhaps increased, consumption of animal products. Welfarists state explicitly that we can "'consume with conscience'"[81] and this position, and comments by groups like PETA that McDonalds is "'leading the way'" in reform of fast-food animal agriculture, are giving rise to a "happy meat" movement that reinforces the welfarist notion that it is our treatment of animals, and not our use of them, that is the moral concern.

Second, as mentioned above,[82] some animal advocates claim that welfarist regulation represents an incremental step in the direction of the abolition of animal use. There is, however, no empirical evidence to support the view that regulation of exploitation leads to abolition of exploitation. There have been animal welfare laws for the better part of 200 years and yet we have more animal exploitation today than at any time in human history. Animal welfare laws tend to make people feel more comfortable about animal exploitation and that comfort is not conducive to abolition.

Related to the claim that animal welfare will lead to abolition is the claim that the animal rights movement is analogous to the civil rights movement and that animal welfare laws are, like civil rights laws, attempts to move closer to full equality. This analogy is flawed because civil rights laws seek to ensure that humans *who are already regarded as persons* are treated as equal persons. Civil rights laws cannot be regarded as incremental steps in the eradication of the status of certain humans as chattel property. Although racial discrimination surely persists, we have abolished chattel slavery and that abolition did not result from incrementally more progressive slave welfare laws, but from a paradigm shift in our moral assessment about the propriety of the property status of other humans. If our response to human slavery was to enact supposedly more progressive slave welfare laws, the result would have been to further enmesh slavery into our culture rather than to move in the direction of the abolition. Similarly, supposedly more progressive animal welfare laws and regulations will serve only to reinforce the prevailing paradigm that animals are things that exist for our use, and not to facilitate the abolition of that use.

Third, welfare advocates claim that the abolitionist approach is "idealistic" or "utopian" and cannot provide any normative guidance concerning incremental change in the short term. This assertion is without foundation. The abolitionist approach provides normative guidance in a number of respects.[83]

The most important form of incremental change proposed by the abolitionist position is the decision by the individual to become vegan. Veganism, which involves not eating or using any animal products, is more than a matter of diet or lifestyle. Although for some it is a matter of physical health alone, for most, veganism represents a political and moral statement that the individual accepts the principle of abolition in her own life; it is the recognition that nonhumans have inherent value and the rejection of the property status of nonhumans. The more people who become vegan for ethical reasons, the stronger will be the cultural notion that animals have a moral right not to be treated as commodities. If we are ever going to effect any significant change in our treatment of animals and to one day end that use, it is imperative that there be a social and political movement that actively seeks abolition and regards veganism as its moral baseline. As long as a majority of people think that eating animals and animal products is a morally acceptable behavior, nothing will change. There may be a larger selection of "happy meat" and other fare for affluent "conscientious omnivores," but that situation is no different from the slave owner who beat his slaves less often or less harshly.

We are amazed and disconcerted at the large number of animal advocates we meet who say that they are "vegetarian but not vegan." Although it seems that "vegetarian" is used loosely, the general distinction is between those who do not eat the flesh of cows, pigs, and birds, but who eat some other animal products, such as fish, dairy products and eggs, and those who do not eat any flesh or any animal products, including dairy products or eggs. Vegans also do not wear clothing made from animals, or use personal care products that contain animal ingredients.

There is no coherent distinction between flesh and dairy or eggs. Animals exploited in the dairy or egg industries live longer, are treated worse, and end up in the same slaughterhouse as their meat counterparts. There is as much if not more suffering in dairy or egg products than in flesh products, but there is certainly no morally relevant distinction between or among them. To say that one does not eat beef but drinks milk is as silly as to say that one eats flesh from large cows but not from small cows. Moreover, there is also no morally relevant distinction between a cow and a fish or other sentient sea animal for purposes of treating either as a human resource. We may more easily recognize the pain or suffering of a cow because, like us, she is a mammal. But that is a matter of our cognitive limitation and does not change the fact that fish and many sea animals are subjectively aware.

Most national animal advocacy organizations focus on animal welfare even if they also advocate veganism. An excellent example of this is PETA. On one hand, PETA claims to encourage veganism. On the other hand, PETA's campaigns are, for the most part, focused on traditional welfare regulation. We discussed above PETA's campaign to get fast-food restaurants to adopt Temple Grandin's slaughter guidelines, which are explicitly aimed at increasing the profitability of corporate exploiters. Another example—and there are many—is PETA's support for Whole Foods, Inc., a large international supermarket chain, which sells organic and "natural" foods, including a great deal of flesh, dairy products, and eggs. According to PETA, which gave Whole Foods a PETA Progress Award in 2004,

> Whole Foods has consistently done more for animal welfare than any retailer in the industry, requiring that its producers adhere to strict standards. Recently, Whole Foods launched the Animal Compassion Foundation. John Mackey, the chair, CEO, and cofounder of Whole Foods Market, observed, "By creating the Foundation, Whole Foods Market is pioneering an entirely new way for people to relate to farm animals—with the animals' welfare becoming the most important goal."[84]

It is important to note that there is a serious question as to whether the "strict standards" that PETA praises have any meaningful effect on the lives and deaths of the animals whose corpses are sold at Whole Foods or anywhere else.[85] However, even putting that question aside, this sort of approach can only encourage confusion where there should be clarity, and encourages people to believe that we can consume "happy meat" as "conscientious omnivores," which serves to perpetuate—and legitimate—the consumption of animal products. Perhaps this is why half of the PETA membership is not even vegetarian.[86] Moreover, to the extent that animal advocates continue to support the consumption of animal products as the "normal" or "default" position, they necessarily keep veganism marginalized and support its characterization as "radical" and "extreme," or as a mere matter of lifestyle choice, rather than as a non-negotiable moral baseline.

Veganism and creative, positive vegan education provide practical and incremental strategies both in terms of reducing animal suffering now, and in terms of building a movement in the future that will be able to obtain more meaningful legislation in the form of prohibitions of animal use rather than mere "humane" welfare regulation. If, in the late-1980s—when the animal advocacy community in the United States decided very deliberately to pursue a welfarist agenda—a substantial portion of movement resources had been invested in vegan education and advocacy, there would likely be many hundreds of thousands more vegans than there are today. That is a very conservative estimate given the tens of millions of dollars that have been expended by animal advocacy groups to promote welfarist legislation and initiatives. The increased number of vegans would reduce suffering more by decreasing demand for animal products than all of the welfarist "successes" put together.[87] Increasing the number of vegans would also help to build a political and economic base required for the social change that is a necessary predicate for legal change. Given that there is limited time and there are limited financial resources available, expansion of traditional animal welfare is not a rational and efficient choice if we seek abolition in the long term. Indeed, traditional animal welfare is not an effective way of reducing animal suffering in the short term as well.

Moreover, it is important for animal advocates to be engaged in efforts to educate society at all levels and through all media about animal exploitation and the moral basis for its abolition. At the present time, the prevailing moral norm, reflected in the law, is that it is morally acceptable to use nonhumans for human purposes as long as animals are treated "humanely." As a result, the social debate focuses on what constitutes "humane" treatment and many advocates spend their time trying to convince members of the public that larger cages are better than smaller cages, or that gassing chickens is better than stunning them. The debate should be shifted in the direction of animal use and the indisputable fact that humans have no coherent moral justification for continuing to use nonhumans, however "humanely" they are treated. This requires that advocates educate themselves about the ethical arguments against animal use and that they engage in creative ways to make those arguments accessible to the general public. Given that most people accept that nonhumans are members of the moral community in some sense—that is, they reject the notion that animals are merely things—it is challenging, but not impossible, to get people to see that membership in the moral community *means* that we stop using animals altogether.

A useful strategy in this regard is to employ something presently in the media that illustrates our "moral schizophrenia" about animals. For example, when football player Michael Vick was publicly excoriated for his involvement with dog fighting, it provided an excellent opportunity to ask those who were outraged by Vick's actions—and that was just about everyone—what they saw as the difference between what Vick did and what the rest of us do when we use animals for food or entertainment, such as rodeos? This approach focused the debate away from the specific issue of dog fighting and toward the more interesting and troubling question of how those of us who eat animals, or exploit them in other ways, are in any way fundamentally different from Michael Vick.[88]

Advocates do not have to have graduate degrees to be able to engage in effective abolitionist education. They need only have the willingness to learn some fundamental notions about moral philosophy and to think about how to bring those ideas to life in a way that will resonate with the public, much of which does care about animals and is surprisingly receptive to arguments about animal rights and the abolition of animal use.

Some advocates are drawn to single-issue campaigns, such as restrictions on the use of the gestation crate or modification of battery cages. Those campaigns may or may not involve legislation or voluntary industry compliance, but all such campaigns are similar in that they that focus on a particular animal use or aspect of treatment. As we discussed above, we do not think that the traditional welfarist single-issue campaigns promoted by the large, national animal groups, do anything to move nonhumans away from property status and, for the most part, reinforce that status and the cornerstone of welfarist ideology—that animals are "here" to be used by us as long as we treat them "humanely." But grassroots groups often ask us whether single-issue campaigns can ever be consistent with abolitionist ideology. This is a difficult question. We believe that, at least at this point, single-issue campaigns, particularly those that seek legislative change, do not represent a good use of time or resources. There is not sufficient public support for any meaningful change, and the compromise necessary to secure passage of legislation makes it highly unlikely that advocates will succeed in getting anything beyond traditional welfare regulation, which merely make animal exploitation more efficient, economically beneficial, and socially acceptable. To the extent that advocates want to pursue single-issue campaigns, they should at least pursue prohibitions of significant animal uses rather than regulations that supposedly ensure more "humane" treatment, and they should do so in a context that explicitly recognizes the inherent value of nonhumans and makes clear that *no* animal exploitation can be justified morally.[89] A campaign that seeks to stop all animal use in circuses based on the inherent value of animals and as an explicit part of an overall effort to end all animal exploitation may at least represent movement away from the property paradigm in a way that a campaign that seeks larger cages for circus animals does not. A campaign by university students to stop animals being used in the classroom that is part of an overall opposition to vivisection and animal exploitation generally, is better than a campaign that seeks more "humane" treatment for animals used in the classroom. But again, we favor veganism and creative vegan-abolitionist education and advocacy as the primary form of abolitionist incremental change.

Finally, although abolitionist theory says that we should stop bringing domesticated nonhumans—including dogs, cats, and other "companion" animals—into existence, it does not entail that we should not engage in and support efforts to find good homes for those nonhumans who exist now. Rescue and adoption efforts that lead to situations in which nonhumans are accorded inherent value are not analogous to efforts to make animal exploitation more "humane," primarily when the latter is limited, as it almost always is, to situations in which the supposed reform merely makes animal use more economically beneficial and socially acceptable. Spay/neuter programs are consistent with the abolitionist approach, as are programs where feral cats are trapped, neutered, and returned to managed colonies.

THE ROLE FOR LAWYERS IN ABOLITIONIST ADVOCACY:
THE RUTGERS ANIMAL RIGHTS LAW CLINIC[90]

At this point, the reader, likely a law student or lawyer, may ask: "what is the role for the lawyer if we employ the abolitionist approach?" That is a fair question because we have argued previously that the prevailing model of "animal law" will do nothing more than to further embed animals in traditional property doctrines and that traditional animal welfare will rarely move beyond making animal exploitation more economically efficient for animal exploiters.

The lawyer can certainly play an important role in the abolitionist movement, but that role will not focus on pet trusts, pet custody, or veterinary malpractice cases. Rather, the abolitionist lawyer will use her skills to provide much-needed protection to abolitionist advocates as they seek to build a vegan movement and to educate the public about ending animal use rather than regulating it. For a decade, we had an enterprise in which we attempted to develop an approach to "animal law" consistent with the abolitionist model. In 1990, we founded the Animal Rights Law Clinic at Rutgers University Law School in Newark. Rutgers had a long history of an emphasis on clinical legal education taught in the context of furthering progressive social causes including civil rights, women's rights, and the rights of the poor. Students who took the Clinic received six academic credits per semester. Their work was broken down into two components. There was a weekly seminar in which students discussed and debated the relevant moral and legal theories. Our goal in the seminar was to introduce law students, many of whom had no familiarity with philosophy or ethical theory, to the basic concepts so that they were comfortable discussing the meaning of "animal rights" or the differences between rights and non-rights or welfarist approaches. As part of the seminar, we often invited defenders of animal exploitation, such as vivisectors or hunters, to present their viewpoints to the class. Two academic credits were allocated to this part of the enterprise. The remaining four credits required that students learn litigation and negotiation skills in the context of working with us on actual cases.

We took our inspiration from the late civil rights attorney William Kunstler, who, with our late colleague at Rutgers, Arthur Kinoy, founded the Center for Constitutional Rights in New York. Kunstler was a neighbor of ours in Manhattan and was a great friend to the Rutgers Law School community. He was sensitive to animal issues and he wrote the foreword to *Animals, Property, and the Law*. Kunstler maintained that the primary role of a progressive lawyer was to protect the rights of those who were trying to effect social and political change. We did not do any veterinary malpractice cases, or draft any custody agreements or trusts concerning animals. We saw ourselves first and foremost as a resource center to assist organizations and individuals who were pursuing the abolition of animal exploitation. That is, we embraced Kunstler's view, and did not see the role of the lawyer as the primary engine of change, but as providing support to animal advocates who were attempting to educate society about the need to abolish animal exploitation and to engage in lawful actions that undermined the property status of animals. In this sense, our enterprise differed dramatically from the model of "animal law" that maintains lawyers can play the central role through litigation or legislation that will, it is claimed, change the legal status of animals or otherwise compel significant changes in our treatment of nonhumans. We did and continue to believe that animals will remain property and will receive minimal protection until there is a fundamental change in our moral attitudes about nonhumans and we saw our role as providing assistance to those who were trying to effect that change through their educational activism.

Much of the work that we did at the Clinic did not involve litigation but involved advising advocates who were pursuing abolitionist activities and negotiating on behalf of those who were seeking objectives consistent with an abolitionist approach. For example, we assisted groups who were seeking to have peaceful demonstrations to promote some abolitionist objective, such as veganism, or the abolition of the use of animals for particular purposes, such as vivisection, as part of an overall animal rights agenda. These groups would often have difficulties with local authorities in obtaining permission for their protests and we would work with the authorities to get the necessary permits. We advised advocates who were involved in trapping, altering, and returning feral cats to managed colonies as these advocates often encountered problems with local authorities. We also worked with advocates involved in rescue and fostering, and we advised animal shelters on various legal issues. Working with advocates who promoted the abolition of hunting, we assisted in stopping a controversial suburban deer hunt. We helped existing grassroots groups focused on abolitionist goals with a wide range of legal problems and we assisted new organizations in getting established and in obtaining tax-exempt status.[91] We represented advocates who engaged in nonviolent protest at various events, including at the Hegins Pigeon Shoot and other similar events. In all of these cases, the advocates were seeking to abolish the animal use and not make it more "humane." We represented advocates who tried to stop the round-up and removal of wild horses in western states,[92] and advocates who, invoking state access laws, tried to get information about federally-funded experiments involving nonhuman animals.

We advised advocates on legislative matters, and often persuaded these advocates not to pursue legislation that would merely reinforce the property status of animals, or advised them as to how they could make proposed legislation less welfarist. For example, when advocates proposed that treatment be made more "humane," we urged them to seek instead prohibitions on particular types of animal use.

A good part of our efforts involved working with students at all levels (grammar school, high school, college, university, veterinary, medical) who, based on their conscientious objection, did not want to engage in vivisection or dissection as part of their class activities.[93] The only students we represented were those who refused to use any animals for this purpose. For example, if a student were willing to have her lab partner use an animal, or to observe a dissection or use of live animals in a videotape, we would not represent her. In the overwhelming number of the cases, we were able to obtain a satisfactory resolution of these cases by negotiating with the particular school. In several instances, we were forced to litigate and in all cases, the students received acceptable alternatives. These cases were, for the most part, based on the claim of the student to the free exercise of her religious and spiritual beliefs concerning the exploitation of nonhuman animals.

When we represented the human companions of Taro, a dog scheduled to be killed under New Jersey's law concerning dangerous dogs, we (with the permission of our human clients) took every opportunity offered to emphasize in the considerable world-wide media coverage of the case, that the nonhumans that we eat are no different morally than the dogs, cats, and other animals whom we regard as members of our families. We succeeded in persuading Governor Christine Whitman to "pardon" Taro.[94]

Finally, as part of our educational function, we often held workshops and seminars at Rutgers for animal advocates at which we discussed abolitionist theory and practical strategy. We regularly spoke on animal rights and the law at the conferences of large national organizations and we hosted several conferences at Rutgers at which we discussed the relationship between animal rights and other progressive social causes, and effective methods of abolitionist advocacy.

CONCLUSION

As a moral theory, animal welfare rests on the indefensible notion that there are differences between humans and nonhumans that make humans morally superior and justify our use of nonhumans as our property. As a practical strategy for improving animal treatment, animal welfare limits protection to what is required to exploit animal property in an economically efficient manner. To work within the welfarist paradigm means trying to convince pork producers that they will make more money from exploiting pigs if they adopt a production system other than conventional gestation crates, or trying to convince poultry producers that they will profit more if they gas chickens rather than stun them. This *may* have some benefit for the animals, but any benefit is marginal at best and comes at a cost of making the public feel better about animal exploitation. And it has nothing to do with moving toward recognition that pigs or chickens have intrinsic or inherent value.

The alternative is to shift the debate away from issues of treatment and toward an abolitionist approach focused on animal use. This requires a sociopolitical movement committed to veganism as a baseline principle both as an individual expression of the abolitionist position and as a defining educational mission. To the extent that advocates pursue single-issue campaigns, they should seek prohibitions that explicitly recognize the inherent value of nonhumans as part of an overall abolitionist approach. The role of the lawyer is to assist the abolitionist educator-activist in changing the paradigm by facilitating her educational activities and her efforts to prohibit animal uses. "Animal law," understood as a focus on veterinary malpractice, pet trusts, and pet custody issues, anticruelty laws and traditional animal welfare, will not move animals away from property status but will enmesh them further in it.

* Distinguished Professor of Law and Nicholas deB. Katzenbach Scholar of Law and Philosophy, Rutgers University School of Law, Newark.

** Adjunct Professor of Law, Rutgers University School of Law, Newark.

1. Throughout the paper, we use "nonhumans" and "animals" to refer to nonhuman animals. To keep matters in perspective, it is advisable to remember that humans are animals as well.

2. For a discussion of animal use, see GARY L. FRANCIONE, INTRODUCTION TO ANIMAL RIGHTS: YOUR CHILD OR THE DOG? 9–49 (2000).

3. *See generally* GARY L. FRANCIONE, ANIMALS, PROPERTY, AND THE LAW (1995) (discussing animal welfare laws).

4. For a further discussion of the distinction between use and treatment, see the introductory chapter in GARY L. FRANCIONE, ANIMALS AS PERSONS: ESSAYS ON THE ABOLITION OF ANIMAL EXPLOITATION (2008).

5. Even if animal use in vivisection is "necessary" in that it cannot be dismissed as trivial and justified only by human amusement, pleasure, or convenience, animal use in this context cannot be justified morally. *See* Gary L. Francione, *The Use of Nonhuman Animals in Biomedical Research: Necessity and Justification*, 35 J.L. MED. & ETHICS 241 (2007), *reprinted in* FRANCIONE, *supra* note 4, at 170–85.

6. *See* FRANCIONE, *supra* note 3, at 142–56.

7. *See* Darian M. Ibrahim, *The Anticruelty Statute: A Study in Animal Welfare*, 1 J. ANIMAL L. & ETHICS 175, 194–98 (2006).

8. 4 Mo. App. 215 (Mo. Ct. App. 1877).

9. In *Bogardus*, the court denied a motion for rehearing, and Judge Lewis, writing for the court, stated that although he joined the court's initial opinion, he emphasized that the killing of the birds could not be justified by a policy to promote superiority in marksmanship for the benefit of the state because any such skill could be developed without killing animals. Judge Lewis stated that the reversal was required solely because the legislature could not have intended the statute to cover actions which, although not necessary for human sustenance, could not be considered as not necessary "for man's enjoyment of his legitimate dominion over the brute creation" given the prevailing sentiments at the time.

10. It is interesting to note how the British and American animal protection communities have focused on vivisection, a use that cannot be dismissed as transparently trivial, more than they have focused on uses involving much larger numbers of animals where the use cannot be regarded as anything but trivial, such as using animals for food. *See* Francione, *supra* note 5, at 242.

11. *See infra* notes 57–70 and accompanying text.

12. (1887) 18 Q.B.D. 532.

13. For a further discussion of these approaches to animal advocacy, see GARY L. FRANCIONE, RAIN WITHOUT THUNDER: THE IDEOLOGY OF THE ANIMAL RIGHTS MOVEMENT (1996).

14. For a theoretical discussion of how animal welfare reform can supposedly provide significant protection to animal interests even if animals remain as human property, see, for example, ROBERT GARNER, ANIMALS, POLITICS AND MORALITY (2d ed. 2004); MIKE RADFORD, ANIMAL WELFARE LAW IN BRITAIN: REGULATION AND RESPONSIBILITY (2001); Jerrold Tannenbaum, *Animals and the Law: Property, Cruelty, Rights*, 62 SOC. RES. 539 (1995).

15. For an extended discussion of recent developments in animal welfare and how they do not disprove the position that the property status of nonhumans militates strongly against the significant protection of animal interests, see Gary L. Francione, *Reflections on*

Animals, Property, and the Law *and* Rain Without Thunder, 70 LAW & CONTEMP. PROBS. 9 (2007), *reprinted in* FRANCIONE, *supra* note 4, at 67–128.

16. PETER SINGER, ANIMAL LIBERATION (2d ed. 1990).

17. Peter Singer, *Animal Liberation at 30*, N.Y. REV. BOOKS, May 15, 2003, at 26.

18. *Id.*

19. Stephanie Simon, *Killing Them Softly: Voluntary Reforms in the Livestock Industry Have Changed the Way Animals Are Slaughtered*, L.A. TIMES, Apr. 29, 2003, at A10 (quoting Bruce Friedrich of PETA).

20. David Shaw, *Matters of Taste: Animal Rights and Wrongs*, L.A. TIMES, Feb. 23, 2005, at F2 (quoting Lisa Lange of PETA).

21. Humane Methods of Slaughter Act of 1958, Pub. L. No. 85–765, 72 Stat. 862 (codified at 7 U.S.C. §§ 1901–1907 (2000)). The Act originally applied to animals slaughtered for sale to the federal government, but was reauthorized in 1978 and covers animals slaughtered in federally-inspected plants. Humane Methods of Slaughter Act of 1978, Pub. L. No. 95–445, 92 Stat. 1069. For a discussion of the considerations that motivated the Humane Slaughter Act, see FRANCIONE, *supra* note 13, at 95–102.

22. The "Findings and declarations of policy" of the Humane Slaughter Act make clear the importance of economic considerations in assessing matters of animal welfare:

> The Congress finds that the use of humane methods in the slaughter of livestock prevents needless suffering; results in safer and better working conditions for persons engaged in the slaughtering industry; brings about improvement of products and economies in slaughtering operations; and produces other benefits for producers, processors, and consumers which tend to expedite an orderly flow of livestock and livestock products in interstate and foreign commerce.

7 U.S.C. § 1901 (2000).

23. For a discussion of Grandin, see FRANCIONE, *supra* note 13, at 99–100, 199–202.

24. TEMPLE GRANDIN, RECOMMENDED ANIMAL HANDLING GUIDELINES AND AUDIT GUIDE 6 (2007), *available at* http://www.animalhandling.org/ht/a/GetDocumentAction/i/1774.

25. Temple Grandin, Humane Slaughter: Recommended Stunning Practices, http://www.grandin.com/humane/rec.slaughter.html (last visited Oct. 27, 2007).

26. Temple Grandin, Stress and Meat Quality: Lowering Stress to Improve Meat Quality and Animal Welfare, http://www.grandin.com/meat/meat.html (last visited Oct. 27, 2007).

27. McDonald's Corp., Animal Welfare Update: North America (Mar. 3, 2003), http://www.mcdonalds.com/content/corp/values/report/archive/progress_report/north_america.html (Q & A between Bruce Feinberg and Terry Williams).

28. Wendy's, Wendy's Animal Welfare Program Fact Sheet (2007), http://www.wendys.com/community/animal_welfare.jsp.

29. Simon, *supra* note 19.

30. *See* PETA, 2004 PETA Proggy Awards (2004), http://www.peta.org/feat/proggy/2004/winners.html#visionary.

31. THE HUMANE SOCIETY OF THE UNITED STATES, AN HSUS REPORT: THE ECONOMICS OF ADOPTING ALTERNATIVE PRODUCTION SYSTEMS TO GESTATION CRATES 1 (2006), *available at* http://www.hsus.org/web-files/PDF/farm/econ_gestation.pdf (internal citations omitted).

32. *Id.*

33. *Id.* at 2 (internal citation omitted).

34. *Id.* (internal citation omitted).

35. *Id.* (internal citation omitted).

36. *Id.*

37. *Id.* at 1.

38. The United States Department of Agriculture, which enforces the Humane Slaughter Act, interprets the Act to exclude poultry. *See* 9 C.F.R. pt. 313 (2006). Poultry accounts for the largest number of nonhumans slaughtered for food. The exclusion of poultry from coverage under the Act mirrors the exclusion of rats and mice, the nonhumans most used in vivisection, from coverage under the federal Animal Welfare Act, Pub. L. No. 89–544, 80 Stat. 350 (1966), which regulates the use of animals in experiments.

39. THE HUMANE SOCIETY OF THE UNITED STATES, AN HSUS REPORT: THE ECONOMICS OF ADOPTING ALTERNATIVE PRODUCTION PRACTICES TO ELECTRICAL STUNNING SLAUGHTER OF POULTRY 1 (2006), *available at* http://www.hsus.org/web-files/PDF/farm/econ_elecstun.pdf (internal citation omitted).

40. *Id.* (internal citation omitted).

41. *Id.*

42. *Id.* (internal citations omitted).

43. *Id.* at 2.

44. *Id.* (internal citations omitted).

45. *Id.* (internal citations omitted).

46. *Id.*

47. *Id.* (internal citation omitted). For another economic analysis of controlled-atmosphere killing, see PEOPLE FOR THE ETHICAL TREATMENT OF ANIMALS, ANALYSIS OF CONTROLLED-ATMOSPHERE KILLING VS. ELECTRIC IMMOBILIZATION FROM AN ECONOMIC STANDPOINT (n.d.), *available at* http://www.peta.org/CAK/CAK+economic+synopsis+with+letterhead.pdf.

48. THE HUMANE SOCIETY OF THE UNITED STATES, AN HSUS REPORT: THE ECONOMICS OF ADOPTING ALTERNATIVE PRODUCTION SYSTEMS TO BATTERY CAGES 1 (2006), *available at* http://www.hsus.org/web-files/PDF/farm/econ_battery_1.pdf (internal citations omitted).

49. *Id.* at 2 (internal citation omitted).

50. *Id.* (internal citations omitted).

51. Robert Garner, *Animal Welfare: A Political Defense*, 1 J. ANIMAL L. & ETHICS 161, 171 (2006).

52. GARNER, *supra* note 14, at 118.

53. *Id.* at 112.

54. *Id.* at 204.

55. *Id.* at 264.

56. For example, in Britain, hunting foxes with dogs is supposedly prohibited but the ban is being evaded in numerous ways. *See Calls to Scrap 'Derided' Hunting Ban*, BBC NEWS, Feb 18, 2006, http://news.bbc.co.uk/2/hi/uk_news/4726566.stm.

57. For a further discussion, see Gary L. Francione, *Taking Sentience Seriously*, 1 J. ANIMAL L. & ETHICS 1 (2006) *reprinted in* FRANCIONE, *supra* note 4, at 129–47.

58. JEREMY BENTHAM, AN INTRODUCTION TO THE PRINCIPLES OF MORALS AND LEGISLATION, 311 n.1 (Hafner Publishing Co. 1948) (1780).

59. *Id.*

60. *See* SINGER, *supra* note 16, at 228–30; FRANCIONE, *supra* note 2, at 130–50 (discussing Bentham's and Singer's position on the interest of animals in continued existence). The view that animals do not have an interest in continued existence and, therefore, that animal use per se is not problematic is proposed by other theorists as well. *See* Gary L. Francione, *Equal Consideration and the Interest of Nonhuman Animals in Continued Existence: A Response to Professor Sunstein*, 2006 U. CHI. LEGAL F. 231, *reprinted in* FRANCIONE, *supra* note 4, at 148–69 (discussing the views of Cass R. Sunstein, who accepts the views of Bentham and Singer).

61. SINGER, *supra* note 16, at 228–29.

62. *Id.* at 229 (footnote omitted).

63. PETER SINGER & JIM MASON, THE WAY WE EAT: WHY OUR FOOD CHOICES MATTER 81–183 (2006).

64. TOM REGAN, THE CASE FOR ANIMAL RIGHTS (1983).

65. *Id.* at 324. For a further discussion of this issue, see Gary L. Francione, *Comparable Harm and Equal Inherent Value: The Problem of the Dog in the Lifeboat,* 11 BETWEEN THE SPECIES 81 (1995), *reprinted in* FRANCIONE, *supra* note 4, at 210–29. It should also be noted that Regan limits his theory to those nonhumans who have preference autonomy. *See, e.g.*, REGAN, *supra* note 64, at 73–81, 243–48. The authors maintain that sentience alone is necessary for a nonhuman to have full membership in the moral community.

66. DONALD R. GRIFFIN, ANIMAL MINDS: BEYOND COGNITION TO CONSCIOUSNESS 274 (2001).

67. *Id.*

68. *Id.*

69. *Id.*

70. *See* Matthew Scully, DOMINION: THE POWER OF MAN, THE SUFFERING OF ANIMALS, AND THE CALL TO MERCY (2002).

71. For a further discussion of the welfarist approach to "animal law," see Francione, *supra* note 15, at 47–53.

72. Douglas Belkin, *Animal Rights Gains Foothold as Law Career: Harvard Hosts Court Competition for 50 Students,* BOSTON GLOBE (Mass.), Mar. 6, 2005, at 6. These traditional welfarist topics are the primary focus of the "animal law" casebook used in a number of courses. *See* SONIA S. WAISMAN ET AL., ANIMAL LAW: CASES AND MATERIALS (3d ed. 2006).

73. Belkin, *supra* note 72.

74. *See, e.g.*, STEVEN M. WISE, RATTLING THE CAGE: TOWARD LEGAL RIGHTS FOR ANIMALS (2000).

75. For a further discussion of the similar-minds approach, see Francione, *supra* note 57.

76. THE GREAT APE PROJECT: EQUALITY BEYOND HUMANITY (Paola Cavalieri & Peter Singer eds., 1993). One of the present authors had a chapter in *The Great Ape Project. See* Gary L. Francione, *Personhood, Property and Legal Competence, in* THE GREAT APE PROJECT, *supra*, at 248. However, the author stressed that only sentience was required for full membership in the moral community. *See id.* at 253.

77. *See, e.g.*, Cass R. Sunstein, *Slaughterhouse Jive*, NEW REPUBLIC, Jan. 29, 2001, at 40, 44 (reviewing FRANCIONE, *supra* note 2).

78. *See, e.g.*, David S. Favre, *Equitable Self-Ownership for Animals*, 50 DUKE L.J. 473 (2000). The authors confess to finding Favre's notion to be conceptually confused and inapplicable to most nonhumans who are used by humans.

79. For a further discussion of the abolitionist perspective, see Animal Rights: The Abolitionist Approach, http://www.abolitionistapproach.com (authors' website).

80. For a further discussion of the right not to be property, see FRANCIONE, *supra* note 2, at 90–100.

81. Patricia Leigh Brown, *Is Luxury Cruel? The Foie Gras Divide*, N.Y. TIMES, Oct. 6, 2004, at F10 (quoting Paul Waldau).

82. *See supra* note 13 and accompanying text.

83. For an extended discussion of the normative guidance provided by abolitionist theory, see FRANCIONE, *supra* note 13, at 147–89.

84. *See* PETA, 2004 PETA Proggy Awards (2004), http://www.peta.org/feat/proggy/2004/winners.html#retailer.

85. Professor Ibrahim maintains that the "strict standards" do not amount to much protection for animals. *See* Darian M. Ibrahim, *A Return to Descartes: Property, Profit, and the Corporate Ownership of Animals*, 70 LAW & CONTEMP. PROBS. 89 (2007).

86. *See* Steve Lowery, *How to Stuff a Lettuce Bikini*, ORANGE COUNTY WKLY. (Cal.), July 24, 2003, available at http://www.ocweekly.com/features/features/how-to-stuff-a-lettuce-bikini/20768 ("Half of our members are vegetarian and half think it's a good idea." (quoting Dan Mathews of PETA)).

87. An average omnivore in the United States is responsible for at least 32 nonhuman deaths per year. This number is based on an estimate of 9.5 billion animals killed in the U.S. and consumed by a population of 300 million. The number of animals killed does not include fish or other sea animals, and only reflects animals use for food and not for other purposes.

88. *See, e.g.*, Gary L. Francione, *We're All Michael Vick*, PHILA. DAILY NEWS (Pa.), Aug. 22, 2007, at 25.

89. *See* FRANCIONE, *supra* note 13, at 190–219.

90. For some of the materials that were produced as part of the Clinic work, see Animal Rights: The Abolitionist Approach, *supra* note 79.

91. We worked with many of the larger organizations to the extent that they promoted abolitionist campaigns but eventually shifted our efforts away from the larger groups.

92. For a further discussion of this matter, see Anna E. Charlton, *The Politics of Western Wild Horse Management, in* ETHICS AND WILDLIFE 177 (Priscilla N. Cohn ed., 1999).

93. For a further discussion of student rights, see GARY L. FRANCIONE & ANNA E. CHARLTON, VIVISECTION AND DISSECTION IN THE CLASSROOM: A GUIDE TO CONSCIENTIOUS OBJECTION (1992); Anna E. Charlton, *Student Rights and the First Amendment, in* ENCYCLOPEDIA OF ANIMAL RIGHTS AND ANIMAL WELFARE 148–50 (Marc Bekoff & Carron A. Meaney eds., 1998).

94. Whitman had the power under state statutory law to remit forfeitures and she exercised this power to prevent the killing of Taro. *See* Exec. Order No. 7 (N.J. Jan. 28, 1994), *available at* http://www.state.nj.us/infobank/circular/eow7.htm.

Chapter 2

ANIMAL SACRIFICE AND THE FIRST AMENDMENT

CHURCH OF THE LUKUMI BABALU AYE, INC. v. CITY OF HIALEAH
508 U.S. 520, 113 S.Ct. 2217, 124 L.Ed.2d 472 (1993).

Church brought action challenging city of Hialeah's ordinances dealing with ritual slaughter of animals. The United States District Court for the Southern District of Florida denied relief. The Eleventh Circuit affirmed.

MR. JUSTICE KENNEDY delivered the opinion of the Court except with respect to Part II–A–2.*

* * *

The principle that government may not enact laws that suppress religious belief or practice is so well understood that few violations are recorded in our opinions. * * *

Our review confirms that the laws in question were enacted by officials who did not understand, failed to perceive, or chose to ignore the fact that their official actions violated the Nation's essential commitment to religious freedom. The challenged laws had an impermissible object; and * * * the principle of general applicability was violated because the secular ends asserted * * * were pursued only with respect to conduct motivated by religious beliefs. We invalidate the challenged enactments and reverse the judgment of the Court of Appeals.

I.

A.

This case involves practices of the Santeria religion, which originated in the 19th century. When hundreds of thousands of members of the Yoruba people were brought as slaves from western Africa to Cuba, their traditional African religion absorbed significant elements of Roman Catholicism. The resulting syncretion, or fusion, is Santeria, "the way of

* THE CHIEF JUSTICE, Justice SCALIA, and Justice THOMAS join all but Part II–A–2 of this opinion. Justice WHITE joins all but Part II–A of this opinion. Justice SOUTER joins only Parts I, III, and IV of this opinion.

36

the saints." The Cuban Yoruba express their devotion to spirits, called *orishas,* through the iconography of Catholic saints. * * *

The Santeria faith teaches that every individual has a destiny from God, a destiny fulfilled with the aid and energy of the *orishas.* The basis of the Santeria religion is the nurture of a personal relation with the *orishas,* and one of the principal forms of devotion is an animal sacrifice. * * * Animal sacrifice is mentioned throughout the Old Testament and it played an important role in the practice of Judaism before destruction of the second Temple in Jerusalem. In modern Islam, there is an annual sacrifice commemorating Abraham's sacrifice of a ram in the stead of his son.

According to Santeria teaching, the *orishas* are powerful but not immortal. They depend for survival on the sacrifice. Sacrifices are performed at birth, marriage, and death rites, for the cure of the sick, for the initiation of new members and priests, and during an annual celebration. Animals sacrificed in Santeria rituals include chickens, pigeons, doves, ducks, guinea pigs, goats, sheep, and turtles. The animals are killed by the cutting of the carotid arteries in the neck. The sacrificed animal is cooked and eaten, except after healing and death rituals.

Santeria adherents faced widespread persecution in Cuba, so the religion and its rituals were practiced in secret. * * * The religion was brought to this Nation most often by exiles from the Cuban revolution. The District Court estimated that there are at least 50,000 practitioners in South Florida today.

B.

Petitioner Church of the Lukumi Babalu Aye, Inc. (Church), is a not-for-profit corporation organized under Florida law in 1973. The Church and its congregants practice the Santeria religion. * * * In April 1987, the Church leased land in the City of Hialeah, Florida, and announced plans to establish a house of worship as well as a school, cultural center, and museum. * * *

The prospect of a Santeria church in their midst was distressing to many members of the Hialeah community, and the announcement of the plans to open a Santeria church in Hialeah prompted the city council to hold an emergency public session on June 9, 1987. * * *

* * * First, the city council adopted Resolution 87–66, which noted the "concern" expressed by residents of the city "that certain religions may propose to engage in practices which are inconsistent with public morals, peace or safety," and declared that "[t]he City reiterates its commitment to a prohibition against any and all acts of any and all religious groups which are inconsistent with public morals, peace or safety." Next, the council approved an emergency ordinance, Ordinance 87–40, which incorporated in full, except as to penalty, Florida's animal cruelty laws. Fla.Stat. ch. 828 (1987). Among other things, the incorpo-

rated state law subjected to criminal punishment "[w]hoever ... unnecessarily or cruelly ... kills any animal." § 828.12.

The city council desired to undertake further legislative action, but Florida law prohibited a municipality from enacting legislation relating to animal cruelty that conflicted with state law. § 828.27(4). To obtain clarification, Hialeah's city attorney requested an opinion from the attorney general of Florida as to whether § 828.12 prohibited "a religious group from sacrificing an animal in a religious ritual or practice" and whether the city could enact ordinances "making religious animal sacrifice unlawful." The attorney general responded in mid-July. He concluded that the "ritual sacrifice of animals for purposes other than food consumption" was not a "necessary" killing and so was prohibited by § 828.12. The attorney general appeared to define "unnecessary" as "done without any useful motive, in a spirit of wanton cruelty or for the mere pleasure of destruction without being in any sense beneficial or useful to the person killing the animal." He advised that religious animal sacrifice was against state law, so that a city ordinance prohibiting it would not be in conflict.

The city council responded at first with a hortatory enactment, Resolution 87–90, that noted its residents' "great concern regarding the possibility of public ritualistic animal sacrifices" and the state-law prohibition. The resolution declared the city policy "to oppose the ritual sacrifices of animals" within Hialeah and announced that any person or organization practicing animal sacrifice "will be prosecuted."

In September 1987, the city council adopted three substantive ordinances addressing the issue of religious animal sacrifice. Ordinance 87–52 defined "sacrifice" as "to unnecessarily kill, torment, torture, or mutilate an animal in a public or private ritual or ceremony not for the primary purpose of food consumption," and prohibited owning or possessing an animal "intending to use such animal for food purposes." It restricted application of this prohibition, however, to any individual or group that "kills, slaughters or sacrifices animals for any type of ritual, regardless of whether or not the flesh or blood of the animal is to be consumed." The ordinance contained an exemption for slaughtering by "licensed establishment[s]" of animals "specifically raised for food purposes." Declaring, moreover, that the city council "has determined that the sacrificing of animals within the city limits is contrary to the public health, safety, welfare and morals of the community," the city council adopted Ordinance 87–71. That ordinance defined sacrifice as had Ordinance 87–52, and then provided that "[i]t shall be unlawful for any person, persons, corporations or associations to sacrifice any animal within the corporate limits of the City of Hialeah, Florida." The final Ordinance, 87–72, defined "slaughter" as "the killing of animals for food" and prohibited slaughter outside of areas zoned for slaughterhouse use. The ordinance provided an exemption, however, for the slaughter or processing for sale of "small numbers of hogs and/or cattle per week in accordance with an exemption provided by state law." All ordinances and resolutions passed the city council by unanimous vote. Violations of each of the four ordinances were punishable by fines not exceeding $500 or imprisonment not exceeding 60 days, or both.

Following enactment of these ordinances, the Church * * * filed this action pursuant to 42 U.S.C. § 1983 in the United States District Court for the Southern District of Florida. Named as defendants were the city of Hialeah and its mayor and members of its city council in their individual capacities. Alleging violations of petitioners' rights under, *inter alia,* the Free Exercise Clause, the complaint sought a declaratory judgment and injunctive and monetary relief. The District Court granted summary judgment to the individual defendants, finding that they had absolute immunity for their legislative acts and that the ordinances and resolutions adopted by the council did not constitute an official policy of harassment, as alleged by petitioners.

After a 9–day bench trial on the remaining claims, the District Court ruled for the city, finding no violation of petitioners' rights under the Free Exercise Clause. * * *

* * *

The Court of Appeals for the Eleventh Circuit affirmed in a one-paragraph *per curiam* opinion. * * *

* * *

* * * We must consider petitioners' First Amendment claim.

In addressing the constitutional protection for free exercise of religion, our cases establish the general proposition that a law that is neutral and of general applicability need not be justified by a compelling governmental interest even if the law has the incidental effect of burdening a particular religious practice. Neutrality and general applicability are interrelated, and, as becomes apparent in this case, failure to satisfy one requirement is a likely indication that the other has not been satisfied. A law failing to satisfy these requirements must be justified by a compelling governmental interest and must be narrowly tailored to advance that interest. * * * We begin by discussing neutrality.

A.

In our Establishment Clause cases we have often stated the principle that the First Amendment forbids an official purpose to disapprove of a particular religion or of religion in general. These cases, however, for the most part have addressed governmental efforts to benefit religion or particular religions, and so have dealt with a question different, at least in its formulation and emphasis, from the issue here. Petitioners allege an attempt to disfavor their religion because of the religious ceremonies it commands, and the Free Exercise Clause is dispositive in our analysis.

At a minimum, the protections of the Free Exercise Clause pertain if the law at issue discriminates against some or all religious beliefs or regulates or prohibits conduct because it is undertaken for religious reasons. Indeed, it was "historical instances of religious persecution and intolerance that gave concern to those who drafted the Free Exercise Clause." See J. Story, Commentaries on the Constitution of the United States §§ 991–992 (abridged ed. 1833) (reprint 1987). These principles, though not often at issue in our Free Exercise Clause cases, have played a role in some. In *McDaniel v. Paty*, 435 U.S. 618 (1978), for example, we invalidated a State law that disqualified members of the clergy from holding certain public offices, because it "impose[d] special disabilities on the basis of . . . religious status," *Employment Div., Dept. of Human Resources of Ore. v. Smith*, 494 U.S. 872, 877 (1990). On the same principle, in *Fowler v. Rhode Island*, 345 U.S. 67 (1953), we found that a municipal ordinance was applied in an unconstitutional manner when interpreted to prohibit preaching in a public park by a Jehovah's Witness but to permit preaching during the course of a Catholic mass or Protestant church service.

1.

Although a law targeting religious beliefs as such is never permissible, if the object of a law is to infringe upon or restrict practices because of their religious motivation, the law is not neutral, and it is invalid unless it is justified by a compelling interest and is narrowly tailored to advance that interest. There are, of course, many ways of demonstrating that the object or purpose of a law is the suppression of religion or religious conduct. To determine the object of a law, we must begin with its text, for the minimum requirement of neutrality is that a law not discriminate on its face. A law lacks facial neutrality if it refers to a religious practice without a secular meaning discernable from the language or context. Petitioners contend that three of the ordinances fail this test of facial neutrality because they use the words "sacrifice" and "ritual," words with strong religious connotations. We agree that these words are consistent with the claim of facial discrimination, but the argument is not conclusive. The words "sacrifice" and "ritual" have a religious origin, but current use admits also of secular meanings. The ordinances, furthermore, define "sacrifice" in secular terms, without referring to religious practices.

* * * Facial neutrality is not determinative. The Free Exercise Clause, like the Establishment Clause, extends beyond facial discrimination. The Clause "forbids subtle departures from neutrality," *Gillette v. United States*, 401 U.S. 437, 452 (1971), and "covert suppression of particular religious beliefs," *Bowen v. Roy*, 476 U.S. [693,] 703. Official action that targets religious conduct for distinctive treatment cannot be shielded by mere compliance with the requirement of facial neutrality. The Free Exercise Clause protects against governmental hostility which is masked, as well as overt. "The Court must survey meticulously the circumstances of governmental categories to eliminate, as it were, religious gerrymanders." *Walz v. Tax Comm'n of New York City*, 397 U.S. 664, 696 (1970).

The record in this case compels the conclusion that suppression of the central element of the Santeria worship service was the object of the ordinances. * * * Resolution 87–66, adopted June 9, 1987, recited that "residents and citizens of the City of Hialeah have expressed their concern that certain religions may propose to engage in practices which are inconsistent with public morals, peace or safety," and "reiterate[d]" the city's commitment to prohibit "any and all [such] acts of any and all religious groups." No one suggests, and on this record it cannot be maintained, that city officials had in mind a religion other than Santeria.

It becomes evident that these ordinances target Santeria sacrifice when the ordinances' operation is considered. Apart from the text, the effect of a law in its real operation is strong evidence of its object. To be sure, adverse impact will not always lead to a finding of impermissible targeting. For example, a social harm may have been a legitimate concern of government for reasons quite apart from discrimination. The subject at hand does implicate, of course, multiple concerns unrelated to religious animosity, for example, the suffering or mistreatment visited upon the sacrificed animals and health hazards from improper disposal. But the ordinances when considered together disclose an object remote from these legitimate concerns. The design of these laws accomplishes instead a "religious gerrymander," *Walz, supra,* 397 U.S. at 696, an impermissible attempt to target petitioners and their religious practices.

It is a necessary conclusion that almost the only conduct subject to Ordinances 87–40, 87–52, and 87–71 is the religious exercise of Santeria church members. The texts show that they were drafted in tandem to achieve this result. We begin with Ordinance 87–71. It prohibits the sacrifice of animals, but defines sacrifice as "to unnecessarily kill ... an animal in a public or private ritual or ceremony not for the primary purpose of food consumption." The definition excludes almost all killings of animals except for religious sacrifice, and the primary purpose requirement narrows the proscribed category even further, in particular by exempting kosher slaughter. We need not discuss whether this differential treatment of two religions is itself an independent constitutional violation. It suffices to recite this feature of the law as support for our conclusion that Santeria alone was the exclusive legislative concern. The net result of the gerrymander is that few if any killings of animals are prohibited other than Santeria sacrifice, which is proscribed because it occurs during a ritual or ceremony and its primary purpose is to make an offering to the *orishas,* not food consumption. Indeed, careful drafting ensured that, although Santeria sacrifice is prohibited, killings that are no more necessary or humane in almost all other circumstances are unpunished.

Operating in similar fashion is Ordinance 87–52, which prohibits the "possess [ion], sacrifice, or slaughter" of an animal with the "inten[t] to use such animal for food purposes." This prohibition, extending to the keeping of an animal as well as the killing itself, applies if the animal is killed in "any type of ritual" and there is an intent to use the animal for food, whether or not it is in fact consumed for food. The ordinance exempts, however, "any licensed [food] establishment" with regard to "any animals which are specifically raised for food purposes," if the activity is permitted by zoning and other laws. This exception, too, seems intended to cover kosher slaughter. Again, the burden of the ordinance, in practical terms, falls on Santeria adherents but almost no others: If the killing is—unlike most Santeria sacrifices—unaccompanied by the intent to use the animal for food, then it is not prohibited by Ordinance 87–52; if the killing is specifically for food but does not occur during the course of "any type of ritual," it again falls outside the prohibition; and if the killing is for food and occurs during the course of a ritual, it is still exempted if it occurs in a properly zoned and licensed establishment and involves animals "specifically raised for food purposes." A pattern of exemptions parallels the pattern of narrow prohibitions. Each contributes to the gerrymander.

Ordinance 87–40 incorporates the Florida animal cruelty statute, § 828.12. Its prohibition is broad on its face, punishing "[w]hoever ... unnecessarily ... kills any animal." The city claims that this ordinance is the epitome of a neutral prohibition. The problem, however, is the interpretation given to the ordinance by respondent and the Florida attorney general. Killings for religious reasons are deemed unnecessary, whereas most other killings fall outside the prohibition. The city, on what seems to be a *per se* basis, deems hunting, slaughter of animals for food, eradication of insects and pests, and euthanasia as necessary. There is no indication in the record that respondent has concluded that hunting or fishing for sport is unnecessary. Indeed, one of the few reported Florida cases decided under § 828.12 concludes that the use of live rabbits to train greyhounds is not unnecessary. See *Kiper v. State,* 310 So.2d 42 (Fla.App.), cert. denied, 328 So.2d 845 (Fla.1975). Further, because it requires an evaluation of the particular justification for the killing, this ordinance represents a system of "individualized governmental assessment of the reasons for the relevant conduct," *Employment Div., Dept. of Human Resources of Ore. v. Smith,* 494 U.S. [872,] 884. As we noted in *Smith,* in circumstances in which individualized exemptions from a general requirement are available, the government "may not refuse to extend that system to cases of 'religious hardship' without compelling reason." *Ibid.,* quoting *Bowen v. Roy, supra,* 476 U.S., at 708. Respondent's application of the ordinance's test of necessity devalues religious reasons for killing by judging them to be of lesser import than nonreligious reasons. Thus, religious practice is being singled out for discriminatory treatment.

We also find significant evidence of the ordinances' improper targeting of Santeria sacrifice in the fact that they proscribe more religious conduct than is necessary to achieve their stated ends. It is not unreasonable to infer, at least when there are no persuasive indications to the contrary, that a law which visits "gratuitous restrictions" on religious conduct, *McGowan v. Maryland,* 366 U.S. [420,] 520, seeks not to effectuate the stated governmental interests, but to suppress the conduct because of its religious motivation.

The legitimate governmental interests in protecting the public health and preventing cruelty to animals could be addressed by restrictions stopping far short of a flat prohibition of all Santeria sacrificial practice. If improper disposal, not the sacrifice itself, is the harm to be prevented, the city could have imposed a general regulation on the disposal of organic garbage. It did not do so. Indeed, counsel for the city conceded at oral argument that, under the ordinances, Santeria sacrifices would be illegal even if they occurred in licensed, inspected, and zoned slaughterhouses. Thus, these broad ordinances prohibit Santeria sacrifice even when it does not threaten the city's interest in the public health. The District Court accepted the argument that narrower regulation would be unenforceable because of the secrecy in the Santeria rituals and the lack of any central religious authority to require compliance with secular disposal regulations. It is difficult to understand, however, how a prohibition of the sacrifices themselves, which occur in private, is enforceable if a ban on improper disposal, which occurs in public, is not. The neutrality of a law is suspect if First Amendment freedoms are curtailed to prevent isolated collateral harms not themselves prohibited by direct regulation.

Under similar analysis, narrower regulation would achieve the city's interest in preventing cruelty to animals. With regard to the city's interest in ensuring the adequate care of animals, regulation of conditions and treatment, regardless of why an animal is kept, is the logical response to the city's concern, not a prohibition on possession for the purpose of sacrifice. The same is true for the city's interest in prohibiting cruel methods of killing. Under federal and Florida law and Ordinance 87–40, which incorporates Florida law in this regard, killing an animal by the "simultaneous and instantaneous severance of the carotid arteries with a sharp instrument"—the method used in kosher slaughter—is approved as humane. See 7 U.S.C. § 1902(b); Fla.Stat. § 828.23(7)(b) (1991); Ordinance 87–40, § 1. The District Court found that, though Santeria sacrifice also results in severance of the carotid arteries, the method used during sacrifice is less reliable and therefore not humane. If the city has a real concern that other methods are less humane, however, the subject of the regulation should be the method of slaughter itself, not a religious classification that is said to bear some general relation to it.

Ordinance 87–72—unlike the three other ordinances—does appear to apply to substantial nonreligious conduct and not to be overbroad. For our purposes here, however, the four substantive ordinances may be treated as a group for neutrality purposes. * * * We need not decide whether the Ordinance 87–72 could survive constitutional scrutiny if it existed separately; it must be invalidated because it functions, with the rest of the enactments in question, to suppress Santeria religious worship.

2.

In determining if the object of a law is a neutral one under the Free Exercise Clause, we can also find guidance in our equal protection cases. * * *

That the ordinances were enacted " 'because of,' not merely 'in spite of,' " their suppression of Santeria religious practice is revealed by the events preceding their enactment. Although respondent claimed at oral argument that it had experienced significant problems resulting from the sacrifice of animals within the city before the announced opening of the Church, the city council made no attempt to address the supposed problem before its meeting in June 1987, just weeks after the Church announced plans to open. The minutes and taped excerpts of the June 9 session * * * evidence significant hostility exhibited by residents, members of the city council, and other city officials toward the Santeria religion and its practice of animal sacrifice. * * * When Councilman Martinez, a supporter of the ordinances, stated that in prerevolution Cuba "people were put in jail for practicing this religion," the audience applauded.

Other statements by members of the city council were in a similar vein. For example, Councilman Martinez, after noting his belief that Santeria was outlawed in Cuba, questioned: "[I]f we could not practice this [religion] in our homeland [Cuba], why bring it to this country?" Councilman Cardoso said that Santeria devotees at the Church "are in violation of everything this country stands for." Councilman Mejides indicated that he was "totally against the sacrificing of animals" and distinguished kosher slaughter because it had a "real purpose." The "Bible says we are allowed to sacrifice an animal for consumption," he continued, "but for any other purposes, I don't believe that the Bible allows that." The president of the city council, Councilman Echevarria, asked: "What can we do to prevent the Church from opening?"

Various Hialeah city officials made comparable comments. The chaplain of the Hialeah Police Department told the city council that Santeria was a sin, "foolishness," "an abomination to the Lord," and the worship of "demons." He advised the city council: "We need to be helping people and sharing with them the truth that is found in Jesus Christ." He concluded: "I would exhort you ... not to permit this Church to exist." The city attorney commented that Resolution 87–66 indicated: "This community will not tolerate religious practices which are abhorrent to its citizens...." Similar comments were made by the deputy city attorney. This history discloses the object of the ordinances to target animal sacrifice by Santeria worshippers because of its religious motivation.

3.

In sum, the neutrality inquiry leads to one conclusion: The ordinances had as their object the suppression of religion. The pattern we have recited discloses animosity to Santeria adherents and their religious practices; the ordinances by their own terms target this religious exercise; the texts of the ordinances were gerrymandered with care to proscribe religious killings of animals but to exclude almost all secular killings; and the ordinances suppress much more religious conduct than is necessary in order to achieve the legitimate ends asserted in their defense. These ordinances are not neutral, and the court below committed clear error in failing to reach this conclusion.

B.

We turn next to a second requirement of the Free Exercise Clause, the rule that laws burdening religious practice must be of general applicability. All laws are selective to some extent, but categories of selection are of paramount concern when a law has the incidental effect of burdening religious practice. The Free Exercise Clause "protect[s] religious observers against unequal treatment," *Hobbie v. Unemployment Appeals Comm'n of Fla.*, 480 U.S. 136, 148, 107 (1987), and inequality results when a legislature decides that the governmental interests it seeks to advance are worthy of being pursued only against conduct with a religious motivation.

* * *

Respondent claims that Ordinances 87–40, 87–52, and 87–71 advance two interests: protecting the public health and preventing cruelty to animals. The ordinances are underinclusive for those ends. They fail to prohibit nonreligious conduct that endangers these interests in a similar or greater degree than Santeria sacrifice does. The underinclusion is substantial, not inconsequential. Despite the city's proffered interest in preventing cruelty to animals, the ordinances are drafted with care to forbid few killings but those occasioned by religious sacrifice. Many types of animal deaths or kills for nonreligious reasons are either not prohibited or approved by express provision. For example, fishing-which occurs in Hialeah, is legal. Extermination of mice and rats within a home is also permitted. Florida law incorporated by Ordinance 87–40 sanctions euthanasia of "stray, neglected, abandoned, or unwanted animals"; destruction of animals judicially removed from their owners "for humanitarian reasons" or when the animal "is of no commercial value"; the infliction of pain or suffering "in the interest of medical science"; the placing of poison in one's yard or enclosure; and the use of a live animal "to pursue or take wildlife or to participate in any hunting" and "to hunt wild hogs."

The city concedes that "neither the State of Florida nor the City has enacted a generally applicable ban on the killing of animals." It asserts, however, that animal sacrifice is "different" from the animal killings that are permitted by law. According to the city, it is "self-evident" that killing animals for food is "important"; the eradication of insects and pests is "obviously justified"; and the euthanasia of excess animals "makes sense." These *ipse dixits* do not explain why religion alone must bear the burden of the ordinances, when many of these secular killings fall within the city's interest in preventing the cruel treatment of animals.

The ordinances are also underinclusive with regard to the city's interest in public health, which is threatened by the disposal of animal carcasses in open public places and the consumption of uninspected meat. Neither interest is pursued by respondent with regard to conduct that is not motivated by religious conviction. The health risks posed by the improper disposal of animal carcasses are the same whether Santeria sacrifice or some nonreligious killing preceded it. The city does not, however, prohibit hunters from bringing their kill to their houses, nor does it regulate disposal after their activity. Despite substantial testimony at trial that the same public health hazards result from improper disposal of garbage by restaurants, restaurants are outside the scope of the ordinances. Improper disposal is a general problem that causes substantial health risks, but which respondent addresses only when it results from religious exercise.

The ordinances are underinclusive as well with regard to the health risk posed by consumption of uninspected meat. Under the city's ordinances, hunters may eat their kill and fishermen may eat their catch without undergoing governmental inspection. Likewise, state law requires inspection of meat that is sold but exempts meat from animals raised for the use of the owner and "members of his household and nonpaying guests and employees." Fla.Stat. § 585.88(1)(a) (1991). The asserted interest in inspected meat is not pursued in contexts similar to that of religious animal sacrifice.

Ordinance 87–72, which prohibits the slaughter of animals outside of areas zoned for slaughterhouses, is underinclusive on its face. The ordinance includes an exemption for "any person, group, or organization" that "slaughters or processes for sale, small numbers of hogs and/or cattle per week in accordance with an exemption provided by state law." See Fla.Stat. § 828.24(3) (1991). Respondent has not explained why commercial operations that slaughter "small numbers" of hogs and cattle do not implicate its professed desire to prevent cruelty to animals and preserve the public health. Although the city has classified Santeria sacrifice as slaughter, subjecting it to this ordinance, it does not regulate other killings for food in like manner.

We conclude, in sum, that each of Hialeah's ordinances pursues the city's governmental interests only against conduct motivated by religious belief. The ordinances "ha[ve] every appearance of a prohibition that society is prepared to impose upon [Santeria worshippers] but not upon itself." *Florida Star v. B.J.F.,* 491 U.S. 524, 542 (1989). This precise evil is what the requirement of general applicability is designed to prevent.

III.

A law burdening religious practice that is not neutral or not of general application must undergo the most rigorous of scrutiny. To satisfy the commands of the First Amendment, a law restrictive of religious practice must advance " 'interests of the highest order' " and must be narrowly tailored in pursuit of those interests. *McDaniel v. Paty,* 435 U.S. [618,] 628, quoting *Wisconsin v. Yoder,* 406 U.S. 205, 215 (1972). * * * A law that targets religious conduct for distinctive treatment or advances legitimate governmental interests only against conduct with a religious motivation will survive strict scrutiny only in rare cases. It follows from what we have already said that these ordinances cannot withstand this scrutiny.

First, even were the governmental interests compelling, the ordinances are not drawn in narrow terms to accomplish those interests. As we have discussed, all four ordinances are overbroad or underinclusive in substantial respects. The proffered objectives are not pursued with respect to analogous non-religious conduct, and those interests could be achieved by narrower ordinances that burdened religion to a far lesser degree. The absence of narrow tailoring suffices to establish the invalidity of the ordinances.

Respondent has not demonstrated, moreover, that, in the context of these ordinances, its governmental interests are compelling. Where government restricts only conduct protected by the First Amendment and fails to enact feasible measures to restrict other conduct producing substantial harm or alleged harm of the same sort, the interest given in justification of the restriction is not compelling. It is established in our strict scrutiny jurisprudence that "a law cannot be regarded as protecting an interest 'of the highest order' ... when it leaves appreciable damage to that supposedly vital interest unprohibited." *Florida Star v. B.J.F., supra*, 491 U.S., at 541–542. As we show above, the ordinances are underinclusive to a substantial extent with respect to each of the interests that respondent has asserted, and it is only conduct motivated by religious conviction that bears the weight of the governmental restrictions. There can be no serious claim that those interests justify the ordinances.

IV.

The Free Exercise Clause commits government itself to religious tolerance, and upon even slight suspicion that proposals for state intervention stem from animosity to religion or distrust of its practices, all officials must pause to remember their own high duty to the Constitution and to the rights it secures. Those in office must be resolute in resisting importunate demands and must ensure that the sole reasons for imposing the burdens of law and regulation are secular. Legislators may not devise mechanisms, overt or disguised, designed to persecute or oppress a religion or its practices. The laws here in question were enacted contrary to these constitutional principles, and they are void.

Reversed.

* * *

MR. JUSTICE BLACKMUN, with whom JUSTICE O'CONNOR joins, concurring in the judgment.

The Court holds today that the city of Hialeah violated the First and Fourteenth Amendments when it passed a set of restrictive ordinances explicitly directed at petitioners' religious practice. With this holding I agree. I write separately to emphasize that the First Amendment's protection of religion extends beyond those rare occasions on which the government explicitly targets religion (or a particular religion) for disfavored treatment, as is done in this case. In my view, a statute that burdens the free exercise of religion "may stand only if the law in general, and the State's refusal to allow a religious exemption in particular, are justified by a compelling interest that cannot be served by less restrictive means." *Employment Div., Dept. of Human Resources of Ore. v. Smith,* 494 U.S. 872, 90 (1990). The Court, however, applies a different test. It applies the test announced in *Smith,* under which "a law that is neutral and of general applicability need not be justified by a compelling governmental interest even if the law has the incidental effect of burdening a particular religious practice." I continue to believe that *Smith* was wrongly decided, because it ignored the value of religious freedom as an affirmative individual liberty and treated the Free Exercise Clause as no more than an antidiscrimination principle. Thus, while I agree with the result the Court reaches in this case, I arrive at that result by a different route.

When the State enacts legislation that intentionally or unintentionally places a burden upon religiously motivated practice, it must justify that burden by "showing that it is the least restrictive means of achieving some compelling state interest." *Thomas v. Review Bd. of Indiana Employment Security Div.,* 450 U.S. 707, 718 (1981). A State may no more create an underinclusive statute, one that fails truly to promote its purported compelling interest, than it may create an overinclusive statute, one that encompasses more protected conduct than necessary to achieve its goal. In the latter circumstance, the broad scope of the statute is unnecessary to serve the interest, and the statute fails for that reason. In the former situation, the fact that allegedly harmful conduct falls outside the statute's scope belies a governmental assertion that it has genuinely pursued an interest "of the highest order." *Ibid.* If the State's goal is important enough to prohibit religiously motivated activity, it will not and must not stop at religiously motivated activity.

In this case, the ordinances at issue are both overinclusive and underinclusive in relation to the state interests they purportedly serve. They are overinclusive, as the majority correctly explains, because the "legitimate govern mental interests in protecting the public health and preventing cruelty to animals could be addressed by restrictions stopping far short of a flat prohibition of all Santeria sacrificial practice." They are underinclusive as well, because "[d]espite the city's proffered interest in preventing cruelty to animals, the ordinances are drafted with care to forbid few killings but those occasioned by religious sacrifice." Moreover, the "ordinances are also underinclusive with regard to the city's interest in public health. . . ."

When a law discriminates against religion as such, as do the ordinances in this case, it automatically will fail strict scrutiny. * * * This is true because a law that targets religious practice for disfavored treatment both burdens the free exercise of religion and, by definition, is not precisely tailored to a compelling governmental interest.

Thus, unlike the majority, I do not believe that "[a] law burdening religious practice that is not neutral or not of general application must undergo the most rigorous of scrutiny." In my view, regulation that targets religion in this way, *ipso facto,* fails strict scrutiny. It is for this reason that a statute that explicitly restricts religious practices violates the First Amendment. Otherwise, however, "[t]he First Amendment . . . does not distinguish between laws that are generally applicable and laws that target particular religious practices." *Smith,* 494 U.S., at 894.

It is only in the rare case that a state or local legislature will enact a law directly burdening religious practice as such. Because respondent here does single out religion in this way, the present case is an easy one to decide.

A harder case would be presented if petitioners were requesting an exemption from a generally applicable anticruelty law. The result in the case before the Court today, and the fact that every Member of the Court concurs in that result, does not necessarily reflect this Court's views of the strength of a State's interest in prohibiting cruelty to animals. This case does not present, and I therefore decline to reach, the question whether the Free Exercise Clause would require a religious exemption from a law that sincerely pursued the goal of protecting animals from cruel treatment. The number of organizations that have filed *amicus* briefs on behalf of this interest however, demonstrates that it is not a concern to be treated lightly.

ANIMAL SACRIFICE AND THE FIRST AMENDMENT: THE CASE OF LUKUMI BABALU AYE

David N. Cassuto*

Animal sacrifice and religious ritual have intertwined for thousands of years. The practice remains integral to Santería, an Afro–Cuban religion that has many adherents in the United States, particularly in Florida. In 1987, when the Santería Church of Lukumi Babalu Aye announced plans to open in Hialeah, Florida, the city reacted by passing a set of ordinances banning animal sacrifice. The Church sued and the issue of whether the ritual killing of animals constituted protected religious expression eventually made its way to the United States Supreme Court. *Church of Lukumi Babalu Aye, Inc. v. City of Hialeah*[1] asked the Court to resolve two linked constitutional questions: Is the ritual slaughter of animals a form of religious expression protected by the First Amendment of the United States Constitution? And, if so, (or even if not) may the practice be banned or regulated by the State?

These are difficult questions and the Court's attempt to answer them raises more questions still. This chapter examines the Court's reasoning in the *Lukumi* case to determine whether it clarified or further clouded the relationship between animal sacrifice and the First Amendment. It argues that the plurality opinion's attempt to cast the Hialeah ordinances as underperforming animal protection statutes was both misguided and counterproductive.

The Hialeah ordinances aimed to suppress Santería practices within the city limits. As such, they were deeply problematic because they intentionally targeted a particular religion. Yet the Court focused primarily on the ordinances' effectiveness at resolving animal cruelty, an issue well beyond their purview. As a result, the Court's analysis mischaracterizes the laws and leaves crucial questions—that is, whether a non-discriminatory prohibition on animal sacrifice is possible or permissible under the First Amendment—unanswered.

Defining the Hialeah ordinances as anticruelty rather than as antisacrifice enabled the Court to find them both overbroad and underinclusive. For those reasons, the Court deemed the ordinances to be intolerably burdensome to religious practices. This reasoning does not withstand close analysis and falls prey to the same imprecision the Court imputes to the challenged laws. It demands that the laws be both narrowly drawn to accomplish a specific goal and broadly applicable to behavior that lies beyond their stated scope. These conflicting expectations create an impossible standard. In addition, by classifying animal sacrifice laws as failed anticruelty statutes and then invalidating them on First Amendment grounds, the Court jeopardized future attempts to legislate animal protection laws, even when such laws only incidentally impact religious practices.

Background—Santería and South Florida

Santería has its origins in Africa. In the eighteenth century, Spain brought a great many slaves from Yoruba-speaking areas of Africa (including Nigeria, Togo and Benin) to its colony in Cuba. Over time, these diverse cultures, all of whom shared the Yoruba language and religious traditions, came to be known collectively as "Lukumi." The dominant religion among the Lukumi involved the worship of *Oludumare* ("owner of heaven") and *ashe* ("cosmic blood" of the universe). *Orishas*—the spirits or guardians who personify the *ashe*—were worshipped as "people of heaven."[2]

In colonial Cuba, the Yoruba religion merged with Catholicism, the official religion of Spain and its Cuban colony. The result was a unique Afro–Cuban syncretic faith that combined Orisha worship with Catholic religious iconography. Orishas and saints were venerated both on traditional Catholic days of celebration as well as according to traditional Lukumi practices. Leaders among the faith were known as "santeros." Eventually, the religion itself became known as Santería, the "Way of the Saints."

Santería migrated north to the United States with Cuban exiles and expatriates. By the early 1980s, an estimated fifty to one-hundred thousand Santería practitioners lived in South Florida. Following the Mariel boatlift in 1980, in which Fidel Castro deported 125,000 people, the number of Santería faithful in the United States swelled. Many of the refugees from the boatlift settled in the Miami area.[3] As a result, the early 1990s found Santería well ensconced in the United States, particularly in South Florida.

Santería religious rituals often include the killing of animals. Practitioners sacrifice animals to the Orishas, who require blood to sustain them. They kill goats, guinea pigs, potbellied pigs, rabbits, chickens and turtles and other animals on days of thanksgiving, to cure illness, to initiate one into the faith, to ward off enemies, and at other times as well. The method of slaughter involves placing the animal on a table with its head hanging over the side and then slitting its throat so that the blood drains into a bowl below the table. Because the Santería faith has no formal hierarchy or organizational structure, there is no standardized training or certification process for those who slaughter the animals. Depending on the animal and the skill of the santeros carrying out the ritual, killing the animal swiftly and efficiently can present a formidable challenge. A number of well-publicized examples that emerged in the days surrounding the *Lukumi Babalu* case demonstrated that the animals' deaths are sometimes slow and grisly.[4]

The Founding of the Church of Lukumi Babalu Aye

In 1974, a Cuban immigrant Ernesto Pichardo, along with his brother, mother, stepfather and several others, founded the Church of Lukumi Babalu Aye. Pichardo assumed the dual roles of corporate president (the church was founded as a non-profit organization) and chief spokesperson. The church operated for many years without a physical home. In 1987, it negotiated a lease with an option to buy an abandoned used-car dealership in downtown Hialeah, Florida.

The announcement of the church's imminent opening caused a vociferous community backlash in Hialeah. Perhaps not coincidentally, the church also encountered difficulties getting utility hookups and a certificate of occupancy for the building. The community outcry soon aggregated into an organized movement opposing the church's presence in Hialeah. That opposition included local religious leaders. The pastor of one local church proclaimed himself in favor of freedom of speech and worship yet still declared, "that there are still people in this era, in our civilized society of the United States, still sacrificing animals ... is indefensible and repugnant."[5]

At a public meeting held by the city council, fervent denunciations came from all quarters. Participants denounced Santería as satanic and medieval. Even the chaplain of the police department labeled it an abomination to the Lord, noting that "We need to be helping people and sharing with them the truth that is found in Jesus Christ."[6] Pichardo was jeered, hectored, and called the "anti-Christ," as well as Satan himself, among other epithets.[7]

Shortly thereafter, the City Council passed a series of resolutions and ordinances outlawing ritual slaughter of the type practiced by the Santería faithful. Resolution 87–66 acknowledged Hialeah residents' "concern" regarding religious practices that conflict with public morals, peace and safety and "reiterated" the city's commitment to the prohibition of animal sacrifice. Ordinance 87–40 incorporated Florida's animal cruelty law which barred anyone from "unnecessarily or cruelly ... kill[ing]" animals. The Florida Attorney General had earlier opined that killing animals for religious purposes was "unnecessary" under the statute and therefore illegal unless the primary purpose was for food consumption. Consequently, by incorporating the state law, the Hialeah City Council effectively outlawed the form of animal sacrifice practiced in Santería.

Since Hialeah is a part of Florida, the Florida anticruelty statute was already in force, so the Council's adoption of it was partially hortatory. However the attorney general's reading of the state statute (that animal sacrifice outside the context of food consumption was "unnecessary" and, therefore, cruel) had not been tested or upheld by the courts. Thus, the state anticruelty statute gained specificity and clarity in the context of the Hialeah ordinances.

Resolution 87–90 declared it city policy to oppose animal sacrifice within the city's limits. Ordinance 87–52 barred the possession or use of animals for ritual slaughter except in properly zoned and licensed establishments. Ordinance 87–71 outlawed animal sacrifice within the city limits except for the primary purpose of food consumption; and Ordinance 87–72 outlawed the slaughter of any animal on any premises not zoned for such activities and which met all city codes and requirements. Taken together, these enactments meant that the Church and its adherents were prohibited from carrying out animal sacrifice within the city of Hialeah.

The church and Pichardo jointly filed suit in federal court against the city as well as its mayor and the entire city council. They alleged violations of their First Amendment right to freedom of religion and demanded that the court void the ordinances. The city countered that the laws did not discriminate against Santería or the church. Rather, they sought to safeguard the populace against unsanitary and unseemly practices. Consequently, the city argued, the ordinances passed constitutional muster and should be upheld.

The district court held for the city. The judge found much of Pichardo's testimony unconvincing and consequently held that the plaintiffs had failed to make a convincing case for discrimination. The Eleventh Circuit affirmed without opinion. The Supreme Court granted *certiorari* to decide whether Hialeah's statutes banning ritual animal slaughter violated the Free Exercise Clause of the First Amendment.

The Court's action surprised many because there did not appear to be any issue of unsettled constitutional law. As we will shortly see, previous case law showed that states could pass laws incidentally burdening religion so long as the laws were secular in purpose, neutral, and generally applicable. Nor was there a visible circuit split. Circuit splits occur when the courts of appeals from two different regions of the country (or "circuits") reach differing conclusions on the same point of law. In such cases, the law applies one way in one region of the country and in a different way in another. It often falls to the Supreme Court to resolve such conflicts. Yet, despite the absence of any apparent new issue of constitutional law or disagreement among the circuits, the Court felt that the *Lukumi* case raised important First Amendment issues that required its attention. Understanding the issue before the Court, as well as the Court's decisional process requires some background on the nature of the First Amendment and its treatment of religion.

THE FIRST AMENDMENT AND RELIGION

The text of the First Amendment reads straightforwardly. It states in relevant part that:

> Congress shall make no law respecting an establishment of religion, or prohibiting the free exercise thereof. . . .[8]

Embedded in this phrase are two important clauses that exist in delicate counterbalance: the Establishment Clause and the Free Exercise Clause. The Establishment Clause forbids the federal government from favoring religion or favoring one religion over another, while the Free Exercise Clause requires that there be no governmental prohibition of religious practice. The Supreme Court has held that, under the Due Process Clause of the Fourteenth Amendment, these precepts apply to the states as well.[9] Taken in tandem, the two clauses propound state neutrality toward religion. Courts have interpreted this to mean that governmental goals and actions should be secular and accomplished in a religiously neutral manner. Articulating such goals and carrying them out in an acceptable manner presents a significant challenge.

Navigating a path between not favoring religion and not inhibiting its practice is not always easy. It is virtually impossible for the government to completely avoid aiding religion unless it actively undermines religion—something it is likewise forbidden to do. For example, if the fire department (a state entity) responds to a fire alarm at a church, it is aiding religion, theoretically in violation of the Establishment Clause. Yet, if the fire department refuses to put out the fire, it is withholding assistance on the grounds of religious affiliation. Under the Free Exercise Clause, that too is prohibited. It would seem that in many circumstances if the state acts, it violates the Establishment Clause and if it declines to act, it violates the Free Exercise Clause. Thus, if applied inflexibly, the First Amendment's noble rhetoric could effectively paralyze the government.

The nature of this dilemma has led the Court to issue a thicket of opinions that attempt (not entirely successfully) to clarify the state's obligations. As a general matter, the two clauses taken together prevent the government from singling out specific religious groups for either benefits or burdens. If the state provides a benefit solely on the basis of religious affiliation, it runs afoul of the Establishment Clause. If, on the other hand, the government imposes a burden or penalty solely because of religious affiliation, then it violates the Free Exercise Clause.

Over the nation's history, a number of laws have been challenged under the Establishment Clause and the Court has fashioned a strategy (which it modifies from time to time) for adjudicating them. Essentially, the Court looks to whether the challenged law has a secular purpose, whether its effect promotes or inhibits religion, and whether it creates an "excessive entanglement" between the government and religion.[10]

Comparatively little jurisprudence arises from the Free Exercise Clause. This may be because there have been fewer instances where federal, state or local governments attempted to suppress or punish religious beliefs or practices so directly that they inspired Free Exercise clause challenges. However, existing case law makes plain that the Free Exercise Clause prohibits the state from prohibiting an activity because of its religious nature or because the government wishes to suppress or burden a particular faith or practice.

For example, in *Fowler v. Rhode Island*,[11] the Court barred enforcement of a municipal ordinance in a manner that prohibited Jehovah's Witnesses from preaching in a public park while allowing Catholic or Protestant services to take place in public parks. Similarly, in *McDaniel v. Paty*,[12] the Court struck down a Tennessee state law excluding ministers from serving in the state legislature. The state may also not impose special burdens of faith on people. Thus, in *Torcasso v. Watkins*,[13] the Court invalidated a Maryland requirement that state elected officials declare their belief in God prior to taking office.

The Court's recent jurisprudence suggests that if the state acts in a religiously neutral manner, it does not violate the Free Exercise Clause even if its actions incidentally burden practitioners of a particular faith. *Employment Division v. Smith*,[14] held that two drug counselors at an Oregon rehabilitation facility fired for ingesting peyote for sacramental purposes during a Native American ritual were not entitled to unemployment compensation. No one contested that the two men used the peyote for religious purposes or that the law interfered with their ability to do so. Nevertheless, the Court upheld the law and denied compensation because the state did not intentionally target religious practices by enacting or enforcing the law. The state's intent was to prevent drug abuse, not to interfere with religious activity. Any burdens placed on religion were incidental. Consequently, the Court held, the law did not violate the Free Exercise Clause.

The *Smith* case presented a new turn in Free Exercise jurisprudence. While *Smith* did not purport to overrule prior case law, the rule in previous cases had been that if a law burdened religious beliefs it had to pass a strict scrutiny test (that is, be narrowly tailored to meet a compelling state interest) to survive. Strict scrutiny poses a formidable barrier to a law's survival. A finding by the Court that a state action must undergo strict scrutiny usually means that it will be struck down. However, that is not always the case. For instance, in *United States v. Lee*,[15] the Court rejected the contention that members of the Amish faith were exempt from paying Social Security taxes. The Court acknowledged that paying or receiving Social Security benefits interfered with the free exercise of the Amish faith but nevertheless found the law "essential to accomplish an overriding governmental interest."[16] As will be argued later in this chapter, a law banning animal sacrifice could also conceivably withstand strict scrutiny.

Although the *Smith* case did not explicitly overrule previous Free Exercise cases, the rule it propounded represented a clear departure from precedent. In *Sherbert v. Verner*,[17] a case that predates *Smith* by almost two decades, the Court determined that a facially neutral law faces strict scrutiny if a plaintiff could show that the law significantly burdened the exercise of her religion. In *Verner*, the plaintiff, a Seventh Day Adventist, had been denied unemployment benefits because she refused to work on Saturdays despite a statutory requirement that applicants be available to work Monday through Saturday. The Court found for the plaintiff, reasoning that if a plaintiff could show a significant burden on the free exercise of her religion, the state would have to demonstrate that that burden was necessary to a compelling state interest. In this instance, the societal interest was not sufficiently compelling to counterbalance the burden. Consequently, the plaintiff could not be deprived of unemployment benefits because she refused to work on the Sabbath.

The key difference between the *Verner* and *Smith* decisions is that in *Verner,* the Court applied strict scrutiny to a neutral law whereas in *Smith*, it held that for neutral, generally applicable laws, strict scrutiny is unnecessary. However, since *Smith* did not explicitly overrule or modify *Verner*, the *Smith* decision created, in Justice Souter's words, "a free exercise jurisprudence in tension with itself...."[18] As a result, it is difficult to extrapolate a general rule from the Court's Free Exercise cases. Nevertheless, based on the Court's explicit reliance in *Lukumi* on the reasoning of *Smith* (as well as Justice Souter's impassioned critique of that case in his concurrence), it is clear that the *Smith* rule holds sway in *Lukumi*.[19]

The *Lukumi* Decision

When the Court granted *certiorari* in *Lukumi* it galvanized interest groups on both sides of the issue. A flurry of *amici* ensued, with religious organizations generally supporting the church's position and animal advocacy organizations weighing in on the side of Hialeah.

In a plurality opinion authored by Justice Kennedy, the Court held for the church, reversing the holdings of the district and circuit courts.[20] The combination of the plurality and concurrences clearly hold the Hialeah ordinances unconstitutional. In a later settlement, Hialeah agreed to pay the legal fees incurred by Pichardo and the church totaling nearly half a million dollars and to pay one dollar to the church as a symbol of reconciliation. Neither Pichardo nor the church pursued further legal action against the elected officials named in the lawsuit.[21]

In keeping with *Smith*, the Court noted that a law that burdens religious practices need not undergo strict scrutiny if it is neutral and of general applicability. However, if the law is not neutral or generally applicable, it must pass strict scrutiny—that is, it must be justified by a compelling governmental interest and narrowly tailored to advance that interest. Should it fail strict scrutiny, the law will be struck down as violative of the Free Exercise Clause.

In the Court's view, the Hialeah ordinances were neither neutral nor generally applicable and also roundly failed strict scrutiny. The second paragraph of Justice Kennedy's opinion encapsulates the plurality's position:

> [T]he laws in question were enacted by officials who did not understand, failed to perceive, or chose to ignore the fact that their actions violated the Nation's essential commitment to religious freedom. The challenged laws had an impermissible object; and in all events the principle of general applicability was violated because the secular ends asserted in defense of the laws were pursued only with respect to conduct motivated by religious beliefs.[22]

The Court held that the Hialeah ordinances were not neutral because the city had "gerrymandered" the ordinances to exclude virtually all types of animal killings except those carried out by Santería adherents.

Animals could still be killed and/or mistreated in many ways; the ordinances carved out only a very narrow prohibition against specific types of ritual killing. Therefore, they were underinclusive as a means of preventing animal cruelty or safeguarding the public (aims which were among the ordinances' stated objectives).[23] The Court found that this result, when coupled with the discriminatory rhetoric that preceded the ordinances' enactment, impermissibly targeted the Santería faith and, consequently, were neither neutral nor generally applicable.

If a law that burdens religion is neither neutral nor generally applicable, then it is unconstitutional unless narrowly tailored to meet a compelling state interest. The Court concluded that the Hialeah ordinances were not narrowly tailored because they regulated behavior that had little to do with their purported purpose. The city could accomplish its goals of protecting animals and the public through other means than a blanket prohibition of ritual sacrifice.

According to the plurality, "[t]he legitimate governmental interests in protecting the public health ... could be addressed by restrictions stopping far short of a flat prohibition of all Santería sacrificial practice."[24] Similarly, "[w]ith regard to the city's interest in ensuring the adequate care of animals, regulation of conditions and treatment, regardless of why an animal is kept, is the logical response to the city's concern, not a prohibition on possession for the purpose of sacrifice."[25] For example, Florida's anticruelty statute, which Hialeah adopted, outlaws the unnecessary killing of animals or any actions which result in "the cruel death, or excessive or repeated infliction of unnecessary pain or suffering." This statute, taken on its own, does not seem vulnerable to First Amendment challenge (recall that the Court struck down the ordinances because they discriminated against Santería in the aggregate). However, the wording of the Florida statute, which closely resembles New York's, has its own set of (non-constitutional) difficulties, as David Favre makes clear in his chapter in this book.

By prohibiting ritual sacrifice altogether even though the public's concerns could be addressed with narrower rules, the Court reasoned that the impact of the laws far exceeded their intended scope and purpose and were therefore overinclusive as well. "The proffered objectives are not pursued with respect to analogous non-religious conduct, and those interests could be achieved by narrower ordinances that burdened religion to a far lesser degree"[26] Consequently, the laws were neither neutral nor generally applicable nor narrowly tailored to meet a compelling state interest. Therefore, they violated the Free Exercise Clause and could not stand.

This reasoning raises a number of questions. For example, it is not clear what the Court means by "neutral," "narrowly tailored," or "compelling state interest." Such questions are not confined to the *Lukumi* controversy; they pervade much of the Court's strict scrutiny jurisprudence.

Strict scrutiny evolved as a method of protecting "preferred" or fundamental rights from governmental intrusion. While the state must occasionally impinge on individual rights to protect the common good, certain rights, such as those enumerated in the Bill of Rights, those guaranteeing access to the political process, and those that protect "discrete and insular minorities" against discrimination receive greater protection. State intrusions into these areas and against such groups therefore meet with a higher degree of judicial skepticism. Strict scrutiny evolved in the 1960s as a way of codifying that judicial skepticism.[27]

Nevertheless, the Court's approach to strict scrutiny remains highly variable. As constitutional scholar Richard Fallon explains, it falls into three main categories: (1) the nearly categorical prohibition version; (2) the weighted balancing test; and (3) the illicit motive test.

The first category works much as one might expect. If a state action threatens fundamental rights, the Court will permit the action only to avoid an impending catastrophe. For example, if there is an imminent danger of death, serious injury, or violent social upheaval, the state can pass a law constraining fundamental rights. Barring an imminent catastrophe, however, any attempt to pass such a law will fail.

The weighted balancing test balances the state's interest in carrying out a particular action against the public interest in protecting fundamental rights. The scales are so heavily weighted in favor of the fundamental rights, the state interest must be quite strong to override them. However, there need not be a showing of imminent calamity. Professor Fallon cites the Court's upholding of a statute giving the government custody of President Richard Nixon's presidential papers despite the apparent violation of Nixon's First Amendment rights. In that case, though the need was compelling and urgent, no impending cataclysm loomed.[28]

The illicit motive test focuses on sussing out whether the government purposely (and improperly) targeted a fundamental right or protected group. If so, the government's behavior will not stand. This test concerns itself more with motive than with outcome. Consequently, a law enacted with illicit motives but whose impact does not burden any protected rights or groups may nonetheless be struck down.[29]

The Court's approach in *Lukumi* seems to combine elements of all three tests. The combination of approaches generates a lack of internal consistency. As a result, the Court's reasoning is often hard to comprehend.

THE NEUTRALITY AND GENERAL APPLICABILITY ANALYSIS

The Court's neutrality and general applicability discussion lays out the legislative history behind the ordinances and shows how it demonstrates the City Council's intent to target the Santería faith. It describes the actions at the City Council's public hearing and the community resistance to the church's presence in Hialeah. The rhetoric of elected officials during the lawmaking process reflected a demonstrable bias against the Lukumi Babalu Church and against Santería practices generally. That bias manifested itself in the enactment of laws that plaintiffs claimed disproportionately impacted Santería practices. The Court's analysis underscores how each of the ordinances seemed more directed at deterring Santería rituals than in protecting animals or safeguarding the public.

For example, Ordinance 87–71 bans animal sacrifice that is "not for the primary purpose of food consumption." This excludes ritual slaughter for purposes of creating kosher meat[30] while effectively isolating and outlawing Santería practices. Similarly, the Court finds that Ordinance 87–52, which enjoins the possession, slaughter or sacrifice of animals with intent to use them for food purposes but exempts "licensed food establishments" with regard to animals "specifically raised for food purposes" intended to exempt kosher (and halal) slaughter while specifically targeting Santería practices. Santerians typically do not conduct their rituals in licensed food establishments nor are the animals they kill necessarily raised for food purposes. As a result, the law's onus fell on Santerians as opposed to followers of other faiths. In this sense, the law was not neutral in its applicability.

The Court's analysis goes awry in its examination of Ordinance 87–40, which incorporates the Florida anticruelty statute and holds liable anyone who "unnecessarily . . . kills any animal." It makes no attempt to prohibit most forms of animal killing, including fishing, hunting, and extermination yet it outlaws animal sacrifice. In the Court's view, this selective prohibition of only certain types of killing demonstrates an impermissible targeting of religious expression. Though facially persuasive, this position raises as many questions as it answers.

MUST A NEUTRAL ANTI-SACRIFICE STATUTE REGULATE ALL ANIMAL-RELATED BEHAVIOR?

The Court's determination that the Hialeah ordinances were both over and under inclusive is logically suspect. The laws purportedly aimed to accomplish a narrow goal—prohibiting ritual animal sacrifice—a type of killing the city (and state) deemed "unnecessary."[31] The city did not take a position on or attempt to ban many other types of animal killing. The Court concluded that this omission demonstrated a clear bias against Santería practices. However, there are other possible explanations. One could argue, for example, that killing animals for food and/or for sport has little in common with ritual sacrifice other than the fact that each involves animals dying.

It is possible to maintain that killing animals for food is ethically defensible while killing them for ritual is not. The argument might be that food is necessary to continued existence and animal protein has been a primary food source for humans for millennia. Therefore, the consumption of animal flesh transcends ethics and resides squarely in the realm of biological necessity.

One could likewise argue the converse—that ample alternative sources of protein and calories exist and that there is no need to consume animal flesh. By contrast, there are no substitutes for the commands of faith. In order to live an ethical life and find peace in the hereafter, one must obey the will of the gods. Both positions, while diametrically opposed, share the view that the two forms of animal slaughter are distinct and unrelated.

For present purposes, the persuasiveness of the various rationales is irrelevant. What matters is that each of the methods of animal killing cited by the Court can lay claim to different normative justifications. Therefore, grouping them together and claiming that regulating one necessarily means regulating them all does not comport with either logic or history.

The ability to differentiate between and among these activities indicates that they are normatively distinct and therefore potentially subject to different restrictions. Indeed, hunting and fishing are each regulated differently, and pest control is regulated differently than either. The slaughter of animals for food is likewise controlled by specific regulations and guidelines.

While broad statutory guidelines could apply to animal treatment (that is, a general anticruelty statute might apply but for the standard exemption for animals used in agriculture), each form of animal killing is governed by a narrow set of guidelines that apply to that activity alone. Lumping them together under the broad rubric of animal cruelty fails to acknowledge the diversity of actions involved. It also ignores the large body of pre-existing codes and regulations governing their practice. To say that hunting and cattle ranching must be covered by the same set of laws because both involve animals is akin to arguing that baseball and tennis ought to have the same rules because both involve hitting balls.

The Hialeah Statutes Were Narrowly Drawn

The Hialeah anti-sacrifice statutes were quite specific; they reached only animal sacrifice, which was the behavior they sought to regulate (as opposed to animal cruelty in general). This narrowness of scope suggests not that the ordinances sought to impose "a prohibition that society is prepared to impose upon [Santería worshippers] but not upon itself,"[32] (as the Court presumes) but rather that the statutes aimed to accomplish a defined goal—the prevention of ritual animal killing for non-food purposes.[33] Indeed, the Court acknowledges the laws' narrowness of purpose when it observes, "The net result [of the ordinances] is that few if any killings of animals are prohibited other than Santería sacrifice, which is proscribed because it occurs during a ritual or ceremony and its primary purpose is ... not food consumption."[34] Yet the Court treats this narrow scope as a flaw even as it criticizes the laws for a perceived lack of precision. It demands a breadth of coverage from the ordinances that extends well beyond what the drafters intended or what a City Council could hope to regulate.

The same dichotomy arises when the Court takes up the question of general applicability. Statutes must be generally applicable and not single out one particular entity for regulation or special treatment. While it is appropriate for the Court to strike down legislation that specifically disallows Santerians but not other religious groups from engaging in religious sacrifice, the Court does not rest its argument about general applicability on that basis. Instead, it concludes that the ordinances are not generally applicable because they are underinclusive with respect to their goals of, *inter alia*, preventing cruelty to animals. This leads back to a discussion of the statutes' narrow ambit—that they do not regulate non-sacrificial modes of animal killing, including hunting, fishing, medical research, and euthanasia. The plurality maintains that because the ordinances do not reach these other forms of animal killing and mistreatment, they are not generally applicable and therefore fail the second prong of the test for constitutionality.

This reasoning raises the same questions of practicability and scope that we saw in the neutrality discussion. Furthermore, it complicates the strict scrutiny analysis. When the Court determined that the Hialeah statutes burdened religion and were neither neutral nor generally applicable, that conclusion triggered a strict scrutiny review. Yet, it seems impossible to have a statute that is both narrowly tailored, as the strict scrutiny test requires, while still encompassing the many disparate behaviors that the plurality's interpretation of neutrality and general applicability demands. It is to the tension between these competing requirements that we now turn.

An Unworkable Strict Scrutiny Analysis

In finding that the ordinances fail to pass strict scrutiny, the Court references its earlier conclusion that the ordinances are not narrowly tailored because they do not cover a raft of behaviors other than ritual sacrifice that also kill or mistreat animals. It would seem that the Court objects to statutes that prohibit a particular type of animal killing unless they also prohibit virtually all manners of animal killing. As noted earlier, this approach mandates that the statutes be simultaneously narrow in scope and breathtakingly broad in application. Few if any laws could meet such a requirement.

Consider the following fictional example:

> The Polaricer faith requires that its adherents snowmobile at midnight through the streets of Oshkosh, Wisconsin every year during the month of January. Thousands of the faithful make the annual pilgrimage. They gather each January evening and trundle through the streets of Oshkosh, the rumbling of their snow machines echoing through the city. The noise problem is exacerbated by the fact that the roaring of the snowmobiles' engines melds with the traffic sounds (particularly the noise from trucks traveling on nearby highways).

> The ritual dismays and disrupts many of the town's inhabitants and has generated considerable friction between the locals and the Polaricers. The Oshkosh City Council, declaring its concern about detrimental impacts on public health, noise and safety from snow-

mobile use, passes an ordinance banning snowmobiles from city streets after dark.

A group of Polaricers sue, claiming violations of their rights under the Free Exercise Clause. They argue that the city government unfairly singled out their particular practice for regulation. Since the ordinances did not attempt to regulate all forms of transportation that impact the public welfare, noise and safety, Polaricer practices have been wrongfully suppressed.

The plaintiffs note the lack of any similar ban on trucks, despite their considerable noise quotient. They note as well that other modes of transportation (toboggans, for example) are potentially hazardous to health and safety yet remain unregulated. Clearly, they argue, the town's concern with public health and safety is pretextual and the real reason for the ordinances is the town's growing dislike for the annual influx of religious pilgrims. Therefore, the Polaricers claim, the statute is unconstitutionally underinclusive and void.

The Polaricers further maintain that the statute is overinclusive because there are more circumscribed ways of accomplishing the town's stated goals. The City Council could, for example, limit the size of the snowmobile engines permitted after ten p.m. and/or require extra soundproofing as well as lights and safety flags. Instead, the Council passed a law effectively rendering it impossible for members of a particular religious group to obey the tenets of their faith. This constitutes unlawful discrimination under the Free Exercise Clause. The plaintiffs seek damages and injunctive relief.

Based on the *Lukumi* court's reasoning, shouldn't the Polaricers prevail? The City Council singled out a specific form of winter transportation for regulation in a manner that directly burdencd the religious practices of a particular group. Even though it could have opted for any number of other ways of safeguarding the public safety and welfare and decreasing noise, the Council chose a method that directly and detrimentally impacted the Polaricer faith. In addition, public welfare and safety as well as the peace of the evening remain at risk because the ordinance did not regulate all possible sources of noise or disruption. Shouldn't the statute be invalidated because it enjoins religiously motivated behavior while failing to address other activities that pose a similar threat to the Council's stated goals?

The problem with this reasoning is that it simultaneously demands too much and too little. On the one hand, it requires that the statute be narrowly tailored to accomplish its goal. On the other hand, it broadens the statute's goal to the point where narrow tailoring becomes impossible.

The issue in Oshkosh is not *all* noise and *all* dangers to public health and safety. The City Council's concern lay with the noise from snowmobile use at night on town streets and its accompanying disturbances. It defies logic and the principles of statutory construction to require that the Oshkosh legislature regulate all noise just because it has concerns with one particular kind of noise. Such a requirement would effectively render any legislative undertaking quixotic and unworkable. Yet, this is apparently the condition that the Supreme Court imposed on the city of Hialeah.

Since the Hialeah anti-sacrifice ordinances target religiously motivated behavior, the Court properly demands that they be narrowly tailored. However, the opinion also requires that the ordinances concurrently address all behavior that negatively impacts animals. No statute could successfully negotiate such a gauntlet and it follows that the Hialeah ordinances were doomed from the outset.

As noted earlier, a law faces strict scrutiny when it burdens a protected group or fundamental right (in a non-neutral manner). Strict scrutiny requires that the law be narrowly tailored to further a compelling state interest. If the law does not further that state interest, it creates a burden on religion for no reason. It follows that a law that burdens religion must have a compelling purpose. An ineffective law that burdens religion would necessarily fall short of this standard. Therefore, though efficacy is not explicitly enumerated in the test, an ineffective law could not pass strict scrutiny.

The chief problem with the Court's approach lies less in its methodology than in its characterization of the city's goals. No statute could eliminate all animal cruelty, not least because of the multifarious definitions of "cruelty." And the Hialeah ordinances—as the Court points out—made no such attempt. Instead, the ordinances prohibited a *certain type* of animal cruelty—the cruelty that stems from ritually killing animals for purposes not explicitly linked to food consumption. Thus, the Court held the ordinances to a standard they could not (and did not attempt to) reach. It then invalidated the laws because they fell short of this artificial standard. Returning to Professor Fallon's terminology, the Court's approach resembles a "weighted balancing test" with the scale so weighted in favor of invalidating the ordinances that it becomes more of a "nearly categorical prohibition." In effect, the Court erected a set of straw men, substituted them for the Hialeah ordinances, and then struck them down.

A Different Approach to Strict Scrutiny

A. *Narrow Tailoring*

The Court determined that the city structured its ordinances to accomplish a religious gerrymander—an "impermissible attempt" to target Santería religious practices. This assessment seems entirely accurate in light of the xenophobic testimony by council members and community leaders at the public hearing prior to the laws' passage. However, determining if these particular ordinances illegitimately targeted a religious group presents an entirely different issue than determining whether a law enjoining ritual animal slaughter for non-food purposes is illegitimately underinclusive. The Court's conflation of these two issues unnecessarily complicates an already complicated body of Free Exercise jurisprudence.

The latter question—whether it would be constitutionally legitimate to prohibit ritual animal slaughter for non-food purposes—raises a host of interesting issues that the *Lukumi* court sidestepped. For instance, the Court's rhetorical linkage of animal sacrifice with all other forms of animal killing/cruelty demands further inquiry. While killing and cruelty are often linked, they are not always—a fact that the law routinely recognizes in both the human and animal realms.

In the human arena, killing and cruelty are distinct and severable phenomena. The law recognizes certain types of killing as acceptable while condemning others. One cannot imagine, for example, the Court striking down a statute prohibiting human sacrifice. It would not matter that other circumstances exist in which people are routinely killed (execution, military combat, etc). Nor would it matter that the anti-human sacrifice statute proscribes killing in certain situations and places and not in others and that the statute targets specifically religious behavior. The law would survive because, despite its apparent underinclusiveness and focus on a specifically religious practice, it still satisfies a compelling state interest (avoiding "unnecessary" human deaths) and is narrowly tailored to accomplish that goal.

"Cruelty" to humans is a similarly fluid concept. The Constitution forbids "cruel and inhuman" punishment yet so-called "Supermax" prisons routinely confine inmates to a tiny cell in solitary confinement for twenty-three hours per day (the other hour is spent in an exercise pen known as a "kennel"). This type of confinement can and often does lead to deep psychological trauma and is considered highly punitive. Yet, it remains both legal and widely tolerated. Clearly, there exist certain situations where treatment that might otherwise be labeled cruel has been found to be expedient and socially acceptable.

The debate between the Bush administration and Congress, as well as the Courts, as to what exactly constitutes "torture" provides another example of the state sanctioning cruelty in some circumstances but not in others. That cruelty is tolerated in some contexts and not in others does not mean that all laws seeking to limit cruel behavior under certain prescribed conditions are useless or underinclusive. It rather indicates that the laws aim to prohibit certain behaviors that society finds particularly objectionable. Since other forms of cruelty do not give rise to the same level of societal concern, it follows that killing and cruelty are not objectionable *per se*. Instead, society allows certain kinds of killing and cruelty while prohibiting others.

A similar tolerance for certain forms of killing and cruelty extends to animals. While numerous laws—both state and federal—ban the mistreatment or killing of animals, those laws are narrowly circumscribed to permit activities which might otherwise fall within their purview. Hunting, for example, involves the killing of animals, but it is regulated rather than prohibited. The same holds true for fishing.

Similarly, one cannot simply butcher one's house pets and the federal Humane Slaughter Act lays out federal guidelines regarding the slaughter of animals for food.

This selective prohibition of animal mistreatment results from a normative (and legislative) choice. While much gratuitous killing of animals still occurs, it does not mean that the laws governing hunting and house pets are failures because they do not regulate or prohibit the various other methods in which animals are killed. Rather, the laws are underinclusive by design. They are narrowly tailored to accomplish the state's particularized interest in preventing the killing and mistreatment of animals in those particular ways that do not meet with state approval.

With this clarification in mind, the Court's position in the *Lukumi* case that the Hialeah statutes are underinclusive because they focus on ritual sacrifice and do not address other methods of animal cruelty or slaughter begins to look strained. Putting aside the fact that hunting, fishing, and medical research are regulated by other statutes, invalidating a law because it fails to regulate behavior that it does not seek to regulate is fundamentally illogical. The Hialeah statutes were narrowly tailored to accomplish the goal of enjoining animal sacrifice within the city limits. If they had a broader scope, they would lose their narrow tailoring. Furthermore, the Court's reasoning demands a breadth of coverage from the ordinances that is well beyond what the drafters intended or what a City Council could hope to accomplish. The Court's complaint seems not to be that the statutes are insufficiently narrow, but rather that they are *too* narrow.

B.   If the Statutes are Narrowly Tailored, Is their Purpose Compelling?

If, as now seems clear, the statutes were narrowly tailored, that does not complete the strict scrutiny test. The second prong of the test requires determining if the challenged law furthers a compelling state interest. The *Lukumi* Court found the interests at issue in the Hialeah ordinances insufficiently compelling. Yet, it is not at all clear to which interests the Court referred when it made that determination.

The opinion is highly critical of the manner in which the ordinances were gerrymandered to burden the Lukumi Babalu church and Santería practices. But that gerrymander does not seem to form the basis—or at least not the sole basis—for the Court's decision to invalidate the laws. Instead, the Court focuses at length on the scope of the laws and their efficacy with respect to preventing animal mistreatment.

Few would disagree that a law enacted for the purpose of excluding a religious organization from a community fails to satisfy any compelling state interest. The record in the *Lukumi* case indicates that such a gerrymander did occur in Hialeah. However, the Court's attention is primarily directed elsewhere. It cites with approval the 1989 case of *Florida Star v. B.J.F.*,[35] which notes that "a law cannot be regarded as protecting an interest 'of the highest order' ... when it leaves appreciable damage to that supposedly vital interest unprohibited."[36] The Court then declaims that the Hialeah ordinances are underinclusive with respect to preventing animal cruelty and/or deaths and that only religiously motivated conduct is impacted by the laws' restrictions.

As we have seen, this critique is only partially accurate. While the ordinances do disproportionately impact religious conduct, they are not underinclusive. They are rather narrowly tailored to accomplish their stated goal of preventing animal sacrifice. When the Court assumes that the statutes seek to remedy all animal cruelty within the city limits, it misapprehends their intent. It then offhandedly notes that "there can be no serious claim that *those interests* justify the ordinances."[37]

The phrase "those interests" in the sentence quoted above does not have a clear referent. It could refer to the prevention of animal cruelty *or* the burdening of religiously motivated conduct. If the former, then the statement is exaggerated and derogates the cause of animal protection. If the latter, then the Court's dismissiveness arguably deprives it of an opportunity to evaluate the ordinances on the terms under which they were enacted. Had the Court focused more explicitly on the religious gerrymander, it would have avoided imposing a significant burden on future animal protection legislation. The Court's insistence that anticruelty legislation be all-encompassing could hinder the enactment of specific statutes in the future that address particular types of cruelty to animals. This intolerance for targeted legislation is particularly problematic because the notion of what constitutes cruelty continues to evolve.

C. *Statutes That Aim to Discriminate Against Religion Will Fail*

The behavior and statements of the Hialeah City Council members (and the members of the community) at the public hearing prior to the ordinances' enactment demonstrate an unmistakable bias against the Santería faith and the Lukumi Babalu Church. The plurality acknowledges this, observing that "the record in this case compels the conclusion that suppression of the central element of the Santería worship service was the object of the ordinances" and that this represented "an improper attempt to target Santería."[38] That obvious bias means that the Court could have taken a much different approach in its analysis.

The examination of the statute's neutrality and general applicability would have been short, swift and irrefutable. Though arguably of general applicability, the ordinances were not neutral; they aimed directly at Santería. That fact alone would have triggered strict scrutiny, requiring that the ordinances be narrowly tailored to accomplish a compelling state interest in order to survive. This analytical approach fits Professor Fallon's "illicit motive test."

Assuming the aim of the statute was to exclude Santería practices from Hialeah, the Court's analysis makes clear that the ordinances were indeed narrowly tailored to accomplish this goal. However, the last prong of the test—determining whether the ordinances satisfy a compelling state interest—is where the ordinances run into difficulty. The state has no compelling interest in discriminating against a particular religious faith or practice. Indeed, under the Free Exercise Clause, such interests are constitutionally impermissible. If the state's interest in passing the anti-sacrifice ordinances centered on suppressing the Santería faith, then the ordinances cannot survive.

Rather than avail itself of this framework, the Court instead dwells on the laws' inclusiveness and efficacy (or lack thereof) with respect to animal cruelty. In light of the Court's lengthy disquisition on the inclusiveness of the ordinances as well as the omission of a straightforward analysis of their discriminatory nature, it is at least plausible that the statement, "there can be no serious claim that those interests justify the ordinances," referred to the state's interest in protecting animals from cruelty and unnecessary death. Both Justice Blackmun and Justice Souter's respective concurrences make plain that they did not believe the plurality opinion addressed the issue of whether animal protection can rise to the level of a compelling state interest. Nevertheless, the language of the plurality opinion with respect to this issue is far from clear.

Assuming the Court intended to refer to animal protection, the decision needlessly undermines that goal while erecting gratuitous hurdles to future laws aimed at safeguarding animals from ritual sacrifice. It conflates the general goal of alleviating animal *suffering* with the narrower goal of eliminating animal *sacrifice* and in so doing needlessly complicates the free exercise analysis. We have already established that, under the Court's jurisprudence, laws can burden and/or constrain religious practices if those constraints are incidental to the enforcement of a neutral law. Unfortunately, when the Court classified animal sacrifice as a protected form of religious expression while finding that laws seeking to regulate it must also address all other types of animal cruelty, it all but eliminated the possibility that a law seeking to regulate and/or ban animal sacrifice could be neutral.

CAN AN ANTI-SACRIFICE STATUTE BE NEUTRAL?

At first reading, the idea of a religiously neutral law prohibiting animal sacrifice may appear self-contradictory. After all, the notion of animal sacrifice has powerful religious connotations. Any law aiming to regulate it would have to negotiate the attendant burden such a law would place on religion. Nevertheless, according to the Court, though "[t]he words 'sacrifice' and 'ritual' have a religious origin, ... current use admits also of secular meanings.... *The ordinances, furthermore, define 'sacrifice' in secular terms*, without referring to 'religious practices.' "[39] Thus, even as the Court struck down the Hialeah ordinances because they unconstitutionally burdened Santería religious practices, it acknowledged that the term sacrifice can be defined secularly and that the Hialeah ordinances did just that.

Ordinance 87–52 defines "sacrifice" as to "unnecessarily kill, torment, torture, or mutilate an animal in a public or private ritual or ceremony not for the primary purpose of food consumption." The dictionary defines a ritual as "the performance of actions in a set, ordered, and ceremonial way." Numerous types of secular animal killing meet this definition. For example, "crush" videos, in which, leggy, spike-heeled women are filmed grinding small animals underfoot meet the definition of sacrifice. So too do many forms of laboratory experiments in which animals are killed according to precise guidelines. Indeed, the common term used to refer to the slaughter of laboratory animals is "sacrifice."

The key term in the ordinance is "unnecessarily." The Attorney General of Florida opined that ritual sacrifice not for the purpose of food consumption was unnecessary and therefore illegal under the state anticruelty statute. The Hialeah ordinances simply adopted the state law. The Court found that the Hialeah ordinances were discriminatory against Santería when viewed in the aggregate because they effectively excluded all forms of animal killing except Santería sacrifice.

One need not quarrel with this conclusion to take issue with the notion that a law banning animal sacrifice must necessarily be discriminatory. If the term can have a secular definition that encompasses the gratuitous killing and torment of animals, then it seems an appropriate area for state regulation. It should likewise be possible to regulate the practice in a neutral, generally applicable way. And, if that regulation is neutral, generally applicable and narrowly tailored, albeit incidentally burdensome to religion, then, under *Smith*, it should pass constitutional muster.[40]

A thornier issue arises when an anti-sacrifice ordinance is not neutral and instead aims to suppress a particular religious practice. The question then becomes whether the regulation is narrowly tailored to further a compelling state interest. Such a law could be narrowly tailored (as evidenced by the Hialeah statutes). And, while the suppression of religion is not (and cannot be) a compelling state interest, suppressing religion need not be the point of the law. It may rather be that the practice is offensive to the majority of society and the legislature wishes to put an end to it (the practice, not the religion). In that case, the legislature would be focusing on the eradication of a certain offensive practice (animal sacrifice). The burden on religion would be incidental, with no intent to suppress religious expression.

Nor must such a law address animal mistreatment in all its forms. The law could simply seek to ban a particular form of animal mistreatment that American society finds intolerable. The pivotal question then becomes: can such a narrow form of animal protection form a compelling state interest? If so, then a properly drafted law banning animal sacrifice should withstand constitutional challenge.

Unsurprisingly, determining if a ban on animal sacrifice can rise to the level of compelling state interest is no simple task. As we have seen, the term "compelling state interest" defies easy categorization. As the Court makes clear, certain types of animal mistreatment and killing are socially acceptable. Others are not. The reasons for society's acceptance of some forms of mistreatment and its flat prohibition of others are far from obvious. Even the laws designed to protect animals are filled with exemptions that often gut their capacity for enforcement.

FEDERAL LAWS ARE RIVEN WITH EXCEPTIONS

At the federal level, the Animal Welfare Act[41] is the principal federal statute mandating protections for animals and setting standards for their care. Yet the Act specifically excludes farm animals from its ambit.[42] Without an umbrella statute that gives it authority to prevent industrial practices that cause farmed animals to suffer, the U.S. Department of Agriculture ("USDA") cannot promulgate regulations to safeguard the health and wellbeing of food animals. Since over nine billion farm animals are killed each year, this regulatory gap looms highly significant.

Similarly, the Humane Slaughter Act,[43] enacted to protect livestock from the often agonizing deaths awaiting them at industrial slaughterhouses, mandates that livestock be slaughtered using "humane methods."[44] However, the USDA has determined that the term "livestock" excludes poultry.[45] Thus, the billions of chickens, turkeys and ducks slaughtered every year need not be—and usually are not—rendered insensible to pain before being hoisted, shackled and cut. In addition, the Humane Slaughter Act exempts ritual slaughter as well as state-inspected slaughterhouses from its ambit. Numerous instances of egregious cruelty have been documented in such facilities.[46]

STATE LAWS ARE LIKEWISE UNPRODUCTIVE

Twenty-eight states have anticruelty statutes that specifically exempt farming practices that are generally accepted in the industry.[47] This exemption effectively strips the laws of any force or normative component. Standard industry practices are typically those that best serve the industry. Removing those practices from legal oversight enables regulated entities to tailor their practices to their maximum benefit, regardless of societal standards or impact on the affected animals.

State criminal anticruelty statutes have also proven ineffective. First, the state must prove intent, a task complicated by the enormous number of animals processed by industrial food producers.[48] Given the hundreds of thousands of animals in their custody, producers can easily claim that they did not know the condition of any given animal. Thus, indifference to the animals' well being actually becomes a defense to prosecution.[49]

Furthermore, criminal statutes do not spawn regulations. Without guidelines for the industry or an administrative agency tasked with the laws' enforcement, no regular inspections take place. This means the job falls to local law enforcement officials who, absent a search warrant, cannot enter private property to ensure compliance.[50] Even if they could enforce the statutes, these officers would have little incentive to do so; penalties for violations are generally quite low.

The low penalty for violations of animal cruelty statutes indicates a low societal interest in deterring such behavior. This lack of interest in protecting animals from harm stems from the fact that the animals' value is often enhanced through their mistreatment (in the sense that the less money invested in their welfare, the greater the profit realized from their sale). Stated differently, the efficacy of animal protection statutes is inversely proportional to the potential profit to be gained from animals' mistreatment. In light of these statutory deficiencies, it becomes fair to ask whether animal protection could realistically be characterized as a compelling state interest. Given the porous nature of existing state and federal statutes, it seems unrealistic to classify protection of all animals as a state interest at all, much less a compelling one.

All fifty states have animal cruelty statutes and the trend in recent years has been to widen rather than narrow the reach of those statutes. For example, several states recently passed laws banning some of the most inhumane factory-farming practices. Florida passed a constitutional amendment prohibiting the use of gestation crates for sows[51] (and another limiting marine net fishing).[52] Similarly Arizona passed a statute effective December 31, 2012 that bans gestation crates for pigs and veal crates for calves.[53]

It also bears mention that federal laws (including those discussed above), while truncated in scope, nevertheless demonstrate a state interest in safeguarding the welfare of at least some animals. Recent trends also indicate a slight shift toward increased protections for animals at the federal level. For example, the Twenty–Eight Hour Law[54], originally enacted in 1873, requires that animals not be confined for more than twenty-eight continuous hours when being transported across state lines in a "rail carrier, express carrier, or common carrier (except by air or water)" without at least five hours of rest, watering and feeding.[55] Yet, the USDA steadfastly maintained that the statute applied only to rail transport and not to trucks.[56] Since trucks form the primary means of transporting animals, this interpretation excluded most animals from the little protection that the statute purported to offer. In 2006, following the filing of a legal petition against the USDA by several advocacy organizations, the agency finally conceded that the statute did indeed apply to trucks.

CAN ANIMAL WELFARE RISE TO THE LEVEL OF COMPELLING STATE INTEREST?

The haphazard approach to animal protection under the current legal regime suggests that animal welfare lies far from the forefront of the nation's consciousness. However, that does not mean the state (and the public) evinces no interest in the issue. Some animals (for example, endangered species, companion animals, service animals) benefit from a clear state interest in their protection, even if that interest lies less with the animals themselves than in the benefits humans gain from their protection. A second possibility is that the nation's laws do not accurately reflect society's strong interest in animal protection and welfare. Still another possibility is that the current animal legal regime overstates society's bent toward animal protection and that, but for the government's proactive legislating, animals would have even fewer legal protections.

The latter possibility (that extant laws are overly strict and out of step with lax contemporary notions of animal welfare) seems least likely. Animal welfare issues have enjoyed increasing visibility and support both in the press and by statute.[57] In addition, as the American public has become more familiar with industrial agriculture, the resulting outcry at its methods has spurred a shift away from some of the most inhumane practices. For example, Smithfield Foods, the world's largest producer of pork, has pledged to move away from gestation crates for sows;[58] Burger King has agreed to transition away from battery cage raised eggs;[59] and celebrity chef Wolfgang Puck will not serve battery cage-raised eggs, pig products from companies that use gestation crates, or foie gras, a duck liver product created through force feeding.[60] These recent developments, as well as the favorable press these and other initiatives have received, and the aforementioned national trend toward tightening animal welfare statutes, militate against the notion of a small and dwindling base of public support for animal welfare.

The second possibility—that current laws do not accurately reflect the public's increased interest in animal welfare—again in light of recent developments in the statutory and corporate realms—seems possible and even likely. Many of the companies that changed their business practices did so in response to public pressure. Similarly, much of the recent legislation has been propelled by public interest groups.[61] Surveys and other data demonstrate that, when informed of the way animals are treated in industrial agriculture and elsewhere (for example, in medical research or puppy mills), the public response tends toward calls for stronger protection for the animals.[62] It therefore seems reasonable to conclude that public interest in animal welfare is both real and growing and that current laws do not satisfactorily reflect the public's concern.

It remains true, however, that the public's concern for animals is not boundless. Even companion animals remain property in the eyes of the law. This means that the animals' interests are always subordinate to the interests of the people who "own" them.[63] Consequently, their legal rights and ability to enforce those rights remain minimal.

Even more dire is the situation of non-companion animals. Though many if not most Americans believe farm animals ought to be better treated during their lives, only a small minority believes that animals should not be killed for food. An even smaller percentage condemns the use of animals for producing dairy products. Nor do most Americans oppose hunting or fishing. In addition, despite questions of efficacy and ethics, experimentation on animals remains an integral part of scientific methodology.

It would seem that American laws lack consistency of purpose when it comes to animal welfare. Most animal protection statutes exempt most animals from their coverage. Many types of animal mistreatment are legal and, in some cases, actively encouraged. In addition, as the *Lukumi* decision demonstrates, religiously based animal cruelty can potentially claim constitutional protection. Nevertheless, there remains a powerful undercurrent of concern for animals and their welfare. In the wake of *Lukumi*, the question lingers whether animal sacrifice can be regulated or whether it must always be protected religious behavior. In order to answer that question we must first determine whether preventing animal sacrifice can rise to the level of a compelling state interest. If so, then despite an inevitable burden on religious behavior, a law banning animal sacrifice should survive challenge under the Free Exercise Clause.

CAN AN ANTI-SACRIFICE STATUTE SURVIVE A FREE EXERCISE CHALLENGE?

The range of protections and public attention afforded animals suggests that the nation's interest in animal protection varies. It further indicates that existing laws do not necessarily reflect the depth of public concern (or lack thereof). The degree of interest depends on the affected animals and the circumstances. Under the current set of laws, one can kill (and eat) some animals but not others. Even among those animals raised for slaughter, some must be killed "humanely" while others need not. Still other animals may not be killed under any except the most exigent of circumstances.

Clearly, the laws protect some animals more than others. It follows that the state possesses a compelling interest in protecting certain animals from certain types of mistreatment. Other animals facing other (or similar) types of harm do not engender the same level of interest. Determining whether a compelling state interest exists requires a fact-specific inquiry focusing on existing laws, the degree of public concern, and other competing societal priorities.

If the legislature enacted additional laws protecting certain animals from mistreatment while leaving others exposed to peril, those laws would blend readily with the current legal regime. Those additional laws might, for example, protect certain animals from certain types of death viewed as not needful while allowing those same animals to be killed in other ways for other reasons. For example, a dog living in domestic situation cannot be poisoned, mutilated or sensorily deprived, yet if that same dog were to find itself the subject of a sanctioned scientific research project, it could suffer any or all of those fates. Similarly, the state could conceivably prioritize killing animals for food while strictly regulating other types of animal slaughter. Ritual killing for purposes other than food consumption might then fall into a state-defined category of non-needful uses. Consequently, barring animal sacrifice might rise to the level of compelling state interest even as the state permits other forms of animal killing and mistreatment.

Thus contextualized, a law banning animal sacrifice seems no more inconsistent or underinclusive than most other animal protection laws. Furthermore, the Court acknowledges that laws prohibiting sacrifice need not specifically aim to burden religion, even if they incidentally do so. Under *Smith* and its progeny, any anti-sacrifice statute that incidentally burdened religion would have to be neutral and generally applicable. If it singled out religious practices, it would also have to be narrowly tailored and necessary to further a compelling state interest. A well-drafted ordinance that defined animal sacrifice carefully and prohibited it for compelling (secular) reasons might well pass such strict scrutiny.

By contrast, the Hialeah ordinances would likely fail because they were neither neutral nor generally applicable. The record overwhelmingly demonstrates that the ordinances' specifically targeted and sought to suppress Santería religious practices. Suppressing religion is *never* a compelling state interest.

Had the Court focused its analysis in this manner, its conclusion would not have changed but it would have avoided opining on the relative worth of animal protection versus religious freedom. The plurality opinion arguably strays into this uncertain territory and its analysis does little to clarify the issue. Indeed, it is not even clear if the opinion actually takes up the question. The concurrences claim that it does not. According to Justice Blackmun, the plurality opinion did not reach the question of "whether the Free Exercise Clause would require a religious exemption from a law that sincerely pursued the goal of protecting animals from cruel treatment." For him, that is a question for another day and one that the outpouring of *amici* demonstrates should not be taken lightly.[64]

Justice Blackmun apparently read the phrase, "there can be no serious claim that *those interests* justify the ordinances" to refer to the interest in discriminating against religious practices—an uncontroversial assertion with a clear constitutional predicate. If he is correct, then the Court's lengthy analysis regarding the alleged over and underinclusiveness of the Hialeah statutes and their relationship to animal cruelty becomes simply dicta. If he is wrong, however, then the plurality opinion enshrined the ritual killing of animals in the pantheon of constitutionally protected behavior. It did so based on a vision of animal protection that has little correlation with contemporary laws or norms. And it did so needlessly.

* Professor of Law, Pace Law School. I am much indebted to Taimie Bryant for her very useful comments and superb editing. I am very grateful as well to Steven Sarno and Danielle Cole for their outstanding research assistance and help with every stage of the project. Finally and as always, Elizabeth Downes and Jesse Cassuto are the unsung heroes of everything I do.

1. 508 U.S. 520 (1993).

2. Much of the description of Santería and the history of the Church of the Lukumi Babalu Aye are drawn from DAVID M. O'BRIEN, ANIMAL SACRIFICE AND RELIGIOUS FREEDOM (2004).

3. Following the exodus, U.S. government agents determined that many of the refugees had been chosen for release due to their status as "undesirable" whether because of religious affiliation, prior criminal record, sexual orientation, political dissidence, or other quality. Having decried Castro's totalitarian regime for decades, the U.S. government was effectively forced to accept the 125,000 refugees or risk appearing to support the concept of the island prison. *See, e.g.*, Stephen Webbe, *Flight from Cuba*, CHRISTIAN SCI. MONITOR, May 8, 1980, at B2 (describing the processing procedures for asylum seekers and the efforts of Cuban–Americans to collect their relatives from Mariel); Paul Montgomery, *1,774 People Without a Country: Cuban Refugees Sit in U.S. Jails*, N.Y. TIMES, Dec. 7, 1980, at 1 (discussing the classification and detention of Cuban refugees based on alleged criminal backgrounds); Steven Weisman, *Havana Government Unilaterally Cuts Off Refugee Boat Exodus*, N.Y. TIMES, Sept. 27, 1980, at 1 (discussing the end of the exodus and the political implications of the relocation efforts).

4. *See* Mirta Ojito, *Santeria Priest Faces Charges in Animal Slaughter*, MIAMI HERALD, June 12, 1995, at 2B (describing the prosecution of a Santerìa priest who publicly sacrificed 15 animals in celebration of the Lukumi decision, but was arrested for the violent manner in which he attempted to kill the animals); Mike Williams, *Santeria Priest Challenges Fla. City's Ban on Ritual Animal Sacrifice: Freedom of Religion Claim Vies with Cruelty Charges*, ATLANTA J.-CONST., Aug. 31, 1989, at A10 (describing the painful techniques employed during Santerìa's ritual sacrifices); G. Savage, *Justices Revisit Unsettled Issue in Santeria Case Law*, L.A. TIMES, Nov. 1, 1992, at A22 (discussing the differences between Santerìa sacrifices and slaughterhouse practices).

5. O'BRIEN, *supra* note 2, at 35.

6. *Id.* at 43.

7. *Id.*; *see also* Church of Lukumi Babalu Aye, Inc. v. City of Hialeah, 508 U.S. 520, 541 (1993).

8. U.S. CONST. amend. I.

9. *See* Everson v. Bd. of Educ., 330 U.S. 1 (1947) (holding that the Establishment Clause applies to the states via the Fourteenth Amendment); Cantwell v. Connecticut, 310 U.S. 296 (1940) (holding that the Free Exercise Clause also applies to the states via the Fourteenth Amendment).

10. *See* Lemon v. Kurtzman, 403 U.S. 602 (1971). The Court revisited and modified the so-called *"Lemon* test" in Agostini v. Felton, 521 U.S. 203 (1997), particularly the "excessive entanglement" prong to focus more on whether the challenged law or government program had the impermissible effect of aiding or inhibiting religion. However, the *Agostini* Court left the *Lemon* test largely intact.

11. 345 U.S. 67 (1953).

12. 435 U.S. 618 (1978).

13. 367 U.S. 488 (1961).

14. 494 U.S. 872 (1990).

15. 455 U.S. 252 (1982).

16. *Id.* at 257–60.

17. 374 U.S. 398 (1963).

18. Church of Lukumi Babalu Aye, Inc. v. City of Hialeah, 508 U.S. 520, 564 (1993) (Souter, J., concurring in part and concurring in the judgment).

19. The plurality opinion cites directly to *Smith* for the proposition that, "our cases establish the general proposition that a law that is neutral and of general applicability need not be justified by a compelling governmental interest even if the law has the incidental effect of burdening a particular religious practice." *Id.* at 531 (plurality opinion).

20. *Lukumi*, 508 U.S. at 547.

21. *See* O'BRIEN, *supra* note 2, at 160.

22. *Lukumi*, 508 U.S. at 524.

23. While the Official Code of Hialeah no longer contains the relevant provisions, the ordinances are included in the appendix to the opinion of the Supreme Court. *See id.* at 548. Resolution No. 87–66 and Ordinance No. 87–90 specifically identify the prevention of animal cruelty and the protection of public safety as goals of the ordinances.

24. *Id.* at 538.

25. *Id.* at 539.

26. *Id.* at 546.

27. Robert H. Fallon, Jr., *Strict Judicial Scrutiny*, 54 UCLA L. REV. 1267, 1270–71 (2007) (citing United States v. Carolene Prods. Co., 304 U.S. 144, 152 n.4 (1938)).

28. *Id.* at 1306 n.228 (citing Nixon v. Adm'r of Gen. Servs., 433 U.S. 425, 467–68 (1977)).

29. *Id.* at 1302–09.

30. The Court does not address halal practices but they would be exempt as well.

31. Church of Lukumi Babalu Aye, Inc. v. City of Hialeah, 508 U.S. 520, 537 (1993). The fact that the city had ulterior motives in enacting the law (discriminating against Santería practices) does not mean that the laws *as written* did not claim a different motivation.

32. *Id.* at 545.

33. The Court quotes several Hialeah officials stating their clear opposition not to the killing of animals but rather to the use of animals in religious sacrifice. *See id.* at 541–42.

34. *Id.* at 536.

35. 491 U.S. 524 (1989).

36. *Id. at* 541–42.

37. Church of Lukumi Babalu Aye, Inc. v. City of Hialeah, 508 U.S. 520, 547 (1993) (emphasis added).

38. *Id.* at 534.

39. *Id.* at 534 (emphasis added).

40. A number of municipalities have anti-sacrifice statutes that are in many respects identical to the challenged Hialeah ordinance 87–52. *See, e.g.,* L.A., CAL., MUN. CODE § 53.67 (1990) (prohibiting animal sacrifice except for food purposes). The Los Angeles Municipal Code defines animal sacrifice to mean "the injuring or killing of any animal in any religious or cult ritual or as an offering to a deity, devil, demon or spirit, wherein the animal has not been injured or killed primarily for food purposes, regardless of whether all or any part of such animal is subsequently consumed." *Id.* The City of Chicago Municipal Code bans the possession or slaughter of animals for food purposes and explicitly states that the ban "is applicable to any cult that kills (sacrifices) animals for any type of ritual, regardless of whether or not the flesh or blood of the animal is to be consumed; except that Kosher slaughtering is exempted from this ordinance." CHI., ILL., MUN. CODE § 7–12–300 (LexisNexis 2007). The City of Euless, Texas passed an ordinance that prohibits the slaughter of animals except for poultry intended for consumption. EULESS, TEX., CODE § 10–3 (1974). Recent friction between a local Santería church and the Euless city council over a municipal sacrifice ban led to a suit against the city. *See Suit Over Animal Sacrifice Ban Highlights Growing Religious Clashes in a More Diverse U.S.*, INT'L HERALD TRIB., Mar. 27, 2007, http://www.iht.com/articles/ap/2007/03/28/america/NA–FEA–REL–US–Suburban–Sacrifices.php.

41. Animal Welfare Act of 1970, Pub. L. No. 91–579, 84 Stat. 1560. Six years later, Congress passed the Animal Welfare Act Amendments of 1976, Pub. L. No. 94–279, 90 Stat. 417.

42. 7 U.S.C. § 2132(g) (1970).

43. Humane Methods of Slaughter Act of 1978, Pub. L. 95–445, 92 Stat. 1069 (codified at 7 U.S.C. §§ 1902–1907 (2000)).

44. 7 U.S.C. § 1902 (2000).

45. 9 C.F.R. § 3012 (2006).

46. *See, e.g.*, Matthew Wagner, *Rabbinate OKs Meat Despite Cruelty to Animals*, JERUSALEM POST (Israel), Mar. 14, 2006, at 8 (discussing the rabbinical approval of slaughtered meat in Iowa that violated U.S. cruelty laws because hooks were used to rip out the esophagus and trachea of conscious animals); Donald G. McNeil, Jr., *KFC Supplier Accused of Animal Cruelty*, N.Y. TIMES, July 20, 2004, at C2 (describing a long list of cruel acts observed by an undercover investigator who infiltrated a KFC plant in West Virginia); David J. Wolfson, *Beyond the Law*, 2 ANIMAL L. 123 (1996) (noting that federal anticruelty laws do not apply to state-inspected slaughterhouses and have no effect on the often cruel, common practices in these facilities).

47. Other states, including Maine, North Carolina, Ohio, Vermont, and Wisconsin, exempt specific industry practices from regulatory scrutiny. Still others, including Louisiana and South Carolina, exempt specific animals (in this case, birds) from state protection. *See* Wolfson, *supra* note 46, at 137; William A. Reppy, *Broad Exemptions in Animal–Cruelty Statutes Unconstitutionally Deny Equal Protection of the Law*, 70 LAW & CONTEMP. PROBS. 255, 307–23 (2007).

48. *See* David J. Wolfson & Mariann Sullivan, *Foxes in the Hen House*, in ANIMAL RIGHTS: CURRENT DEBATES AND NEW DIRECTIONS 209 (Martha Nussbaum & Cass Sunstein eds., 2004); *see also* Paula J. Frosso, *The Massachusetts Anti–Cruelty Statute: A Real Dog–A Proposal for a Redraft of the Current Law*, 35 NEW ENG. L. REV. 1003 (2001).

49. *See* David N. Cassuto, *Bred Meat: The Cultural Foundation of the Factory Farm*, 70 LAW & CONTEMP. PROBS. 59, 66 n.44 (Winter 2007) citing Wolfson & Sullivan, *supra* note 48, at 209 (citing New Jersey v. ISE Farms, Inc. (Super. Ct., Warren County, Mar. 8, 2001) (unreported decision on the record) (vacating conviction for animal cruelty because the hundreds of thousands of chickens owned by defendant and the few people actually responsible for them meant that the two sick but still living chickens found in a garbage bin full of dead chickens might not have been "knowingly" discarded)).

50. *See* Wolfson & Sullivan, *supra*, note 48, at 209–10.

51. FLA. CONST. art. 10, § 21.

52. *Id.* art. 10, § 16.

53. ARIZ. REV. STAT. ANN. § 13–2910–07 (2007).

54. Livestock Transportation Act, 45 U.S.C. §§ 71–74 (2000).

55. *Id.* § 71; *see also* Wolfson, *supra* note 46, at 125.

56. *See* 49 U.S.C. § 80502(c) (2000); 9 C.F.R. pt. 89 (2006).

57. *See, e.g.,* Carol Ness et al., *What's New*, S.F. CHRON., Jan. 10, 2007, at F2 (comparing humane treatment labels for meat producers such as "certified humane" and "animal welfare approved"); Nancy Luna, *Restaurants Adopt Humanity*, ORANGE COUNTY REG. (Cal.), May 11, 2007 (describing animal welfare as an important social issue for diners at restaurants and chef's belief that animals raised with compassion create healthier and tastier food); Elizabeth Weise, *Food Sellers Push Animal Welfare*, USA TODAY, Aug. 13, 2003, at 01D (describing efforts of Food Marketing Institute and National Council of Chain Restaurants to spearhead reforms of animal food producers); David Barboza, *Animal Welfare's Unexpected Allies*, N.Y. TIMES, June 25, 2003 at C1 (describing efforts of fast food industry to devise standards for humane treatment of animals raised in factory farms); Michael Leidig, *Government to Farmers: Be Kind to Your Swine*, CHI. SUN TIMES, Feb. 19, 2002, at 34 (discussing Germany's Agriculture Ministry's directive to farmers to provide for welfare of pigs by keeping the pigs happy with toys, exposure to daylight, and with "quality time" of twenty seconds per day with a farmer); Commission Directive 2001/93/EC, 2001 O.J. (L 316) 36 (EC) (European Union legislation laying down minimum standards for the protection of pigs raised for farming purposes).

58. Alexi Barrionuevo, *Pork Producer Says It Plans to Give Pigs More Room*, N.Y. TIMES, Jan. 26, 2007, at C8.

59. Andrew Martin, *Burger King Shifts Policy on Animals*, N.Y. TIMES, Mar. 28, 2007, at C1.

60. Kim Severson, *Celebrity Chef Announces Strict Animal–Welfare Policy*, N.Y. TIMES, Mar. 22, 2007, at A17.

61. *See* Brian T. Murray, *A New Crop for the Amish Pennsylvania Farmers Have Found Raising Puppies Is a Lucrative Business, but They're Reaping an Increasingly Bitter Harvest of Cruelty Charges*, STAR LEDGER (Newark, N.J.), Nov. 20, 2005, at 1 (discussing U.S. Senate bill to add retail dog operations to licensing and inspection authority of U.S. Department of Agriculture that was propelled by activists including the Humane Society); April M. Washington, *Circus Acts or Ax Circus? Animals Mistreated, Groups' Report Says*, ROCKY MOUNTAIN NEWS (Denver, Colo.), July 29, 2004, at 7A (discussing report detailing animal abuse at Ringling Bros. and Barnum & Bailey Circus written by national animal protection groups American Society for the Prevention of Cruelty to Animals, the Fund for Animals, and the Animal Welfare Institute which prompted a ballot initiative in Denver aimed at banning circuses from using exotic animals in their acts); John Horton, *More Oversight of Wild Animal Ownership Sought*, PLAIN DEALER (Cleveland, Ohio), May 26, 2006, at B3 (discussing appeals from the Humane Society of the United States and People for the Ethical Treatment of Animals to support a proposed ban on the private ownership of wild animals in Ohio).

62. *See* Marni Goldberg, *Bill Aimed at Research Trade, Activists Target Dealers Who Collect Animals—Including, Some Say, Stolen Pets—For Sale to Science Facilities*, CHI. TRIB., June 30, 2006, at 3 (crediting momentum from HBO documentary *Dealing Dogs* for public pressure on Congress to pass Pet Safety and Protection Act aimed at prohibiting dealers from selling random source dogs and cats to laboratories); Jeff Mosier, *Bills Seek To Overturn Horse Slaughter Ban : Humane Society Condemns Proposals in State House and Senate*, DALLAS MORNING NEWS (Tex.), Mar. 10, 2007, at 10B (discussing Texas state and Federal Congressional bills pursued by the Humane Society, horse racing associations, and celebrities to end the slaughter of horses for human consumption and citing a poll of Texans showing that about three-quarters of them opposed the slaughter would be less likely to support a legislator who voted to ease a ban); David Crary, *U.S. Activists Revive War on Canadian Seal Hunt*, GLOBE & MAIL (Toronto, Can.), Jan. 29, 2004, at A12 (discussing seal hunt's history as early target of animal welfare movement when public outcry was aroused by grisly videos of baby seals being brutally slaughtered); Bryn Nelson, *Science at a Price, Ethics as the Argument, New Questions Are Raised About Whether the Gains of Animal Research Are Worth the Ethical Uncertainties*, NEWSDAY, Sept. 27, 2004, at A06 (discussing the evolving debate over the use of animals in medical research).

63. *See* Gary Francione, *Taking Sentience Seriously*, 1 J. ANIMAL L. & ETHICS 1, 17 (2006) ("Property status stops us from perceiving animal interests as similar to ours in the first instance and subordinates animal interests to human interests. . . ."); Gary Francione, *Animal Rights Theory and Utilitarianism*, 3 ANIMAL L. 75, 96 (1997) ("[W]e will almost always presume that property owners are the best judges of whether a particular use of their property, including their animal property, will be a 'benefit' to them.").

64. Church of Lukumi Babalu Aye, Inc. v. City of Hialeah, 508 U.S. 520, 581 (1993) (Blackmun, J., concurring).

Chapter 3

THE REGULATION OF COMMON FARMING PRACTICES

NEW JERSEY SOCIETY FOR PREVENTION OF CRUELTY TO ANIMALS v. NEW JERSEY DEPARTMENT OF AGRICULTURE
No. A–6319–03TI, 2007 WL 486764 (N.J. Superior Ct. App. Div. Feb. 19, 2007).

PER CURIAM.

Appellants, various individuals, animal protection and environmental groups, appeal the promulgation by respondent New Jersey Department of Agriculture (the Department) of regulations that establish standards for the care of domestic livestock. The subject regulations were promulgated in response to legislation enacted in 1996 directing the Department to issue standards regarding the humane care, treatment, raising, keeping, marketing and sale of domestic livestock. * * *

* * *

On appeal, appellants assert that a substantial number of these regulations authorize industry practices that are not humane, and are in violation of the legislative command. Accordingly, they argue the regulations cannot be sustained. The regulations also include an exemption for routine husbandry practices, namely, those practices that are taught at veterinary schools and other agricultural institutions, which appellants claim are not humane. Finally, appellants argue the regulations impermissibly curtail the enforcement authority of the New Jersey Society for the Prevention of Cruelty to Animals (SPCA), the entity charged with enforcing the animal cruelty code.

* * *

Essentially, appellants argue that the animal husbandry practices adopted by the Department cause unnecessary pain to the animals; that many of the challenged practices provide no benefit to the animal itself and instead only provide convenience to the particular farmer or producer; and that the regulations are not "science-based" and are therefore arbitrary. Accordingly, they contend that the regulations violate the legislative mandate requiring the Department to specify standards for the "humane raising, keeping, care, treatment, marketing and sale of domestic livestock." *N.J.S.A.* 4:22–16.1.

The Department, in response, argues that in discharging its responsibilities in connection with the rulemaking, it embarked on a full and careful review of the 6,500 written and sixty-five oral comments it received prior to the close of the comment period. The Department argues that it examined scientific texts and journals, as well as reports of governments and academic institutions related to the keeping and care of domestic livestock. Agency staff met with the legislative committee of the State Board of Agriculture and with the New Jersey Agricultural Experiment Station, in order to ensure that the Department has appropriately addressed concerns raised by the thousands of individuals or groups submitting comments.

The Department further argues that it has based the regulations on objective criteria to assess animal health, such as the maintaining of adequate body condition, assessment of the animal's ability to sustain its reproductive capacity, data measuring adrenal gland activity as an indicator of animal stress, manifestation of signs of injury or disease and the rate of the morbidity and mortality. The Department further contends that where professionals were evenly divided on the advantages and disadvantages of a particular practice, it relied on its own expertise to make legitimate and protected judgments about the content of particular regulations. Finally, the Department asserts that an appellate court presented with a challenge to agency rulemaking is obliged to apply a deferential standard of review, and must avoid substituting its judgment for that of the agency. The Department argues that, when the proper standard of review is applied, the regulations will be found manifestly reasonable and in full compliance with the legislative mandate.

We have carefully considered appellants' arguments in light of applicable law. Affording the regulations the presumption of reasonableness and validity to which they are entitled by settled law, we conclude that the challenged regulations are consistent with the agency's legislative mandate, and are neither arbitrary, nor unreasonable. Accordingly, we affirm. *In re Distrib. of Liquid Assets upon Dissolution Reg'l High Sch. Dist. No. 1*, 168 *N.J.* 1, 10 (2001).

I.

On January 5, 199[6], the Legislature approved amendments to *N.J.S.A.* 4:22–16.1, to adopt standards for the humane "raising, keeping, care, treatment, marketing and sale of domestic livestock." The 1996 amendments also directed the Department to enact regulations governing enforcement of those standards. The statute provides, in relevant part:

> The State Board of Agriculture and the Department of Agriculture, in consultation with the New Jersey Agricultural Experiment Station and within six months of the date of enactment of this act,[3]

---

3. The Department did not adopt the regulations within the six month period specified by the Legislature. Instead, the promulgation was delayed for seven years. The Department attributes the delay to its competing obligations, which included "addressing issues related to West Nile Virus, Foot and Mouth Disease, anthrax, and ultimately post 9/11 terrorism concerns."

shall develop and adopt, pursuant to the "Administrative Procedure Act" ... (1) standards for the humane raising, keeping, care, treatment, marketing, and sale of domestic livestock; and (2) rules and regulations governing the enforcement of those standards.

The next subsection, which appellants characterize as a "safe harbor," provides an immunity from prosecution for any person engaging in an approved animal husbandry practice specified in the adopted regulations. It provides, in part:

Notwithstanding any provision in this title to the contrary:

(1) there shall exist a presumption that the raising, keeping, care, treatment, marketing, and sale of domestic livestock in accordance with the standards developed and adopted therefor [sic] pursuant to subsection a. of this section shall not constitute a violation of any provision of this title involving alleged cruelty to, or inhumane care or treatment of, domestic livestock.

On June 7, 2004, the Department adopted its first set of regulations. * * *

The regulations expressly govern and establish requirements for humane treatment of domestic livestock. The regulations define a "humane" practice as one "marked by compassion, sympathy and consideration for the welfare of animals." *N.J.A.C.* 2:8–1.2(a). The regulations define animal welfare as the "physical and psychological harmony between the animal and its surroundings, characterized by an absence of deprivation, aversive stimulation, over stimulation or any other imposed condition that adversely affects health and productivity of the animal." *N.J.A.C.* 2:8–1.2(a). * * *

* * *

We analyze the challenge to these regulations under our standard of review. It is well established that agency regulations are presumed valid and are accorded a presumption of reasonableness. *In re N.J. Am. Water Co.*, 169 *N.J.* 181, 188 (2001); *N.J. State League of Municipalities v. Dep't of Cmty. Affairs*, 158 *N.J.* 211, 222 (1999).

An appellate court's review of the actions of state agencies is "severely limited." *In re Musick*, 143 *N.J.* 206, 216 (1996). * * * Further, a court may not substitute its judgment for the expertise of an agency, "so long as that action is statutorily authorized and not otherwise defective because arbitrary or unreasonable." *In re Distrib. of Liquid Assets, supra*, 168 *N.J.* at 10. On appeal, a court may reverse agency action only if the regulations: (1) violate the enabling statute's express or implied legislative policies; (2) are unsupported by substantial evidence in the record; or (3) result from an unreasonable application of the legislative policy to the facts, and the agency clearly erred by reaching a conclusion that could not reasonably have been made upon a showing of the relevant factors. *In re Rulemaking, N.J.A.C. 10:82–1.2 and 10:85–4.1*, 117 *N.J.* 311, 325 (1989). The party challenging the regulation bears the burden of proving its invalidity. *N.J. State League of Municipalities, supra,* 158 *N.J.* at 222.

Reviewing courts accord substantial deference to the interpretation an agency gives to a statute that it is charged with enforcing because "agencies have the specialized expertise necessary to enact regulations dealing with technical matters and are particularly well equipped to read and understand the massive documents and to evaluate the factual and technical issues that . . . rulemaking would invite." *Ibid.*

The process of administrative rulemaking does not require findings of fact sufficient to justify the regulations. *Heir v. Degnan,* 82 *N.J.* 109, 119 (1980). Instead, "facts sufficient to justify the regulation must be presumed. The burden is not upon the Commissioner [or administrative agency] to establish that the requisite facts exist; [r]ather, the burden is on petitioners to establish that they do not." *In re Adoption of N.J.A.C. 10:52–5.14(d) 2 & 3,* 276 *N.J.Super.* 568, 575 (App.Div.1994), *certif. denied,* 142 *N.J.* 448 (1995). As we have previously explained:

> Findings may be based on an agency's expertise, without supporting evidence, and findings resting on an agency's expertise may be especially important to the judicial review process when the court does not share the agency's expertise. . . . This is especially true of determinations which, as here, are primarily of a judgmental or predictive nature.

> [*In re Regulation of Operator Serv. Providers,* 343 *N.J.Super.* 282, 332 (App. Div.2001).]

It is against this deferential standard that we consider appellants' challenge to these regulations.

II.

Appellants first argue that "the final regulations codify numerous existing factory farming practices that the record overwhelmingly demonstrates cause severe hunger, pain, stress, disease, and even mortality in animals." They assert that because the regulations are at odds with the expressed purpose of the enabling statute, they must be invalidated.

A. Veal Calves

The regulation at issue, *N.J.A.C.* 2:8–2.4(g), permits farmers to tether veal calves in stalls so narrow that the animal cannot turn around, and that are, in appellant's words, "barely wider than the animals themselves." The regulations incorporate the standards of the American Veal Association's Guide, and permit a 450–pound veal calf to be tethered and housed in an individual crate twenty-six inches wide. *N.J.A.C.* 2:8–2:4(h).

Appellants argue that this inability to turn around causes abnormal coping behaviors in the calf, compromises its immune system and increases disease and mortality. Appellants claim it is arbitrary for the Department to permit other animals, such as poultry, the ability to turn around while denying calves sufficient space to do the same. They conclude that there is no basis in the record to conclude that the American Veal Association's Guide complies with the Department's definition of "humane."

The Department acknowledges that it has adopted the American Veal Association Guide, which provides producers with four alternative housing arrangements. These include individual stalls, individual pens, group rearing in pens and a combination of individual and group rearing.

The Department states that it considered more than 100 studies on the subject of veal calf housing and considered the arguments both for and against tethering and individual stall housing, and ultimately concluded that science supported the practices permitted by the regulations.

In its rule adoption, the Department specified the factors it relied on, and identified the scientists whose research underlies the veal tethering regulation. * * *

* * *

[*The Department indicated that tethering provides the following benefits: tethering prevents the calf from defecating in its water and feed buckets, restricts the licking of the backs and rumps of neighboring calves, allows for individual calf stalls to be larger by preventing unwanted contact with the backs and rumps of neighboring calves, permits head and neck licking of neighboring calves, thus increasing social contact among calves, prevents unwanted or aggressive behaviors because some calves are more aggressive and antagonistic towards timid calves, and, among dairy calves, allows them to become accustomed to the method of restraint they will experience as adult dairy cattle in the milking barn. Opponents of tethering argued that confinement by tethering leads to increased stress on calves; and tethering leads to inhibition of muscular development. The court found these arguments not to be adequately supported by science.*]

It is clear from the Department's comments surrounding the rule adoption that the agency thoroughly reviewed and evaluated a number of scientific studies regarding housing and tethering of veal calves. Where the technical and scientific data is in conflict, an agency is entitled to rely on its own expertise. In such circumstances, judicial deference to the agency is appropriate. When, as here, the "appellants' arguments are merely plausible, and not clearly convincing, we will not interfere with the [agency's] determination on these scientific matters." *In re Adoption of N.J.A.C. 7:26E–1.13*, 377 *N.J.Super.* 78, 101 (App.Div.2005), *aff'd o.b.*, 186 *N.J.* 81 (2006).

B. *Sow Gestation Crates and Tethering of Sows*

Appellants argue that gestation crates "prevent pigs from exercising or performing even the most basic, natural movements, such as simply turning around." This practice, they claim, causes the sow physical and psychological ailments, such as decreased muscle mass, decreased bone strength, cardiovascular disease, boredom, apathy and stereotypic behavior. They argue that pregnant sows should be raised in enclosures that permit them to turn around freely.

Appellants assert that several state and foreign governments have "denounced gestation crates ... as inhumane." Moreover, they claim that the regulation does not establish any stall size or make it clear that a sow must have sufficient space to turn around in its crate. Therefore, they contend that the regulation is inhumane.

The Department, in promulgating the regulations, consulted with the New Jersey Agricultural Extension Station, veterinarians, academicians, and animal scientists. Specifically, the agency relies on a European Commission report, entitled *Report on the Welfare of Intensively Kept Pigs*, to support its conclusion that individual stalls ensure that fighting between sows is minimized; provide each sow with a full ration of food; and permit swine producers to identify signs of morbidity, and treat the sow accordingly. As a result, the Department claims that the scientific community supports its conclusion that individual stall systems are not inhumane.

The Department also addressed gestation crates in the rule adoption. The comment to the regulation states:

> * * * Studies have shown that there are fewer injuries in sows individually housed. Group pens may result in increased aggression and biting which appears to increase stress levels. Reproductive performance is in general better in stall-housed versus group-penned sows.... In addition, the health of the animals is more easily monitored when housed individually.

[36 *N.J.R.* at 2681.]

The Department also points to the proceedings of the American Veterinary Medicine Association that reviewed the impact of gestation stalls on pregnant sows, concluding that "no one system is clearly better than others under all conditions and according to all criteria of animal welfare." (AVMA Position Statement on Pregnant Sow Housing).

As we concluded concerning tethering of veal calves, here the use of sow gestation crates finds support in the veterinary literature, and there is no evidence that this determination is arbitrary or unreasonable. Accordingly, we see no basis to interfere.

C. Mutilation Practices

Appellants assert that the regulations permit various inhumane practices, such as tail docking, castration, debeaking, and toe trimming, all without the use of anesthesia and without any benefit to the individual animal.

The Department, in response, argues that appellants ignore the requirement set forth in the regulation that these "husbandry practices" must be performed "by a knowledgeable individual, in a sanitary manner, and in a way to minimize pain." *N.J.A.C.* 2:8–2.6(f),–4.7(e),–7.6(d).

The Department further contends that because these husbandry practices are taught at veterinary schools, land grant colleges and agricultural extension services by veterinarians and animal scientists, when a trained person conducts these practices any pain the animal experiences will be minimized. This, it claims, is a practical and desirable standard.

1. Tail Docking

Tail docking is the removal of the lower portion of a dairy cow's tail. The purpose is improved cow hygiene by reducing the incidence of udder infection and maintaining milk quality by reducing [sic] of fecal contamination. Appellants argue that the majority of scientists have concluded that there is no benefit to the animal and no human health justification for tail docking. Moreover, appellants assert that the practice causes pain and interferes with the cow's ability to perform natural behaviors, such as flicking its tail to swat at flies. Appellants explain that the American and Canadian Veterinary Medical Associations oppose tail docking. Accordingly, they argue that the Department's conclusion that the practice is humane violates the agency's own record.

The Department acknowledges that there is a controversy regarding the practice of tail docking. It relies on the report prepared by the American Association of Bovine Practitioners, which concluded that there was not enough scientific evidence to condone or condemn the practice. The agency claims that there is a lack of evidence that the procedure, when performed in accordance with the regulations by a knowledgeable individual to minimize pain, is cruel or inhumane. Accordingly, it declined to deny cattle producers the option of tail docking.

In reaching its conclusion that tail docking should be permitted, the Department reviewed and relied on materials from Penn State's College of Agricultural Studies, Purdue University, University of Wisconsin, the School of Veterinary Medicine at University of California, Davis, the North Mississippi Branch Experiment Station, and the Journal of the American Veterinary Medical Association.

Here, too, the Department made a scientific judgment after considering arguments on both sides. Appellants' arguments fail to persuade us that our intervention is warranted.

2. Castration without Anesthesia

Appellants next assert that the record is clear that castration without anesthesia is "devastatingly painful." They argue that scientists who have reviewed the issue have concluded that castration has no benefit to animal welfare. Accordingly, appellants argue that this regulation unquestionably is not humane.

The regulation, *N.J.A.C.* 2:8–7.6(d), provides that castration may be performed by knowledgeable individuals in a manner that minimizes pain. * * *

* * *

* * * [T]he Department * * * relies on the fact that this is a routine husbandry practice and may be performed only by individuals who have been trained by veterinarians and animal scientists. The agency also relies on studies by the National Pork Board, the American Association of Swine Veterinarians, the California Pork Industry Group and the University of California, Davis. Based on these scientific reports, and the fact that trained individuals will perform piglet castrations, the Department has concluded that the practice is not inhumane.

There are two distinct issues here. One is the practice of castration itself; the other is performing it without anesthesia. Analytically, they are not intertwined. The practice of castration itself finds support in the record. Notably, the record contains a fact sheet authored by two university professors, who cite castration of male pigs before weaning as useful in avoiding the "tainting of pork with foul odors and off flavors" and in "reduc[ing] aggressiveness and handling problems associated with intact males." Appellants argue that the principal purpose of castration is an economic one and that the procedure does not normally result in any benefit to pig welfare. We conclude the agency is entitled to determine that ease of management and avoiding "off flavors" are consistent with the Legislature's expressed mandate directing the Department to develop standards governing "marketing and sale of livestock." That interpretation of its mandate is an exercise of agency discretion protected by law, and we decline to substitute our judgment on the relative benefits of castration for that of the agency.

Turning to the issue of castration without anesthesia, materials in the record support the Department's conclusion that the short-term pain associated with the practice is reduced when performed prior to weaning by experienced handlers. Again, our deferential standard of review and our obligation to respect an agency's technical expertise persuade us that any interference by us with this practice would be unwarranted.

3. Debeaking of Chickens and Turkeys

Appellants challenge the section of the regulations permitting chicken and turkeys to undergo a procedure known as beak-trimming or "debeaking," in which a hot blade is used to cauterize and remove part of the beak. *N.J.A.C.* 2:8–4.7(e). They claim the record shows that birds experience both short term and chronic pain as a result of the procedure. Additionally, appellants contend that alternatives such as providing birds with more space and selectively breeding birds to be less aggressive would reduce the incidence of pecking, and the need for beak trimming. The practice, they argue, is therefore not humane because it causes pain and stress in birds and turkeys.

The Department, in turn, argues that beak trimming is not inhumane, although it may cause acute or transient pain. This pain is offset by the benefit to the animal and the flock as a whole. Beak trimming, the agency asserts, reduces the incidence of cannibalism and pecking within the flock. Although certain studies show that analgesics should be used, the Department relies on studies by the United Egg Producers, the

California Poultry Working Group and the Cornell Cooperative Extension to conclude that as long as a knowledgeable person performs the trimming, that individual will be aware of the appropriate techniques and will be able to determine whether the particular bird will require an analgesic.

* * *

There is nothing to indicate that this response is arbitrary or unreasonable.

4.   Toe Trimming of Turkeys

N.J.A.C. 2:8–4.7(f) permits the practice of removing some of a turkey's toes so that the animal will be unable to scratch its handlers. Appellants claim the record demonstrates that this practice causes animals acute pain and stress for varying lengths of time. Accordingly, appellants argue the practice is not humane.

The Department counters that the practice of toe trimming is necessary to prevent injury to other birds in a flock. It addressed the practice in the rule adoption, stating that:

> toe trimming is a practice employed to prevent injury to other birds in the flock (for example, turkeys will climb onto other birds). Such behavior is not necessarily remediated by the availability of space. Appropriate flock management may include the need for this routine husbandry practice which is taught in poultry science departments at agricultural colleges. The Department declines to prohibit this practice and believes its rules related to time in which the procedure may be performed is [sic] appropriate.

[36 *N.J.R.* at 2667.]

The Department states it "embarked on a full and careful" review of all of the submissions it received, and that it examined scientific texts and journals pertaining to toe-trimming, and it relies on its extensive adoption notice to establish its rationale for the rulemaking. We are unable to conclude that the Department's assessment of the benefits of toe-trimming is arbitrary or unreasonable.

5.   The Requirement that Mutilations be Performed in a Way that "Minimizes Pain"

The regulations provide that knowledgeable individuals may dehorn, disbud, remove extra teats, tail dock, tattoo, brand and castrate cattle, provided that these practices are performed in a sanitary manner in such a way as to minimize pain. *N.J.A.C.* 2:8–2.6(f). The regulations also provide that knowledgeable individuals may detusk, remove needle teeth, castrate, ear notch, tattoo and tail dock swine, again provided that these practices are performed in a sanitary manner in such a way as to minimize pain. *N.J.A.C.* 2:8–7.6(d). Finally, the regulations provide that knowledgeable individuals may trim the beaks of poultry, provided it is done in a sanitary manner in a way that minimizes pain. *N.J.A.C.* 2:8–4.7(e).

Appellants argue the "minimize pain" requirement does not "establish any meaningful standard by which the regulated community, enforcement agents, or the courts can determine whether conduct actually complies" with the standard. Accordingly, they contend that the regulation does not meet the "baseline" standards the Department sought to promulgate so that enforcement agents could identify and address inhumane practices. Appellants argue these regulations are arbitrary and capricious because they "allow producers to mutilate livestock as long as they 'minimize pain' without any additional guidance."

The Department defends the regulation, arguing that because animal husbandry practices are taught in veterinary schools and to agricultural extension agents by veterinarians and animal scientists, individuals learn how to properly perform these routine practices. The Department's rules provide that a knowledgeable individual, i.e., one who has been trained, must perform these practices in a way that minimizes pain. The Department argues that each procedure must be evaluated in light of the individual animal and that it is not necessary to eliminate all pain in order for the practice to be "humane." Instead, the agency argues that if the practice is beneficial to the animal or to the flock or herd as a whole, the transient pain may be assessed in a "holistic" way, looking at the benefits to the animal in light of its overall welfare.

The Department's conclusion, which is supported by its expertise and vast experience, is neither arbitrary nor unreasonable.

D. Transport of Downed and Emaciated Animals

Appellants next argue that the regulations permit producers to transport emaciated and downed animals even though the process of loading these animals onto transport trucks causes significant pain. They claim that, to reduce their suffering, these animals should be humanely euthanized at the farm instead of being transported to slaughter, adding that the animals suffer greatly when they are dragged from trucks or moved with bucket loaders or fork lifts. Appellants explain that this practice has been denounced by the European Commission's Scientific Committee on Animal Health and Animal Welfare. They assert that this part of the regulation is arbitrary and capricious and inconsistent with *N.J.S.A.* 4:22–16.1.

For its part, the Department argues that because federal regulations already prohibit the slaughter of disabled cattle for use in the food chain, the transportation of sickly cattle for slaughter will be virtually eliminated. The agency argues that such animals will likely be euthanized on the farm, and therefore the only sick animals to be transported will be those taken for veterinary care. The agency also correctly notes that the regulation provides that non-ambulatory disabled cattle and swine may not be dragged while conscious and must be handled humanely at all times even if they are to be slaughtered or euthanized. *N.J.A.C.* 2:8–2.6(a)(3)(ii), (v); *N.J.A.C.* 2:8–7.6(a)(3)(ii), (v).

Because most sickly animals will likely be euthanized on the farm, and because disabled animals cannot be dragged while conscious, we conclude that the agency's rationale is not arbitrary or unreasonable, and reject appellant's argument that the regulation in question author-izes an inhumane practice.

III.

Under the regulations, practices that are not expressly prohibited are permitted provided they are "routine husbandry practices" taught at veterinary schools, land grant colleges and agricultural extension agents. Appellants claim that this exemption is inconsistent with the Legisla-ture's mandate because it creates a vast exemption for practices regard-less of whether they are humane. They argue that "If the New Jersey Legislature had wanted to exempt 'routine husbandry practices' from the reach of the State's animal cruelty statute it could clearly have amended the statute to accomplish this result." Appellants further argue that the Department engaged in impermissible delegation of authority by violating the principle that it may not subdelegate a power or duty delegated by statute where the Legislature did not so intend.

The Department argues that it has complied with the enabling legislation by adopting standards protecting animals from inhumane treatment and at the same time protecting public health, enhancing worker safety, ensuring a safe food supply and helping to sustain agriculture. This, the agency argues, is consistent with the legislative mandate. The humane routine husbandry practices permitted by the challenged regulation include techniques used in animal restraint, iden-tification, training, manure management, restricted feeding, watering and exercising, vaccination, and fencing. *N.J.A.C.* 2:8–1.2(a). The De-partment explains that "[h]ealthy livestock and high-quality livestock products will maintain demand from the public for livestock and their products, thereby helping to maintain the viability of the livestock industry in New Jersey." 36 *N.J.R.* at 2567.

In its rule proposal, the Department explained that "[t]hese stan-dards are not intended to modify those routine animal agriculture practices that are performed each day by farmers in New Jersey, but rather to protect animals from only those practices that are inhumane or cruel." 35 *N.J.R.* at 1874.

A. *Impermissible Delegation*

[Appellants relied on three cases to support their argument that the Department impermissibly delegated the Legislature's mandate to pro-mulgate humane standards to veterinary schools, land grant colleges, and agricultural extension agents. The court distinguished these cases by interpreting them to bar delegation of functions where the legislature previously had specifically delegated those functions to a particular state agency.]

* * *

Here, the Department did not delegate to a private individual or private entity duties or functions it is required by statute to perform. Individual farmers are not creating the humane standards but are, rather, continuing to perform practices that are taught in veterinary schools, land grant colleges and agricultural extensions. These farmers must either be knowledgeable, or have a knowledgeable individual perform routine husbandry practices according to the regulations, and must perform them in a sanitary way that minimizes pain. If the farmer does not do so, he or she will violate the rules and be subject to enforcement. Routine husbandry practices are humane because of who teaches them and who may perform them.

We agree with the Department's contention that it would be essentially impossible, and certainly impractical, for it to list every possible routine husbandry practice taught in veterinary schools, land grant college and agricultural extension schools, and then create specific humane standards for each and every practice. The Legislature has also expressly allowed the Department to draw upon agricultural educational sources. There is nothing arbitrary or capricious about exempting routine husbandry practices commonly taught in veterinary schools, land grant colleges and agricultural extensions. There is no reason to invalidate the Department's reliance on the curricula and expertise of the veterinarians and animal scientists who develop and teach these routine husbandry practices, especially in light of the Department's clearly articulated twin goals to provide humane standards and also promote sustainable agriculture. As a result, the Department has not delegated its duty to set standards.

B. *Whether the "Routine Husbandry Practices" Exemption Fails to Set a Standard*

Appellants next claim that the routine husbandry practices exemption is arbitrary and capricious because it fails to set a standard to inform enforcement agents, the courts or the public of exactly what conduct is prohibited. They argue that by failing to set such a standard, the Department has failed to meet the requirement of the enabling legislation. This is readily apparent, they claim, because there are hundreds of veterinary schools, land grant colleges and agricultural extensions in this country that "teach a wide variety of practices." Accordingly, it is impossible to determine what practices are "commonly taught." By extension, it is then impossible to determine which practices are sheltered by the "safe harbor" provisions of *N.J.S.A.* 4:22–16.1b, and thus, presumptively exempted from prosecution. They claim that the exemption leaves the regulated community and enforcement agents completely unclear as to which routine practices are permitted and which are prohibited.

* * *

Here, contrary to appellants' arguments, the Department has provided sufficient guidance and objective standards in the regulations. The

Department changed the definition of routine husbandry practices between proposal and adoption to provide that only those practices commonly taught in certain institutions are included in the definition.

* * *

The Department relies on the American Veterinary Medical Association Handbook, which describes the curricula at veterinary schools. According to the Handbook, these schools provide "knowledge, skills, values, attitudes, aptitudes and behaviors necessary to address responsibly the health and well-being of animals." By ensuring that only the practices taught at these institutions would be included, we conclude that the permitted practices are not so vague as to fail to constitute a standard. Moreover, we agree with the Department's assertion that because it would be impractical to list all of the potential routine husbandry practices performed on a working farm, this is a valid limitation. We are also persuaded by the argument that because the Department reviewed the curricula of these schools and was convinced that they teach the latest farming techniques and instruct students in the most recent scientific innovations, that a standard has indeed been established.

* * * Here, the process reveals that the Department's actions were not unreasoned, and appellants have failed to satisfy their burden of establishing the invalidity of the "routine husbandry practices" regulation. This conclusion is entitled to our deference because the Department has the specialized knowledge to protect animal welfare. We defer to the Department's expertise in assessing the need for routine husbandry practices in the day to day operation of the farms. *In re Zahl*, 186 *N.J.* [341,] 353–54 [2005].

C. *Whether the "Routine Husbandry Practices" Exemption Created a Vacuum That Impermissibly Authorizes Practices that Are Not Humane*

In addition to their other challenges to the routine husbandry practices exemption, appellants argue that the regulation's failure to specifically identify practices that are authorized creates a vacuum, resulting in inhumane practices being allowed. They point to two such inhumane practices: forced feeding of ducks and geese for foie gras and genetic manipulation.

1. Forced Feeding of Ducks and Geese for Foie Gras

Appellants argue that forced feeding of ducks and geese to produce foie gras is inhumane. In order to produce foie gras, a tube is forced down the bird's throat and food is pumped directly into its stomach. Appellants claim this unquestionably causes birds significant pain and suffering, but because it is not specifically addressed by the regulations, this inhumane practice is permitted under the regulations.

The Department counters by explaining that the AVMA House of Delegates unanimously declined to prohibit the practice of force feeding birds for foie gras. The AVMA found that there was insufficient peer-reviewed evidence related to animal welfare during the production of foie gras. Accordingly, the Department refused to ban the practice because there is no scientific evidence that the procedure is detrimental to animal welfare. In the absence of such evidence, we are unable to conclude that the practice is not humane. Stated differently, because there is no conclusive evidence that the practice is detrimental to animal welfare, the agency's decision not to ban it cannot be considered arbitrary or unreasonable.

The Department has consistently stated that, in the absence of evidence that a practice is detrimental to animal welfare, it will refuse to prohibit the practice but will continue to monitor the practice and propose amendments when appropriate. We conclude that it was not unreasonable or arbitrary for the Department to rely on the AVMA position on the production of foie gras and to continue to research the issue. Accordingly, we reject appellants' claim that the routine husbandry exemption will allow inhumane practices.

2. Genetic Manipulation

Appellants claim that the routine husbandry exemption also permits producers to use intensive genetic selection, authorizing them, for example, to breed larger, faster-growing broiler chickens and turkeys. They assert that the record shows that these chickens and turkeys "suffer chronic pain from skeletal deformities, muscle disease, and cardio-pulmonary disease, increased susceptibility to painful contact dermatitis, reduced immune function and increased mortality."

There is only one article in the record that addresses genetic manipulation, namely the European Commission's Scientific Committee on Animal Health and Animal Welfare's 2000 Report entitled *The Welfare of Chickens Kept for Meat Production (Broilers)*. According to this article, "a wide range of metabolic and behavioral traits in broilers have been changed by selection practices. Major concerns for animal welfare are the metabolic disorders resulting in leg problems, ascites and sudden death syndrome and other health problems."

The Department addressed this concern by including in the regulations an obligation to adequately care for, feed and hydrate poultry. The regulation also requires prompt treatment of sick or injured chickens. *N.J.A.C.* 2:8–4.6(c). The Department argues that the regulation will ensure that poultry maintain adequate body condition, and that sound animal husbandry practices will avoid the pitfalls of genetic manipulation. The agency's determination is entitled to our deference and appellants' examples of genetic manipulation do not show that the routine husbandry practice exemption is arbitrary or capricious.

IV.

Appellants argue next that the enforcement provisions of the regulations are beyond the scope of the Department's authority because the Department has adopted regulations that modify "the enforcement of the entire animal cruelty code, as applied to livestock." By so doing, they argue, the Department has curtailed the authority of the New Jersey SPCA and local law enforcement agencies and has created unnecessary barriers to enforcement. Appellants contend, therefore, that the Department has acted unreasonably, outside of its authority, and in a manner contrary to legislative policy. We review these claims individually.

A. Whether the Department Can Regulate Enforcement of the Cruelty Laws

Appellants argue that when the Legislature directed the Department to promulgate rules and regulations to enforce humane standards, the Legislature did not authorize the Department to regulate cruelty investigations. They further argue that the Department cannot dictate to other agencies with primary enforcement authority "requirements for investigating and enforcing animal cruelty complaints and violations."

* * *

A determination of whether a regulation is within the agency's delegated authority begins with the terms of the enabling statute. *N.J. State League of Municipalities*, *supra*, 158 *N.J.* at 224. "When construing a statute, courts initially consider the statute's plain meaning." *Ibid.* If a statute is clear and unambiguous on its face, courts will enforce the statute as written and need not review legislative history or extrinsic matters. *Nobrega v. Edison Glen Assoc.*, 167 *N.J.* 520, 536 (2001).

Here, the plain language of the statute makes it clear that the Department, in consultation with the New Jersey Agricultural Experiment Station, was charged to develop and adopt "(1) standards for the humane raising, keeping, care, treatment, marketing, and sale of domestic livestock; and (2) rules and regulations governing the enforcement of those standards." *N.J.S.A.* 4:22–16.1a. The legislative history of this statute reveals that it was the intent of the bill "that it should be construed to allow the New Jersey Society for the Prevention of Cruelty to Animals, and its [county] societies, in cooperation with the Department of Agriculture, to continue in the SPCA's statutory capacity to enforce the State's animal cruelty laws." *Senate Senior Citizens, Veterans Affairs and Agricultural Committee, Statement to S. 713* (June 2, 1994). Accordingly, we reject appellants' argument that the Department's enforcement provisions are beyond the scope of its authority.

B. Whether the Enforcement Regulations are Inconsistent with the Statutory Authority of Law Enforcement and Are Unduly Burdensome

Appellants claim that *N.J.S.A.* 4:22–16.1 does not authorize the Department to restrict the existing authority of the SPCA and that the regulations interfere with the SPCA's ability to investigate violations and enforce cruelty laws relating to farm animals. We disagree. The Legislature expressly provided that the SPCA and the Department cooperate in the enforcement of the prevention of cruelty laws. *N.J.S.A.* 4:22–16.1.

Further, by amending the enforcement scheme for the protection of livestock in 2005, the Legislature placed new limits on the authority of the SPCA. Until 2005, any member, officer or agent of the SPCA could exercise and perform the powers and duties exercised and performed by agents of the society who had been deputized by a sheriff. Additionally, any member, officer or agent of the SPCA could make arrests for violations of the animal cruelty law and arrest, without warrant, anyone violating any provision of the cruelty law in the presence of that member.

In 2005, the Legislature passed an act to supplement, amend and repeal certain portions of chapter 22 of Title 4. It essentially "reorganized" the State and county SPCAs. * * *

The Department correctly argues that the reorganization of the SPCA imposes new limits on the authority of the SPCA. Now, not all of its members possess arrest authority, but rather only humane law enforcement officers may make arrests and arrests without warrants.

These changes reflect the Legislature's intent to place humane enforcement in the hands of law enforcement. Stated differently, the SPCA no longer has unfettered discretion to enforce the cruelty laws but must now do so in cooperation with local law enforcement.

The humane standards under review here also demonstrate the Legislature's trend toward more cooperative arrangements between the SPCA and other New Jersey agencies and entities. * * *

We find no basis upon which to disturb the Department's effort to work cooperatively with the SPCA.

Appellants' final argument is that the regulations require "unnecessary procedures that do nothing to further the legislative mandate." Specifically, appellants claim that the requirement that all investigations be conducted in accordance with biosecurity protocols will prevent investigators from walking among and inspecting animals at a facility. Appellants take issue with the reporting and notice requirements, claiming that they are senseless and deter "an already under-funded and understaffed New Jersey SPCA." These arguments lack sufficient merit to warrant discussion in a written opinion.

CONCLUSION

Having carefully considered appellants' arguments, we conclude that many of their contentions find support in the literature and in the veterinary community. So, too, do those of the Department. When the material in the record presents such divergence of opinion, the agency's expertise and experience are entitled to our deference. We are obliged to avoid encroaching on the Department's exercise of its expertise where, as here, that expertise is a pertinent factor in the enactment of the subject regulations. The regulations are not arbitrary or unreasonable or in derogation of the statutory mandate. Accordingly, the challenged regulations are valid.

Affirmed.

IF IT LOOKS LIKE A DUCK . . .
NEW JERSEY, THE REGULATION OF COMMON
FARMING PRACTICES,
AND THE MEANING OF "HUMANE"

Mariann Sullivan*
David J. Wolfson**

It is hard to comprehend the number of animals killed for food in the United States. More than ten billion animals (excluding fish) die every year. This number represents over ninety-eight percent of all animals with whom humans interact, including companion animals; animals in zoos and circuses; and animals killed by hunters and trappers, in animal shelters, biomedical research, product testing, dissection, and on fur farms.[1]

In order to turn this unimaginable number of living creatures into the meals eaten by most Americans several times a day, at the lowest cost possible, it is now considered necessary to keep most of these animals tightly packed into small indoor areas. Farmed animals live out their short lives knowing nothing of sunshine, grass, trees, fresh air, unfettered movement, sex, and many other simple conditions of contentment—a physiological and psychological shadow world. They never experience many of the things that make up most of what we think of as the ordinary pattern of life on earth. They are castrated and mutilated without anesthesia, may be deliberately starved, live in conditions of extreme and unrelieved crowding, and sometimes suffer genetic manipulation which results in physical deformities.[2]

Two of the more egregious examples of the grim conditions in such factory farms involve breeding pigs and veal calves, many of whom are kept for their whole lives in enclosures barely bigger than themselves (known as "gestation crates" in the case of pigs, and "veal crates" in the case of calves). These breeding pigs spend nearly all of their three to four years on earth in metal stalls, generally able to take no more than one step forward or back, never able to turn around. Likewise, veal calves are confined in wooden stalls so small that the young animal cannot turn around. They are also kept in an anemic state through a diet deficient in iron solely to maintain the whiteness of their flesh, only to be slaughtered at the young age of four to six months.[3]

Other animals, while not kept in individual stalls, live in quarters so close that they must be mutilated so that the inevitable fighting caused by crowding does not result in injuries that reduce their economic value to the producer. Examples include the searing off of the beaks of laying hens, who would otherwise cause each other injury or death by pecking at each other in the small cages in which they spend their lives; or the clipping of pigs' tails, which is, diabolically, designed to increase the pain the pigs experience when bitten so as to encourage them to avoid being bitten, thus reducing infections and deaths.[4]

Many animals are genetically engineered to make them grow unnaturally fast, which causes painful health problems, but allows them to be slaughtered and eaten in as short an amount of time as possible. Like veal calves, pigs raised for pork are slaughtered at only four to six months. "Broiler" chickens, who are raised to be slaughtered for meat (as opposed to laying hens raised to lay eggs), are genetically programmed to grow so fast that by the time they are slaughtered, at six to seven *weeks* old, their legs frequently cannot hold them up and often break under their weight.[5]

Most of us are uncomfortable thinking about the ways in which farmed animals are treated. This discomfort is appropriate given that it is difficult to avoid the conclusion that the lives of these animals are extremely harsh. The farming practices to which these animals are subjected, which many view as inhumane, are, by and large, modern developments. After the Second World War, the farming industry began to adopt techniques very different from traditional husbandry. Prior to the rise of such modern industrial farming it may be that what most people consider cruelty to farmed animals occurred outside of the normal bounds of agriculture. But, as a result of the development of modern industrial farming methods, cruelty to farmed animals has become embedded in the methods of production themselves, and the life of each individual animal has become much less valuable to the producers who raise them for food. Unfortunately, as farming methods have become more unpleasant, the legal regime governing the welfare of farmed animals has been significantly weakened.

Farmed Animals and the Law

While animals have always been raised for food, most societies have recognized some obligation to treat farmed animals with some level of consideration. In fact, the first legal code in the United States, The Body of Liberties of 1641, which governed the Massachusetts Bay Colony, contained anticruelty provisions relating to farmed animals:

Of the Brute Creature.

Liberty 92

No man shall exercise any Tyranny or Cruelty toward any brute creature which are usually kept for man's use.

Liberty 93

If any man shall have occasion to lead or drive Cattle from place to place that is far off, so that they may be weary, or hungry, or fall sick, or lame. It shall be lawful to rest or refresh them, for a competent time, in any open place that is not corn, meadow, or enclosed for some peculiar purpose.[6]

As time went by, states enacted anticruelty statutes, initially focused on farmed animals and then including other animals within their protection, prohibiting acts of cruelty in general terms. To this day, farmed animal law remains, by and large, a state issue. Federal law is essentially irrelevant to the raising of farmed animals; the Animal Welfare Act, the primary piece of federal legislation relating to animal protection, exempts farmed animals.[7] No other federal law applies to the *raising* of farmed animals, and, as a result, the United States Department of Agriculture has no statutory authority to promulgate regulations relating to the welfare of farmed animals on farms. While there is a federal law relating to *slaughter*, the Humane Methods of Slaughter Act,[8] this statute to date has been interpreted by the United States Department of Agriculture, the agency entrusted with enforcing it, to not apply to poultry, it has no fines for violations, and it is very poorly enforced. Finally, there is also a federal statute entitled the Twenty–Eight Hour Law,[9] limiting the time animals can be *transported* when traveling across state lines. This law, too, is rarely enforced, and, even if enforced, the maximum penalty is a mere $500 fine.

As a result, the only hope for the legal protection of farmed animals while being raised is at the state level, where, as noted above, state anticruelty laws historically applied to farmed animals. There are, however, numerous problems with existing anticruelty statutes, particularly when they are applied to industrial farming. Among them are the facts that such criminal statutes place the burden of proof on the prosecutor and require proof beyond a reasonable doubt, a very high standard of proof, and they require proof of a mental state on the part of the accused, either intent or knowledge, that is hard to demonstrate. Anticruelty statutes can only very rarely be enforced by someone other than a public prosecutor, often carry minimal penalties, and do not contain inspection powers by which there can be regular assessments of compliance. Anticruelty statutes may explicitly exclude certain animals from statutory coverage, and courts have, on occasion, interpreted such statutes to exclude animals that are not explicitly excluded. Finally, rather than setting forth specific affirmative requirements of humane care and treatment, they are often worded in a very broad, arguably vague, way that leaves a court or jury with the difficult task of deciding when and how much an animal is suffering and if so, whether such suffering should be considered "necessary" or "justifiable," with little or no explanation of what those terms mean. Not only does such vagueness work to the animals' detriment when harm to them is found justifiable, but the breadth of statutory wording has also led to defendants' arguing that such statutes are unconstitutional because they did not explicitly prohibit the specific conduct for which they are being prosecuted. For all of these reasons, the introduction and widespread use of modern industrial farming methods, although causing a great amount of suffering, has not been limited to any significant extent by state anticruelty statutes.

Despite the ineffectiveness of anticruelty statutes, as new, arguably cruel, farming methods became more prevalent, agribusiness determined that such statutes nevertheless posed a potential threat of interference. In response to fears that the general prohibitions of cruelty to animals on the books in every state might be interpreted to prohibit the industrialized farming practices that were coming to dominate the industry, agribusiness lobbies persuaded legislators in a growing number of states, now a majority, to enact wholesale exemptions to the statutes for "customary," "accepted," "common" or "normal" farming practices.[10]

For those with no familiarity with, or insight about, the changes in the industry and how animals were being treated under new factory farming methods, an exemption from prosecution for "customary" farming practices might sound reasonable. After all, slaughter for food might be seen by some as cruel in and of itself. In the minds of the uninformed, such an exemption could be seen as simply an attempt to prevent an overzealous, animal-loving prosecutor from prosecuting farmers for doing what farmers had always done. But, in fact, farmers were doing very different things to animals than had ever been done before, and the enactment of these statutes created a legal regime in which cruelty to farmed animals theoretically had no limits. Farmers now had complete authority to define what was, or was not, an acceptable common farming practice for animals in their possession. Judges, prosecutors, and societies for the prevention of cruelty to animals became irrelevant in deciding what was cruel, as long as it was customary.

Thus, as of 1996, when the story that is the subject of this chapter begins, the law that related to the raising of farmed animals throughout the United States could be summarized as inadequate state law, either by way of an antiquated and largely ineffective anticruelty statute, or by way of a common farming practice exemption to the antiquated and ineffective anticruelty statute. There was only one exception—the state of New Jersey.

New Jersey and "Humane" Standards

New Jersey's long-standing general anticruelty statute is similar to the anticruelty statutes on the books in all 50 states. It provides that a person who "shall abuse or needlessly kill a living animal or creature" or shall "inflict unnecessary cruelty upon a living animal or creature, by any direct or indirect means ... or unnecessarily fail to provide a living animal or creature of which the person has charge either as an owner or otherwise with proper food, drink, shelter or protection from the weather" shall be guilty of a criminal offense.[11] Also, New Jersey's anticruelty statute did not have an exemption for common farming practices.

But in 1996, for reasons that are not completely clear, the New Jersey legislature amended the anticruelty statute to provide that the "raising, keeping, care, treatment, marketing and sale of domestic livestock" will be presumed not to be illegally cruel if these animals are kept in accordance with "*humane* standards to be developed and adopted by the State Board of Agriculture and the New Jersey Department of Agriculture in consultation with the New Jersey Agriculture Experiment Station."[12] (Emphasis added) With the addition of one word—"humane"—the New Jersey legislature became the first in the nation to attempt to draw a line that would limit the cruel treatment of farmed animals in industrial farming.

While New Jersey's imposition of a regulatory system, rather than a simple criminal statute, to govern farmed animal welfare is unique in the United States, it is the way in which most other large industries are governed. Also, it is the way other, more progressive jurisdictions, including the European Union, have chosen to govern farmed animal welfare. There are reasons why such a system may make sense so long as the system contains certain safeguards. In instituting a regulatory system, a legislature may set forth requirements for an industry with whatever level of specificity, or lack of specificity, it wants. After that, creating and enforcing regulations are tasks placed in the hands of an administrative agency. The agency can promulgate clearer and more detailed requirements than are present in enabling statutes. When it comes to regulating animal welfare, unlike many criminal anticruelty statutes, regulations almost always require affirmative acts, which, in regards to animals, could include adequate exercise, space, light, ventilation and clean living conditions, and could do so in very specific terms.

Theoretically, regulatory schemes governing animal welfare can have significant enforcement advantages over criminal statutes. They can provide for civil penalties, in addition to criminal penalties, and they generally do not require proof beyond a reasonable doubt. Judicial review of agency actions can be permitted, although it is usually of a very limited nature. Crucially, regulatory regimes can provide for inspection powers by which the enforcement agency can regularly assess compliance.

Unfortunately, in the instant case, these advantages were not fully realized. New Jersey's statute is a hybrid between a criminal statute and a regulatory scheme and, therefore, has many of the enforcement disadvantages inherent in criminal laws. The law does not provide for inspections. Moreover, as discussed below, both the Department's interpretation of the statute and the process for judicially challenging the Department's actions were highly problematic. These factors significantly impaired the advantages of a regulatory approach.

By requiring regulatory standards that would set forth exactly what farmers could do to farmed animals in order to remain presumptively within the law, the New Jersey legislature no doubt sought to simplify the process of enforcement and protect both farmers and animals. But, in doing so, it foisted upon the New Jersey Department of Agriculture (the "Department"), the agency that took the lead in drafting the regulatory standards, difficult and contentious questions: What farming practices could be endorsed as humane for an industry that had become used to treating animals in any manner it wished? More fundamentally, how do we produce billions of animals for human consumption while treating those animals "humanely," at least within some defensible definition of that word?

While the Department may seem, at first blush, to be the logical arbiter of these questions, it was in reality poorly suited to this task. Like most departments of agriculture, whether state or federal, it is primarily tasked with promoting agriculture, and, like any other industry, agribusiness often sees attempts to regulate its behavior as a hindrance. Indeed, the Department had never before been asked to consider animal welfare as part of its job in overseeing and promoting agriculture and had no experience in enforcing laws protecting animals from cruelty. The New Jersey anticruelty law was a criminal law that, like any other criminal law, was enforced by the police and prosecutors. It was also enforced by the New Jersey Society for the Prevention of Cruelty to Animals, a quasi public-private organization entrusted with certain enforcement powers (the "NJSPCA").[13]

Not surprisingly, the Department did not welcome the task set before it, which, in its defense, was not something it had requested. At best, the task was particularly tricky for the Department given how far the industry, which the Department was responsible for supporting, had departed from common understandings of what is "humane." The challenging nature of the task was, perhaps, most clearly reflected in the amount of time that passed before its completion. Although statutorily required to produce the regulations within six months, the Department did not do so until 2004, and then only after it had been pressured by campaigns headed by animal protection organizations, including threats of lawsuits.

Given that animal protection organizations pushed for the regulations, it is worth asking the question: what were they hoping to gain? Did they expect the Department to leave numerous common farming practices off its list of "humane" practices, potentially causing significant change to industrial farming in New Jersey? Probably not. Still, these groups must have believed that there was some hope that the Department would, at least, not actually endorse, as "humane," the most egregiously inhumane practices. Some practices had already been prohibited in other countries and in the European Union (in part because of scientific evidence of animal suffering), and there was also evidence that the general public did not support such practices due to their obvious cruelty. These practices could include the use of the gestation crate, battery cage and the veal crate, which force animals to live their entire lives in intensive states of confinement.

Animal protection organizations in other jurisdictions had also achieved significant success in persuading the public that some of the worst common farming practices should be banned. In 2002, before promulgation of the New Jersey regulations, the gestation crate had been prospectively prohibited in Florida. Since the promulgation of the regulations, Arizona prospectively prohibited the gestation crate in 2006, as did Oregon in 2007; the veal crate was prospectively prohibited in Arizona in 2006; and the force feeding of birds for the production of foie gras was prospectively prohibited in California in 2006.[14] In the cases of both Arizona and Florida, these bans were effected through the use of a ballot initiative. Essentially, animal protection groups took a public referendum on whether such practices were acceptable and found out, resoundingly, that they were not. Given this, there may have been reason to expect that the New Jersey regulatory approach could bring a modicum relief to animals from some practices associated with intensive confinement.

At the same time, animal advocates presumably determined that there was little to lose, and that even bad regulations were not likely to make things substantially worse for animals than they already were. To the extent industrial farming existed in New Jersey, there was already widespread use of practices that would likely be considered inhumane by most people, and virtually no challenges had been made to them under the state anticruelty law. That was true even in the absence of an exemption for "common farming practices." Nor was there any reason to believe that, if such challenges were made, they would be successful. In what was perhaps the only case brought under the New Jersey anticruelty statute concerning the customary treatment of farmed animals, which involved the successful prosecution of an egg factory farm for discarding living, half-strangled, hens in the garbage, the conviction had been overturned on appeal on the ground that there was no evidence that the principals of the facility knew what its workers were doing, given the enormous size of the facility.[15] At the time of the lawsuit (and as of the writing of this chapter) there has not been a successful prosecution of a standard practice for the rearing of farmed animals *in any state* pursuant to a general anticruelty statute. Perhaps a set of regulatory standards could avoid the enforcement problems inherent in anticruelty statutes and create a higher level of accountability.

In any case, encouraging the Department to promulgate regulations was apparently seen as a risk worth taking, and animal protection organizations no doubt always knew that they could go to court to challenge what the Department did. In this respect, courts in other countries had, on occasion, held certain common farming practices to be inhumane. Perhaps a New Jersey court could do the same thing; perhaps a lawsuit would initiate a wave of change.

The "Humane" Regulations

Even given such modest expectations, the resulting standards, which finally took effect in 2004, as amended in 2005, could only be seen as very disappointing to animal advocates. The Department did set relatively appropriate standards for practices that were in the industry's own interest and without which animals would perish, such as feeding and watering. When, however, it came to practices where the industry's desires conflicted with animal welfare, the regulations almost unfailingly sided with industry. Thus, the Department codified as "humane" virtually every industrial farming practice condemned by animal protection groups, including gestation crates and veal crates, and numerous types of standard mutilations. As just one example, the provisions governing stalls for sows indicate that a pig is confined in a humane manner as long as:

    i.   The sow's head must not have to rest on an adjacent feeder.

ii.   The sow's rear quarters must not be in contact with the back of the stall with her nose in contact with the front of the stall.

iii.   The sow's head must not have to rest in the water trough.

iv.   A pregnant sow's stall must be wide enough to allow the sow to stand up and lie down unimpeded, rest and move its head freely.[16]

Stated more simply, as long as the sow lives her life out in a space that is not smaller than she is, she is being housed humanely. In fact, with the possible exception of two practices discussed below, every common farming practice that existed prior to the enactment of the regulations was endorsed as humane.[17]

What was perhaps most troubling was that the Department built into the regulations a presumption that all "routine husbandry practices" would be considered humane, and thus exempt from prosecution, unless otherwise restricted by the regulations.[18] By adding this provision, the Department erased the one key distinction between the New Jersey statute and all other common farming practice exemptions in other state anticruelty statutes: the regulation did not rely on demonstrable humaneness in allowing a practice; common usage constituted humaneness. This is exactly the approach from which the New Jersey legislature had, to its credit, attempted to depart. After an initial round of criticism, the Department modified this provision by codifying as "humane" only those practices "commonly" taught at land-grant colleges, veterinary schools and by agricultural extension agents.[19] But, as discussed below, it is hard to view this as anything other than window dressing to make the regulation seem more palatable.

Finally, as noted, the regulations did appear to take two steps forward. First, producers must provide caged hens with sufficient room to spread their wings and turn around.[20] If this provision were interpreted in a straightforward manner and duly enforced, it could result in significant improvements with respect to the general industry practice of confining egg-laying hens in "battery cages," where the birds are generally unable to fully spread their wings. Unfortunately, at this time, the provision has not been enforced and battery cage production continues in New Jersey. Second, subsequent to their issuance, the regulations were amended to revise the rule that authorized "forced molting" of laying hens by complete feed withdrawal for up to two weeks, a practice that had been followed in the industry since it caused hens to lay more eggs when feed was restored. The new regulations permit feed reduction to induce more egg production, but not complete feed withdrawal.[21] Tellingly, this practice was removed from the list of "humane" standards only after the leading industry trade group, United Egg Producers, issued a guideline for its producers disapproving of the practice, which has been long condemned by animal advocates on humane grounds. This appears to be an obvious example of the Department simply following, rather than truly regulating, the industry.

THE LAWSUIT

As soon as the regulations were promulgated, animal advocates went to court. In 2005, a coalition, which included the NJSPCA, other animal protection organizations such as Farm Sanctuary and The Humane Society of the United States, small farmers, veterinarians, environmental and consumer organizations, and certain individuals who shared a concern for animal welfare, challenged the regulations. They argued to the New Jersey Appellate Division (an intermediate appellate court which, among other things, hears appeals from final decisions of state administrative agencies[22]) that the Department of Agriculture did not follow the statutory mandate and/or was "arbitrary and capricious" in promulgating certain regulations.

The lawsuit focused on what were no doubt considered the most egregious violations of the statutory "humane" standard, i.e., those regulations authorizing gestation crates, veal crates, and various mutilations such as debeaking, tail docking, and castration without anesthesia. The lawsuit also focused on the "routine husbandry practice" provision, which would endorse numerous common practices not otherwise listed in the standards, including force feeding for foie gras production, and the rapid growth production of "broiler" chickens, which results in leg abnormalities and disorders, skeletal and cardiovascular disease, and other disabilities. The appellants argued that the Department had failed to follow the statutory standard of "humaneness," and had, instead, approved practices that were clearly inhumane. They argued further that the "routine husbandry practice" provision was utterly detached from any humane analysis.

This lawsuit was truly unique—a legal first in the United States. No other court in the United States had been asked to examine common methods of rearing farmed animals to determine if such practices were humane, although, as noted above, a few foreign courts had ruled in this area. Animal protection organizations looked to those decisions with some hope that an American court would similarly reject at least some common farming methods. It is worth briefly examining two particularly notable examples. In Israel, the Supreme Court had annulled regulations permitting the force-feeding of geese for foie gras because they allowed suffering of the birds in violation of a standard anticruelty statute.[23] In England, a judge held that two individuals had successfully defended themselves in a defamation case brought by McDonald's by proving that they had spoken truthfully when they claimed that certain farming practices for which McDonald's was responsible, including the gestation crate, battery cage, the gassing of male chicks and leg-problems in broiler chickens, were "cruel".[24]

It is important to note, however, that the New Jersey case differed dramatically in terms of substance and procedure from those cases. First, the New Jersey court was being asked to review numerous common farming practices, involving virtually every sector of animal agriculture, to determine whether the Department had acted arbitrarily in finding such practices to be "humane." By contrast, the Israeli court had examined only one farming practice, and a relatively obscure one at that, to determine if that practice was illegally cruel. The English court's decision was also more limited in scope than the New Jersey litigation. The decision, in the context of a civil defamation case against a retailer with respect to alleged cruel farming practices, did not directly mandate any changes to the farming industry. Second, the burden in the New Jersey litigation was significantly different than in either of the other two cases. In Israel, where standard principles of administrative law permit courts much greater latitude in reviewing the decisions of administrative agencies than in the United States, the court was entitled to review the way in which the agency had weighed the arguments in favor of and against the questionable regulations without significant deference to the agency. In England, the court was asked to determine whether defendants had demonstrated, by a preponderance of the evidence, that a reasonable person would view the relevant common farming practices as "cruel." In the instant case, as discussed below in more detail, the appellants' burden was far more onerous. Finally, in both foreign cases the courts were focused on determining whether practices had been shown to be cruel, or inhumane, whereas in New Jersey the court was, or should have been, focused on determining whether practices were shown to be humane. As we shall see, this is far from a distinction without a difference.

THE DECISION

After reciting the procedural history of the case, the Appellate Division (the "Court") laid forth its very limited power to review the determinations of administrative agencies. The Court indicated that it would presume that the regulations were valid and reasonable until proven otherwise and characterized its review as "severely limited."[25] The Court made clear that it would intervene only if the Department had done something clearly inconsistent with its mission or state policy. The Court would not substitute its judgment for that of the Department as long as the Department's action was authorized by the statute, supported by substantial evidence in the record, and not based on an arbitrary or unreasonable application of the law to the facts. The burden lay on appellants to establish that the regulations were invalid and unsupported by the facts. By contrast, the Department had no burden of persuasion. The Department was under no obligation to show the Court that it had relied on anything other than its own specialized expertise in making its judgments.

The Court then proceeded to analyze each practice that appellants had singled out as obvious examples of inhumane practices: veal crates; gestation crates; "mutilation practices," such as tail docking, castration, debeaking, and toe-trimming; and the transport of downed (non-ambulatory) and emaciated animals. The Court also considered whether the provision that required mutilation practices to be conducted in a way that "minimized pain" was too vague to constitute a standard since it did not specifically require anesthesia or any other method of controlling pain.

In its analysis of these practices, the Court first noted the appellants' argument that the record "overwhelmingly" demonstrated that the practices caused severe pain, stress and "even mortality."[26] As to each practice, it set forth appellants' specific claims regarding the types of pain or deprivation caused. For example, as to veal calves, the Court summarized appellants' arguments:

> The regulation at issue ... permits farmers to tether veal calves in stalls so narrow that the animal cannot turn around, and that are, in appellants' words, "barely wider than the animals themselves." The regulations incorporate the standards of the American Veal Association's Guide, and permit a 450–pound veal calf to be tethered and housed in an individual crate twenty-six inches wide.

> Appellants argue that this inability to turn around causes abnormal coping behaviors in the calf, compromises its immune system and increases disease and mortality. Appellants claim it is arbitrary for the Department to permit other animals, such as poultry, the ability to turn around while denying calves sufficient space to do the same. They conclude that there is no basis in the record to conclude that the American Veal Association's Guide complies with the Department's definition of "humane."[27]

After setting forth appellants' arguments against each practice, the Court then noted the Department's assertion that it had considered voluminous scientific evidence in relation to each practice. The Court also set forth a number of the benefits that the Department attributed to each practice. For example, as to the tethering of veal calves, one of the claimed benefits is that "[t]ethering permits head and neck licking of neighboring calves, thus increasing social contact among calves."[28] Or, as to toe trimming of turkeys, alleged to cause acute pain and stress, "toe trimming is necessary to prevent injury to other birds in a flock."[29] Finally, as to each practice, the Court concluded that there was conflicting scientific evidence, and that the Department was entitled to decide what evidence it found persuasive, or rely on its own expertise, without being second-guessed.

Separately, the Court dealt at length with appellants' arguments against the creation of a global provision endorsing all practices that are "commonly taught by veterinary schools, land grant colleges, and agricultural extension agents for the benefit of animals, the livestock industry, animal handlers and the public health."[30] Appellants argued that the Department's re-delegation of its authority to such entities as veterinary schools was impermissible because the Legislature had expressly vested responsibility for the promulgation of humane standards solely in the Department and that there was no reason to suppose that, merely because practices were taught at such institutions, they were necessarily humane. They also argued that the regulation failed to set a standard that could inform law enforcement officials, and others, of exactly what is prohibited since they would have no way of knowing what was taught at these institutions. The Court rejected these arguments, finding that there was no impermissible delegation of authority because it was appropriate for veterinary schools, land grant colleges and agricultural extension agents, as opposed to private individuals or entities, to set humane standards. The Court noted

> There is no reason to invalidate the Department's reliance on the curricula and expertise of veterinarians and animal scientists who develop and teach these routine husbandry practices, especially in light of the Department's clearly articulated twin goals to provide humane standards, and also promote sustainable agriculture. As a result, the Department has not delegated its duty to set standards.[31]

The Court also held that the Department had directly established a standard when it provided that whether a practice is humane would be determined by reference to what is taught in veterinary and agricultural schools. That is "because the Department reviewed the curricula of these schools and was convinced that they teach the latest farming techniques and instruct students in the most recent scientific innovations."[32] The Court noted further that the American Veterinary Medical Association Handbook describes the curricula at veterinary schools as providing "knowledge, skills, values, attitudes, aptitudes and behaviors necessary to address responsibly the health and well-being of animals."[33]

In summary, the Court completely rejected all of appellants' arguments. Many individuals would likely view this decision as counterintuitive. Surely, most people do not believe that agricultural methods that involve mutilation of animals and such severe restriction of movement fall within the common view of what is "humane." Indeed, as noted above, the ballot initiatives in Arizona and Florida indicate that the public does not agree with the Court. Recent polling also supports this position. A 1995 poll found that approximately ninety percent of respondents disapproved of the standard practices of confining veal calves, pigs and hens.[34] A poll conducted by Zogby in 2004 found that seventy-seven percent of Americans supported a ban on force feeding ducks and geese for foie gras production.[35] Most notably, eighty-three percent of *New Jersey residents* felt that it was cruel to confine pigs in gestation crates and veal calves in veal crates! This poll was conducted by the Eagleton Institute of Politics at Rutgers University in 2003 in order to determine the views of New Jersey residents in relation to the proposed regulations.[36] Unfortunately, despite the effort expended to gather these views, neither the Department nor the Court appear to have taken into account the views of the vast majority of New Jersey's citizens who would define "humane" to exclude the very methods that the Department authorized as meeting the definition of "humane."

So why did the Court rule the way it did? Was the decision the product of an unusually hidebound court predisposed to rubber stamp a government agency? Were the claims of the appellants overly emotional, reflecting a lack of awareness of the realities and needs of modern farming; did the appellants simply fail to understand that common farming practices are, in fact, humane, regardless of the beliefs of everyday citizens, who are, after all, not farmers or scientists? Is there a possibility that the Court, while doing its best to come to a just result, was limited by an onerous standard of judicial review or a misunderstanding of certain essential factors, such as the science relevant to animal welfare? Or was the Court unduly influenced by concern about the consequences of determining that numerous common farming practices are actually outside of the statutory protection from prosecution provided by the legislature?

The following discussion, which examines certain aspects of the decision in closer detail, will hopefully shed further light on these issues. Notably, at this writing, the Supreme Court of New Jersey has agreed to hear an appeal in this case.[37] It will be interesting to see how it addresses the issues raised in this chapter, and if it finds its way to a different result.

What Does "Humane" Mean?

The task before the Court was to determine whether the practices authorized by the regulations promulgated by the Department fit within the statutory requirement that such practices be "humane." But what does "humane" mean? Even for the same person, what is humane may depend on the context, including the species of the animal, the use to which the individual animal is being put, and the benefit to humans created by the practice. As animal advocates continuously point out, if a dog were kept for her whole life, or even for a day, in a cage in which she could not turn around, it would be grounds for cruelty charges. Yet, this is how breeding pigs and veal calves are often kept, as approved by the Court. Along the same lines, if a dog (or a horse) were killed for food, many people, and not just vegetarians, would find that inhumane in and of itself.

Even solely within the context of farmed animals, it seems clear that "humane" means very different things to different people. At one end of the spectrum are those like industry commentator Trent Loos, who states,

> Animal welfare is quite simple. We need to provide the animals in our care with adequate food, water and protection from predators and the environment. Anything we worry about in addition to these basic needs is satisfying the emotions of humans not food animals.[38]

At the other end of the spectrum are those who believe that, given the availability of plant foods, the entire process of raising animals only to exploit their reproductive processes or slaughter them for food is inherently inhumane. Bruce Friedrich, of People for the Ethical Treatment of Animals, in his essay, *Humane Meat: A Contradiction in Terms*, clearly expresses this point of view:

> Not only are many of the humane labels—like "Swine Welfare" and "Animal Care Certified"—entirely meaningless, describing animals

treated in nearly exactly the same way as unlabeled products, but please ask yourself a basic question: Would you be willing to cut an animal's throat? For most of us, taking an animal's life is anathema; we just wouldn't do it. And then ask yourself in what other areas of your life do you pay others to do things you find too repulsive? And how ethical is it to pay someone to do things that are wholly unnecessary and too atrocious to watch?[39]

Despite this range of opinions, the New Jersey legislature apparently believed, as do most people, that it was possible to reach an uncomfortable consensus, embraceable by a majority of the citizens of that state, as to how much, if any, pain, immobility, fear, concrete, crowding, stench, darkness, discomfort, boredom, loneliness, misery, and deprivation, a farmed animal should be permitted to experience when balanced against the benefit to humans of having available less expensive meat, dairy and eggs. As the first jurisdiction in the United States to require that such judgments be made by anyone other than industry or the individual consumer, New Jersey chose an approach that was directly contrary to the trend of simply exempting common farming practices from laws protecting animals. In doing so, the New Jersey legislature adjusted the scale upon which that balancing was to be performed. Its legislative decision to require the Department to develop standards that are "humane" suggests a rebalancing of interests and priorities to include significant consideration for the interests of the animals. At the same time, it must not be forgotten that the legislature obviously intended that large numbers of animals would be raised for food under modern farming systems in a manner that would definitely cause such animals some negative outcomes, and must have believed that this could be accomplished with methods that could be considered "humane."

Unfortunately, the New Jersey legislature saw no need to undertake the difficult task of providing a definition of humaneness itself. Accordingly, the statute adhered to an outdated formulation not dissimilar to the lack of guidance found in 19th century anticruelty statutes that utilize terms such as "unnecessary suffering." It required nothing more than that the farming standards be "humane," with no elucidation as to what that meant. In short, the legislature, while recognizing the need for specificity, dumped the task of providing it onto the Department.

The legislature's failure to offer guidance as to what ethical considerations were to be used in the evaluation of what is "humane" left the Department, in the first instance, and then the Court, in reviewing the Department's decisions, with the necessity of ascertaining the meaning of that word. While this could have been an enormous bone of contention, the definition set forth by the Department was not contested by the appellants in the lawsuit. This allowed the Court to rather easily accept and ostensibly apply the following regulatory definitions: a "humane" practice is one "marked by compassion, sympathy and consideration for the welfare of animals"[40] and "animal welfare" is "physical and psychological harmony between the animal and its surroundings, characterized by an absence of deprivation, aversive stimulation, over stimulation or any other imposed condition that adversely affects health and productivity of the animal."[41]

While the two regulatory definitions at first blush appear promising from an animal welfare perspective, and certainly set forth a lofty goal, they are far from ideal in terms of clarity. "Compassion" and "sympathy" are strong words, but they hardly provide more guidance than the word "humane" itself and their use in a situation in which animals are being raised to be killed obviously contextualizes them in a way that influences their meaning. The definition of "animal welfare" also sets a very high, and arguably unobtainable, goal of physical and psychological harmony between the animal and the animal's surroundings. It also, admirably, refers to an "absence of deprivation." This somewhat extraordinary double negative appears to create an affirmative obligation to fulfill the animal's needs and, even, significant desires. A legitimate interpretation of "absence of deprivation" could include the requirement to satisfy all needs and desires, including things like adequate space, mental stimulation, and emotional relationships, that animals would experience as "deprivations" if these things were denied. However, the definition does not permit only that interpretation. There is ambiguity as to whether the absence of deprivation, like the other characteristics of good welfare, is only relevant if the deprivation adversely affects health and productivity. Ambiguity arises from the fact that it is not clear whether "adversely affects health and productivity" only modifies "any other imposed condition" or also modifies the preceding three characteristics as well. Still, despite their susceptibility to different interpretations, these definitions certainly provided more specific guidance than the statute's bald statement that the standards must be "humane."

Unfortunately, as we will discuss in more detail below, the Court did no more than recite the regulatory definitions and did not review whether the Department appropriately applied compassion and sympathy, along with the other aspects of the definitions, to its analysis of specific farming practices. Nor is there any indication that the Court did so *sub silentio*. As a result of this failure, the Court allowed the Department to authorize numerous practices that most people would agree are not humane and surely would not endorse if principles of compassion and sympathy for the animal's fate were properly applied. In effect, it could be argued that the Department, and the Court, ended up treating the word "humane" as philosopher Tom Regan has accused the industry of doing, i.e., in the way that Humpty Dumpty treated words in his famous exchange with Alice in Lewis Carroll's *Alice in Wonderland*, "Words mean what I decide they mean, neither more nor less." Regan continues:

> Humane is a word that actually has an established meaning, and if you look it up, you'll find that it means to treat with kindness, mercy, consideration, compassion—very positive ways of treating another being. You debeak an animal; you put an animal in a cage, it can't turn around, it can't dust bathe, it has no access to fresh air, every natural instinct is frustrated except they're being fed 24 hours

a day, and you call that humane? That is merciful, kind, considerate, compassionate? I don't think so. They're making up the meanings of words. What they're saying is not what they're doing.[42]

The Reasons for the Court's Decision

It is worth asking how the Court came to what is arguably such a completely counter-intuitive conclusion when it, and the Department, built their determinations on scientific studies. There is certainly no question that science can be extremely relevant in determining whether a farming practice is humane. Shouldn't the reliance on science to determine humaneness have guaranteed an equitable result for farmed animals?

Initially, it must be recognized that, in general, it was the Court's obligation to leave the resolution of scientific questions largely in the Department's hands. When judging whether an administrative agency has effectively balanced scientific studies, courts will generally defer to an agency's determination unless it had no support for its position at all.[43] It could not be expected that the Court would re-examine the scientific evidence itself in order to decide whether, in its opinion, the Department had appropriately weighed that evidence in determining whether each practice was "humane." That was not the Court's responsibility, given the very limited role of judicial review in administrative law in New Jersey, which is typical of many jurisdictions in the United States. As the Court pointed out, the burden of proving to the Court that the Department had come to the wrong conclusion lay on the appellants.

> Facts sufficient to justify the regulation must be presumed. The burden is not upon the [Department] to establish that the requisite facts exist; [r]ather, the burden is on appellants to establish that they do not.[44]

The appellants' burden was very heavy. As is common in judicial review of agency rulemaking, the New Jersey court had to find that the Department's findings were "arbitrary and capricious," or not authorized by the statute, in order to set those findings aside. The threshold for finding an agency's conduct "arbitrary and capricious" is extremely high.

This heavy burden certainly stacked the cards against the animals from the start. Essentially all the Department had to do to avoid a determination of "arbitrary and capricious" decision making was to cite to some scientific evidence for its position or rely on its own expertise. Even though the Court acknowledged that the appellants were able to submit large amounts of plausible competing scientific evidence as to whether specific practices are humane, the Court was required to side with the Department unless the Department was so obviously wrong as to render such a result arbitrary and capricious or not authorized by the statute. As the Court stated,

> Having carefully considered appellants' arguments, we conclude that many of their contentions find support in the literature and in the

veterinary community. So, too, do those of the Department. When the material in the record presents such divergence of opinion, the agency's expertise and experience are entitled to our deference.[45]

But, even given the extraordinary procedural burden that appellants faced, the Court appeared to understand that it was still required to decide whether the Department actually made its judgments about specific practices after considering the competing arguments. And the Court purported to do exactly that, citing to the various scientific studies cited by the Department or occasionally pointing out where the Department had chosen to rely on its own expertise and vast experience.

Ultimately, given these factors, it would be logical to conclude that the burden of proving "arbitrary and capricious" conduct sufficiently explains why the appellants lost the case. The Department simply produced enough (even if only barely enough) legitimate scientific evidence to defend the regulations and satisfy the Court. But a closer analysis of the Court's own discussion of the scientific evidence will demonstrate that, in fact, this was not the sole reason for the determination of the Court. Other factors appear to be extremely relevant. First, the Court made the fundamental error of seeing "humaneness" as a purely scientific standard, rather than recognizing that a determination of "humaneness" necessarily involves an ethical judgment. The Court also simply accepted any reference to a scientific study as being relevant to humaneness, making no effort either to determine what such study actually said about animal suffering, misery, happiness, or any other aspect of animal welfare, or to weigh such factors against the costs to the animals or humans of changing the particular practice being examined. In addition, the Court failed to note that some cited studies were not relevant to humaneness at all. Second, the Court failed to recognize the Department's admission that it had endorsed a number of practices in the absence of any findings as to humaneness. As a result, the Department violated the statutory mandate that practices, in order to receive protection from criminal prosecution, should first be determined to be humane. Third, the Court ignored the Department's reliance on industry-funded, incomplete, and obviously flawed scientific studies, which were based on an outmoded method of studying animals. Finally, the Court failed to recognize that science itself may not be able to tell us everything we need to know about the experience of animals in order to determine what is humane, and that the Court, or the Department, may, in some cases, need to rely on common sense.

HUMANENESS IS AN ETHICAL DETERMINATION

Not only did the Court give mere lip service to the Department's own definition of "humane" but the Court appears to have assumed that the question of whether a practice is or is not "humane" is purely a scientific inquiry. Industry has encouraged this approach when confronted with concerns about animal welfare in factory farming. But is this the correct approach? Can science completely answer the question of how society wishes to treat animals?

Of course, the question of what is "humane" probably cannot be decided in the complete absence of scientific inquiry. But the Court's apparent assumption is highly problematic. The question of what is humane, and other similar moral issues, can be answered only by the combination of an ethical inquiry (to set the standard) and a scientific inquiry (to see if the standard has been met). Unless one believes that it is possible to raise and kill animals for food in such a way that does not cause them any detriment whatsoever, and then follows that method exclusively, it is necessary to decide, according to an ethical standard, how much suffering can be imposed upon an animal and still have her treatment classifiable as "humane." As one prominent animal welfare scientist has pointed out,

> [A]lthough science can be of enormous help in solving animal welfare problems, readers should remember that the driving force behind this science is society's ethical concern about the quality of life experienced by farm animals. Therefore, we need to keep in mind what the concerns of society are. Is it morally acceptable to keep laying hens in battery cages, gestating sows in dry sow stalls and veal calves in crates? Should animals be de-horned, castrated or tail-docked? These are questions that are often heard. Science can provide some evidence about these topics, but the questions are fundamentally ethical.[46]

The Court did not attempt to see if the Department had answered the ethical questions that inevitably arise when one is developing or applying a definition of humaneness. Instead, the Court simply examined the actions of the Department to confirm that the Department had cited to some type of a scientific text as to each practice it endorsed. If the Department was able to point to any science at all, the Court looked no further. The following exemplify the Court's approach: "[a]s we concluded concerning tethering of veal calves, the use of sow gestation crates finds support in the veterinary literature,"[47] as to tail docking, "the Department made a scientific judgment after considering arguments on both sides;"[48] as to castration without anesthesia, "our obligation to respect an agency's technical expertise persuade[s] us that an interference by us with this practice would be unwarranted;"[49] and as to toe trimming of turkeys, the Department "examined scientific texts and journals."[50]

The Court did express some reluctance to rule the way it did in a few cases, but it also expressed its sense that it could not second guess the Department as to its "scientific" determinations. For example, as to the Department's wholesale adoption of the standards of the American Veal Association for the treatment of veal calves, including crating and tethering, the Court noted that the appellants' arguments were plausible, but not so "clearly convincing" as to warrant judicial intervention.[51]

The Court's uncritical acceptance of the Department's exclusive reliance on the scientific studies cited by the Department implies that it was acceptable for the Department to rely on such studies without applying any ethical judgment. The Court did not require the Department to justify its designations based on ethical considerations of compassion and sympathy, to consider the judgments of the people of the state of New Jersey as to the ethical boundaries of harming animals, or to engage directly in balancing harms to animals against the benefits to animals and humans from causing them harm. Indeed, the Court not only failed to question whether the Department had made any ethical judgments about when to apply the designation of humane, it failed to consider how, or even whether, the studies cited by the Department actually did relate to humaneness, in any sense of that term. In fact, at best, some of the studies and reports cited by the Department demonstrated only the most tenuous relevance to animal welfare, such as showing that a practice provided some, however marginal, advantage for the animal over another practice.

For instance, permanent individual confinement may well provide the advantage of less fighting among animals, but that does not mean that the practice of intensive confinement is humane. Indeed, the need for individual confinement arises only when there has already been such distortion of an animal's needs and failure to supervise and apply time-honored traditions of animal husbandry that fighting erupts. The Department's consideration of the use of gestation crates for pregnant pigs provides a glaring example of the Department's failure to understand the underlying ethical nature of a determination of what constitutes humane treatment. Both the Department and the Court cited a report issued by the American Veterinary Medical Association summarizing the research on the use of such crates. For such a report to relate to whether the practice was *humane* it would need to determine whether the advantage of using crates outweighed the disadvantage to pigs of being confined in them. It would also be necessary to consider whether there is some other, less restrictive means of providing the advantage conferred by use of the crates. The primary claimed advantages of gestation crates is the prevention of pigs from fighting and ability to more conveniently treat health problems. However, such fighting and health problems are negative possibilities that are exaggerated, indeed made inevitable, by factory farming. The disadvantage to pigs is confinement so severe that even the ability to turn around or move one step forwards or backwards is frustrated. Is the benefit worth that cost to pigs? Are there alternative housing arrangements that do not provoke fighting or permit the administration of adequate veterinary care and allow pigs full range of movement?

Our point is that, if it is to comport with commonsense notions of what is humane, a designation of a practice as humane cannot turn only on the identification of some benefit to the animals without any consideration of concomitant harm and alternatives, as well as the costs to humans. Fundamentally, a determination of humaneness would require consideration of, *inter alia*, what it is that animals experience and how much various deprivations cause them to suffer. Indeed, the AVMA report relied on by the Department *itself* concludes that there is no scientific way, for example, to say how much freedom of movement is equal to how much freedom from aggression or how many scratches are equal to how much frustration. In such cases, science can identify problems and find solutions but cannot calculate and compare overall welfare in very different systems.[52]

The Department did not take those next steps; it did not compare animal welfare in different systems and then decide, by balancing animal suffering with the economic and perhaps other advantages or costs of industrial farming, what was tolerable in New Jersey. Instead the Department simply acted as if the existence of this study entirely resolved an issue that the study itself clearly proclaimed it did not, and could not, address.

A similar route is seen in the Court's discussion of the practice of cutting the beaks of chickens and turkeys, known to animal advocates as "debeaking" and to industry as "beak trimming," or, more recently, "beak conditioning." The Court pointed out that appellants argued that this practice does not pass muster under a calculation of costs and benefits. The practice undisputedly causes the birds pain and would not be necessary to reduce fighting if the birds were provided with more space, thereby reducing the likelihood of aggression. The Court then cited to the Department's position that studies showed that beak trimming, while painful, is not inhumane because it is offset by the benefit to the bird and to the flock of reduced injury from fighting. What was missing was a discussion of whether the Department had considered the costs and benefits of the alternative of reducing crowding. There was also no judicial discussion of the failure of the Department even to attempt to make an informed decision as to whether any increase in the price of eggs or poultry caused by giving the birds adequate room so outweighed the conceded harm to the birds as to make the practice sufficiently acceptable to be deemed "humane."

Certain factors cited by the Department, and, in turn, by the Court, as evidence that the standards were humane, had nothing to do with humaneness at all. For example, among the benefits listed for the permanent tethering, by the neck, of calves, were that "[a]mong dairy calves, tethering allows them to become accustomed to the method of restraint they will experience as adult dairy cattle in the milking barn."[53] Similarly, castration of pigs is useful in "avoiding the 'tainting of pork with foul odors and off flavors'."[54] A number of practices used with birds, including debeaking, were noted to be of benefit to the "flock."[55] There was no effort to separate out these benefits to the industry and weigh them against the concomitant harm to the individual animal, or the costs and benefits of any alternatives.

For a final example, consider the issue of castration without anesthesia: "Turning to the issue of castration without anesthesia, materials in the record support the Department's conclusion that the short-term pain associated with the practice is reduced when performed prior to weaning by experienced handlers."[56] Notably, and oddly, in spite of this conclusion on the part of the Department, the regulations did not require that castration take place prior to weaning, only that it be done in a way that "minimized pain." But even if the Department had required pre-weaning castration, the fact that pain is reduced, or "minimized" (whatever that means in a context that does not require anesthetics), does not make a practice humane. To determine humaneness it is first necessary to balance, at the very least, how much pain the practice causes, (not just whether it could be worse), the reasons for using the practice (while the Court discussed the reasons for castration, it did not discuss the reasons for performing castration without anesthesia), and what the alternatives are. Following these determinations, it would have been possible for a judgment to be made as to whether that amount of suffering is tolerable given the benefits of the practice. The Department never conducted the balancing necessary to such an analysis—a failing ignored by the Court.

In stark contrast, the Supreme Court of Israel's decision invalidating regulations authorizing the force-feeding of geese was based *entirely* on such an analysis. The Court held that although the regulations were intended to prevent the suffering of geese, the regulations did not achieve a "proper balance" between the suffering of animals and the needs of farming. The regulations

> to some extent, measure up to the appropriateness between the means and end, but they are not sufficient to stand up to this test. They do not establish the means that will minimize the injury nor do they answer the test of proportionality, which measures the relation between the benefit and harm.[57]

SWITCHING THE STATUTORY MANDATE

The Court compounded its error in treating "humaneness" as a purely scientific standard by allowing the Department to classify practices as "humane" in the absence of such scientific proof. A plain reading of the statute indicates that the legislature mandated that the Department specify farming practices that are humane, a designation which would result in "safe harbor" protection from prosecution for violation of the state's anticruelty laws for the specified practices. For example, if the Department determined that indoor group housing for pigs (with no access to the outdoors) met the standard of "humane," then a pork producer who houses pigs in that way would presumptively escape prosecution for cruelty even if free-range production that allowed pigs access to the outdoors met more of a pig's needs and desires. A producer who used gestation crates would not receive a presumption that his or her conduct was legal. If the Department did not make a determination that any method of housing pigs was humane, then the matter of housing pigs would be left completely open to interpretation of the state's anticruelty statute. Only if the Department made an affirmative decision that a practice is humane and therefore included it in the "safe harbor" of the regulations would there be an effect on the anticruelty statute.

This, however, was not how the Department understood the statute. In undertaking the legislatively mandated task to designate certain farming practices as humane, the Department decided that *humane* should mean any practice that had not been "scientifically" determined to be *inhumane*. So, in the example of the crating of pregnant pigs, the Department did not understand its task to be determining whether the gestation crate was, in fact, humane. Rather, the Department understood its task to be determining whether or not the gestation crate has been scientifically determined to be inhumane. If the Department decided that the gestation crate has not been scientifically determined to be inhumane, then the Department believed it should designate the gestation crate as humane. Since inclusion in the regulations would result in safe harbor protection from prosecution under the anticruelty law, as a result, "not proven inhumane" practices were validated as "humane" practices. The Department's way of undertaking its mandated duty dramatically increases the breadth of the legislative impact on the anticruelty law since it designated as humane every farming practice in the United States that, in its opinion, could not be scientifically proven to be *in*humane. Thus, any practice as to which there was no proof, or, in the Department's ungenerous view, insufficient proof, of inhumaneness, was nevertheless classified as humane and presumptively immune from prosecution.

This problem of Departmental mischaracterization of its authority is compounded by its additional mistaken belief that failing to designate a practice as humane would result in a prohibition of the practice. As the Court noted, without any hint that it saw the inherent flaw in the Department's understanding of its role, "The Department has consistently stated that, in the absence of evidence that a practice is detrimental to animal welfare, it will refuse to prohibit the practice ..."[58] But there is nothing in the statute to support the idea that the legislature intended such a sweeping Departmental impact on the state's anticruelty statute. The Department was charged only with designating humane practices, which would provide safe harbor protection from prosecution for cruelty, not with *prohibiting* anything. Perhaps the Department's misunderstanding of the scope of its obligations was what led it to err so far on the side of industry. It may have been afraid to exclude any common practice from its regulations on its false assumption that to do so would be to immediately prohibit it, causing substantial disruption to New Jersey's farmers. Whatever the reason, the Department, and then the Court, turned the statute on its head, and vastly expanded its reach.

Moreover, as previously noted, not only did the Department presume humaneness in the absence of evidence, and misunderstand its obligation as requiring it to either endorse each and every farming practice or prohibit it entirely, it appears to have concluded that the only evidence it should consider was scientific studies; in the absence of *scientific* proof that the practice was inhumane, it should automatically deem a farming practice humane without making any attempt to consider what a reasonable observer of such activity might think. Thus, the

Department was operating under three misunderstandings: (1) that it was at liberty to define "humane" practices as synonymous with "not proven inhumane" practices; (2) that failure to designate a practice as humane by virtue of its not being proven inhumane would result in that practice violating the anticruelty statute; and (3) that the absence of *scientific* proof that a practice is inhumane should result in the protection of that practice by way of designating it to be humane. As a consequence, certain practices that appear to a reasonable observer to be inhumane were sanctioned as humane without any scientific evidence (or any other reasonable basis for judgment on the part of the Department) that those practices were actually humane.

The Court concluded that the Department's approach was authorized by the statute and was not arbitrary. For example, regarding the tail docking of dairy cows, the Court approvingly noted,

> The Department acknowledges that there is a controversy regarding the practice of tail docking. It relies on the report prepared by the American Association of Bovine Practitioners, which concluded that there was not enough scientific evidence to condone or condemn the practice. The agency claims that there is a lack of evidence that the procedure, when performed in accordance with the regulations by a knowledgeable individual to minimize pain, is cruel or inhumane. Accordingly, it declined to deny cattle producers the option of tail docking.... Here too, the Department made a scientific judgment after considering arguments on both sides.[59]

If the legislature had required the Department to set forth standards that prohibited practices when they were proven to be inhumane, then the Department's refusal to prohibit tail-docking, and the Court's validation of such determination, would be appropriate given the Department's determination that the evidence did not support a finding of inhumaneness. Similarly, if the legislature had required the Department to authorize practices that had not been proven to be inhumane, the Department's designation and the Court's validation would also be justified. However, what the legislature did do was to require the Department to designate practices that were affirmatively humane. To accomplish that task, the Department was to approach the question neutrally, without assigning a burden of proof to either side of the question.

The most obvious, and far-reaching, example of the Department's presumption in favor of upholding industry practices as long as they had not been proven inhumane was the Department's treatment of routine husbandry practices. Every single existing and future common farming practice, as taught by veterinary schools, land grant colleges, and agricultural extension agents, was deemed to be humane, and, therefore, to fall within the safe harbor exemption from prosecution under the state's anticruelty statutes. The fact is that there is no reason to suppose that practices are reviewed for humaneness before they are included in the curricula of schools or training programs. Thus, practices will be deemed humane simply because they are taught and not because there has been any determination of their humaneness.

The Court accepted this approach, and this exemption, stating, "because the Department reviewed the curricula of these schools and was convinced that they teach the latest farming techniques and instruct students in the most recent scientific innovations,"[60] that a standard of humaneness has been established. Aside from the complete inaccuracy of the Court's claim that the Department reviewed such curricula,[61] the fact is that the "latest farming techniques" and "most recent scientific innovations" do not necessarily take animal welfare into account. Sadly, the truth is that scientific innovation on the farm has, as a general rule, been consistently the *cause* of increased animal suffering.

The harmful impact of this provision is evidenced in the Department's defense, accepted by the Court, of its inherent authorization of the commonly taught practice of force-feeding of ducks and geese for foie gras. When considering whether forcibly feeding geese was inhumane (and, as a result, proof that farming practices customarily taught in veterinary schools and land-grant colleges violated the statute), the Department rejected the argument that force-feeding had been proven inhumane, even though the European Council's Scientific Committee on Animal Health and Animal Welfare had determined that force-feeding is "detrimental to the welfare of the birds"[62] and the Israeli Supreme Court had accepted that report as a basis for holding that force-feeding is cruel. In support of its decision to designate force-feeding, as a customarily taught practice, as humane, the Department cited to a report of the American Veterinary Medical Association that stated that "there was insufficient peer-reviewed evidence related to animal welfare during the production of foie gras."[63] The Court pointed out that, as a result of this report, the Department "refused to ban the practice because there is no scientific evidence that the procedure is detrimental to animal welfare." Not only is this statement factually incorrect, as noted above, but it is, again, based on a presumption that practices not included in the regulations will be considered "ban[ned]" and, in the absence of scientific proof, the Department should deem a practice humane. Nevertheless, in this instance, as in all others, the Court simply deferred to the Department's misapplication of this presumption.

> In the absence of such evidence, we are unable to conclude the practice is not humane. Stated differently, because there is no conclusive evidence that the practice is detrimental to animal welfare, the agency's decision not to ban it cannot be considered arbitrary or unreasonable.[64]

The reversal of the statutory mandate from protecting practices from prosecution when they are proven to be humane to protecting practices from prosecution when there is allegedly no scientific proof that they are inhumane is fully in line with industry policy. This policy no doubt influenced the Department, and thus the Court's, approach.

For example, three very prominent "animal welfare" researchers, Temple Grandin, John McGlone and Stanley Curtis, recently stated:

> To call for changing animal production and processing systems on the basis of erroneous premises ultimately will be of no use to any human or any animal. Until we know much more about the causation and function of the behaviors an animal exhibits and the correlated physiological responses in challenging settings, we should not change production systems willy-nilly.[65]

At first blush, the idea that farming practices should be allowed to continue until scientifically proven inhumane may seem reasonable. Why should an industry be forced to change its ways without conclusive evidence? One answer may be that the question assumes the wrong starting point. Such changes may be called for because many of the practices that are in use should never have been allowed in the first place. Because of a dearth of regulation of the farmed animal industry on welfare grounds for the past half-century, industry has created a status quo that is causing horrendous suffering on an unimaginable scale. The idea that we should allow industry to continue to do anything it finds profitable to animals until all of these practices are conclusively proven inhumane is extremely problematic for a number of reasons. One reason is that the industry is continually funding science to produce studies in ostensible support of its current practices. If industry is funding the research, how likely is it that truly objective studies will be done or that conclusive determinations proving industry practices unacceptable will be made? How do we even know that scientists are examining each and every common farming practice in regard to the suffering they cause? A second reason is that, as the size of the farming industry grows, practices it deems efficient become further entrenched. Since efficiency and humane objectives are often at odds with one another, cruelty becomes more and more enmeshed into the process of farming animals, and it simply becomes harder and harder to change farming practices in the direction of humane treatment.

Perhaps the most basic reason that industry should be required to prove practices to be humane before they are authorized, as we will discuss further below, is that the animal welfare science that industry has relied upon is rarely situated to produce valid conclusions about animal sentience. As a result, industry will be able to continually claim that we need to "know much more about the causation and function" of animal behavior before it should have to change its treatment of animals. How long should animals be forced to wait for us to prove that they are suffering? They will wait quite literally forever if we do not have the scientific expertise or desire to produce such proof.

THE USE OF SCIENCE

The Court's willingness to accept that it was appropriate to presume that practices were humane until scientifically proven otherwise appears to be rooted, at least in part, in a fundamental naiveté about the controversies involved in using science to evaluate animal welfare and how that should inform what society chooses to consider humane. Three different types of factors are generally identified in evaluating animal welfare: biological, which include the animals' health and productivity; behavioral, which include the animals' ability to live in a manner consistent with their nature; and, affective, which include the avoidance of pain, hunger, fear and other forms of suffering, as well as the presence of pleasure. For a long time, industry relied solely on the first measure (an animal's biological health and productivity) to its advantage. Without support, industry argued that any profitable factory farm could be assumed to be treating their animals well because production would drop if the animals were suffering. Indeed, such assertions by industry spokespersons are still frequent. For example, in 2007, a dairy farmer and veterinarian testified before a Congressional committee on behalf of the National Milk Producers Federation that, "[s]imply put, what's good for our cows is good for our business."[66] Similarly, the Connecticut Agriculture Commissioner, in response to a proposed ban on battery cages, asserted:

> The concept [that] housing laying hens in cages is necessarily inhumane is based on conjecture and not supported by scientific evidence. Hens that are contented tend to lay more eggs, and in all the studies we've seen, caged hens lay more eggs than free-roving hens. So to say they're not content is incorrect.[67]

There is, however, really no question that productivity, in and of itself, is not an accurate measure of animal welfare. As Bernard E. Rollin has stated,

> Productivity may be relevant to welfare, in that productivity testifies that at least certain animal needs are being met. But because productivity is fundamentally an economic notion, it is conceptually and often actually present in the absence of animal well-being. Indeed, productivity is itself ambiguous. It may refer to the economic success of an operation as a whole or to the performance of an individual animal. In neither case does it ensure absence of suffering. [P]rofitable production systems may be the causes of certain production diseases. Many individuals may suffer and die, yet the operation as a whole may still be profitable; individual animals may produce, for example, gain weight, in part because they are immobile, yet suffer because of the inability to move.[68]

Despite assertions like those made by the National Milk Producers Federation described above, in more serious arenas industry itself no longer relies solely on productivity as establishing good animal welfare. Yet, even when industry purports to be broader in its scientific approach, its reliance on, and use of, science is very unsatisfying. Initially, there is the obvious fact that nearly all of the scientific research industry uses is industry funded, to one extent or another. At the very least, it is reasonable to assume that the results of such research are biased in its favor. Accordingly, the additional "scientific" factors that industry looks at in addition to production measures are generally very limited and are based more on biological measurements than on behavioral or affective factors. For example, industry-funded research may well focus on such indicators as the health of the animal, but those measurements may be limited to aspects of health that relate to production. Physiological evaluations may be limited to measurements of various hormones to measure the level of stress that the animal is under. Negative states may be measured only by gross behavioral abnormalities such as repetitive, "stereotypic" bar biting, licking, etc.

That an animal is not exhibiting extreme stress or physical deterioration does not mean that the animal is even moderately comfortable or healthy. While all of the factors discussed above can be, to some extent, relevant to welfare, the problem is that they cannot even begin to provide a full picture. The industry, including the Department, tends to approach the entire issue of animal welfare with a purely behaviorist view that only observable behavior and physiology can be evaluated scientifically. Thus, in discussing the regulations, the Department noted that "objective scientific measurement of an animal's feelings has not been uniformly developed to the extent it could be applied uniformly and consistently."[69] This kind of thinking is common in industry circles. For example, Dr. Anna Johnson, director of animal welfare for the National Pork Board, when asked what makes a happy pig, responded,

> It's very, very difficult to put human feelings and emotions over into an animal setting....From a production standpoint, we look at the brain and try and understand how the brain functions. We look at the animal's behavior, physiology and production and try and balance all three to keep an animal in a healthy state.[70]

It is hardly "scientific" to think that, in order to make sure an animal is "happy" one need consider only those states that may be represented by a limited range of biological measures and abnormal coping behaviors. That is true even if one adheres strictly to behaviorism. As pointed out by Marian Stamp Dawkins, behaviorism

> does not deny the existence of animal consciousness altogether, as is sometimes claimed. It just says that the existence of conscious feelings cannot be tested empirically, and so the study of conscious emotions is outside the realm of science.[71]

The bottom line is that industry has taken a position that is arguably quite deceptive. First, it argues that scientific research is the only way to determine whether farmed animals are suffering. Tellingly, industry next argues that science, which it views through a purely behaviorist lens, can only tell us very few things about the suffering of farmed animals. It then asserts that the few things that can be demonstrated either prove that a farmed animal *is not* suffering or, more commonly, fail to demonstrate that an animal *is* suffering. Finally, industry argues that, in the absence of proof of suffering, a practice should continue.

Experience, including the experience of suffering, does not fail to exist merely because it cannot be measured. Unfortunately, it can be *treated* as non-existent if it cannot be measured. But is it true that it cannot be measured? In fact, not only does industry use the alleged inability to scientifically understand animal consciousness to support its policies, it ignores the fact that mainstream scientific thinking has moved far away from strict behaviorism. It is now widely accepted that it is possible to measure animals' subjective states, at least to some extent. After decades of what has been termed "the banishment of our fellow beasts from psychological literature by the predominance of behaviorism,"[72] there is extraordinary interest in the subjects of animal cognition, emotions and personality. Current research is rapidly revealing evidence of the astounding abilities of many animals, and the claims of "sentimental" animal lovers that many animals have complex personalities are being confirmed.

While most of this research has not dealt with farmed animals, some research by more progressive farmed animal researchers has started to take into account this "newer" mode of thought. An important consequence for farmed animals of a rejection of purely behaviorist thinking has been the evaluation of farming systems in terms of how many natural behaviors they allow. Bernard E. Rollin, the foremost proponent of this school of thought, has identified this agenda as "preserving the common-sense insight that 'fish gotta swim and birds gotta fly,' and suffer if they don't."[73] Another development has been the use of "preference testing," which is the use of experiments to determine what animals feel. Preference testing involves giving animals choices and then drawing conclusions from the choices the animals have made. For example, researchers can determine how much hens value access to litter by seeing how often they peck or stand on a switch to open a door that gives them such access.[74] One example cited by Ian Duncan, a strong proponent of such testing, demonstrates that

> [a] population of broiler[] [chickens], some of which were lame, were given a choice of two different coloured feeds, one of which contained an analgesic. The lame broilers ate more of the drugged feed than did broilers with no lameness, and ate enough of it to improve their lameness. These birds are indicating very clearly that lameness hurts, and if given the chance they will take steps to alleviate it.[75]

Animals can also be tested to see how strongly they will avoid painful or frightening situations.[76] This modern science, although certainly not yet at a point where it gives us a full picture of animal experience, is becoming increasingly sophisticated, and underlies many of the changes in Europe.

Neither the Department nor the Court recognized that the overwhelming majority of scientific conclusions upon which the Department relied are based on flawed assumptions improperly drawn from outmoded studies. In one particularly startling example, the Court noted, without any hint of disapprobation, the Department's reliance on a

European Commission report entitled, 'Report on the Welfare of Intensively Kept Pigs', to support its conclusion that the gestation crate was humane.[77] The report, as the Court notes, was adopted in 1976 by the Council of Europe. Yet it has long been refuted by subsequent European scientific research. That subsequent research was the basis for the European Union's decision to prohibit the gestation crate on welfare grounds, effective in 2013.

Ironically, unlike the Department or the Court, even industry is starting to realize that its positions are indefensible and is beginning, albeit very slowly, to move away from some of the most egregiously cruel methods of production. Within the last year, Smithfield Foods, Maple Leaf Foods, and Cargill Meat Solutions, all major "pork" producers, have pledged to slowly phase out or greatly reduce their use of gestation crates.[78] Perhaps most ironically, in view of the Department's complete reliance on its guidelines to approve of crating and tethering calves, in 2007, the American Veal Association board of directors unanimously approved a new policy that the veal industry fully transition to group housing by the end of 2017.[79] This change provoked Randy Strauss, co-president and CEO of Strauss Veal (the leading US veal producer), to comment that veal crates are "inhumane and archaic" and "do nothing more than subject a calf to stress, fear, physical harm and pain."[80] Notably, other than Strauss, industry spokespersons are generally careful to attribute these changes to consumer demand and not to any decision to embrace scientific developments that show that the systems currently in use are inhumane. Perhaps industry is generally reluctant to attribute changed policies to anything other than consumer demand because any hint of acceptance of the findings of modern animal science could result in far wider changes than they are prepared to make at this juncture. Regardless, the consumer demand for less inhumanely produced products is real, and it is based on consumers' common sense understanding that such practices as gestation crates, veal crates and battery cages are not humane. That common sense understanding stands in stark contrast to the Department's, and the Court's, conclusions.

THE ROLE OF REASONABLE INTUITION

Even if industry were forthrightly and straightforwardly using the very best science available, there is inevitably a grey area in drawing conclusions about animals in which intuition begins to play an important role. Science cannot tell us everything. The point at which the line is drawn between scientific understanding and what feels like simple common sense is not always clear or explicitly discussed. Nevertheless, courts are expected to use common sense. This is readily observable in judicial decisions regarding matters ranging from child abuse[81] to first amendment law[82] to environmental law.[83] Is there a role for common sense when determining how we should treat animals?

It appears that the Department and the Court did not think so. In this respect, the decision is deafeningly silent, especially when compared to the decisions of other courts that have examined common farming practices. For example, the English court in the McLibel case noted, in the context of another common farming practice (the gassing of male chicks),

> I bear in mind the danger of substituting one's own imagination of what it must be like to be gassed in this way. I bear in mind that a very young chick's awareness must be limited. But as chickens are living creatures we must assume that they can feel pain, distress and discomfort in some form . . . I find the practice cruel.

The same court, in discussing gestation crates, stated, "pigs are intelligent and sociable animals and I have no doubt that keeping pigs in [gestation crates] for extended periods is cruel."[84] Similarly, in Israel, the first step laid out by the Court in determining whether force-feeding of ducks and geese was cruel had nothing to do with science. Instead, it was whether that act "would be seen by a bystander as constituting either torture, cruelty or abuse."[85] The Court had no trouble concluding that force-feeding ducks and geese to make foie gras would be seen as such.

There is no reason to reject intuitive understanding out of hand. Intuition can be very valuable in an area where science has not been successful in devising ways to provide more objective measures of welfare. It has particular value when industry-funded science and industry practice conflict with the type of strong intuition demonstrated by polling and consumer choices. Intuitive judgments about animals' experiences are often criticized as mere anthropomorphism or as non-scientific nonsense. Yet there is a growing awareness that we are not so different from other animals as to make all of our assumptions about them valueless. According to philosopher Martha Nussbaum,

> All human descriptions of animal behavior are in human language, mediated by human experience. As [Peter] Singer has noted, there is a real risk of getting things wrong through anthropomorphic projection. But we should remind ourselves that the same problems vex our human relationships. . . . All of our ethical life involves, in this sense, an element of projection, a going beyond the facts as they are given. It does not seem impossible for the sympathetic imagination to cross the species barrier.[86]

Indeed, even the Department appeared to understand that there was a role for intuition in determining what was, and was not, humane, as demonstrated by its use of the terms "compassion" and "sympathy," in its definition of "humane." These terms are difficult to understand as anything other than a call to apply intuitive understanding and emotion.

How should a court deal with such intuitions? Of course, were many of the questions regarding animals that come before a court to involve humans instead of animals, scientific expertise would hardly be considered necessary. Expert opinion testimony is normally required only when evaluating a particular matter requires more of the fact finder than the exercise of common sense and good judgment.[87] No litigant would bring in a scientist to establish that requiring a human being to live in a space barely larger than herself causes suffering. But, inherent in the determination that such a decision can easily be made by the average person is the fact that it is considered appropriate for such a person, sitting in the role of fact-finder, to intuit that his or her reasonable experiences of life are not so different from those of any other human. Because of a presumed basic similarity in human experience and interpretation of that experience, it is assumed that a person can make such an obvious objective judgment without the need for expert testimony. Is there any role for such judgments when the question is whether an animal, rather than a human being, is suffering?

It is often the case in non-legal and non-scientific settings that animal advocates eager to persuade others of the suffering of, say, pigs, will compare pigs to the animals whom most humans know best, dogs. Most people familiar with dogs have the sense that they can truly understand what dogs are feeling in a certain situation. It seems almost absurd to posit otherwise. If a dog jumps up and down at the sight of her leash, runs around in circles, and takes on a different facial expression that makes people smile in response, could it possibly be wrong to say that she is almost certainly happy and excited? And if it is possible to make that assumption, isn't it possible to make many other such assumptions based on interactions with dogs? Based on those assumptions, is it not reasonably safe to say that one knows enough about dogs to know that, if a dog were forced to live her whole life in a space barely bigger than herself, she would be very unhappy? What, then, can be inferred in regard to an animal such as a pig or a calf? Inferences drawn from experiences with or observations of animals are not necessarily less reasonable, valuable, or pertinent than are inferences drawn from experiences with or observations of humans.

Skepticism about humans' ability to understand animals without the aid of scientific research increased dramatically with the ascendance of behaviorism in the 1940s. Perhaps not coincidentally, intensive confinement factory farming was taking hold of animal agriculture in the United States at the same time. Before that time the sense that animals think and feel much as we do was not considered "unscientific." Charles Darwin's *The Expression of the Emotions in Man and Animals*, published in 1872, and numerous other works, including standard human psychology textbooks, were based on the belief in a comprehensible cognitive and emotional continuity between animals and humans. Such ideas underlay the early laws prohibiting cruelty to animals, including the ones on the books in each of the 50 states today. These intuitive beliefs continue to guide many of our dealings with animals. They are why we enjoy the company of pets and why we cringe when we hear of or witness acts of cruelty.

This applies even to farmed animals, even though we rarely interact with them while they are still whole living animals. When decisions about whether pigs and calves suffer when kept for life in spaces so small they can never turn around are left to ordinary citizens, the results are quite different than when such decisions are delegated to industry or departments of agriculture. Such questions have been placed before voters in ballot initiatives in Florida and Arizona, and the results have been landslide votes to ban such practices. Numerous polls, including, as noted above, the 2003 polling in New Jersey, result in similar conclusions. There is every indication that an increasing majority in our society is convinced that modern common farming practices are not ethically acceptable. These people are not reaching those conclusions based on obscure scientific studies. It is more likely that people's intuitive protective response is triggered by increasing awareness and access to information about how farmed animals are treated and by their gut reaction that such treatment is cruel. If people are making common sense decisions about animals based on an intuitive appreciation for how animals may well be experiencing farming practices, why should courts reject out-of-hand common sense and intuition as bases for determining such questions as whether a particular practice is "humane?" Why should they completely ignore such beliefs? Is it because of difficulty in assessing the limits of intuitive judgment? Even if that difficulty is real, it is a poor reason to give intuition and common sense no role whatsoever, particularly since they are used without question in order to resolve other kinds of legal problems.

CONCLUSION

The Court's decision demonstrates that access to the courts will not, by itself, necessarily lead to decisions that benefit farmed animals subject to institutionalized cruelty. At the same time, however, the decision sheds light on several questions that must be addressed by policy makers in order to lead to positive legal change.

First, how much suffering should animals endure to justify a resulting benefit to humans? This is a normative, not a scientific, decision. Science, if it is up-to-date and informed by ethical inquiry, can tell us how an animal reacts to certain stimuli and, increasingly, can tell us what those reactions mean about what animals are experiencing subjectively. Science cannot, however, make up our minds, or help us avoid a decision as to whether a particular amount of discomfort, or any amount of discomfort, is justified by a concomitant benefit to humans. That decision must be infused with the common understanding shared by society as to what constitutes the humane treatment of animals.

Second, who should make this decision? Clearly, departments of agriculture do not appear to be the best institutions to determine standards of farmed animal welfare. Such agencies are not necessarily well-equipped to resolve this issue and are likely to be too tied to the agricultural industry to fairly evaluate industry's obligations. While it would be ideal to have an administrative agency that could be entrusted to exercise ethical judgment in an objective evaluation of science regarding animals, failing that, who should be making these evaluations? At the very least, given the problems seen with departments of agriculture in performance of this task and the limitations of judicial review, legislatures should enact statutes that not only require that farmed animals be treated "humanely" but specifically spell out what that means and what practices will not be tolerated.

In cases such as the instant one, when a legislature has not provided specific guidance but has, as in New Jersey, provided for an administrative agency to determine specific humane standards, courts should vigorously review and reject agency decisions that fly in the face of common sense ideas about what is humane. Courts in other countries have managed to make principled and carefully nuanced decisions with no more guidance than the New Jersey Appellate Division had here.

Third, what are the implications of reforming cruel farming practices? Whether made by legislatures, administrative agencies, or courts, these decisions must be made with an understanding of their enormous practical implications. In trying to understand why, in this case, the Court ignored its obligations to the legislature and to the animals it appears obvious that a background concern must have been the potential impact on New Jersey agribusiness. If New Jersey agribusiness must operate on a significantly more humane basis than agribusiness in other states, New Jersey businesses would be economically disadvantaged.

This concern certainly points towards the need for federal, rather than state, reforms, although, at this time, federal reforms hardly seem likely. One way in which this concern has been addressed in virtually every jurisdiction that has required changes in common farming practices is to provide for a substantial phase-out period. The institution of such a phase-out can, at the very least, allow farmers time to adjust and retool equipment, thereby reducing the economic impact. Of course, the lack of a phase-out period does not fully explain the result in this case since, here, there was no need for a phase-out because the statutory mandate, if properly carried out, would have only resulted in a safe harbor from cruelty prosecution for certain practices, not the prohibition of any practices that would have to be phased out. The problem in this case was a Department that improperly assumed the task of validating the entirety of industrialized animal agriculture and a lack of judicial will to invalidate the Department's erroneous designations of humane practices and put New Jersey in the lead, in even the slightest way, in protecting farmed animals from the institutionalized cruelty that has become the American norm.

Fourth, can science be trusted? The results of scientific studies can be used in misleading ways. Claims based on scientific studies should be examined closely to assess bias in research design and the interpretation of results. At the very least, neither the industry nor administrative agencies like the Department should be allowed to rely on a misinterpretation of an outmoded behaviorist theory that holds that animal experiences cannot be understood and therefore need not matter. Too many scientists are failing to ask the questions that need to be answered in order to properly understand farmed animals' experiences and feelings. No doubt the major reason for this fact is that control over animal science in the United States lies largely with agribusiness. Given the intertwined nature of agribusiness, agricultural education, and departments of agriculture, there may be little hope that the funding of farmed animal welfare science in the United States will be removed from the control of agribusiness. Nevertheless, at the very least, European scientific findings, which are often funded in a government bureaucracy less dependent on agribusiness, and other more modern and accurate scientific findings based on sophisticated scientific methods, should play some role in decision making about animal welfare issues in this country.

Finally, is there a place for common sense and reasonable intuition? Even if access to better designed and unbiased science is increasing, we should recognize that common sense, based on reasonable intuition, must have a role in the determination of how farmed animals are treated, analogous to the role common sense plays in many other areas of law and ethics. The complete replacement of intuition with "science" as a basis for policy making has not done farmed animals any favors. Instead, it has created distance between industry practices and common sense understandings of animals' experience. Heavy reliance on behaviorism has resulted in policies and practices that are far less rooted in reality than they were in the past. When it comes to the law, there are extraordinary real world consequences resulting from refusing to draw any conclusions about whether animals have consciousness or cognitive abilities. The combination of a reluctance to draw scientific conclusions regarding animal consciousness and suffering, no matter how intuitively compelled, and the creation of a legal presumption that failure to prove the inhumaneness of a practice will result in the practice being deemed to be "humane," dramatically stacks the deck against animals. Legally, if something is impossible to prove (such as the suffering of animals), the creation of a presumption (that animals are not suffering unless scientifically proven to be suffering) carries the day. Our reasonable intuitions about animals should play some role in the creation of presumptions or allocation of the burden of proof when science cannot provide definitive answers. If it seems to us, given our common sense understanding of the world and of animals (as demonstrated by numerous polls), that a particular practice must cause suffering, industry should be required to prove that it does not before it can engage in that practice. Ultimately, if it walks like a duck, quacks like a duck, and looks like a duck, we should accept that it is a duck, until industry proves otherwise. This would not only reduce animal suffering, it would create incentives for the industry, as well as other entities, to fund studies that look at the real questions. It would also result in the law appropriately reflecting the concerns of most citizens.

Fundamentally, the Department, and then the Court, derailed New Jersey's attempt to be the first state to modestly address the entrenched cruelty of modern farming. The Court created a legal precedent, now under appellate review, that the Department did not act arbitrarily or contrary to the statutory mandate when it determined that practices are humane merely because they have not been scientifically proven to be inhumane and that it could ignore evidence of grave animal suffering when deciding that a practice was "not proven inhumane." In doing so, the Department and the Court validated practices that disregard the most basic needs of intelligent, social, and emotional beings, including rendering them immobile for their whole lives. Hopefully, the decision of the Court in this case will, at some point, be seen as the nadir in the relationship between farmed animals and the law. Hopefully, at some point, its flaws will be recognized and rectified, either by the Supreme Court of New Jersey in its review of this decision, by another court faced with similar questions, or by a legislature stepping up to the plate to do the hard work of reforming modern industrial farming.

* Mariann Sullivan is the deputy chief court attorney at the New York State Appellate Division, First Department. She is the former chair of the animal law committee of the Association of the Bar of the City of New York and an adjunct professor at Benjamin N. Cardozo School of Law.

** David J. Wolfson is a partner at Milbank, Tweed, Hadley & McCloy LLP, an adjunct professor at NYU Law School and a lecturer-in-law at Columbia Law School. The views expressed by the authors are solely their own. The authors would like to thank Taimie Bryant, David Cassuto, and Delcianna Winders for their assistance in the preparation of this chapter.

1. David J. Wolfson & Mariann Sullivan, *Foxes in the Hen House: Animals, Agribusiness, and the Law: A Modern American Fable, in* ANIMAL RIGHTS: CURRENT DEBATES AND NEW DIRECTIONS 206 (Cass R. Sunstein & Martha C. Nussbaum eds., 2004).

2. *Id.* at 217.

3. *Id.*

4. MATTHEW SCULLY, DOMINION: THE POWER OF MAN, THE SUFFERING OF ANIMALS 276 (2002).

5. Factory Farming, Poultry Production, http://www.factoryfarming.com/poultry.htm (last visited Nov. 8, 2007).

6. EMILY STEWART LEAVITT & DIANE HALVERSON, THE EVOLUTION OF ANTI-CRUELTY LAWS IN THE UNITED STATES 1 (1990).

7. 7 U.S.C. § 2132(g) (2000).

8. *Id.* §§ 1901–1907.

9. 49 U.S.C. § 80502 (2000).

10. Wolfson & Sullivan, *supra* note 1, at 212.

11. N.J. STAT. ANN. § 4:22–17 (West Supp. 2007).

12. The New Jersey Agriculture Experiment Station is a joint project between the State of New Jersey and Rutgers University, a land-grant university, designed "to be the leading public research and service based institution for the development and delivery of practical science-based solutions that contribute to the vitality, health and sustainability of agriculture, environments, people and communities of New Jersey." Rutgers, New Jersey Agricultural Experiment Station (NJAES), Vision and Mission (July 5, 2007), http://njaes.rutgers.edu/about/mission.asp.

13. N.J. STAT. ANN. § 4:22–3(d).

14. Mariann Sullivan & David J. Wolfson, *What's Good For The Goose . . . The Israeli Supreme Court, Foie Gras, and The Future of Farmed Animals in the United States*, 70 LAW & CONTEMP. PROBS. 139, 170 (2007).

15. New Jersey v. ISE Farms, Inc. (N.J. Super. Ct., Warren County, Mar. 8, 2001) (Kingfield, J.) (unreported decision on the record).

16. N.J. ADMIN. CODE § 2: 8–7.4(b)(2) (2006).

17. Humane Treatment of Domestic Livestock, 36 N.J. Reg. 2367 (June 7, 2004).

18. *Id.*

19. N.J. ADMIN. CODE § 2:8–1.2.

20. *Id.* § 2:8–4.4(d).

21. *Id.* § 2:8–1.2, 4.2.

22. N.J. R. App. Prac. 2:2–3(2).

23. HCJ 9232/01 Noah v. Att'y Gen. [2002–2003] IsrSc 215, 215, *available at* http://elyon1.court.gov.il/Files_ENG/01/320/092/s14/01092320.s14.pdf.

24. The decision is available at The Verdict, Justice Bell's Verdict. The Rearing and Slaughter of Animals (June 19, 1997), http://www.mcspotlight.org/case/trial/verdict/verdict_jud2c.html; *see also* Wolfson & Sullivan, *supra* note 1, at 219.

25. NJSPCA v. N.J. Dep't of Agric., No. A–6319–03T1, 2007 WL 486764, at *4 (N.J. Super. Ct. App. Div. Feb. 16, 2007) (per curiam).

26. *Id.* at *5.

27. *Id.* (citations omitted).

28. *Id.* at *6 (citations omitted).

29. *Id.* at *10.

30. N.J. Admin. Code § 2:8–1.2 (2007).

31. *NJSPCA*, 2007 WL 486764, at *14.

32. *Id.* at *16.

33. *Id.*

34. Gaverick Metheny & Cheryl Leahy, *Farm-Animal Welfare, Legislation, and Trade*, 70 Law & Contemp. Probs. 325, 333 (2007).

35. Press Release, Farm Sanctuary, Poll Shows New York Consumers Favor Ban on Cruel Practice of Force–Feeding Birds to Produce Foie Gras: Pending Legislation Reflects Will of State Residents (Mar. 29, 2005), *available at* http://www.commondreams.org/news2005/0329–03.htm.

36. Sherry Morse, Poll: NJ Residents Oppose Cruel Farm Industry Standards (2003), http://www.vet.com/rural_news/cruel_farm.html.

37. 927 A.2d 1291 (N.J. 2007).

38. Posting of Trent Loos to Truth Be Told, Fighting for What We Know is Right, http://loostales.blogspot.com/2007_07_15_archive.html (July 20, 2007, 10:24 CST).

39. Posting of Bruce Friedrich to The Huffington Post, Humane Meat: A Contradiction in Terms, http://www.huffingtonpost.com/bruce-friedrich/humane-meat-a-contradict_b_58547.html (July 31, 2007, 10:49 EST).

40. N.J. Admin. Code § 2:8–1.2(a) (2007).

41. *Id.*

42. *See* Patrick O'Neill, *Trappist Monks' Egg Factory Under Fire as Cruel to Chickens*, Nat'l Catholic Rep., Feb. 21, 2007, http://ncrcafe.org/node/933 (quoting Tom Regan).

43. *See* Animal Legal Def. Fund, Inc. v. Glickman, 204 F.3d 229, 235 (D.C. Cir. 2000) ("Where 'Congress delegates power to an agency to regulate on the borders of the unknown, courts cannot interfere with reasonable interpretations of equivocal evidence'; courts are most deferential of agency readings of scientific evidence." (citing New York v. EPA, 852 F.2d 574, 580 (D.C. Cir. 1988) (quoting Citizen Health Research Group v. Tyson, 796 F.2d 1479, 1505 (D.C. Cir. 1986)))).

44. *In re* Adoption of N.J.A.C. 10:52–5.14(d) 2 & 3, 276 N.J. Super. 568, 575 (N.J. Super. Ct. App. Div. 1994), *cert. denied*, 142 N.J. 448 (1995) (citation omitted).

45. No. A–6319–03T1, 2007 WL 486764, at *20 (N.J. Super. Ct. App. Div. Feb. 16, 2007) (per curiam).

46. Ian J.H. Duncan, *Science-Based Assessment of Animal Welfare: Farm Animals*, 24 Rev. Sci. Tech. Off. Int. Epiz. 483, 483 (2005).

47. *NJSPCA*, 2007 WL 486764, at *7.

48. *Id.* at *8.

49. *Id.* at *9.

50. *Id.* at *10.

51. *Id.* at *6.

52. Task Force Report, *A Comprehensive Review of Housing for Pregnant Sows*, 227 J. Am. Veterinary Med. Ass'n 1580 (2005).

53. *NJSPCA*, 2007 WL 486764, at *6.

54. *Id.* at *9.

55. *Id.* at *9–10.

56. *Id.* at *9.

57. *See* HCJ 9232/01 Noah v. Att'y Gen. [2002–2003] IsrSc 215, 268.

58. *Id.* at *17.

59. *Id.* at *8.

60. *Id.* at *16.

61. An inquiry sent by a Department veterinarian to land grant colleges *after* the decision was issued stated, "In defense of the current treatment of farm animals, the NJDA is trying to gather information pertaining to the education of veterinarians, animal science researchers, and food animal producers from veterinary schools, land grant colleges, and agricultural extension agencies. As a land-grant school, I was hoping you might be able to provide us with a list of your animal science curriculum, course syllabi, and list of required/suggested text books for your animal science courses pertaining to farm animals." Mass e-mail from Shari C. Silverman, V.M.D., Senior Veterinarian, N.J. Dep't of Agric., Division of Animal Health to professors of animal science at universities throughout the United States (July 15, 2007) (on file with authors).

62. Sullivan & Wolfson, *supra* note 14, at 150.

63. *NJSPCA*, 2007 WL 486764, at *16.

64. *Id.* at *17.

65. Stanley Curtis, Temple Grandin & John McGlone, *Time for United Position on Animal Welfare: Three Leading Animal Welfare Experts Take United Position on Key Animal Welfare Issues*, FEEDSTUFFS, July 20, 2007, at 8.

66. AVMA, Congressional Hearing Examines: Welfare of Farm Animals (June 15, 2007), http://www.avma.org/onlnews/javma/jun07/070615a.asp.

67. Ken Dixon, *Egg Farmers Clucking at Cage Ban*, CONN. POST ONLINE, Mar. 10, 2007, http://www.connpost.com/localnews/ci_5404113.

68. BERNARD E. ROLLIN, FARM ANIMAL WELFARE: SOCIAL, BIOETHICAL, AND RESEARCH ISSUES 41 (1995).

69. Respondent's Brief at 8–9, NJSPCA v. N.J. Dep't of Agric., No. A–6319–03T1, 2007 WL 486764 (N.J. Super. Ct. App. Div. Feb. 16, 2007).

70. *Animal Welfare Efforts Are Anchored in Science*, 21 PORK REPORT 12 (Spring 2002), *available at* http://www.pork.org/NewsAndInformation/News/docs/porkrept% 20spring% 2002.pdf.

71. Marian Stamp Dawkins, *Feelings Do Not a Science Make: Review of Pleasurable Kingdom: Animals and the Nature of Feeling Good, by Jonathan Balcombe*, 57 BIOSCIENCE 83 (Jan. 2007).

72. Charles Siebert, *The Animal Self*, N.Y. TIMES, Jan. 22, 2006 (Magazine), *available at* http://www.nytimes.com/2006/01/22/magazine/22animal.html.

73. ROLLIN, *supra* note 68, at 17.

74. Marian Stamp Dawkins & T.M. Beardsley, *Reinforcing Properties of Access to Litter in Hens*, 15 APPLIED ANIMAL BEHAV. SCI. 351 (1986).

75. Duncan, *supra* note 46, at 487.

76. *See, e.g.*, S. Mark Rutter & Ian J.H. Duncan, *Shuttle and One–Way Avoidance as Measures of Aversion in the Domestic Fowl*, 30 APPLIED ANIMAL BEHAV. SCI. 117 (1991).

77. *NJSPCA*, 2007 WL 486764, at *7.

78. Vincent ter Beek, *Group Housing for Sows*, 23 PIG PROGRESS 6 (2007), *available at* http://www.agriworld.nl/public/file/pdf/20070917–07_ppr_grouphousing.pdf.

79. Rod Smith, *Veal Group Housing Approved*, FEEDSTUFFS, Aug. 6, 2007, at 3.

80. Factory Farming, Strauss Veal and Marcho Farms Eliminating Confinement by Crate (Feb. 22, 2007), http://www.hsus.org/farm/news/ournews/strauss_and_marcho_veal_crates.html.

81. *See* United States v. Bailey, 169 Fed. App'x 815 (5th Cir. 2006) ("Common sense and the x-rays presented to the jury alone make the argument that the [two month old] child was not in pain almost ridiculous.")

82. Doe v. Gonzales, 449 F.3d 415, 422 (2d Cir. 2006) (Cardamone, J., concurring) ("The government's urging that an endless investigation leads logically to an endless ban on speech flies in the face of human knowledge and common sense: witnesses disappear, plans change or are completed, cases are closed, investigations terminate.").

83. Ethyl Corp. v. EPA, 541 F.2d 1 (D.C. Cir. 1976) (en banc) ("Sometimes, of course, relatively certain proof of danger or harm ... can be found. But, more commonly, 'reasonable medical concerns' and theory long precede certainty. Yet the statutes—and common sense—demand regulatory action to prevent harm, even if the regulator is less than certain that harm is otherwise inevitable.")

84. Wolfson & Sullivan, *supra* note 1, at 220–21.

85. HCJ 9232/01 Noah v. Att'y Gen. [2002–2003] IsrSc 215, 233 (Grunis, J., dissenting).

86. Martha C. Nussbaum, Frontiers of Justice, Disability, Nationality & Species Membership 354–55 (2006).

87. *See, e.g.*, Salem v. U.S. Lines Co., 370 U.S. 31, 35 (1962) ("[T]he general rule is ... that expert testimony ... is unnecessary ... 'if all the primary facts can be accurately and intelligibly described to the jury, and if they, as men of common understanding, are as capable of comprehending the primary facts and of drawing correct conclusions from them as are witnesses possessed of special or peculiar training, experience or observation in respect of the subject under investigation.' " (quoting U.S. Smelting Co. v. Parry, 166 F. 407, 411, 415 (8th Cir. 1909))).

Chapter 4

THE DUTY OF OWNERS TO PROVIDE VETERINARY MEDICAL CARE TO ANIMALS

PEOPLE v. ARROYO
3 Misc.3d 668, 777 N.Y.S.2d 836 (2004).

Margarita Lopez Torres, J.

* * *

Defendant is charged with Overdriving, Torturing and Injuring Animals and Failure to Provide Proper Sustenance (Agriculture and Markets Law § 353). Defendant has moved for dismissal of the information on the grounds that the statute is unconstitutionally vague.

Relevant Facts

The factual part of the information in this case states as follows:

Deponent [a special investigator of the ASPCA] states that, at the above time and place, the deponent observed a dog sitting behind a fence at the above-mentioned location and that said dog did have difficulty walking due to large tumor hanging from said dog's stomach and that said tumor was bleeding.

The deponent is further informed by the defendant's own statements that the defendant resides at the above-mentioned location and that the defendant is the owner of the dog and that the defendant owned the dog for approximately six years, he knew that she had a tumor and was in pain, he decided not to provide medical treatment for the dog because it was to [sic] expensive.

The deponent is informed by Doctor Bunni Tan of the ASPCA, that the informant did examine the above-mentioned dog, and that said dog did have a very large mammory [sic] gland tumor on the lower stomach area, and that the surface of said tumor had several ulcerations that leaked fluid causing a chronic medical condition, which was neglected to the point where her tumor was uncomfortable and painful for the dog, and that the tumor was approximately the size of a large grapfruit [sic]

132

and that said tumor required a painful and extensive surgery and that said dogs [sic] condition is terminal.

* * *

Upon his return from vacation, at Ms. Lucas' request, defendant went to the A.S.P.C.A. offices to meet with her. The minutes of a hearing held before another judge of this court, pursuant to *People v. Huntley*, 15 N.Y.2d 72 (1965), reveal that during that meeting, defendant acknowledged to Ms. Lucas that he was the owner of the dog, that he knew the dog had a tumor, and that he had not provided medical care to the dog because of his limited finances. Defendant added that he was familiar with cancer because a relative had had cancer and painful chemotherapy and stated that he believed that the dog should live out her life without intervention. Ms. Lucas then arrested defendant.

THE PARTIES' CONTENTIONS

In support of his motion, defendant argues that A.M.L. § 353 is vague because the terms "necessary sustenance" and "unjustifiable physical pain" (this latter one included in the definition of "torture" and "cruelty" of A.M.L. § 350) are not specific enough to provide notice that an owner must provide medical care to a terminally ill animal.

In opposition, the People argue that A.M.L. § 353 is not so vague as to violate Due Process standards and that the statute gave enough notice to defendant that he was required to get veterinary care for his dog. In particular, the People argue that "[t]he intent of the legislature and wording of the applicable statute" make it clear that the term sustenance means more than food and drink. The People also argue that the statute's failure to define the term "unjustifiable" does not make the statute vague because that term has "an extremely common" meaning in the vernacular.

THE STATUTES IN QUESTION

Section 353 of the Agriculture and Markets Law provides:

A person who overdrives, overloads, tortures or cruelly beats * * *, or deprives any animal of necessary sustenance, food or drink, or neglects or refuses to furnish it such sustenance or drink, or causes, procures, or permits any animal * * * to be deprived of necessary food or drink, or who wilfully sets on foot, instigates, engages in, or in any way furthers any act of cruelty to any animal, or any act tending to produce such cruelty, is guilty of a misdemeanor, punishable by imprisonment for not more than one year, or by a fine of not more than one thousand dollars, or by both.

"Torture" or "Cruelty" is defined by section 350 of the Agriculture and Markets Law as "includ[ing] every act, omission, or neglect, whereby unjustifiable physical pain, suffering or death is caused or permitted."

* * *

DISCUSSION

* * *

Necessary Sustenance

The court in this case must then determine whether A.M.L. § 353 gives sufficient notice to a pet owner that not providing medical care to an ill animal is a crime. In particular, the court should determine whether the term "necessary sustenance" includes the provision of medical care to an animal, such that defendant should have been on notice that his decision not to provide veterinary care to his pet was a crime. Defendant does not argue that the phrase "necessary sustenance" as used in the statute is vague per se or on its face, but that it is vague as applied to the facts of this case. As stated above, the People argue that the wording of A.M.L. § 353 makes clear that the term "sustenance" refers to more than food or drink, and that it also includes medical care.

When constructing a statute, the intention of the Legislature is first to be sought from a literal reading of the act itself. The language of the statute in this case is anything but clear. The first time the statute mentions the term "sustenance," it refers to depriving an animal of *"necessary sustenance, food or drink."* Then, within the same sentence, the statute refers to neglecting or refusing to furnish the animal *"that sustenance or drink."* Finally, the statute states, again within the same sentence, that it is also a violation of the statute to permit any animal to be deprived *"of necessary food or drink."* From the grammatical construction employed the first time the phrase is used, i.e, the use of an appositive set off by commas, the court infers that the legislature intended to define sustenance as "food or drink." The use of the term "sustenance" in place of the word "food," as in "sustenance or drink," the second time the phrase is used within the same sentence, supports this inference. The third time the phrase is used, the statute omits the word sustenance and refers merely to "necessary food or drink," which further supports the notion that the legislature meant "food or drink" when it wrote "sustenance."

* * *

Unjustifiable Physical Pain

The court must also determine whether, when measured by common understanding and practice, as well as society's sense of morality, the language of the statute, and specifically, the term "unjustifiable," conveys sufficient notice to a person that his or her decision not to provide a pet with medical care is a crime. The answer to this question requires the court's analysis of common understanding, practice and moral standards and how these notions inform the meaning of the term "unjustifiable" in the context of laws protecting animals.

* * *

Thus, anti-cruelty statutes, including A.M.L. § 353, do not prohibit causing pain to animals but causing "unjustifiable" pain. *People v. Downs*, 136 N.Y.S. 440, 445 (City Magistrates' Court, 1911); *Hammer v. American Kennel Club*, 304 A.D.2d 74, 78 (1st Dept. 2003). In the context of these statutes, an act is considered justifiable, "where its purpose or object is reasonable and adequate, and the pain and suffering caused is not disproportionate to the end sought to be attained." 4 Am Jur 2d, Animals, § 29, at 370. That is, not all pain and suffering is prohibited and some pain, even if substantial, is considered justifiable. For instance, branding is allowed, even though it causes pain, because it is found to be justified by the owner's need to enjoy his or her property. Hunting and fishing as sports are not prohibited by anti-cruelty statutes, even though they are arguably the ultimate form of cruelty, because these activities are found to be justified by the need of some people to engage in killing animals as a recreational activity. Similarly, the killing of animals for their pelts to adorn clothing and accessories is permitted.

The question of what is justifiable—or unjustifiable—in the context of anti-cruelty statutes protecting either children or animals has also been the subject of discussion in judicial opinions from several states. A review of these decisions reveals that courts across the nation are split on the issue of whether the term "unjustifiable" is a vague term, incapable of conveying a proscription. Appellate courts of at least two states have held that statutes containing the phrase "unjustifiable physical pain" are unconstitutionally vague as a result of the uncertainty of that phrase. See, *State v. Meinert*, 225 Kan. 816 (1979); *State v. Ballard*, 341 So.2d 957 (Ct.Crim.App.Alabama, 1976). The opposite result was reached in *People v. Smith*, 35 Cal.3d 798 (1984); *State v. Eich*, 204 Minn. 134 (1938); and *State v. Comeaux*, 319 So.2d 897 (La.1975).

* * *

It is clear from the above discussion that what is "unjustifiable" in the context of anti-cruelty statutes is what is not reasonable, defensible, right, unavoidable or excusable. This court agrees with the reasoning in *People v. Rogers*, [703 N.Y.S.2d 891 (City Ct., Watertown, 2000)] and is not inclined to accept that merely adding the term "unjustifiable" to the word "pain" transforms conduct that is inherently innocent, like allowing an animal to die of natural causes without providing medical care, into a crime. As the Court of Appeals held more than a century ago, "purely statutory offenses cannot be established by implication, and [...] acts otherwise innocent and lawful do not become crimes, unless there is a clear and positive expression of the legislative intent to make them criminal. The citizen is entitled to an unequivocal warning before conduct on his part, which is not *malum in se*, can be made the occasion of a deprivation of his liberty or property." *People v. Phyfe*, 136 N.Y. 554 (1893).

Neither does the court believe that society's current practice or the moral standards of our community expand the meaning of the term "unjustifiable" to include a duty on owners to provide their animals with medical care. This is especially true in the case of a terminally ill pet. Reading into A.M.L. § 353 an affirmative duty to provide medical care in all cases, regardless of the expenses or the owner's ability to meet them, implies a standard of morality and decency that the court is not persuaded society has adopted. Judging by the current lack of national consensus regarding the provision of affordable health care for our less affluent citizens, to impose seemingly limitless mandates on owners to provide health care for their pets based on the vague language of this statute would be overreaching on the part of this court. The court concludes that, as used in § 350, the term "unjustifiable physical pain" is too vague to warn pet owners that not providing medical care for their pets is a crime.

* * *

Furthermore, the court is troubled by the imposition of a duty to provide care in light of a statute that, like § 353, is so general in its terms. Reading this duty into the statute will create a myriad of logistical problems. For instance, how is the standard of medical care that must be provided to be determined? (i.e., To what extent must treatment be provided to avoid prosecution? Is providing regular veterinary care sufficient? Or, in light of the sophisticated medical procedures that are now available for animals—chemotherapy, radiation therapy, organ transplants—will that level of treatment be required? Will mental health treatment be required?); and how would that standard be judged? (What kind of expense is it mandated to be incurred to avoid prosecution?) It will also create ethical issues that are difficult to discern in the absence of a legislative pronouncement (When is extending a pet's life permissible? When is putting an animal to death mandated? Up to what point do we respect the owners' choice to refuse invasive treatment for their pets and allow them to die at home in the company of their human and non-human companions, rather than in a strange and antiseptic environment?).

CONCLUSION

The court finds that A.M.L § 353 is unconstitutionally vague as applied to the facts of this case. In particular, the court finds that § 353 does not give notice to a person of ordinary intelligence that he or she is obligated to provide veterinary care to a terminally ill animal. Therefore, defendant's motion to dismiss is granted.

HOW MUCH "CARE" DOES THE LAW REQUIRE?

David Favre*

The case of *People v. Arroyo* requires analysis of specific phrases in New York's anticruelty law but it more generally raises the issue of whether, and to what extent, the law should require an owner of an animal to provide veterinary care. Before getting to the particulars of the case or the matter of owners' responsibilities to provide veterinary care, it will be helpful to review the origin of the existing New York anticruelty law at issue. It is also necessary to consider generally what social issues are or are not dealt with in anticruelty laws. One hundred and forty years ago the same person who formed the American Society for the Prevention of Cruelty to Animals in New York City, Henry Bergh, was the individual who was able to persuade the New York legislature to adopt the first law in the United States that sought to balance the interests of animals in being free from suffering with the interests of humans in using animals in ways that can cause animals to suffer.[1]

The language of this New York law reflected a political consensus that working animals, primarily horses on New York streets, were often abused by their owners as people and freight were being moved from place to place. Although not stated in these words at the time, in effect, the laws acknowledged that animals had moral status and, as a result of that status, had a right to be free from unnecessary pain and suffering that might otherwise be inflicted by humans. These primary concerns resulted in the adoption of statutory anticruelty language that is still found in the criminal law of all states today. For example, it was made illegal to "overload, overdrive or torture an animal." However, the law was much broader than the focus on working horses, which gave it political acceptability in the New York legislature and the impetus to enact the anticruelty law. Within the 1867 New York anticruelty law three general categories of prohibited activities were set out: prohibition of certain intentional acts on animals committed by humans, prohibition of the abandonment of animals, and prohibition against not providing sustenance (or, after eliminating the double negative, the imposition of a modest duty to provide care for animals).

Embedded within the first section of this old New York law is language that reflects the basic legislative approach to a most difficult social and political issue. It is an issue that is critical to the case of *People v. Arroyo* and also to most animal-human conflicts. That issue is reflected in the phrase "unnecessarily beat, or needlessly kill ... any living creature." The words "unnecessary" and "needless" are extraordinarily complex from the perspective of juries who are asked to apply those words to the acts of particular defendants charged with violating the anticruelty law. Included within those words "unnecessary" and "needless" is an acknowledgement that there is to be a balancing of interests between humans and animals but also the legal recognition that humans will get to decide how to strike that balance.

Consider the simple and frequent circumstance of a pet owner who goes on vacation and places her pet in a kennel. Many animals will suffer from disruption in their daily routine, loss of companionship, new frightening experiences, changes in food, and confrontations with other animals. The decision of the owner to go on vacation creates these experiences that most pets would prefer to avoid. But the human has decided that the human's need for a vacation outweighs the negative impact on the pet and, therefore, that the pet's suffering is necessary. Thus, while the pet's suffering is real, the social judgment of today would find the pet owner's conduct acceptable and, therefore, far removed from the scope of criminal anticruelty laws.

Some other examples are the following:

- An owner or private third party may decide that her need for entertainment or an emotional release justifies setting a cat on fire or kicking a dog.

- An owner of a cat may decide that it is necessary to remove part of the skull of a cat in order to insert and maintain electrodes so that the cat's brain waves may be measured.

- An owner of sheep may decide as part of her standard husbandry procedures to cut off the tails of her sheep in order to reduce "fly-strike."[2]

- An owner of egg-laying hens may decide to keep those hens in very small cages in order to reduce the cost of egg production.

Should society, through the legal system, seek to intervene in any of those decisions? Beginning in 1867 with the enactment of the New York law, all states have restricted or prohibited some decisions that people can make with regard to animals. Anticruelty laws set minimum standards for how animals are to be treated and what owners must do or may not do to the animals they own. In drafting such laws, legislatures have three broad approaches available to them. First, a legislature can focus upon a particular act or type of act and decide whether that act or type of act will be lawful. Second, a legislature can create general standards but then delegate to a government agency the authority to fill in the details of legal conduct through the adoption of regulations. Third, a legislature can create broad standards which will be applied by judges and juries in courts of law on a case by case basis.

LEGISLATIVE APPROACHES TO ANTICRUELTY STATUTES

As an example of the first category (focus on particular acts), a law can be enacted that makes it a criminal offense to dock (cut off) the tails of sheep. A legislature could distinguish between docking the tails of sheep and docking the tails of dogs, making it illegal in one case and leaving it as lawful conduct in the other case. When a legislature makes an act illegal, the legislature is substituting its judgment for that of the owner of sheep or dogs as to a particular act that can be performed on individual animals. A legislative decision to prohibit a practice is the result of a legislature's balancing of human and animal interests such that the benefits to the human, if any, from cutting off the tail does not justify the pain and suffering inflicted upon animals; it is not a legally justified action. In making that decision, the legislature may reject arguments that a practice is good for the animal, such as cutting off a sheep's tail to reduce the incidence of "fly strike," because the legislature does not agree that the benefit to the animal offsets the pain, suffering, or other problems associated with the practice, regardless of whether there is an effective alternative. Or, the legislature may have been made aware of alternative treatments that protect sheep without causing as much suffering.

Of course, a legislature could also decide that some human activities are so necessary or acceptable that, regardless of the pain and suffering imposed upon animals, the legislature will protect those activities by explicitly exempting them from the application of the anticruelty statutes. For instance, the anticruelty statute enacted in New York in 1867 contained a specific exception stating that the law did not apply to animal experiments carried out at universities.[3] Such exemptions for scientific research are now common.[4] This means that the example of cutting a cat's skull open, as an act of science at a university, would be found acceptable and would not result in criminal culpability even though the cutting open of a cat's skull could result in criminal culpability under other circumstances. The result of an exemption for scientific research is that no judge or third party can legally question the professional decision of a scientist working at an appropriate institution and under appropriate circumstances to conduct scientific research. That is true even as to experiments that many people, including many scientists, might not agree are valuable.

There are many other examples of legislative decisions that certain types of human activities should be protected. Although not part of that first New York anticruelty law, hunting and fishing are also usually explicitly exempted in anticruelty laws because they are considered socially acceptable activities, regardless of the pain or suffering inflicted upon individual animals.[5] As in the example of scientific research, no third party or judge can bring a lawsuit to challenge as "cruel" a practice that the legislature has explicitly deemed to be outside the scope of the anticruelty statute and, therefore, a legally protected activity.

The second approach a legislature can take when enacting anticruelty statutes is to enact general standards but also delegate the development of specific standards to agencies the legislature deems best-suited for that purpose. For example, Congress could enact a law providing that the Department of Agriculture adopt standards for the humane transport of sheep and chickens in interstate commerce. Thereafter, the Department of Agriculture would adopt specific standards about the allowable density of animals, the type of shipping containers that must be used, and the extent to which animals must be given access to food and water. Until the regulations are adopted, it would not be known how the word "humane" was to be judged within the legal system. Such a delegation could also occur at the state level as when the New Jersey legislature enacted in 1996 the requirement that the New Jersey Department of Agriculture develop standards for "humane" animal husbandry practices for raising and maintaining animals owned by agricultural businesses in New Jersey. For reasons explained by David Wolfson and Mariann Sullivan in Chapter Three of this book, it is very difficult to challenge agency determinations as to what is "humane."[6] When legislatures give an agency, and not members of the public, the right to define what is "cruel" or "humane," the agency's decisions are reviewable only if it can be shown that the agency abused its discretion in reaching its decision.

The focus of this chapter is the third category of legislative approaches to anticruelty laws, the creation of broad standards to be applied by judges and juries. In the case of *People v. Arroyo*, the question before the court was whether the failure of an owner to provide veterinary care constituted a violation of the New York anticruelty statute. The law did not specifically provide that such care should be given but it also did not specifically exempt owners from providing such care. But, before turning to the details of this legal question about veterinary care, it is worth examining, as a matter of historical development, the language from the 1867 law and the law in effect at the time of the court's decision in 2004.

1867 NY law: "If any person shall overdrive, overload, torture, torment, deprive of necessary sustenance, or unnecessarily or cruelly beat, or needlessly mutilate or kill ... any living creature, every such offender shall, for every such offence, be guilty of a misdemeanor.	2004 NY law: "A person who overdrives, overloads, tortures or cruelly beats ... deprives any animal of necessary sustenance, food or drink, or neglects or refuses to furnish it such sustenance or drink, or ... in any way furthers any act of cruelty to any animal...is guilty of a ... misdemeanor."[7] The law further defines cruelty as: "includ[ing] every act, omission, or neglect, whereby unjustifiable physical pain, suffering or death is caused or permitted."[8]

Note that the first act identified as illegal under both the old and the newer law is the "overdriving" of an animal. As an example of the application of the legislature's priority, consider the activity of horses pulling wagons. Is it cruel to make a horse pull a wagon? Our society's answer, both 150 years ago and today, is that it is not cruel to make a horse pull a wagon. Animals have worked for humans for so long that it is doubtful that any legislature has debated the basic issue of whether or not it is proper for humans to "work" a horse. Instead the legislative policy debate begins with the premise that animals are working for humans and then asks the question: when should we constrain owners in their pursuit of work output by their horses or other animals? When it sets limits of any kind, the legislature creates a generic line that is legally unacceptable to cross. At some point, the interests of a horse in his or her own well-being becomes greater than the marginal additional work that might be performed by the horse to carry out human interests in having the horse work; that tipping point in favor of the horse's interests is called "overdrive" or "overload." The only way to know for sure if the line has been crossed in any given case is to bring criminal charges against a person and present a jury with the particular facts of the case. The jury does not have to decide if overloading a horse should be criminal; the legislature has already decided that it is. The jury must decide if the facts presented fall into the category of "overloading." The collective judgment of a jury, or perhaps just a judge or magistrate, will decide if the law has been breached.

One of the first cases brought under the original 1867 New York anticruelty law dealt with this issue of "overloading." Consider the facts and the instructions to the jury presented in the case of *People v. Tinsdale*:[9]

> The police officer who appears to be perfectly disinterested, and who has been complimented for his fairness by the counsel for the accused, testifies that the car was unusually crowded, that one of the horses slipped twice, and that some of the passengers were compelled to aid the horses in putting the car in motion. If the testimony did not expressly establish the fact, the right belongs to you to infer the fact that without the aid of the passengers and also of the conductor, the car could not have been set in motion. You are to regard all the testimony in determining the question, whether or not the car was overloaded upon the occasion referred to. Mr. Bergh testifies that the car was crowded and was ascending the steepest grade in the city; that the horses attached were light in weight and strength; that they slipped, and one of them fell twice, whilst straining propel the overloaded car, and were evidently unsuited for such labor. Mr. Bergh further states that, in his opinion, the car could not have been placed in motion without the aid of the passengers and conductor. Mr. Hill, a witness for the defense (a driver by occupation, and on the occasion a passenger upon the car), testifies that the stoppage was occasioned by the passage of a truck in front, and when the horses started, one slipped; but corroborates the statement that the passengers had to aid the horses in their endeavor to start the car.

Depending on the jury members' views about the nature of horses and about what was expected of the horses in this situation, the jury could decide that the horses were "lazy" or that the horses were "overloaded." In either case, the jury would be deciding on the basis of their general human experience whether too much was being asked of the horses, and whether, therefore, the law against "overloading" had been violated. The jury in this case was asked by the defendants to consider, and thereby to balance against the burden placed on the horses, the need for the employees to follow the directive of their bosses. In assessing that balance, the jury rejected the defendants' justification and decided that the horses had been "overloaded."

In *People v. Tinsdale*, the legislature's general standard of not "overloading" animals had to be considered in light of what actually happened to particular horses as a result of specific actions by humans responsible for the treatment of the horses. The case illustrates the fallacy of assuming that owners of work horses would take into account those horses' abilities to pull heavy loads because of the need to conserve the horses' capacities to work. First, the humans directly responsible for the horses are not the owners of the horses, and so the costs of replacing the horses or caring for the horses would not directly fall on their shoulders. Second, depending on the cost of replacement horses and the financial success of the business, it may be cost-efficient from an owner's point of view to run the risk of harming a horse by forcing him or her to pull too heavy a load. When it enacted the law prohibiting overloading, the legislature determined that it was cruel to overload an animal even when doing so was efficient for the human owner. What remained for the jury to decide was whether in this particular instance the horses had been overloaded within the meaning of the words the legislature enacted.

As in the case of determining the meaning of the term "overloading," juries and judges would be required to determine whether an act that causes pain and suffering was "necessary" or "needless" when pain and suffering is inflicted on animals outside of the context of legislative exemptions for such activities as scientific research, hunting and fishing, and pest control. The legal question would be, does a particular act constitute pain and suffering that is "unnecessary"? That is because anticruelty laws prohibit only "unnecessary" pain and suffering. Consider the example above of a person choosing to set a living cat on fire for entertainment purposes. Although a researcher could set a living cat on fire without violating the law, kids engaged in burning a living cat could be charged with violating a law that prohibits the infliction of "unnecessary" pain and suffering. Most likely, a jury would decide that setting a living cat on fire for entertainment purposes violates the anticruelty statute.

Note that, as a general prohibition on cruelty to animals, the law does not say that it is illegal to set a living cat on fire. Rather, the law says that it is illegal to "torture" an animal. Nor does the law say that it is illegal to inflict pain on an animal. Prohibited acts of "torture" or "cruelty" include the notion of "needless" harm to animals and explicitly provide only that "unnecessary" infliction of pain and suffering is prohibited. The level of pain experienced by the cat in being set on fire is only one factor; another factor is the reason for the suffering imposed on the cat. Linguistically, the words "torture" and "cruelty" have as part of their meanings the notion of socially unacceptable conduct, such as setting a living animal on fire for no better reason than entertainment. Indeed, so strong is the public's condemnation of that act that even unowned cats or stray cats would be protected from such an act.

By contrast, what if a teenager seeks entertainment by throwing pebbles at a sleeping cat for the amusement of startling the cat? Would that violate the legislatively created standard of "torture" or "cruelty"? It is doubtful that a jury would convict the teenager of cruelty to animals. While the teenager's motivation is as trivial as in the case of setting a cat on fire and results in an "unnecessary" act of startling the cat, the degree of harm experienced by the cat would most likely not rise to the level that it would be condemned as a criminal act of torture.

While it seems safe to assume that juries can determine in many cases what constitutes pain and suffering from an animal's perspective, it is not always easy to make that determination or to decide when the suffering an animal experiences is "necessary." While in the case of *People v. Tinsdale* the jury was called upon only to determine the meaning of "overload" in the specific context of horses required to pull a heavy load, in the case of a more general charge of "cruelty" or "torture," a jury is called upon to make a much more complex determination. To be found guilty of the crime of torturing an animal the jury must first find that the animal did suffer, but then the jury must also decide whether the animal's suffering was justified. The combination of the extent of suffering and the justification for inflicting that suffering comprises the moral balancing required of the jury.

For purposes of considering the calculus in which juries engage, let us return to the example of the person who boards her pet in a kennel while going on vacation. If the pet was so upset that she did not eat and howled the entire time, should her owner (or the kennel operator) be charged with cruelty for having boarded her? What if the owner knows that her pet always reacts with strong fear and distress when she is left at a boarding facility? Due to society's view that vacations are necessary and that boarding animals at kennels is a responsible way to provide an animal's needs while his or her owner is on vacation, it is unlikely that a jury would find that the mere use of a boarding kennel was itself a criminal act. After all, juries are required to balance interference with the animal's interests and fulfillment of the human's interests and not simply consider the degree of suffering the animal experienced. The pet's behavior indicated that she was suffering a great deal. But the law does not make illegal the infliction of that suffering when it is sufficiently justified. What constitutes "sufficient" justification is a matter for the jury to decide.

Included in a jury's analysis is attention to the motivation of the human who inflicts suffering on an animal. In the case of a pet owner's leaving a pet at a boarding kennel, a jury could find that the pet owner's intentions were admirable, particularly if she took care in choosing the boarding facility. At the very least, the pet owner did not intend by boarding the pet to cause the distress the pet experienced; the pet's distress was an unfortunate byproduct of the pet owner's vacation. By comparison, the intention of the person who sets fire to a cat for the purpose of amusing himself is intentionally engaging in an act known to cause extreme suffering. In that case the human is actually deriving pleasure from the suffering of the animal and the purpose of setting the cat on fire was to experience that pleasure. As these examples show, the concept of "unjustified" suffering is a moral pivot point for jury decision, requiring case by case determination of the acceptability of a particular act that has caused an animal to suffer.

Such questions of moral responsibility and causation are even more complex in the case of animals in commercial contexts. Could a prosecutor charge a local farmer for violation of the anticruelty law by claiming that the keeping of chickens in small cages known as "battery cages" is "torture"? Let us assume that expert testimony was available about how being kept in such cages frustrates almost every natural instinct of a chicken and that the conditions often result in observable adverse medical conditions and death. The jury would have to decide several different questions. Does the average hen "suffer" and experience pain from such caging? If the average hen does suffer, is the infliction of such suffering justified? What are the farmer's justifications for the practice? How might the farmer's interest in profitability factor in to the calculus of human interests and animal interests? Should profitability of a commercial enterprise ever be considered as a factor? If so, is there a limit to what a farmer can do to animals in the name of profitability?

Another example in the commercial context is the use of a whip to cause horses to work. Could a prosecutor charge a person with cruelty if he uses a whip? The horse's reaction makes it clear that pain is felt. The issue for the prosecutor and the jury would be whether the infliction of pain is "necessary." Perhaps the human used the whip with malice toward the horse, either because his original purpose was exclusively to cause the animal to suffer or because he lost his temper, hitting the horse fifty times resulting in cut skin and blood flowing. Or, perhaps the human used the whip only once and for the purpose of causing the horse to start pulling a wagon. Or, perhaps the human used the whip as part of a training exercise during which he struck the horse ten times but without drawing blood. How does a jury decide what is "unjustified" pain and when would such a conclusion result in a conviction for "cruelty"? Pain is "justified" by reference to the amount of pain an animal suffers, by reference to the motivation of the human, and by the reference to social norms as to each. In many circumstances it is a difficult calculation.

Consider the number of human-animal interactions that occur on a daily basis. Consider also the number of animals that are hurt or killed each day by humans. It is impossible to expect a legislature to decide in each case whether or not the action is inappropriate, immoral, or unethical. Therefore, such decisions must be delegated to others under general principles. A prosecutor is the first person who has to balance the factors to be considered by a jury, as a matter of deciding whether to charge an individual with animal cruelty at all. If the prosecutor decides that there are sufficient factors present to enable a judge or jury to find that the person so charged is guilty of animal cruelty, the matter is submitted to a judge or jury to engage in the actual assessment of those factors.

Thus far I have been considering animal anticruelty laws from the standpoint of the legislature's choice among three approaches: (a) deciding that specific acts will or will not be considered "cruel" as a matter of legislative determination; (b) deciding on a general ground that conduct should be regulated but delegating that authority to an agency; and (c) deciding on general principles what constitutes "cruelty" but expecting judges and juries to make determinations as to whether an animal has been treated "cruelly" in individual cases. The case of *People v. Arroyo* is a case in which a jury was asked to decide whether in the particular case of an owner's failure to provide veterinary care there had been a violation of the state's prohibition of "cruel" conduct. Before turning directly to that case and the specific issue it raises, it is important to consider another distinction that is commonly made in anticruelty statutes: the extent to which an animal's suffering is caused by humans' acts or caused instead by humans' failures to act. Anticruelty statutes can prohibit humans from engaging in acts that constitute cruelty or torture, and they can also require that humans do certain things or provide certain things that animals need in order to experiencing pain and suffering.

The first category, the prohibition of cruel acts, applies regardless of the ownership status of the animals; such prohibitions exist without regard to the property relationship between the animal and the person who causes them to suffer. If an act constitutes "torture," then neither total strangers nor owners may engage in it. In fact, one of the explicit features of the 1867 New York anticruelty law was that owners had duties to not to cause their own animals to suffer needlessly; the law did not apply only to the acts of strangers that harm animals owned by someone else.

The second category of laws, the obligation to act on behalf of an animal, is imposed only on owners or keepers of animals. In the case of the 1867 New York law, the only such provision was one stating that the law was violated if any person "deprives [an animal] of necessary sustenance."[10] The current New York anticruelty law still contains this duty, and it is still stated in terms of "deprivation" of "necessary sustenance" rather than the affirmative obligation to provide "necessary sustenance."[11]

Stating duties in terms of negative commands is common. Even states that have substantially revised their anticruelty laws still state the duty in the negative. For instance in Michigan the duty is stated as follows:

> An owner, possessor, or person having the charge or custody of
> an animal shall not do any of the following:

(a) Fail to provide an animal with adequate care.[12]

The reason for this form of imposing a duty is that historically legislatures have been reluctant to state, as a matter of criminal law, duties in terms of actionable failures rather than actionable duties to refrain from acting in a harmful way. Thus striking a cat is more likely to be prohibited than is stating the duty by way of requiring that discipline be accomplished through specified means that exclude striking a cat. A legislature can more easily in a criminal law context condemn the "failure to provide care" rather than dictate specified actions of care, such as requiring owners of cats to brush their cats' teeth regularly, on pain of a criminal prosecution for cruelty. Framing the obligation to provide care in terms of failure that can result in punishment for cruel conduct is compatible with the general idea that criminal laws have legitimacy by virtue of their providing punishments for failures of basic duties.

THE CASE OF PEOPLE v. ARROYO

Having considered several aspects of criminal anticruelty statutes it is now profitable to turn to the application of New York's anticruelty statute in the case of *People v. Arroyo*. The facts of the case are not at issue: the owner of a dog was aware that the dog had a visible, painful, terminal tumor. Rather than having the dog medically treated or euthanized, the owner decided to allow the dog to live out its natural, if pain-filled, life without medical intervention. At the outset, it is worth reflecting on why this person was prosecuted for cruelty. Some might contend that the owner's conduct, even if wrongful, was not so egregious as to warrant the time and effort expended by the prosecutor and the courts. However, perhaps the dog's suffering was particularly troubling to those who observed it. Or, perhaps the American Society for the Prevention of Cruelty to Animals, which conducted the investigation, was influential in persuading the prosecutor to bring charges.

One motivation for prosecution might be the desire to establish a statewide common law precedent for the proposition that compliance with New York's anticruelty law requires owners to provide veterinary care to their animals, even if there is no explicit requirement of such care in the statute itself. Indeed, the case is difficult for both the prosecution and the Court because the statute does not explicitly state that "failure to provide veterinary care" is a violation of the anticruelty statute. If the statute did so state, then the question for the jury would be whether failure to provide veterinary care *under these circumstances* was a violation of the obligation to provide veterinary care. Without any explicit statutory requirement to provide veterinary care, the question for the jury would be whether failure to provide veterinary care under these circumstances violated the general anticruelty statute. If the jury found that there was a failure to provide veterinary care under these circumstances and that these circumstances violated the anticruelty statute, it still would not be clear what the extent of required veterinary medical care is under the anticruelty statute. All that would be established is that—under circumstances *such as these*—veterinary medical care would be required. Nevertheless, the case would be important in establishing precedent because of the decision that *some* veterinary medical care under *some* circumstances would be necessary.

While the Court's analysis focused primarily on the legal issue of whether the law covers this fact pattern, the Court also raises broader policy issues about what the legislature ought to consider about this complex issue of veterinary medical care as a requirement of pet ownership. Before getting to the broader social policy issues, it is useful to review what the Court had to say about the scope of existing law. First, the State claimed that the affirmative legal obligation to provide "necessary sustenance" includes within it the affirmative duty to provide veterinary care.[13] By fairly straightforward analysis the Court rejects that interpretation of the statutory language and holds that the phrase "necessary sustenance" refers only to the provision of food and water and not veterinary care.[14]

The second argument of the State is more complex and legally interesting. The law makes illegal "any act of cruelty to any animal."[15] This is stated as a prohibition of wrongful affirmative acts toward an animal. Therefore, the *failure* to act would not initially seem to be within the scope of the term. However, the word "cruelty" is defined in the law as "including every act, omission or neglect whereby unjustifiable physical pain, suffering or death is caused or permitted."[16] This extends the definition to include not only affirmative acts of harm to an animal; the law was also explicitly intended to include inaction that causes an animal to suffer.

From the facts that the dog was in pain and that the defendant did omit to provide veterinary medical care to relieve that pain, it would seem clear that there was a violation of the law that causing an animal to suffer through either acts of commission or acts of omission constitutes a criminal offense. Nevertheless, as the Court noted, an animal's suffering, even if that suffering could be averted, will not result in culpability under the anticruelty statutes unless that suffering is "unjustifiable."[17] The term "unjustifiable" is not further defined in the law under which the defendant was prosecuted. That term, or its equivalent, exists in most anticruelty laws and, therefore, the issues raised by reason of the qualifier "unjustifiable" are nearly universal in the United States when it comes to prosecution under state anticruelty laws.

The word "unjustifiable" relates to both the suffering an animal endures and to the conduct of humans in relation to that suffering. The suffering of an animal might be justified by the reasons for which he or she is caused to suffer. One example is animals' suffering in the context of scientific research. Human conduct that causes animals to suffer is "justified" by virtue of the ends to be achieved through scientific research that includes experimentation on animal subjects. When the concept or term "unjustified" or "unjustifiable" is without definition in an anticruelty statute, then it is a jury or a judge that fills in the substantive content of that concept, in accordance with their life experiences. It is not a fixed judgment as to what is "justifiable"; rather what a judge or jury would consider "justifiable" might change with time. In the 1880s it was noted by a court that it would be acceptable to put kittens in a bag and drown them.[18]

> Society, for instance, could not long tolerate a system of laws, which might drag to the criminal bar, every lady who might impale a butterfly, or every man who might drown a litter of kittens, to answer there, and show that the act was needful. Such laws must be rationally considered, with a reference to their objects, not as the means of preventing aggressions upon property, otherwise unlawful; nor so as to involve absurd consequences, which the Legislature cannot be supposed to have intended. So construed, this class of laws may be found useful in elevating humanity, by enlargement of its sympathy with all God's creatures, and thus society may be improved.[19]

It is doubtful that a judge or jury today would find such an act "justified" or the kittens' suffering "justifiable." The dynamism of the concept of "justifiability" in the context of criminal cruelty prosecutions is the reason anticruelty statutes are more complex than their language suggests at first glance. It is also the reason why such a law enacted in the 1800s can remain relevant and useful in deciding questions of cruelty even in the 21st century. As noted earlier, this dynamic quality of social determinations of what constitutes cruelty is the product of a delegation of authority from the legislature to judges or juries to make determinations of "cruelty" and to fairly punish those who violate commonly held social norms associated with the care and treatment of animals.

It is important to remember that this word is also reflective of a much deeper principle. The concept of "justifiability" is reflective of our social, political, and legal judgment that animals have individual interests that are deserving of at least some level of acknowledgement. By contrast, there is no law that prohibits owners from engaging in the destruction, justified or not, of their computers. As discussed previously, an acknowledged interest of animals is freedom from pain. However, the law does not provide unlimited or absolute freedom from pain. And thus, the concept of "justifiability" calls for humans' judgment to balance the multiple and diverse interests of humans in causing suffering incident to their uses of and relationships with animals against the interest of animals to be free from pain caused by humans.

Why might there be the need to do any balancing? Why not have an absolute rule: humans shall not inflict pain on animals? Consider first the fact that humans do not have an absolute right to be free from pain. For example, one human can be legally (and morally) justified in the killing, hitting, or knifing of another human if in self-defense. Society, through its laws has the duty to articulate the boundary between acceptable and unacceptable infliction of pain or death.

I do not mean to suggest that humans are legally justified by reason of self-defense in causing all of the pain they cause animals to suffer. I mean to suggest only that the phrase "self-defense" is like that of "unjustified." It is the doorway through which juries and judges must pass before deciding the guilt or innocence of an individual's action. It is the legislatively sanctioned point at which a balancing test is to be applied, and that balancing test requires the application of social judgments that may change over time. The argument of those seeking legal rights for animals is that, at the moment, the interests of humans are very often accorded more weight than they should receive and that the interests of animals receive less weight than they should during the process of humans' balancing those respective interests. How to weigh the competing interests of humans and animals is exactly the issue that our society continually revisits in situations such as the legal prosecution for cruelty under statutes that obligate judges and juries to make determinations about "justifiable" human conduct that results in "justifiable" animal suffering.

In the case of *People v. Arroyo* the Court forthrightly acknowledged that its determination of "justifiability" led to the finding that the defendant was not guilty of cruelty to animals when the defendant failed to provide veterinary care, even in the case of a dog in pain and nearing the end of life due to a bleeding malignant tumor. In considering the threshold duty of providing veterinary medical care, the Court said:

> Neither does the court believe that society's current practice or the moral standards of our community expand the meaning of the term "unjustifiable" to include a duty on owners to provide their animals with medical care. This is especially true in the case of a terminally ill pet. Reading into A.M.L. § 353 an affirmative duty to provide medical care in all cases, regardless of the expenses or the owner's ability to meet them, implies a standard of morality and decency that the court is not persuaded society has adopted.[20]

As a basis for its conclusion the Court compared the rights of humans to medical care:

> Judging by the current lack of national consensus regarding the provision of affordable health care for our less affluent citizens, to impose seemingly limitless mandates on owners to provide health care for their pets based on the vague language of this statute would be overreaching on the part of this court. The court concludes that, as used in § 350, the term "unjustifiable physical pain" is too vague to warn pet owners that not providing medical care for their pets is a crime.[21]

Of course, the Court may only have been signaling to the Legislature that the broad delegation it received from the Legislature was not sufficient for the Court to reach the determination that veterinary medical care is to be included in the requirements of pet ownership. Just as a court is empowered and obligated to make decisions in light of changing social values and consensus, so are legislatures in a position to constantly monitor the development of social norms and to adopt new laws or refine existing laws when a new consensus has been reached. Indeed, if the matter of veterinary medical care were before the New York State Legislature, instead of before the Court in *People v. Arroyo*, the New York State Legislature could consider the argument that a number of states have adopted statutory language that requires pet owners to provide more care to their animals than was previously the case.

One state that has adopted such language is Texas. Under the Texas anticruelty statute:

(b) A person commits an offense if the person intentionally, knowingly, or recklessly:

(1) tortures an animal or in a cruel manner kills or causes serious bodily injury to an animal; ...

(3) fails unreasonably to provide necessary food, water, care, or shelter for an animal in the person's custody ...[22]

The Texas anticruelty statute further provides that:

"Necessary food, water, care, or shelter" includes food, water, care, or shelter provided to the extent required to maintain the animal in a state of good health.[23]

Does the obligation to provide "care," where "care" is "required to maintain the animal in a state of good health," encompass the requirement to provide "veterinary" care? Remember the Court in *People v. Arroyo* found that the obligation to provide "sustenance" did not include an obligation to provide veterinary care. Perhaps the addition of another, separate word ("care") and the required level of "care" being to maintain an animal's "good health" would result in a court including within the ambit of an anticruelty statute a range of caretaking responsibilities that the word "sustenance" does not readily seem to include. On the other hand, a court could still find that the obligation to provide "care" does not include veterinary medical care, despite the explicit statutory reference to maintaining an animal's state of "good health."

By contrast with the Texas statute, let us consider the much more explicit language of the Michigan anticruelty statutes that pertain to owners of animals. Under the Michigan statutes there are three steps in the analysis. First, the law states the following:

An owner, possessor, or person having the charge or custody of an animal shall not do any of the following:

(a) Fail to provide an animal with adequate care....[24]

Second, it is necessary to determine what "adequate care" is. Michigan law provides as follows:

"Adequate care" means the provision of sufficient food, water, shelter, sanitary conditions, exercise, and veterinary medical attention in order to maintain an animal in a state of good health.[25]

Third, although this language seems to resolve the problem of whether veterinary care is required, there is still the need to determine what constitutes the "state of good health" for which veterinary medical care must be provided. The Michigan legislature answers that question with the following language:

> "State of good health" means freedom from disease and illness, and in a condition of proper body weight and temperature for the age and species of the animal, unless the animal is undergoing appropriate treatment.[26]

As compared to the New York statute which requires only the provision of "necessary sustenance," the Texas statute's requirement of "care" as a separately articulated duty could provide a basis upon which a court could decide that pet owners must provide veterinary medical care. What if New York had adopted the Texas statutory requirement of "care"? The *People v. Arroyo* Court might have, but need not have, found the defendant guilty for failing to provide veterinary medical care. There are many possible interpretations of the word "care."

On the other hand, if New York had adopted the language of Michigan's anticruelty statutes, would the Court in *People v. Arroyo* have necessarily found the defendant guilty of failing to provide veterinary medical care? No state legislature has done a better job of articulating an *explicit* requirement of veterinary medical care than has Michigan. However, it is not so easy to state that the Court in *People v. Arroyo* would have decided that the defendant violated the anticruelty statute even if Michigan's statute were in place in New York. It would seem that it applies to the facts at issue, but the Court indicated that there would have been great difficulty finding a defendant guilty unless some hard questions could be answered. The Court reveals its concerns as follows:

> Reading this duty [to provide veterinary care] into the statute will create a myriad of logistical problems. For instance, how is the standard of medical care that must be provided to be determined? (i.e., To what extent must treatment be provided to avoid prosecution? Is providing regular veterinary care sufficient? Or, in light of the sophisticated medical procedures that are now available for animals—chemotherapy, radiation therapy, organ transplants—will that level of treatment be required? Will mental health treatment be required?); and how would that standard be judged? (What kind of expense is it mandated to be incurred to avoid prosecution?) It will also create ethical issues that are difficult to discern in the absence of a legislative pronouncement (When is extending a pet's life permissible? When is putting an animal to death mandated? Up to what point do we respect the owners' choice to refuse invasive treatment for their pets and allow them to die at home in the

company of their human and non-human companions, rather than in a strange and antiseptic environment?).[27]

The threshold issue for the Court of what standard of veterinary medical care might be required is solved under the Michigan law, which requires freedom from disease and illness as well as proper body weight. At least in the facts of that case there was an apparent need for veterinary medical care. Surely in most cases, an expert ought to be able to relay to a jury whether or not a particular animal is in a good state of health. But, there are still questions to be resolved before an individual is criminally sanctioned for cruelty to an animal. For instance, since an animal can be thin without being unhealthy, does the statutory reference to "proper body weight" refer to ideal or minimum weight? Just how wide a margin around an animal's ideal weight will be allowed before it becomes criminal to fail to do something about it. Of course, this same problem arises in the context of failure to provide "necessary sustenance." However, the problem is complicated by the many veterinary therapies that could be employed if an owner has the obligation not only to provide necessary sustenance but also to provide veterinary care. Moreover, what about such matters as an owner's awareness or lack of awareness that an animal's condition indicates the need for veterinary medical care? Is failure to provide care a strict liability criminal law requirement such that an owner will be guilty regardless of knowledge of or an understanding of the animal's condition such that he or she knows to take the animal to a veterinarian on pain of conviction for animal cruelty?

One question raised by the Court in *People v. Arroyo* is what kind of expense is mandated. That question is not addressed at all by the Michigan law. Inability to pay for expensive treatment is not a defense explicitly provided to an owner, so a court would have to interpret the law to allow for an equitable defense of inability to pay or limit the requirement of veterinary care to euthanasia or treatment, whichever is less. That would not result in animals getting veterinary care, however. That would result in increased potential of euthanasia. If a court holds firmly to the explicit language of the law that requires veterinary care, does that simply help more veterinarians than it actually helps animals? While particular individual pet owners may well choose to use up their life savings or go into debt to provide the highest level of care for their animals, there is a question as to whether, as a matter of criminal law, such a duty should be imposed on all animal owners, regardless of financial ability to provide veterinary medical care. It would be very unusual for the law to mandate the expenditure of money that a person does not have, under penalty of jail time or a fine (which the person may not be able to pay, either).

There is an argument that one should not have animals unless one is willing to incur unforeseen and unforeseeable costs of an animal's care. However, the fact is that many people cannot make those assessments easily or have changed financial circumstances by the time the pet needs extensive care. At that point the pet is no longer adoptable, and the pet's owner may already care too much for the animal to let him or her go to a more affluent home in any case. Would it be a necessary interpretation of the Michigan law that the owner relinquish the pet? Would an owner satisfy her responsibility by relinquishing the pet to a shelter? What if the shelter does not have the responsibility to provide veterinary care? Would it be fair if the requirement applied only to the individual owner and not to the institutional owner (the shelter) of animals?

Another question raised by the *People v. Arroyo* Court is whether mental health care should be required. That question seems to be answered in the negative by Michigan law. Legally required veterinary care would be limited to animals' physical health. While some veterinarians do attend to mental health issues, or at least behavioral manifestations of mental health issues, statutory mandates for owners to seek such care would not seem to reflect a social consensus about the extent to which a pet owner should provide care or risk prosecution for animal cruelty. There is increasing awareness of mental health issues, perhaps as reflected by the success of the television show, The Dog Whisperer. Nevertheless, the phrase "psychological well-being" does not appear explicitly in the Michigan law. A judge or jury would have to interpret the requirement of "veterinary medical attention in order to maintain an animal in a state of good health" to include veterinary mental health care.

A problem that often arises is the extent to which a law should be applied when literal application of a law, or even simply the application of a law as it has been applied in other contexts, would result in apparently unfair outcomes. For instance, under the Michigan law, every animal owner has a criminally sanctioned duty to keep his or her animal in good health. So, if an elderly person with a dog but no car is unable to take her dog to be treated for a severe skin condition, should she be considered a criminal? It may seem unfair to raise extreme hypothetical situations in order to argue against particular laws because it may seem that the likelihood of prosecution would be low under extreme, unjust circumstances, and, therefore, the extreme hypothetical situations are not the situations that would be faced in the real world. Unfortunately, there are such cases of questionable prosecution under broad and ill-defined criminal language.

Consider the case of *Martinez v. State*, 48 S.W.3d 273 (Tex. App. 2001). As stated in the appellate decision:

Appellant Andrea Martinez, an eighty-three year old widow, is known in her neighborhood for taking in homeless animals. She was charged with cruelty to animals and convicted by a jury. [The skin condition of the dog was severe enough that the attending veterinarian decided to euthanize rather than treat the dog.] The trial court assessed punishment of one year confinement and fined Martinez one thousand dollars. The trial court probated the sentence and the fine for two years on the condition that Martinez perform one hundred hours of community service at a local animal shelter.[28]

This outcome clearly bothered the appellate court, but the Court claimed that it was unable to change the lower court's decision because, after all, there had been a failure to provide veterinary care under circumstances that caused a dog such grave suffering that the dog was euthanized when taken to a veterinarian.[29] The conviction was upheld even though the defendant was an elderly woman whose only income was her monthly Social Security check and who had no means of taking animals to a veterinary clinic. In a final footnote the judge wrote, "in my view, anyone visiting this home should have realized that Martinez, poor, isolated, and elderly, needed assistance [not criminal prosecution]".[30]

Why was Martinez prosecuted? There may have been circumstances that led prosecutors to believe that many animals were suffering because of her efforts to "assist" homeless animals. Is it better for an animal to be taken in and denied care than not to be taken in at all? If Martinez had not taken them in, would those animals have received any care at all or would they most likely have died in other, equally painful, ways? Without a full understanding of what happened, perhaps it is difficult to pass judgment on the prosecutor. Nevertheless, on the surface it appears that an elderly person whose only intent was to help animals felt the full brunt of a law designed to address the cruelty of those who fail to provide care under other types of circumstances. Animal and human interests appear to have been balanced in such a way that the animal's interest far outweighed that of the human. Without qualifying language being attached to the statutory duty to provide animals with veterinary care, the net of criminal prosecution may be cast too wide.

LEGISLATIVE RESPONSES TO THE QUESTION OF VETERINARY CARE

Thus far, we have dealt with the possibility of a requirement to provide veterinary medical care primarily through the lens of the Court's decision in *People v. Arroyo*. We have considered how the Court interpreted the New York specifically at issue in the case, and we have also considered how the Court might have dealt with the issue if there had been different statutory language, such as the language adopted by the Michigan legislature. At this point it may be instructive to consider a range of state legislative responses to the question of veterinary medical care.

A quick survey of ten states produced mixed results. Much like New York, Ohio and Florida have no provisions using the term veterinary or medical care at all. On the other hand, Pennsylvania decided that it would violate its anticruelty laws if an owner "deprives any animal of necessary veterinary care."[31] Several features of this provision catch the eye. First, the obligation is stated as a negative "act" when it is actually creating a duty of action. Second, the requirement of veterinary care is qualified by the term "necessary." Neither of those terms ("veterinary care" or "necessary") were further defined in the law. As there is almost no risk of an individual being prosecuted for failure to provide "unnecessary" veterinary care, the qualifier "necessary" does not help sort out legal from illegal conduct that could result in conviction for cruelty to animals. Determinations of criminal violations will be strictly up to the judge or jury in a particular case, and there is little a pet owner can do to predict what behavior will turn out to have been compliant with the law. Perhaps an owner's only safe course of action is to provide veterinary care whenever the owner thinks anyone could possibly find that his or her animal could benefit from a trip to a veterinary clinic. This might well make veterinarians happy, but it is not clear that it would necessarily increase the health and well-being of animals.

By contrast, the Virginia legislature chose to use the word "emergency" to qualify the requirement of veterinary care. Under the Virginia anticruelty law it is illegal to deprive an animal of "emergency veterinary treatment."[32] The term "emergency" would appear to limit the obligation to provide care but the term is not further defined by statute. When a reasonable person would consider an animal's situation to require "emergency" care would be matter left up to a judge and a jury. Is the reason for this requirement to limit the circumstances under which a person could be found criminally liable for failure to provide veterinary care? Perhaps that makes some sense, but, in terms of an animal's needs, it makes less sense than the requirement of "necessary" veterinary care. If "necessary" veterinary care is required, some conditions will be treated before they become "emergency" treatment situations in which many animals will simply be euthanized. In other words, what constitutes an "emergency"? A clear example of when such a law would apply is when a pet is hit by a car. The owner must take the animal to a veterinarian. If "emergency" is to have meaning, should it suggest a sudden change of conditions related to the well-being of an animal? What if an animal has a tumor that will definitely kill the animal but it will take six months before the tumor reaches the point of killing the animal. At what point is the owner required to provide "emergency veterinary care to"? Is such a requirement really only the requirement that the worst suffering of an animal be cut short by euthanasia provided by veterinarian?

Colorado approaches the situation similarly to Texas. Colorado law provides that a person has committed animal cruelty if she or he neglects an animal.[33] The law further defines "neglect" to include the failure to provide "care generally considered to be normal, usual, and accepted for an animal's health and well-being consistent with the species, breed, and type of animal."[34] As in the case of the Texas statute, this language requires only "care" without explicitly requiring *veterinary* care. Colorado does provide more language to define "care" than does Texas, but the terms "normal," "usual," and "accepted" do not provide a lot of guidance to a prosecutor, judge, or jury. Apparently, Colorado's legislature decided to leave such determinations to the judge or jury in particular cases. The Legislature's language seems to suggest that evidence about social norms in the usage of veterinarians would be more important for a determination of cruelty than would be the expert testimony of veterinarians about what care should or could have been provided to ease an animal's suffering or to provide for "an animal's health and well-being." This language has the advantage of readily and explicitly allowing for change over time in social norms about the provision of veterinary care, but it contains the disadvantage that there is some lack of predictability on the part of owners who want to know (before they would be prosecuted) whether veterinary care is required by law and, if so, what kind.

Like Michigan and Virginia, Oregon provides more specific language that includes veterinary care requirements. The law requires all owners to provide "minimum care" to their animals.[35] Included within the requirements for "minimum care" is the requirement to provide "veterinary care deemed necessary by a reasonably prudent person to relieve distress from injury, neglect or disease."[36] Oregon's law provides that owners are excused from the obligation to provide "minimum care" when there are "emergencies or circumstances beyond the reasonable control of the owner."[37] Please note that this appears to be the reverse of the Virginia situation in which owners must provide emergency veterinary care. However, a close reading reveals that Virginia's legislation refers to an emergency as to the animal's condition, even if "emergency" medical conditions are not defined, while the Oregon statute is referring to emergencies that befall owners such that they cannot provide the care that they are otherwise required to provide. So, for example, if a wildfire prevents an Oregon owner from taking an animal to a veterinarian, the owner will not be prosecuted for failure to provide veterinary medical care to that animal.

Oregon's requirement to provide "veterinary care deemed necessary by a reasonably prudent person to relieve [an animal's] distress from injury, neglect or disease" imposes an objective standard for determinations about an owner's having met or failed to meet the statutory requirement. However, this may be just another formulation for the requirement that judges and juries decide whether an owner's conduct has violated the statute by reference to the social norms regarding usage of veterinary medical services. There is additional difficulty arising from the use of the word "distress." It is more typical for anticruelty statutes to refer to an animal's "pain and suffering" than it is for a statute to refer to an animal's "distress." Is "distress" meant as a synonym for "pain and suffering"? Is it an attempt to label an animal's state by objective criterion (the appearance of being "distressed") rather than by subjective criteria we cannot fully assess (an animal's experience of pain and of suffering)? It isn't clear why the term was used, but to some judges and jurors "distress" might seem broader than the term "suffering" such that it includes an owner's responsibility to safeguard an animal's psychological well-being as well as physical well-being. While Oregon's legislature has provided more words than many other states in defining the scope of the duty to provide veterinary care, the words it chose raise as many questions as they answer.

Washington's legislature also added the requirement of veterinary care to its anticruelty statutes.[38] The specific language of the statute seems to create a broad statutory duty because of the requirement that owners provide "necessary medical attention."[39] However, despite the breadth of the term, the actual duty may be much narrower than a duty created by the use of the word "care." Arguably, the word "attention" limits the owner's duty to that of providing euthanasia because there is no obligation to "treat" an animal or to otherwise provide medical "care."

Washington's law states that an owner is guilty of animal cruelty if the owner fails to provide necessary medical attention such that an animal suffers "unnecessary or unjustifiable physical pain *as a result of the failure.*"[40] (Emphasis added.) Just as the phrase "necessary medical attention" could be viewed as a limitation on owners' responsibility, this phrase could be seen as an additional limitation on an owner's liability. If an animal would have suffered, regardless of the owner's attempts to alleviate the animal's suffering, then the owner cannot be convicted of cruelty. If an animal would have suffered even if the owner had taken the animal to the veterinarian, then there is no criminal liability. Stated differently, the prosecutor has the explicit burden of showing that *but for* the owner's acts the animal would not have suffered. While that may well be an implicit requirement of prosecutors in other jurisdictions, the Washington legislature chose to make the requirement explicit, with the consequence that prosecutors will have to prove that element in all cases. That could be a significant prosecutorial burden, depending on the facts of a case.

Arizona's statutory requirement of veterinary care seems to be an extension of the Washington approach. Arizona makes it a crime of animal cruelty when an owner "intentionally, knowingly or recklessly fails to provide medical attention necessary to prevent protracted suffering to any animal under the person's custody or control."[41] Arizona's approach is similar to Washington's in that the duty is limited to medical attention, which may not include treatment or care of an animal beyond euthanasia. Arizona's approach also limits prosecutions to cases in which an owner intentionally or recklessly denied an animal necessary medical attention; it does not make an owner criminally liable for simple negligence. If an owner did not know an animal needed care and was not willfully ignorant regarding an animal's need, then an owner cannot be prosecuted for cruelty. Arizona also limits liability to those cases in which the owner's failure to provide medical attention results in "protracted" suffering. The term is not defined, but presumably the statute is intended to cover primarily those situations in which an owner provided no medical attention of any kind to an animal that experienced a long period of visible and extreme suffering as a direct result.

On the other hand, Arizona's statute can be read more expansively. The statute explicitly requires owners to prevent protracted suffering, not just to address it once it appears that the suffering has gone on for some time. The indeterminacy of the word "prevent" means that owners should be alert as to the potential for their animals to suffer and to prevent such circumstances from unfolding. Moreover, the scope of the statutory provision is not explicitly limited to situations in which an animal's suffering is "unnecessary" or "unjustified." While such limitations might well be read into the statute, the fact that the language is not there to begin with could well mean that the owner who knowingly denies attention that prolongs the suffering of her pet will have the burden of persuading the court that the failure was justified.

As in the case of the other state statutes we have examined, the job of judges and juries in Arizona in sorting out a particular defendant's criminal liability is daunting due to the need to apply general legal terms to the facts of specific cases in which animals have suffered and their owners have not provided veterinary medical attention. Arizona is not atypical; to date no state legislature has enacted language that clearly defines the public policies in support of the obligation of owners to provide veterinary care to their pets. That language might go a long way in helping judges and juries to interpret the terms the legislature has chosen to use in creating duties of care that include veterinary medical care. In the next section, I will consider various aspects of the public policy debate about owners' obligations to provide veterinary medical care in order to propose language by which a legislature could participate explicitly in necessary debate and also thereby provide guidance in the interpretation of such statutes.

The Public Policy Debate

Within the United States today most members of the general public hold the view that humans owe a duty of care to the animals they hold in their possession. This has been the view at least since the anticruelty law was enacted in New York in 1867. At that point the view that there are limits to what a person can do to animals without being guilty of the crime of cruelty was codified. Over time there have gradual changes in what constitutes "cruelty," but the specific duty to provide veterinary care is so recent a concept that it has been explicitly codified in relatively few places. Following a discussion of issues that arise when legislatures contemplate this specific duty, I will propose an approach that seeks to accommodate various complexities of enacting a requirement that pet owners provide veterinary care.

As we have seen, it is virtually impossible to draft statutory language that clearly and fairly delineates a duty to provide veterinary care. The source of some of the statutory language difficulty is the benevolent intentions of the drafters, who are often animal welfare organizations and humane societies. These organizations are seeking to accomplish positive changes for animals by imposing standards of ideal conduct by codifying the "best practice" of providing veterinary medical care to animals. However, the criminal law is best understood as setting out standards of minimally acceptable conduct which, if violated, will subject an individual to severe consequences. We should remember that violations of the criminal law create lifetime criminal records and the possibility of incarceration. These consequences are inappropriately harsh penalties to suffer for having failed to live up to ideal "best practices" standards.

An example of what I mean by the "best practices" approach is represented by the statutory language found in a phrase of the Michigan law that requires owners to provide "veterinary medical attention" to their animals when the alternative language of "medical care" might have been used. The difference between the two could be significant. The statutory language of "veterinary medical attention" was most likely suggested by individuals who are thinking about the effect of that language on the owners of pets. In this society in which millions of people own millions of pets, the presumption when the word "animal" is used or the phrase "veterinary medical attention" is used is that sick or hurt pets would be transported to a veterinarian. However, if such a law also applies to domestic animals generally, then the law will affect many more commercially owned animals than animals owned as pets.

In fact, in the United States most animals are owned by agricultural concerns. Except under very unusual circumstances, horses, lamas, sheep, cows, goats and poultry are never taken to a veterinarian when medical problems arise. When these animals receive veterinary care, it is usually provided either by the owner or by some non-veterinarian on the premises. Indeed, some states recognize this by exempting owners from veterinary licensing requirements[42] or from requirements that only veterinarians perform certain procedures;[43] owners are allowed to perform veterinary procedures on their own animals even if they are not allowed to perform such procedures on others' animals. Of course, sometimes owners of commercial animals do use the services of veterinarians who make farm calls, but there are not a lot of such veterinarians and the cost for their services can be high.

The problems of transporting large animals to veterinary facilities and the cost of on-site veterinary services combine to create a pattern whereby many commercial animal owners work with veterinarians but most often provide substantial care, including the giving of shots and drugs, by themselves. To the extent that the law requires "medical care," such owners have met the standard. To the extent that the law requires "veterinary medical attention," such owners may not have met the standard unless "veterinary medical attention" is construed to include owners' provision of veterinary medical care. Unless there is such an interpretation, it would appear that the Michigan law and other similarly worded laws do not allow for owners to provide treatment for their own animals. This simply does not comport with the realities of agricultural practices.

It is hard to believe that a legislature would really intend to put commercial animal owners at risk of criminal sanctions every time an animal is not taken to a veterinarian for treatment or care. The failure to articulate the scope of a criminal law that requires "veterinary medical attention" can cause predictable downstream difficulties when judges and juries seek to apply the law in the context of commercial animals. It is one thing to require that animals receive medical care; it is another thing altogether to codify who is to provide that care.

Even if the law were limited to pet animals, there are four kinds of issues that should be considered before criminal laws requiring veterinary care of companion animals are chiseled in legislative stone. These include the following:

- An owner's ignorance of an animal's having a health problem or of how to handle that problem;
- An owner's lack of resources for handling the problem;
- The lack of available treatment options or veterinarians;
- Judgments about the preference of life with pain versus death.

Experienced individuals know how to read the actions or inactions of individual animals and can thereby detect changes from normal patterns of behavior. Those changes can, but need not, signal that there is a health problem. Even if an experienced person could always make accurate determinations, how many pet owners really know how to judge the health of animals in their possession? How many individuals can distinguish between muscle sprains and a broken bone? Would both require veterinary medical attention? When does a skin condition require treatment? What about gradual deterioration in hearing or sight; at what point would failure to provide veterinary medical care result in criminal liability? Sometimes malignant tumors grow to a considerable size before an owner is aware of it, and, by then, it may well be too late to stop the cancer from further development. Moreover, there are species differences that make some determinations particularly difficult. Reptiles and birds are not as well understood as mammals and, as a result, very little veterinary care may be provided for these types of pets. Do we as a society want to bring criminal charges against those who lack the ability to read an animal and to know when veterinary care is "required"?

Under some existing statutory language, ignorance would not be an exception to the requirement. There may be room for interpretation, which could exclude situations the judge or jury finds problematic for conviction. For instance, the Texas statute that requires owners to provide "care" provides that only "unreasonable" failures to provide care would result in a finding of animal cruelty. Use of the word "unreasonable" may be an attempt to provide more flexibility and protection from unintended consequences because the legislature is empowering the judge or jury to determine whether the failure to provide care was reasonable. But that single word "unreasonable" cannot bear the full weight of managing all the issues that must be considered before imposition of criminal liability for failure to provide veterinary medical care.

What about owners who are in denial about the health condition of loved animals? They may see the lump, the visible manifestation of the tumor, but they may not believe that it is so significant as to warrant treatment. After all, if it turns out to be cancer, that could mean the end of the animal's life is uncomfortably close at hand. Or, what about the many owners who over-feed their animals and end up with obese animals whose health is severely compromised. Do those owners fully understand the risks to their animals of over-feeding? Is there some upper weight limit that would or should trigger prosecution for cruelty? Regardless of what a legislature had in mind, the legislature should anticipate that these kinds of questions will emerge. Is it sufficient to charge the finder of facts with filling in the substantive meaning of phrases such as "unreasonably fails to provide veterinary medical care"?

Second, assume that an owner does recognize that a health problem exists and takes the animal to a veterinarian. Perhaps the veterinarian will say that the animal has a condition which will produce increasing discomfort and death within two years. The treatment for the condition will cost $3,000 and could prolong the animal's life by as much as an additional year. Assume further that the cost of the treatment is not affordable for the owner. Under the present statutory approach the options of the owner are (a) treat the animal and go (further) into debt, (b) not treat the animal and be subjected to criminal charges or, (c) have the animal killed. Under this fact pattern, if the statutory obligation to provide medical care was violated, at what point was it violated? Is it violated because an owner cannot or will not provide the money to pay for the care?

That there is apparently no ceiling on the cost of care is, again, illustrative of the attitude of well-intentioned groups that are seeking to create an ideal world for animals by way of criminal law and its sanctions. Perhaps those organizations and their members would go into debt for the welfare of their animals, but is it fair to expect this of all pet owners on pain of criminal liability? I contend that there is no social consensus regarding the justice of imposing such a burden on pet owners in the first place and that the criminal law is not the appropriate realm for imposing such a burden, even if consensus existed.

The harsh effects of a criminal law that would penalize pet owners for failing to provide care even if they could not afford to provide such care could be mitigated by legislative provision of funding for veterinary care in such circumstances. If an animal's good health is so worthy a social goal, shouldn't society pay for an animal's care and treatment if it is not affordable for individual owners? Yet, if we compare this situation to the analogous situation confronting humans who cannot afford to pay for their own or their families' health care, we see a similar pattern of social failure to provide a safety net. It is not surprising, therefore, that the matter of paying for animal health care does not seem to have been part of the debate when criminal law duties to require veterinary care were imposed.

Finally, society has not yet had an adequate discussion about how to balance the value to an animal of living with pain versus dying. Does the imposition of the requirement of veterinary medical care suggest that owners should do something, even if it is to kill the animal, rather than do nothing and allow the animal to live in pain? That is a judgment embedded in these anticruelty statutes, and it is a judgment we need to excavate and fully consider. Who should make this decision about the life or death of an animal? By requiring the involvement of veterinarians, isn't the law privileging their judgments over those of owners? It seems that criminal requirements of veterinary care would push owners into veterinary offices, but it is the owner of the animal and not the veterinarian who must ultimately judge what quality of life an animal will face. Veterinarians do not generally have any better ethical basis for making that decision than do owners, even if they do possess superior technical knowledge.

On the other hand, many animal owners seem incapable of making ethical decisions about their own conduct, let alone making life and death decisions for animals they own. Perhaps there should be "substituted" judgments by veterinarians in some situations, but what would those situations be? What seems to be missing in the equation is the requirement of consideration of what is in the best interests of an animal whose health is compromised to some extent. While most humans might choose to continue life despite considerable pain and discomfort, is it reasonable or proper to assume that their pets would make the same decisions for themselves? Surely one aspect of considering an animal's best interests would be to consider carefully the amount of pain an animal is experiencing and the degree to which that pain is interfering with an animal's normal activities. A judgment about the animal's best interests might also depend on how temporary the pain appears to be or expectations of future reduction in the pain.

The point here is not to suggest here that a particular calculus should be applied when determining the interests of animals versus their owners; the point is that discussion about how to consider the animal as a patient with interests independent of his or her owner should take place before legislatures enact criminal laws that expose pet owners to risk of conviction for animal cruelty for failure to provide veterinary care. That discussion should be tempered with two realizations. First, regardless of one's philosophy about the status of animals and their best interests, it is not appropriate to have a legal system that requires a human to provide an animal with more medical care than that human can provide for him or herself. Second, pernicious effects result from the fact that we do not have sufficient judicial or prosecutorial resources to enforce laws that require pet owners to provide veterinary care to their pets. The net effect of such legal provisions in a world of limited resources is that nothing will get done to help any of the animals who need help because our resources will be expended prosecuting only the most egregious cases. Meanwhile, there is the illusion that most animals are getting veterinary medical care simply because the criminal law requires it. Our resources should not be expended only on such egregious cases, but that is all that can be done in a world of limited law enforcement resources. The better social policy would be to expend resources on preventing harms to animals rather than investing such effort and resources into punishing owners who fail to provide veterinary care.

PROPOSED LEGISLATIVE INTENT LANGUAGE

Although a certain amount of debate occurs before any law is enacted, when legislatures are dealing with the details of specific language they may not pay adequate attention to the larger issues in which those details are embedded. In order to generate debate about those larger issues, I propose some generalized "legislative intent" language that would preface the enactment of specific requirements that owners provide veterinary care to their pets. It is too early in the social debate about this matter to propose specific language, but perhaps the following could be considered a starting point:

> It is the policy of this state that owners and keepers of animals have an obligation to keep animals in a healthy state and to provide a quality of life for the animals in their care to the extent that is possible. Acknowledging that all owners or keepers are not equally situated in terms of knowledge or resources, the state shall endeavor to provide support for owners and keepers of animals to obtain appropriate information and skill to support the well-being of the animals in their care. Additionally, to the extent financially feasible, the state shall provide support services to those of limited resources. While the state will prefer to intervene before criminal acts or omissions have occurred, failure to provide the expected level of care for an animal will ultimately result in criminal charges being filed against the responsible parties.

A key aspect of this proposed language is its emphasis on intervention before an animal's health has deteriorated to the point that there is an egregious case in the courtroom. Perhaps the area of enforcement of child care obligations can be considered as analogous. While there are criminal laws that prohibit the abuse of children and assume a duty to provide medical care, existing laws also have a number of levels of intervention, which can be triggered to deal with such issues before the line of criminal culpability has been crossed. Public policy seeks to support the parent-child relationship, and, if a parent is not doing all that might be required, the first level of intervention should be to educate the parent. This allows the parent to change his or her attitude and to improve before the matter of jail time is even on the horizon. This may well be a civil law intervention that is undertaken by a government agency other than the prosecutor's office.

Analogously, the goal of improving the access of animals to veterinary care would be most productively pursued by helping owners receive the information and resources they need to provide adequate health care to their animals. If individuals do not understand the needs of their animals, they cannot begin to address those needs. Such individuals should be assisted in acquiring necessary information about their animals' needs as well as where healthcare services may be available for their animals.

Civil procedures to assist owners should be flexible enough to allow different points of entry. Intervention should also involve different levels before criminal processes are invoked. Consider the following plan for increasing intervention:

1. A person knows they are lacking in knowledge or resources and actively seeks assistance.

2. Someone else observes that an animal owner is lacking in knowledge or resources and asks for intervention on behalf of the animal. The owner may voluntarily allow access to the animal and cooperate with the intervening agency. No court action is required, no search warrants are sought.

3. If the number of animals and or conditions of the animals suggests a violation of duty of care standards and the owner is not cooperative, then a search warrant may be obtained to determine the condition of the animals. The options of a visiting agent would include one or more of the following: (a) on-site education with follow up materials or voluntary re-inspections (b) filing of civil charges for violation of care standards or, (c) criminal charges may be filed.

4. In a civil action against the owner a court may be empowered to consider the following alternatives after appropriate hearings: mandated conditions for the care of the animal, payment of civil fines, requiring the owner to obtain education, prohibitions on possession of animals in the future and the ultimate civil sanction, forfeiture of ownership or possession of animals. The remedies available to the court for criminal violations also need to be diverse and robust to deal with the wide variety of fact patterns that might arise.

If this new animal support system can be put in place, early intervention could result in better lives for animals and their human caregivers. While it is possible that a government agency, with some parallel to child support services, could be created to carry out these tasks, financial limitations may make this difficult. A more likely path will be to allow local government to appoint a humane society to carry out the investigative and educational function of the interventions suggested above. Many humane societies presently have trained investigators on staff. The passage of a new law would provide them with a much more useful array of tools which can be used to help animals and their owners. It is more productive to utilize their skills to prevent harm than to use those skills to deal only with egregious cases of owner neglect or mistreatment when it is too late to improve the animal's quality of life.

CONCLUSION

Statutory requirements that owners provide veterinary care reflect the fact that social concern for the health and well-being of animals is increasing. Increasing expectations of owners to provide care is appropriate but should not necessarily be imposed by operation of the criminal justice system. There is a place for criminal sanctions for some kinds of owner conduct, but there is also a legitimate and useful place for civil law to intervene to provide educational and financial resources for owners to better care for their animals.

When the question of allocating governmental resources to assist animals and their owners arises, many difficult questions will emerge. Perhaps the most difficult ethical issue to be addressed is how to decide what level of pain and suffering an animal may endure as a consequence of the fact that his or her owner cannot afford treatment. Another difficult issue is how to deal with commercial animals where current investment in medical care is often limited to the commercial value of the animal and thus seldom is seen to justify the costs of veterinary care. One thing is certain: mere delegation by legislatures to judges and juries to consider these factors in the context of criminal prosecutions of individual owners is insufficient. It is important to attend to these matters with non-criminal procedures and to infuse the establishment of those procedures with serious debate about the circumstances under which owners owe their animals the duty of veterinary medical care.

* David Favre is a Professor of Law at Michigan State University, and creator of the Michigan State University College of Law: Animal Legal & Historical Web Center, *at* http://www.animalaw.info. The author would like to thank Taimie Bryant for taking on this project and her assistance with this chapter.

1. 1867 N.Y. REV. STAT. ch. 375, §§ 2–9. *See generally* David Favre & Vivien Tsang, *The Development of Anti–Cruelty Laws During the 1900's*, 1993 DETROIT C. L. REV. 1.

2. "Fly-strike" is a painful condition caused by infestation with fly maggots. *See* MERRIAM-WEBSTER ONLINE DICTIONARY, http://www.merriam-webster.com/dictionary/fly%strike (last visited Nov. 6, 2007).

3. N.Y. REV. STAT. tit. 6, § 375.10 (1867).

4. *See, e.g.,* CAL. PENAL CODE § 599c (West 1999); GA. CODE ANN. § 16–12–4(e) (2007); MICH. COMP. LAWS ANN. § 750.50(h) (West 2004); N.J. STAT. ANN. § 4:22–16(a) (West 1998).

5. *See, e.g.,* CAL. PENAL CODE § 599c (West 1999); GA. CODE ANN. § 16–12–4(e) (2007); MICH. COMP. LAWS ANN. § 750.50(a), (b) (West 2004); N.J. STAT. ANN. § 4:22–16(c) (West 1998).

6. Mariann Sullivan & David J. Wolfson, *If It Looks Like a Duck . . . New Jersey, The Regulation of Farming Practices, and the Meaning of 'Humane'*, in ANIMAL LAW AND THE COURTS 94 (Taimie L. Bryant, Rebecca J. Huss & David N. Cassuto, eds., 2008).

7. N.Y. AGRIC. & MKTS. LAW § 353 (McKinney 2004 & Supp. 2007).

8. *Id.* § 350.

9. 10 Abb. Pr. (n.s.) 374 (N.Y. 1868).

10. *See* 1867 N.Y. REV. STAT. ch. 375, §§ 2–9.

11. *See supra* note 7.

12. Mich. Comp. Laws Ann. § 750.50(2)(a) (West 2004).

13. 777 N.Y.S.2d 836, 840 (2004).

14. *Id.* at 842.

15. *See supra* note 7.

16. *Id.*

17. *Arroyo*, 777 N.Y.S.2d at 842–43.

18. Grise v. State, 37 Ark. 456 (1881).

19. *Id.*

20. 777 N.Y.S.2d at 844.

21. *Id.*

22. Tex. Penal Code Ann. §§ 42.092(b)(1), (3) (Vernon 2007).

23. *Id.* §§ 42.092(a)(7) (Vernon 2007).

24. *See supra* note 11.

25. Mich. Comp. Laws Ann. § 750.50(1)(a) (West 2004).

26. *Id.* § 750.50(1)(k) (West 2004).

27. *Arroyo*, 777 N.Y.S.2d at 845.

28. 48 S.W.3d 273, 274 (Tex. Ct. App. 2001).

29. *Id.* at 276–77.

30. *Id.* at 277.

31. 18 Pa. Cons. Stat. Ann. § 5511(c)(1) (West 2004).

32. Va. Code Ann. § 3.1–796.122 (1994 & Supp. 2007).

33. Colo. Rev. Stat. Ann. § 18–9–202 (2006).

34. *Id.* § 18–9–201(4).

35. Or. Rev. Stat. Ann. § 167.325 (2005).

36. *Id.* § 167.310(6) (2005).

37. *Id.*

38. Wash. Rev. Code Ann. § 16.52.207(2)(a) (West 2006).

39. *Id.*

40. *Id.*

41. Ariz. Rev. Stat. Ann. § 13–2910.A.2 (2001 & Supp. 2007).

42. *See, e.g.*, Ariz. Rev. Stat. Ann. § 32–2211 (2002); Ind. Code Ann. § 15–5–1.19 (LexisNexis 1998); Vt. Stat. Ann. tit. 26, § 2403 (2006).

43. *See, e.g.*, Cal. Bus. & Prof. Code § 4827 (West 2003); Ky. Rev. Stat. Ann. § 321.200 (West 2001); Minn. Stat. Ann. § 156.12 (West 2005).

Chapter 5

COMPANION ANIMALS
AND HOUSING

NAHRSTEDT v. LAKESIDE VILLAGE
CONDOMINIUM ASSOCIATION, INC.
8 Cal.4th 361, 33 Cal.Rptr.2d 63, 878 P.2d 1275 (Cal. 1994).

KENNARD, J.

A homeowner in a 530–unit condominium complex sued to prevent the homeowners association from enforcing a restriction against keeping cats, dogs, and other animals in the condominium development. The owner asserted that the restriction, which was contained in the project's declaration recorded by the condominium project's developer, was "unreasonable" as applied to her because she kept her three cats indoors and because her cats were "noiseless" and "created no nuisance." Agreeing with the premise underlying the owner's complaint, the Court of Appeal concluded that the homeowners association could enforce the restriction only upon proof that plaintiff's cats would be likely to interfere with the right of other homeowners "to the peaceful and quiet enjoyment of their property."

Those of us who have cats or dogs can attest to their wonderful companionship and affection. Not surprisingly, studies have confirmed this effect. But the issue before us is not whether in the abstract pets can have a beneficial effect on humans. Rather, the narrow issue here is whether a pet restriction that is contained in the recorded declaration of a condominium complex is enforceable against the challenge of a homeowner. As we shall explain, the Legislature, in Civil Code section 1354, has required that courts enforce the covenants, conditions and restrictions contained in the recorded declaration of a common interest development "unless unreasonable."

Because a stable and predictable living environment is crucial to the success of condominiums and other common interest residential developments, and because recorded use restrictions are a primary means of ensuring this stability and predictability, the Legislature in section 1354 has afforded such restrictions a presumption of validity and has required of challengers that they demonstrate the restriction's "unreasonableness" by the deferential standard applicable to equitable servitudes. Under this standard established by the Legislature, enforcement of a restriction does not depend upon the conduct of a particular condominium owner. Rather, the restriction must be uniformly enforced in the condominium development to which it was intended to apply unless the plaintiff owner can show that the burdens it imposes on affected properties so substantially outweigh the benefits of the restriction that it should not be enforced against any owner. Here, the Court of Appeal did not apply this standard in deciding that plaintiff had stated a claim for declaratory relief. Accordingly, we reverse the judgment of the Court of Appeal and remand for further proceedings consistent with the views expressed in this opinion.

I.

Lakeside Village is a large condominium development in Culver City, Los Angeles County. It consists of 530 units spread throughout 12 separate 3–story buildings. The residents share common lobbies and hallways, in addition to laundry and trash facilities.

The Lakeside Village project is subject to certain covenants, conditions and restrictions (hereafter CC & R's) that were included in the developer's declaration recorded with the Los Angeles County Recorder on April 17, 1978, at the inception of the development project. Ownership of a unit includes membership in the project's homeowners association, the Lakeside Village Condominium Association (hereafter Association), the body that enforces the project's CC & R's, including the pet restriction, which provides in relevant part: "No animals (which shall mean dogs and cats), livestock, reptiles or poultry shall be kept in any unit."[3]

In January 1988, plaintiff Natore Nahrstedt purchased a Lakeside Village condominium and moved in with her three cats. When the Association learned of the cats' presence, it demanded their removal and assessed fines against Nahrstedt for each successive month that she remained in violation of the condominium project's pet restriction.

Nahrstedt then brought this lawsuit against the Association, its officers, and two of its employees, asking the trial court to invalidate the assessments, to enjoin future assessments, to award damages for violation of her privacy when the Association "peered" into her condominium unit, to award damages for infliction of emotional distress, and to declare the pet restriction "unreasonable" as applied to indoor cats (such as hers) that are not allowed free run of the project's common areas. Nahrstedt also alleged she did not know of the pet restriction when she bought her condominium. The complaint incorporated by reference the grant deed, the declaration of CC & R's, and the condominium plan for the Lakeside Village condominium project.

---

3. The CC & R's permit residents to keep "domestic fish and birds."

The Association demurred to the complaint. In its supporting points and authorities, the Association argued that the pet restriction furthers the collective "health, happiness and peace of mind" of persons living in close proximity within the Lakeside Village condominium development, and therefore is reasonable as a matter of law.

* * *

[*The Court reviewed the history of the case and provided a broad overview of the general principles governing common interest forms of real property ownership.*]

II.

* * *

Use restrictions are an inherent part of any common interest development and are crucial to the stable, planned environment of any shared ownership arrangement. The viability of shared ownership of improved real property rests on the existence of extensive reciprocal servitudes, together with the ability of each co-owner to prevent the property's partition.

The restrictions on the use of property in any common interest development may limit activities conducted in the common areas as well as in the confines of the home itself. Commonly, use restrictions preclude alteration of building exteriors, limit the number of persons that can occupy each unit, and place limitations on—or prohibit altogether—the keeping of pets.

Restrictions on property use are not the only characteristic of common interest ownership. Ordinarily, such ownership also entails mandatory membership in an owners association, which, through an elected board of directors, is empowered to enforce any use restrictions contained in the project's declaration or master deed and to enact new rules governing the use and occupancy of property within the project. Because of its considerable power in managing and regulating a common interest development, the governing board of an owners association must guard against the potential for the abuse of that power.[6] As Professor Natelson observes, owners associations "can be a powerful force for good or for ill" in their members' lives. Therefore, anyone who buys a unit in a common interest development with knowledge of its owners association's discretionary power accepts "the risk that the power may be used in a way that benefits the commonality but harms the individual." Generally, courts will uphold decisions made by the governing board of an owners association so long as they represent good faith efforts to further the purposes of the common interest development, are consistent with the development's governing documents, and comply with public policy.

---

6. The power to regulate pertains to a "wide spectrum of activities," such as the volume of playing music, hours of social gatherings, use of patio furniture and barbecues, and rental of units.

Thus, subordination of individual property rights to the collective judgment of the owners association together with restrictions on the use of real property comprise the chief attributes of owning property in a common interest development. * * *

* * *

[*The Court then distinguished between restrictive covenants and equitable servitudes.*]

* * *

When restrictions limiting the use of property within a common interest development satisfy the requirements of covenants running with the land or of equitable servitudes, what standard or test governs their enforceability? In California, as we explained at the outset, our Legislature has made common interest development use restrictions contained in a project's recorded declaration "enforceable ... *unless unreasonable.*" (§ 1354, subd. (a), italics added.)

In states lacking such legislative guidance, some courts have adopted a standard under which a common interest development's recorded use restrictions will be enforced so long as they are "reasonable." Although no one definition of the term "reasonable" has gained universal acceptance, most courts have applied what one commentator calls "equitable reasonableness," upholding only those restrictions that provide a reasonable means to further the collective "health, happiness and enjoyment of life" of owners of a common interest development. Others would limit the "reasonableness" standard only to those restrictions adopted by majority vote of the homeowners or enacted under the rulemaking power of an association's governing board, and would not apply this test to restrictions included in a planned development project's recorded declaration or master deed. Because such restrictions are presumptively valid, these authorities would enforce them regardless of reasonableness. * * *

* * *

Indeed, giving deference to use restrictions contained in a condominium project's originating documents protects the general expectations of condominium owners "that restrictions in place at the time they purchase their units will be enforceable." This in turn encourages the development of shared ownership housing—generally a less costly alternative to single-dwelling ownership—by attracting buyers who prefer a stable, planned environment. It also protects buyers who have paid a premium for condominium units in reliance on a particular restrictive scheme.

* * *

III.

[*The Court then analyzed California's statutory scheme governing condominiums and other common interest developments—the Davis-*

Stirling Common Interest Development Act (§ 1350 et seq.) hereinafter referred to as the Act.]

* * *

Pertinent here is the Act's provision for the enforcement of use restrictions contained in the project's recorded declaration. That provision, subdivision (a) of section 1354, states in relevant part: "The covenants and restrictions in the declaration shall be enforceable equitable servitudes, *unless unreasonable,* and shall inure to the benefit of and bind all owners of separate interests in the development." (Italics added.) * * *

* * * The provision's express reference to "equitable servitudes" evidences the Legislature's intent that recorded use restrictions falling within section 1354 are to be treated as equitable servitudes. Thus, although under general rules governing equitable servitudes a subsequent purchaser of land subject to restrictions must have actual notice of the restrictions, actual notice is not required to enforce recorded use restrictions covered by section 1354 against a subsequent purchaser. Rather, the inclusion of covenants and restrictions in the declaration recorded with the county recorder provides sufficient notice to permit the enforcement of such recorded covenants and restrictions as equitable servitudes.

* * *

In choosing equitable servitude law as the standard for enforcing CC & R's in common interest developments, the Legislature has manifested a preference in favor of their enforcement. This preference is underscored by the use of the word "shall" in the first phrase of section 1354: "The covenants and restrictions shall be enforceable equitable servitudes. . . ."

The Legislature did, however, set a condition for the mandatory enforcement of a declaration's CC & R's: a covenant, condition or restriction is "enforceable . . . *unless unreasonable.*" (§ 1354, subd. (a), italics added.) The Legislature's use of the phrase "unless unreasonable" in section 1354 was a marked change from the prior version of that statutory provision, which stated that "restrictions shall be enforceable equitable servitudes *where reasonable.*" Under settled principles of statutory construction, such a material alteration of a statute's phrasing signals the Legislature's intent to give an enactment a new meaning. Here, the change in statutory language, from "where reasonable" to "unless unreasonable," cloaked use restrictions contained in a condominium development's recorded declaration with a presumption of reasonableness by shifting the burden of proving otherwise to the party challenging the use restriction.

* * *

[To determine how the burden is satisfied the Court examined the principles governing the enforcement of equitable servitudes.]

Thus, when enforcing equitable servitudes, courts are generally disinclined to question the wisdom of agreed-to restrictions. This rule does not apply, however, when the restriction does not comport with public policy. Equity will not enforce any restrictive covenant that violates public policy. Nor will courts enforce as equitable servitudes those restrictions that are arbitrary, that is, bearing no rational relationship to the protection, preservation, operation or purpose of the affected land.

These limitations on the equitable enforcement of restrictive servitudes that are either arbitrary or violate fundamental public policy are specific applications of the general rule that courts will not enforce a restrictive covenant when "the harm caused by the restriction is so disproportionate to the benefit produced" by its enforcement that the restriction "ought not to be enforced." When a use restriction bears no relationship to the land it burdens, or violates a fundamental policy inuring to the public at large, the resulting harm will always be disproportionate to any benefit.

* * *

As the first Restatement of Property points out, the test for determining when the harmful effects of a land-use restriction are so disproportionate to its benefit "is necessarily vague." Application of the test requires the accommodation of two policies that sometimes conflict: "One of these is that [persons] should be required to live up to their promises; the other that land should be developed to its normal capacity." Reconciliation of these policies in determining whether the burdens of a recorded use restriction are so disproportionate to its benefits depends on the effect of the challenged restriction on "promoting or limiting the use of land in the locality...."

From the authorities discussed above, we distill these principles: An equitable servitude will be enforced unless it violates public policy; it bears no rational relationship to the protection, preservation, operation or purpose of the affected land; or it otherwise imposes burdens on the affected land that are so disproportionate to the restriction's beneficial effects that the restriction should not be enforced.

With these principles of equitable servitude law to guide us, we now turn to section 1354. As mentioned earlier, under subdivision (a) of section 1354 the use restrictions for a common interest development that are set forth in the recorded declaration are "enforceable equitable servitudes, unless unreasonable." In other words, such restrictions should be enforced unless they are wholly arbitrary, violate a fundamental public policy, or impose a burden on the use of affected land that far outweighs any benefit.

This interpretation of section 1354 is consistent with the views of legal commentators as well as judicial decisions in other jurisdictions that have applied a presumption of validity to the recorded land use restrictions of a common interest development. As these authorities point out, and as we discussed previously, recorded CC & R's are the primary means of achieving the stability and predictability so essential to the success of a shared ownership housing development. In general, then, enforcement of a common interest development's recorded CC & R's will both encourage the development of land and ensure that promises are kept, thereby fulfilling both of the policies identified by the Restatement.

When courts accord a presumption of validity to all such recorded use restrictions and measure them against deferential standards of equitable servitude law, it discourages lawsuits by owners of individual units seeking personal exemptions from the restrictions. This also promotes stability and predictability in two ways. It provides substantial assurance to prospective condominium purchasers that they may rely with confidence on the promises embodied in the project's recorded CC & R's. And it protects all owners in the planned development from unanticipated increases in association fees to fund the defense of legal challenges to recorded restrictions.

* * *

IV.

Here, the Court of Appeal failed to consider the rules governing equitable servitudes in holding that Nahrstedt's complaint challenging the Lakeside Village restriction against the keeping of cats in condominium units stated a cause of action for declaratory relief. Instead, the court concluded that factual allegations by Nahrstedt that her cats are kept inside her condominium unit and do not bother her neighbors were sufficient to have the trial court decide whether enforcement of the restriction against Nahrstedt would be reasonable. For this conclusion, the court relied on two Court of Appeal decisions, both of which had invalidated recorded restrictions covered by section 1354.

* * *

[*The Court distinguished the two cases relied upon by the appellate court and found that the cases failed to apply the deferential standards of equitable servitude law that they analyzed earlier in the case.*]

V.

Under the holding we adopt today, the reasonableness or unreasonableness of a condominium use restriction that the Legislature has made subject to section 1354 is to be determined *not* by reference to facts that are specific to the objecting homeowner, but by reference to the common interest development as a whole. As we have explained, when, as here, a restriction is contained in the declaration of the common interest development and is recorded with the county recorder, the restriction is presumed to be reasonable and will be enforced uniformly against all residents of the common interest development *unless* the restriction is arbitrary, imposes burdens on the use of lands it affects that substantially outweigh the restriction's benefits to the development's residents, or violates a fundamental public policy.

Accordingly, here Nahrstedt could prevent enforcement of the Lakeside Village pet restriction by proving that the restriction is arbitrary, that it is substantially more burdensome than beneficial to the affected properties, or that it violates a fundamental public policy. For the reasons set forth below, Nahrstedt's complaint fails to adequately allege any of these three grounds of unreasonableness.

We conclude, as a matter of law, that the recorded pet restriction of the Lakeside Village condominium development prohibiting cats or dogs but allowing some other pets is not arbitrary, but is rationally related to health, sanitation and noise concerns legitimately held by residents of a high-density condominium project such as Lakeside Village, which includes 530 units in 12 separate 3–story buildings.

Nahrstedt's complaint alleges no facts that could possibly support a finding that the burden of the restriction on the affected property is so disproportionate to its benefit that the restriction is unreasonable and should not be enforced. Also, the complaint's allegations center on Nahrstedt and her cats (that she keeps them inside her condominium unit and that they do not bother her neighbors), without any reference to the effect on the condominium development as a whole, thus rendering the allegations legally insufficient to overcome section 1354's presumption of the restriction's validity.

* * *

[*The Court then discussed Nahrstedt's allegation that the restriction violated her right to privacy under the California Constitution. The Court found that the California Constitution did not confer a right that guarantees condominium owners or residents the right to keep cats or dogs as household pets.*]

* * *

[*The Court remanded the case to the Court of Appeals to reconsider whether Nahrstedt's complaint is sufficient to state the other causes of action claimed invasion of privacy, invalidation of assessments, injunctive relief and damages for emotional distress.*]

CONCLUSION

In section 1354, the Legislature has specifically addressed the subject of the enforcement of use restrictions that, like the one in this case prohibiting the keeping of certain animals, are recorded in the declaration of a condominium or other common interest development. The Legislature has mandated judicial enforcement of those restrictions unless they are shown to be unreasonable when applied to the development as a whole.

Section 1354 requires courts determining the validity of a condominium use restriction in a recorded declaration to apply the deferential standards of equitable servitude law. These standards grant courts no unbridled license to question the wisdom of the restriction. Rather, courts must enforce the restriction unless the challenger can show that the restriction is unreasonable because it is arbitrary, violates a fundamental public policy, or imposes burdens on the use of the affected property that substantially outweigh the restriction's benefits.

By providing condominium homeowners with substantial assurance that their development's recorded use restrictions can be enforced, section 1354 promotes the stability and predictability so essential to the success of any common interest development. Persons who purchase homes in such a development typically submit to a variety of restrictions on the use of their property. In exchange, they obtain the security of knowing that all other homeowners in the development will be required to abide by those same restrictions. Section 1354 also protects the general expectations of condominium homeowners that they not be burdened with the litigation expense in defending case-by-case legal challenges to presumptively valid recorded use restrictions.

In this case, the pet restriction was contained in the project's declaration or governing document, which was recorded with the county recorder before any of the 530 units was sold. For many owners, the pet restriction may have been an important inducement to purchase into the development. Because the homeowners collectively have the power to repeal the pet restriction, its continued existence reflects their desire to retain it.

Plaintiff's allegations, even if true, are insufficient to show that the pet restriction's harmful effects substantially outweigh its benefits to the condominium development as a whole, that it bears no rational relationship to the purpose or function of the development, or that it violates public policy. We reverse the judgment of the Court of Appeal, and remand for further proceedings consistent with the views expressed in this opinion.

CHIEF JUSTICE LUCAS, and JUSTICES MOSK, BAXTER, GEORGE and WERDEGAR, concurred.

ARABIAN, J., dissenting.

"There are two means of refuge from the misery of life: music and cats."—Albert Schweitzer.

I respectfully dissent. While technical merit may commend the majority's analysis, its application to the facts presented reflects a narrow, indeed chary, view of the law that eschews the human spirit in favor of arbitrary efficiency. In my view, the resolution of this case well illustrates the conventional wisdom, and fundamental truth, of the Spanish proverb, "It is better to be a mouse in a cat's mouth than a man in a lawyer's hands."

As explained below, I find the provision known as the "pet restriction" contained in the covenants, conditions, and restrictions (CC & R's) governing the Lakeside Village project patently arbitrary and unreasonable within the meaning of Civil Code section 1354. Beyond dispute, human beings have long enjoyed an abiding and cherished association with their household animals. Given the substantial benefits derived from pet ownership, the undue burden on the use of property imposed on condominium owners who can maintain pets within the confines of their units without creating a nuisance or disturbing the quiet enjoyment of others substantially outweighs whatever meager utility the restriction may serve in the abstract. It certainly does not promote "health, happiness [or] peace of mind" commensurate with its tariff on the quality of life for those who value the companionship of animals. Worse, it contributes to the fraying of our social fabric.[3]

* * *

1. *The Pleadings*

The majority acknowledge that under their interpretation of Civil Code section 1354 "the test for determining when the harmful effects of a land-use restriction are disproportionate to benefit 'is necessarily vague.' [Citation.]" Nevertheless, in their view the foregoing allegations are deficient because they do not specifically state facts to "support a finding that the burden on the affected property is so disproportionate to its benefit that the restriction is unreasonable and should not be enforced." They also fail to make "any reference to the effect on the condominium development as a whole...." This narrow assessment of plaintiff's complaint does not comport with the rule of liberal construction that should prevail on demurrer. When considered less grudgingly, the pleadings are sufficient to allege that the pet restriction is unreasonable as a matter of law.

Generically stated, plaintiff challenges this restriction to the extent it precludes not only her but anyone else living in Lakeside Village from enjoying the substantial pleasures of pet ownership while affording no discernible benefit to other unit owners if the animals are maintained without any detriment to the latter's quiet enjoyment of their own space and the common areas. In essence, she avers that when pets are kept out of sight, do not make noise, do not generate odors, and do not otherwise create a nuisance, reasonable expectations as to the quality of life within the condominium project are not impaired. At the same time, taking into consideration the well-established and long-standing historical and cultural relationship between human beings and their pets and the value they impart enforcement of the restriction significantly and unduly burdens the use of land for those deprived of their companionship. Considered from this perspective, plaintiff's complaint states a cause of action for declaratory relief.

3. The majority imply that if enough owners find the restrictions to oppressive, they can act collectively to alter or rescind it. However, realistically speaking, implementing this alternative would only serve to exacerbate the divisiveness rampant in our society and to which the majority decision itself contributes.

2. *The Burden*

Under the majority's construction of Civil Code section 1354, the pet restriction is unreasonable, and hence unenforceable, if the "burdens [imposed] on the affected land . . . are so disproportionate to the restriction's beneficial effects that the restriction should not be enforced." What, then, is the burden at issue here?

Both recorded and unrecorded history bear witness to the domestication of animals as household pets. Throughout the ages, dogs and cats have provided human beings with a variety of services in addition to their companionship—shepherding flocks, guarding life and property, hunting game, ridding the house and barn of vermin. Of course, the modern classic example is the assist dog, which facilitates a sense of independence and security for disabled persons by enabling them to navigate their environment, alerting them to important sounds, and bringing the world within their reach. Emotionally, they allow a connection full of sensation and delicacy of feeling.

Throughout the ages, art and literature, as well as mythology, depict humans in all walks of life and social strata with cats and dogs, illustrating their widespread acceptance in everyday life. Some religions have even incorporated them into their worship. Dogs and cats are also admired for the purity of their character traits. Closer to home, our own culture is populated with examples of the well-established place pets have found in our hearts and homes.[10]

In addition to these historical and cultural references, the value of pets in daily life is a matter of common knowledge and understanding as well as extensive documentation. People of all ages, but particularly the elderly and the young, enjoy their companionship. Those who suffer from serious disease or injury and are confined to their home or bed experience a therapeutic, even spiritual, benefit from their presence. Animals provide comfort at the death of a family member or dear friend, and for the lonely can offer a reason for living when life seems to have lost its meaning. In recognition of these benefits, both Congress and the state Legislature have expressly guaranteed that elderly and handicapped persons living in public-assistance housing cannot be deprived of their pets. (12 U.S.C. § 1701r–1; Health & Saf.Code, § 19901.) Not only have children and animals always been natural companions, children learn responsibility and discipline from pet ownership while developing an important sense of kindness and protection for animals. Single adults may find certain pets can afford a feeling of security. Families benefit from the experience of sharing that having a pet encourages. While pet ownership may not be a fundamental right as such, unquestionably it is an integral aspect of our daily existence, which cannot be lightly dismissed and should not suffer unwarranted intrusion into its circle of privacy.

---

10. The President and his family often set a national example in this regard. Chelsea Clinton's cat "Socks" is only the latest in a long line of White House pets, including Franklin Roosevelt's "Fala" and the Bushes' "Millie."

3. *The Benefit*

What is gained from an uncompromising prohibition against pets that are confined to an owner's unit and create no noise, odor, or nuisance?

To the extent such animals are not seen, heard, or smelled any more than if they were not kept in the first place, there is no corresponding or concomitant benefit. Pets that remain within the four corners of their owners' condominium space can have no deleterious or offensive effect on the project's common areas or any neighboring unit. Certainly, if other owners and residents are totally *unaware* of their presence, prohibiting pets does not in any respect foster the "health, happiness [or] peace of mind" of anyone except the homeowners association's board of directors, who are thereby able to promote a form of sophisticated bigotry. In light of the substantial and disproportionate burden imposed for those who must forego virtually any and all association with pets, this lack of benefit renders a categorical ban unreasonable under Civil Code section 1354.

The proffered justification is all the more spurious when measured against the terms of the pet restriction itself, which contains an exception for domestic fish and birds. A squawking bird can readily create the very kind of disturbance supposedly prevented by banning other types of pets. At the same time, many animals prohibited by the restriction, such as hamsters and the like, turtles, and small reptiles, make no sound whatsoever. Disposal of bird droppings in common trash areas poses as much of a health concern as cat litter or rabbit pellets, which likewise can be handled in a manner that avoids potential problems. Birds are also known to carry disease and provoke allergies. Neither is maintaining fish without possible risk of interfering with the quiet enjoyment of condominium neighbors. Aquarium water must be changed and disposed of in the common drainage system. Leakage from a fish tank could cause serious water damage to the owner's unit, those below, and common areas. Defendants and the majority purport such solicitude for the "health, sanitation and noise concerns" of other unit owners, but fail to explain how the possession of pets, such as plaintiff's cats, under the circumstances alleged in her complaint, jeopardizes that goal any more than the fish and birds expressly allowed by the pet restriction. This inconsistency underscores its unreasonableness and discriminatory impact.

4. *The Majority's Burden/Benefit Analysis*

From the statement of the facts through the conclusion, the majority's analysis gives scant acknowledgment to any of the foregoing considerations but simply takes refuge behind the "presumption of validity" now accorded *all* CC & R's irrespective of subject matter. They never objectively scrutinize defendants' blandishments of protecting "health and happiness" or realistically assess the substantial impact on affected unit owners and *their* use of *their* property. As this court has often recognized, "deference is not abdication." Regardless of how limited an inquiry is permitted under applicable law, it must nevertheless be made.

Here, such inquiry should start with an evaluation of the interest that will suffer upon enforcement of the pet restriction. In determining the "burden on the use of land," due recognition must be given to the fact that this particular "use" transcends the impersonal and mundane matters typically regulated by condominium CC & R's, such as whether someone can place a doormat in the hallway or hang a towel on the patio rail or have food in the pool area, and reaches the very quality of life of hundreds of owners and residents. Nonetheless, the majority accept uncritically the proffered justification of preserving "health and happiness" and essentially consider only one criterion to determine enforceability: was the restriction recorded in the original declaration? If so, it is "presumptively valid," unless in violation of public policy. Given the application of the law to the facts alleged and by an inversion of relative interests, it is difficult to hypothesize any CC & R's that would not pass muster. Such sanctity has not been afforded any writing save the commandments delivered to Moses on Mount Sinai, and they were set in stone, not upon worthless paper.

Moreover, unlike most conduct controlled by CC & R's, the activity at issue here is strictly confined to the owner's interior space; it does not in any manner invade other units or the common areas. Owning a home of one's own has always epitomized the American dream. More than simply embodying the notion of having "one's castle," it represents the sense of freedom and self-determination emblematic of our national character. Granted, those who live in multi-unit developments cannot exercise this freedom to the same extent possible on a large estate. But owning pets that do not disturb the quiet enjoyment of others does not reasonably come within this compromise. Nevertheless, with no demonstrated or discernible benefit, the majority arbitrarily sacrifice the dream to the tyranny of the "commonality."

5. *Conclusion*

Our true task in this turmoil is to strike a balance between the governing rights accorded a condominium association and the individual freedom of its members. To fulfill that function, a reviewing court must view with a skeptic's eye restrictions driven by fear, anxiety, or intolerance. In any community, we do not exist *in vacuo*. There are many annoyances which we tolerate because not to do so would be repressive and place the freedom of others at risk.

In contravention, the majority's failure to consider the real burden imposed by the pet restriction unfortunately belittles and trivializes the interest at stake here. Pet ownership substantially enhances the quality of life for those who desire it. When others are not only undisturbed by, but *completely unaware of,* the presence of pets being enjoyed by their neighbors, the balance of benefit and burden is rendered disproportionate and unreasonable, rebutting any presumption of validity. Their view, shorn of grace and guiding philosophy, is devoid of the humanity that must temper the interpretation and application of all laws, for in a civilized society that is the source of their authority. As judicial architects of the rules of life, we better serve when we construct halls of harmony rather than walls of wrath.

I would affirm the judgment of the Court of Appeal.

ISSUES RELATING TO COMPANION
ANIMALS AND HOUSING

Rebecca J. Huss*

This chapter provides a general overview of the issues that arise in connection with the desire of humans to have companion animals[1] in their lives, specifically, in their homes. The focus is on various restrictions that the law imposes, with the hope that through the analysis of these restrictions, the reader begins to consider the changing role of these animals in the lives of humans.

The chapter starts with introductory material on the domestication of companion animals. It continues by dividing the legal issues into two broad categories. The first category relates to housing in the private sector. It will briefly discuss issues in rental housing and then turn to restrictions that have been adopted by condominiums and subdivisions. Although these are essentially private contractual relationships, these restrictions may also be subject to laws governing those relationships. Municipal ordinances, which can be very similar to restrictive covenants, as well as the application of nuisance law to companion animals will be discussed next as a transition is made to the second category of issues focusing on the public sector. The final portion of the chapter will analyze federal laws that can pre-empt any private or municipal restrictions.

INTRODUCTION

The way that many people deal with companion animals has changed substantially over time. The specific timeline and history relating to the domestication of dogs and cats is controversial.[2] There is evidence that the dog, as we know it, was in existence between 60,000 and 125,000 years ago. The bond between humans and dogs can be traced to bones found in human graves dated 12,000 to 14,000 years ago. There are several theories that attempt to explain the domestication of dogs from the neotenous traits of dogs to the usefulness of dogs in warning humans of predators. The registration of specific breeds of dogs developed in the nineteenth century, although the breeding of dogs for specific purposes such as hunting, herding and as a source of food occurred well before that time.

The domestication of cats has been estimated at between 4200 and 1000 B.C. with one theory positing that cats were drawn to rodents that concentrated around long-term grain storage buildings in Egypt. Similarly to dogs, specific breeds of cats were formalized in the nineteenth century.

Pets and pet keeping were by no means developed in the modern Western world. There is evidence of pet keeping in ancient Egypt, Greece and Rome as well as other cultures. In the Western world, at one time keeping a pet was primarily limited to the wealthy, but by the mid-nineteenth century the practice of pet keeping had spread to the middle class.

Dogs and cats in our current society have a privileged position in comparison to other domesticated animals such as cattle, sheep and poultry. For example, it is not culturally acceptable in United States society to consume dogs or cats as food. Similarly, the use of dog or cat fur for clothing is not culturally acceptable and is restricted by federal and state laws. In contrast, the use of fur from animals that are biologically quite similar to cats and dogs is not restricted, although there are labeling laws, and some states restrict the methods of production of fur.

Why are these companion animals more "esteemed" (although given the limits on the protection of these animals, this is of course a relative term) than other domesticated animals? As with the domestication of animals there are many theories. One theory that has been the focus of scholars is the impact of urbanization of the United States. Some of these scholars point to the difference in how animals in rural societies are generally considered to have a particular purpose, with the primary role as one to be exploited as a commodity to be sold. As the number of animals, specifically those animals viewed today as farm animals, such as pigs, declined in numbers in urban environments, an increasing number of cats and dogs were kept as pets.

It should not be forgotten that there has been a change in what can be viewed as the "emotional orientation" of humans toward animals. Animals in the wild are often portrayed as idyllic or romantic while domesticated animals, especially dogs and cats, are viewed through the lens of anthropomorhism and neoteny.

Viewed from a broader perspective, it may be controversial to argue that at least some people appear to need to connect with an individual companion animal before they can recognize the suffering of other animals, but the practical matter is that for many people companion animals are the only live animals they deal with on a daily basis. Based on the current culture in the United States, clearly many people are not concerned about the inconsistency in how they treat their beloved companion animals and the way that the rest of animals live in our society. That said, preventing people from living with companion animals, certainly would not appear to make it any easier to make a connection with all nonhuman animals. Allowing people to keep animals in their homes, in addition to providing benefits to the humans, just may provide some hope that people may begin to consider the treatment of all animals in our society.

Other chapters in this book discuss the philosophical, moral and ethical questions of whether it is rational to put dogs and cats in a category that is different from other animals. For purposes of this chapter, it is important to recognize that regardless of whether it is right, or even beneficial to these animals or nonhuman animals as a whole, dogs and cats currently are treated differently by our society and the legal system.

It is important to understand the prevalence of these animals in our society when considering the issues involved with companion animals and housing. In the last few decades, the number of households in the U.S. with pets has increased from approximately 56% to 63%.[3] Of the pets in households, it is estimated that there are 73.9 million dogs and 90.5 million cats with the remainder consisting of fish, birds, small animals and reptiles. Households that include young children and larger sized households report owning more pets on average.

At least in some situations, companion animals are given the role of pseudo family members. In fact, some people view companion animals as analogous to children. Polling data reports that 74% of dog owners and 60% of cat owners agree with the statement that their pets are "like a child/family member." Just as the relationship of adults to children has changed in the last century to focus on children as the sentimental object of affection, the role of companion animals has also changed from one of utility to one of affection. Evidence of the role that companion animals' play in society is supported by polling data asking people how they view their companion animals.

It is perhaps not surprising that people with pets are likely to agree with positive statements relating to pets. Eighty-nine percent of dog and cat owners (to use the prevalent legal term referencing this relationship) agree with the statement "pets are a good source of affection." The positive role of pets in the health of their human owners has been shown by multiple scientific studies. Polling results reinforce this data with the percentage in the high seventies for both dog and cat owners who agree with statements such as "interacting with a pet helps me relax" and "owning a pet can be beneficial to my health." The survey data, of course, focuses only on the benefits of these pets to humans, not whether it is positive for these animals to be kept by humans in this manner.

The amount of money spent on companion animals in the U.S. is significant. A common estimate is that approximately thirty-five billion dollars is spent each year on these animals. Many companion animals are regularly taken to the veterinarian. The percentage of dogs taken to the veterinarian in a twelve-month period is markedly higher at 88% than cats at only 63%. For those owners with the financial resources, there are veterinary specialists such as cardiologists and oncologists. If so desired, there are holistic treatments, such as acupuncture, in addition to traditional veterinary medicine. Given the way that people perceive their pets, and the amount they are willing to spend on them, it is not surprising that they want to have them in their homes and may fight to retain the right to keep their companion animals with them.

RENTAL HOUSING

This section discusses the type of housing that contains the most restrictions on the keeping of animals. As the chapter progresses from discussing the laws applicable to rental housing, to condominiums and then to all housing including single-family housing, fewer limitations on the keeping of animals will apply. As anyone with a companion animal in his or her life knows, it can be challenging to find rental housing that allows animals. In fact, the problem of finding or retaining housing that allows animals is consistently given as one of the top reasons for relinquishing animals to shelters.

Landlords, in the absence of a law stating otherwise, have sole discretion on whether they will allow tenants to have animals on their premises. Landlords articulate many reasons to prohibit or restrict companion animals in their units, including the potential damage done by the animals, noise or other nuisance issues and the threat of litigation if an animal causes harm to another. Estimates on the number of rental units that allow pets vary wildly from five to fifty percent of units allowing animals of some sort.[4] It is common to have significant pet deposits or additional rental assessed if pets are allowed on the premises. Unfortunately for landlords and tenants, the violation of a no-pets policy is all too common. This violation, as with the violation of any clause of a lease, can lead to eviction of the tenant so long as the landlord follows the proper procedure.

A tenant's defense to eviction based on violation of a no-pets clause often is based in equitable arguments such as waiver. Some municipalities have codified these types of equitable arguments into their municipal codes. Perhaps the best-known example of this type of statutory protection is New York City's so called "Pet Law."[5] The New York City Pet Law states that if a tenant harbors a pet (1) open and notoriously, (2) the owner or his or agent has knowledge of that fact, and (3) the owner does not commence proceedings to enforce the lease provision within three months, then (4) the lease provision that would prohibit the pet will be deemed waived. The provision specifies that the waiver will not apply if the pet causes damages to the premises, creates a nuisance or otherwise interferes with the health, safety or welfare of the other tenants. With provisions such as the New York City Pet Law, there is more certainty in the application of equitable arguments but disputes still arise over the application of the provision to individual facts. There have been attempts to change this provision to provide more certainty in its application as it has been left up to the courts to try to determine issues such as the application of the law to replacement pets and the type of knowledge an owner or agent must have in order for the waiver provision to apply.

Laws that are not specifically focused on no-pets clauses may become an issue when there are disputes. The *Young v. Savinon*[6] case in New Jersey illustrates the application of a general Anti–Eviction Act[7] to this issue. In the *Young* case a previous owner had not placed any prohibition on tenants in the building having pets and there were three dogs residing in the building when the building was sold. The new owner testified that his intent was to force the tenants with the animals to move or get rid of their pets and included a no-pets clause in the renewal leases. The New Jersey Anti–Eviction Act requires that lease provisions, as well as any changes to them, be reasonable. The *Young* case is noteworthy because the tenant defendants had an expert testify concerning studies that demonstrated the positive impact of pets on human health as well as the likely negative consequences to these tenants if they were forced to give up their animals. The *Young* court found that it would be unreasonable to enforce the no-pets policy with respect to the tenants and their current pets. The court in the *Young* case was able to come to this conclusion because of the language of the Anti–Eviction Act and the fact that there was such strong testimony on behalf of the tenant defendants. Unfortunately for tenants with animals there is often not an applicable law to argue that the continued presence of their companion animals in violation of a lease provision is warranted. Generally the right of a landlord to ban or restrict animals will prevail.

There are efforts by humane societies and other organizations to promote pet friendly rental housing. These efforts often take a non legal approach to encourage rental housing that allows companion animals. For prospective tenants there may be information on creating a "pet resume" and providing information on local housing options. For landlords, organizations provide model pet agreements and may tout studies that show that tenants with pets are likely to stay in a unit for a longer period of time, thus providing on-going rental income, compared with tenants without pets.

As evidenced by the New York Pet Law there does appear to be a greater understanding by some legislative bodies that the right to have companion animals in rental housing is important to people. Further changes can be made in the law to encourage pet friendly housing such as clarifying the liability of a landlord for damage done by a tenant's animal (which varies substantially by jurisdiction) or providing for financial incentives for landlords that allow animals. After all, if studies show that companion animals are good for human health, why shouldn't the government do what it can to support this interaction?

Without any change in the legal ability of landlords to restrict pets in housing, it appears that any substantial increase in the availability of pet friendly housing may rely primarily on market forces. With the increasing numbers of United States households with pets, it is possible that landlords will feel the need to relax their no-pets policies to attract tenants.

CONDOMINIUMS

There still may be restrictions on keeping a companion animal even if someone owns his or her housing. For many people, because of location or financial constraints, their only choice is to purchase a condominium unit. In a condominium, people have separate ownership of their own units as well as interests in the common areas of the development. Unfortunately for humans with companion animals in their lives, the rules that apply to condominium developments often include substantial restrictions or an outright prohibition on having animals in the units.

Not surprising, as with rental housing, these provisions are often violated and subject to legal disputes.

A.   Declaration and Bylaws

Each state has its own statute governing condominiums but generally the structure is similar. The restrictions on what a condominium owner can do in his or her own unit as well as in common areas (referred to as "use restrictions") are set forth in the governing documents of the condominium development. There are three primary documents or levels of rules that are used to structure the legal relationships within the condominium development. The first is often called a Declaration. This is the so-called "constitution" of the development and may also be referenced as a Master Deed. The developer of the condominium project may draft the Declaration and record it prior to the sale of the individual units. The condominium association itself may also record the Declaration. Similar to other types of recorded instruments in real property law, the restrictions in a Declaration will "run with the land" (to use the proper legal phrase) and bind each subsequent owner of the property.

Courts are very deferential to the language of Declarations and there is generally a strong presumption of validity given to a Declaration.[8] This means if there is a prohibition on the keeping of pets in the Declaration, the court will most likely uphold the restriction, unless the application has been wholly arbitrary or there is an abrogation of a fundamental Constitutional right. On the other hand, if the Declaration expressly allows unit owners to keep pets, the right to keep pets should also be upheld by a court. Unfortunately, it is not uncommon for a Declaration to be silent on this particular issue.

Condominium statutes also often provide for Bylaws for the development to be recorded with the Declaration. Bylaws contain administrative and procedural matters and may be contained in the Declaration. If there is a conflict between the Bylaws and Declaration the terms of the Declaration will prevail.

The application of this type of use restriction can be found in the *Nahrstedt v. Lakeside Village Condominium Assoc. Inc.* case found at the beginning of this chapter.[9] In this 1994 California Supreme Court case, Nahrstedt moved into a 530 unit condominium complex with her three cats. The complex's declaration had a provision stating that "[n]o animals (which shall mean dogs and cats), livestock, reptiles or poultry shall be kept in any unit."[10] When the condominium association learned of the presence of the cats, it demanded that Nahrstedt remove them and assessed fines for each month she continued to violate the restriction. Nahrstedt brought a lawsuit against the association and others asking the court to invalidate the assessments and declare the pet restriction "unreasonable" as it is applied to indoor cats that are not allowed in common areas of the development. The trial court dismissed Nahrstedt's complaint. Nahrstedt was more successful at the Court of Appeals, which revived her case, allowing for the lawsuit to continue.

The California Supreme Court provided background on condominiums generally as well as the role of use restrictions prior to beginning its analysis on the specific facts of the case. The *Nahrstedt* court focused on specific language in the California statute that provides that use restrictions contained in recorded declarations will be enforceable unless unreasonable.[11]

Given the deference that is usually granted by courts to restrictions set forth in declarations, it is not surprising that the *Nahrstedt* court's test to determine the validity of a declaration also would lean towards enforceability. The test set out by the court was that "such restrictions should be enforced unless they are wholly arbitrary, violate a fundamental public policy, or impose a burden on the use of affected land that far outweighs any benefit."[12] The court continued by finding the facts that should be considered are those of the common interest development as a whole rather than that of the objecting homeowner. (This is in contrast to the majority in the Court of Appeals which found that whether the use restriction was reasonable should be determined by the facts of a particular homeowner's case.) Given this test, the California Supreme Court found as a matter of law that the pet restriction was not arbitrary, but was rationally related to the health, sanitation and noise concerns legitimately held by the residents of the development. The court found that the portion of the complaint challenging enforcement of the restriction stated no cause of action, but remanded the case to the Court of Appeals on several other claims raised by Nahrstedt.

If the *Nahrstedt* decision ended at that point, it would likely not be so heavily cited by commentators and other courts. Although the majority in the *Nahrstedt* decision provided a comprehensive review of condominium law and restrictive use provisions useful in future cases, much of the attention brought to the case is due to the eloquent dissenting opinion by Justice Armand Arabian.[13] Justice Arabian found the pet restriction at issue wholly arbitrary, unreasonable, and unduly burdensome on the use of the land within the meaning of the California statutory provision at issue. To support this finding, Justice Arabian began his dissent by discussing the long and cherished association people have with their household animals and the benefits derived from pet ownership.

The dissent continues by performing a burden/benefit analysis of the restriction. Justice Arabian cites to accounts of the domestication of animals and discusses the role of animals in religion and culture as well as studies showing the health benefits of companion animals. He ends his analysis of the burden of the restriction by stating "While pet ownership may not be a fundamental right as such, unquestionably it is an integral aspect of our daily existence, which cannot be lightly dismissed and should not suffer unwarranted intrusion into its circle of privacy."[14] In considering the possible benefits of the restriction, Justice Arabian focused on the facts in this case that illustrated that there was essentially no impact on other unit holders by having an animal solely within one's unit given the allowance of fish and birds in the restriction.

Justice Arabian used the facts set out in the pleadings that alleged that the cats were maintained entirely within the unit, were noiseless and did not otherwise create a nuisance. Justice Arabian's dissent ends by stating that the majority failed to consider the real burden imposed by the pet restriction and trivialized the interest at stake in the case.

B.   Board or Association Rules and Regulations

The last set of rules or documents that apply to a condominium are the rules and regulations that are set by a condominium's board. The structure of the board and the process to adopt rules and regulations are governed by the Bylaws or Declaration. Many times these rules and regulations are adopted by the majority of the board or may be submitted to the vote of the unit holders for majority adoption. Given the inherent fluidity of these rules and regulations, it is perhaps not surprising that there is no presumption of validity granted by courts to restrictions adopted by the board or unit holders. The standard of review for these rules and regulations is generally one of "reasonableness."

An example of a condominium board successfully adopting a rule restricting pet ownership is illustrated by the case of *Board of Directors of 175th East Delaware Place Homeowners Ass'n v. Hinojosa.*[15] In the *Hinojosa* case the condominium board for the residential portion of the John Hancock building in Chicago passed a rule that restricted the condominium unit holders from keeping dogs in their units. Dogs that were in the building at the time of the adoption of the rule were allowed to stay—only additional or replacement dogs were banned. Previously less restrictive measures had been taken to try to regulate dogs but there had been problems, including one dog killing another dog in the building. The Illinois Court of Appeals recognized that rules adopted by boards would not be given a strong presumption of validity but found that the rule was reasonable under the specific facts of the case because it was rational and applied to all owners.

C.   Defenses

If a unit holder is alleged to have violated a restriction, he or she may first attempt to argue that the adoption of the restriction is invalid. These types of regulations are required to be objective, even-handed, nondiscriminatory and applied uniformly. If a regulation does not meet the standards, a unit holder may argue selective enforcement, waiver, or changed conditions.

A case where the argument of selective enforcement was raised is *Prisco v. Forest Villas Condominium Apartments, Inc.*[16] In the *Prisco* case the restriction at issue was added to the Declaration in 1979 and read in part:

> The Board is cognizant that dogs are currently being harbored in units of FOREST VILLA CONDOMINIUM. These dogs shall be permitted to remain so long as they shall live. It is emphatically agreed that upon their demise, these animals shall not be replaced. Further, with the exception of these dogs, no pet of

any kind whatsoever, except fish and/or birds, shall ever be permitted to be harbored in FOREST VILLAS.[17]

Prisco moved into the development in 1995 with her dog and the association filed a complaint against her seeking to enjoin her from keeping a dog in violation of the pet restriction. At the trial there was evidence that cats resided in several units of the development as well as a dog that it had been mistakenly "grandfathered" in under the provision. (The dog was in fact a replacement dog for a dog owned at the time the unit holder left the development. He then returned to the development with a new dog.) The trial court found in favor of the association's summary judgment motion on the issue of selective enforcement finding that "cats are not the same as dogs"[18] and the judgment relating to the other unit holder's dog was based a good faith belief of the board that the dog was entitled to be grandfathered in under the provision.

The Florida Court of Appeals rejected the trial court's analysis and found that the restriction was clear and unambiguous stating that both cats and dogs would be prohibited under the provision. In addition, the appellate court agreed with Prisco's argument that by allowing the other unit owner to keep his dog, the board was selectively and arbitrarily enforcing the pet restriction, thus Prisco could raise the defense of selective enforcement at a new trial.

It is interesting to compare these common interest development cases. Clearly the trial court in *Prisco* may have been swayed by the arguments raised by the cat owner in *Nahrstedt*. Even given a clear and unambiguous statutory provision, the *Prisco* trial court distinguished between cats and dogs and the impact of each animal on the common areas. The *Hinojosa* court as well focused on the perceived practicalities of living with a dog in a common environment to find that the board rule was reasonable. This does not take into account dogs that are litter box trained, and thus from the perspective of access to common areas, are similar to cats. Even if you take into account the fact that dogs bark, there may not be a significant distinction between barking and the yowling of a cat or the squawk of a bird if considering the potential noise of an animal.

Of course, another avenue of change is the recognition of Justice Arabian in the *Nahrstedt* dissent of the importance of animals in the lives of humans. Can an argument be made that, as the role of these animals has changed, having an animal with you in housing that is owned (perhaps continuing to distinguish from rental property) could rise to the leval of a fundamental right? Although no case has found that animals will be treated on the level of other human family members, can an argument be made, based on what we know people think of their companion animals, that these animals should have similar status—or is this contrary to our society's core beliefs?

It is clear that if people want to make certain that they can have their companion animals in their condominium units, it is necessary to review the governing documents carefully. In addition to determining what the current restrictions on pets may be, it is necessary to make certain that the amendment process is one that they are comfortable with in the event that a restriction may be proposed in the future. Even if any new restriction grandfathers in existing animals, the ability to replace a pet that passes away is an important right that they would likely want to retain.

D. *Statutory Provision Impacting Common Interest Developments*

Given the ability of condominium associations to amend their governing documents, protection at the state level is especially useful. Partially in response to the *Nahrstedt* case discussed above, the California Civil Code was amended to provide that no governing documents shall prohibit the owner of each separate interest in a common interest development (or a mobile home park) from keeping at least one pet in the development subject to reasonable rules and regulations.[19] Pet is defined as domesticated birds, cats, dogs or aquatic animals kept within an aquarium. The provision applies to governing documents entered into or amended on or after January 1, 2001. The definition of governing documents includes rules and regulations. Thus common interest developments established prior to 2001 will fall within the provision, if they amend their rules and regulations, even if such an amendment does not relate to companion animals.

Clearly, the California statutory provision provides valuable protection for owners of companion animals residing in common interest developments, although it is limited in scope. Given the challenges with making changes under the common law due to the precedent establishing that animals are simply another form of personal property, legislative action may be a more viable approach to making changes in the current system.

As seen when discussing the federal and state laws relating to persons with a disability later in this chapter, absent an intervening law, owners of companion animals are subject to significant restrictions in the ability to keep their animals in all types of housing.

ALL TYPES OF HOUSING—RESTRICTIVE COVENANTS AND MUNICIPAL ORDINANCES

There are limits on the ownership of companion animals even when real property is acquired outside of a condominium common development. Restrictive covenants and municipal ordinances often cover the same issues. In both cases the number and type of animals kept by each household may be limited. Ordinances may be enacted by cities or by larger divisions of states such as counties. Restrictive covenants (found in a subdivisions) are similar to the use restrictions in condominiums. Just as with condominiums, restrictive covenants that are located in recorded documents are given significantly more deference than limits that are imposed via vote of a homeowners association or board.

In order to determine whether a municipal ordinance is valid, the first step is to determine the authority granted by the state. Some states provide very broad grants of authority while others require municipalities to have approval at the state legislative level for particular types of restrictions. State legislatures will often, either explicitly or inferentially, delegate a significant amount of police power to municipalities for the regulation of companion animals. Just as federal law may preempt state law, state law may preempt local law. Note that there are some municipalities that are given more power to determine their laws because of their status as "home rule" jurisdictions. (A discussion of this land use issue is beyond the scope of this chapter.)

Courts will uphold state and local laws if the issue of the law is within the allowed concerns of public health, safety or welfare. The limitations of the law must also be rationally related to the goals of the legislature and must meet general standards of statutory construction. As illustrated below, the power of municipalities to regulate animals kept as pets is generally broadly construed. This section will address three ways that the keeping of animals is often limited. It will first discuss ordinances based on the number of animals, and pet licensing generally. The section will also address, to a lesser extent, ordinances based on the breed of dog or if a dog is deemed dangerous and ordinances restricting the type of animals allowed in a community.

A. Limits on Number of Animals

1. Content of Ordinances

It is quite common to have a limit on the number of cats or dogs or a combination of the two allowed in each household as the core of an ordinance. This common restriction is usually upheld if attacked on Constitutional grounds. Generally, if homeowners have a greater number of these types of animals on their property than the ordinance allows, they are required to obtain a special license from the relevant authority.

A county ordinance that was found to be unconstitutionally vague is illustrated by the Georgia Supreme Court case of *Foster v. State*.[20] The problematic ordinance language in the *Foster* case was as follows:

> It shall be unlawful for there to be more than four dogs and/or cats on any residential lot that is less than five acres in size, subject to the following exceptions: (1) Animal owners who have an approved permit issued by the animal control board shall be excepted from this section.[21]

The problem in this ordinance was not the pet limit itself (which was clear) but the fact that there were no ascertainable standards to grant or deny the permit that would except an animal owner from the section. The uncontrolled discretion this provided to the animal control board was considered to be incompatible with due process requirements.

Municipalities are provided with a great deal of discretion in drafting their ordinances. An example is an ordinance that limits the number of animals based in part on the weight of the animals. (Note that weight restrictions are quite common in common area development restrictions.) In *City of Marion v. Schoenwald*,[22] the South Dakota Supreme

Court considered the Constitutionality of a city ordinance that limited households to a total of four dogs with the additional restriction that only two out of the four dogs could weigh over twenty-five pounds. The ordinance also allowed each household to have four adult cats. Even though the city cited no cases where a similar weight restriction was upheld, or any authority based on animal science as to the impact of larger dogs versus smaller dogs, the ordinance was upheld. The court found that the weight limit did not unreasonably exceed the city's regulatory authority because it was sufficiently related to the purpose of protecting public health and safety. The *Schoenwald* court stated, apparently with no evidence supporting these findings, that "larger dogs have a greater potential for harm" and the "limit on the number of dogs assuredly advances public welfare."[23]

Ordinances may consider the type of housing when setting limitations on the number of pets. The *Village of Carpentersville v. Fiala*[24] case in Illinois provides an example of this type of restriction. In the Village of Carpentersville ordinance, single-family residences were allowed to have two dogs while single-family units in multiple family residences were only allowed to have one dog. The court found that there are real and substantial differences between these two types of residences. Similar to the analysis found in condominium and other common area development cases, issues such as proximity to others, noise levels and structural differences were cited to support the ruling. Treating these types of residences differently was rationally related to the object of the ordinance. The rational basis test was applied even though there was a difference in treatment based on classification because the classification in the ordinance was not a 'suspect classification' and did not involve 'fundamental interests.' (If either of these had been triggered, a higher standard of review would have been implicated.)

The usefulness of arbitrary pet limit laws has been challenged by organizations as diverse as the American Society for Prevention of Cruelty to Animals, The Association of Pet Dog Trainers, the National Animal Interest Alliance, the American Kennel Club and the Cat Fancier's Association. Proponents of pet limit laws argue that such ordinances are a way to combat overpopulation, hoarding, nuisances and cruelty. The argument that pet limit laws combat overpopulation doesn't make much sense given that the source of new animals is, of course, intact animals. A limit on the number of sterilized animals in a household serves only to limit the number of homes available to companion animals. Given that conservative estimates are that three to five million dogs and cats are killed each year due to homelessness it would seem that governmental entities should be encouraging the responsible adoption of these animals rather than discouraging it.

The hoarding issue is raised in many contexts dealing with companion animals. So far there has not been systematic reporting of hoarding cases, however criteria have been developed by researchers to determine whether hoarding may be an issue. The criteria used set forth three specific behaviors or circumstances. First, there is generally more than a typical number of companion animals in the household. Second, there is an inability to provide minimum standards of care resulting in illness or death to the animals. The final indication of hoarding is that the person would deny that he or she is not able to provide minimal care and that there is a negative impact on the animals or other members of the household. Of these criteria, only the first relating to the number of animals is addressed in a pet limit law.

Hoarding has been characterized as a symptom of obsessive-compulsive disorder and obsessive-compulsive personality disorder and the little research that exists indicates that hoarders are particularly resistant to treatment using commonly prescribed medications and psychotherapy. Unfortunately, as of the date of the writing of this chapter, only the State of Illinois has a specific statutory provision dealing with hoarding.[25] If a person fits within the criteria for a hoarder in the statute (based on the criteria set forth above), the statute allows the court to order a psychological or psychiatric evaluation and treatment at the convicted person's expense.

Along with preventing hoarding, proponents of pet limit laws say that such laws are necessary to stop neglect and abuse caused when people take in more animals than they can adequately provide care. As discussed above, a well-crafted hoarder law would address this issue. A pet limit law does not address the setting of any minimum standards of care. It is possible that one household may be unable to care for even a single animal but another can care for many.

Finally, proponents argue that pet limit laws can prevent nuisances from arising or can be used to combat nuisances. As discussed below, nuisance laws can deal directly with issues relating to animals. Opponents of pet limit laws point to the fact that one animal can be deemed a nuisance if its behavior causes problems while numerous well-behaved animals may have no impact on neighborhood. (The nuisance issue is an especially weak argument if you have animals that are consistently kept confined such as cats that are not allowed to roam.)

Opponents of pet limit laws argue that enforcement of these laws is often arbitrary. If the law is enforced on a complaint basis, such a provision can be used as a weapon in disputes between neighbors that may be unrelated to the animals. Opponents also point to the fact that these laws regulate people's behavior in their homes, thus the issue of an individual's right to privacy is raised by these restrictions.

Ultimately, opponents of pet limit laws point to the fact that these types of laws are counterproductive since they discourage people from complying with licensing laws due to the fear that they will be found to be in noncompliance with the limit. Even when an exemption is made allowing a person to apply for a permit to have more than the restricted number of animals, there is the possibility that the request will be denied leaving the applicant in a position of potentially losing his or her animals.

2.   Pet Licensing

In addition to and in conjunction with, pet limit laws, many jurisdictions have licensing statutes. These licensing statutes may be solely local in nature or be required by state law. For example, in Indiana there is a "dog tax" established by state statute that allows counties to adopt a County Option Dog Tax.[26] A part of the proceeds of this tax are apportioned to an account disbursed to the state's veterinary college for canine research and education. The remainder of the proceeds of this tax is allocated to the local jurisdictions for the purpose of establishing and maintaining animal care and control services, reimbursements to farmers for livestock kills and reimbursement to persons who have undergone rabies post exposure prophylaxis.

Other justifications for licensing include ensuring vaccination enforcement as well as funding educational programs. Note that the licensing requirements discussed here are separate from the common requirement by states that companion animals receive a rabies vaccination on a set schedule. The rabies vaccination requirement is often met through contact with veterinarians who will issue the rabies tag and certification directly.

A positive aspect of licensing is that if an animal has a current license (especially if the ordinance requires microchipping of an animal since tags can often be lost) it will be easier to reunite the animal with his or her original owners. Since the percentage of pets that are never identified and recovered by their owners is estimated to be quite high, reunification is certainly a valid goal.

Differential licensing can also be used to encourage the sterilization of animals. Differential licensing requires a substantially higher fee for licenses for intact animals over sterilized animals and thus provides an incentive for owners to spay or neuter their pets.

The problem of course, is that a significant percentage of companion animals are not licensed, even when a licensing ordinance is applicable. There are many reasons for this lack of compliance. Certainly limited education or knowledge about a relevant licensing requirement is common. Enforcement of licensing violations alone is unlikely to be a priority for animal control services. Finally, given the pet limit laws, there is a disincentive for people to license their animals because of the realistic problem of being in violation of an arbitrary limit.

B.   *Dangerous Dog versus Breed Specific Statutes*

State and local laws also have been passed to deal with the problem of dangerous dogs. A dangerous dog statute itself is not connected to where the animal resides (ownership or control of the animal is key to liability) but it obviously directly impacts a person's ability to have certain dogs on his or her property. There is no question that there are serious issues relating to dogs causing injury to people. According to estimates by the Insurance Information Institute, seventy percent of dog bite incidents occur on the dog owner's property and half of all children in the United States will be bitten by the age of twelve. The Insurance

Information Institute has also stated that dog bites account for one-third of all homeowner's insurance claims.

Dog bite laws vary from state to state. Some states approach the issue in a strict liability fashion with very few defenses while others consider whether the owner knew or should have known of an animal's vicious propensities. Liability for condominium associations and landlords most often turns on whether those parties had control over the animal. If the landlord or association does not have control, the injured person's remedy remains with the legal owner of the animal.

Some municipalities have targeted certain breeds of dogs—referred to as "breed discriminatory legislation" ("BDL"). These provisions either ban certain dogs outright (pit bulls and pit bull mixes are the current target) or place significant restrictions on ownership of those dogs. Several states have banned municipalities from having BDL. Even in a state that has banned municipalities from passing BDL there may be jurisdictions within the state with enforceable laws due to the application of a clause that provides for such a ban to be applied only to new ordinances passed by municipalities. An example of a city that currently has an enforceable BDL due to prospective application of an anti-BDL statute is Miami, Florida. The application of the concept of home rule jurisdiction, which provides certain large municipalities with greater control over their legislation, also may allow a municipality to have BDL even though a state statute may prohibit it. An example of home rule being applicable, thus allowing a ban to exist, is Denver, Colorado.

Even absent a municipal breed ban, it may be impossible for owners of certain types of dogs to keep them as some insurance companies now refuse to insure households that contain certain breeds. These insurance breed bans are based solely on the breed of dog, regardless of the individual dog's history. Some BDL mandates that an owner maintain liability insurance. In such jurisdictions, the inability to obtain insurance, because of a widespread insurance breed ban may be an insurmountable problem for these owners. As of the time of the writing of this chapter, although legislation has been introduced in several states, no state legislature has implemented a restriction on the ability of insurance companies to refuse to insure based on the presence of a specific breed of dog. There has been action on this issue at the administrative level. An example is the Michigan Insurance Commissioner issuing a ruling in 2003 that prohibits insurance companies from refusing to issue insurance or renew policies based solely on the breed of a dog or dogs in a household.

C. *Animals Other than Dogs and Cats*

Another common restrictive covenant or municipal ordinance is one that limits the type of animals that can be kept on the property. These prohibitions may address concerns over potentially dangerous animals or be drafted in order to maintain a particular appearance or preserve the residential nature of the community. Some states also have laws that relate specifically to the keeping of wild or exotic animals.[27] Just as with the ordinances relating to dangerous dogs, so long as the language in the ordinance is carefully drafted, the ordinance is likely to be upheld by the courts.

Domesticated animals that are identified as "livestock" are often prohibited by ordinance. One type of animal that grew in popularity as a pet in the 1990s was the potbellied pig. There have been several cases that have analyzed whether a potbellied pig should be considered livestock or a household pet. The results in these cases have been mixed depending in large measure on the specific language of the statute as well as the evidence in the case.

In *Gebauer v. Lake Forest Property Owners Ass'n*,[28] the owner of a potbellied pig named Taylor prevailed and was allowed to keep the pig on her property. The restrictive covenant in this case provided that no livestock could be kept on the property other than dogs, cats and other animals that were qualified as household pets. The court considered evidence such as a 'day in the life' videotape of Taylor and spent a significant amount of time analyzing the distinction between potbellied pigs and pigs used for human consumption. Ultimately the court found that Taylor should be considered a household pet.

NUISANCE LAW

There are two categories of nuisance laws. The type of harm and type of person who may bring the cause of action determines the category. A public nuisance focuses on a person interfering with the rights of the community at large and the city (or other governmental entity) brings the cause of action. A private nuisance is based on a disturbance of rights in land and the remedy lies with the private landowner who has been harmed.

The issue of nuisance is closely related to the pet limit laws and restrictions on keeping animals other than dogs and cats discussed above. In some jurisdictions, the keeping of dogs and cats above a set number may be considered a nuisance per se. In others, the pet limit law itself may be based on the ability of a jurisdiction to regulate nuisances.

One of the cases often cited in this area is *Commonwealth v. Creighton*.[29] A cat owner in this case appealed from a summary conviction for violating an ordinance limiting the number of cats and/or dogs that could be kept within the borough to a total of five. As with many states, the Pennsylvania state legislature delegates to the boroughs the power to prohibit and remove any nuisance, and to make regulations necessary for the health, safety, and general welfare of the borough.

The *Creighton* court considered the arbitrary limit of animals to be enacted by a borough under the power to regulate nuisances. A prior Pennsylvania case required that ordinances enacted pursuant to this authority be phrased in a way that required the municipality to affirmatively establish that a nuisance in fact existed. In this case, the application of this requirement would mean that the mere presence of the animals alone cannot support the nuisance claim. The *Creighton* court continued its analysis under the general power of the borough to enact laws that it perceives are necessary to protect the public health, safety and general welfare. The court reiterated that the test to review such a law is that the "goal sought to be achieved is legitimate and that the means used to achieve that goal are reasonably necessary and not unduly oppressive."[30] The preamble to the ordinance did not state what legitimate goal the borough sought to advance. The appellate court remanded the case for the lower court to determine whether the goals were legitimate and the means used to achieve them reasonable. Although this case is often cited to illustrate a possible restriction on a jurisdiction's ability to limit the number of animals, in fact, it is just an illustration of problematic statutory construction. If the borough had set forth a legitimate goal (which based on the overwhelming majority of cases finding pet limit laws Constitutional is has been fairly easy to do), and set forth the basis for finding a nuisance in fact, this law would likely have been upheld.

More common than nuisance cases brought solely on the basis of the number of animals kept on a property are those based on odor and noise. *Barnes v. Board of Adjustment of the City of Bartlesville*[31] provides an example of a case where the maintenance of an animal, in this case a potbellied pig, constituted a nuisance sufficient to deprive the owner of a special zoning permit. The primary evidence that the pig constituted a nuisance was the testimony of one neighbor as well as the Chief Building Inspector, Code Enforcement Officer of Bartlesville who testified that they could distinguish between the odor of pig and dog feces. There were several neighbors who testified that they had not noticed a problem with the pig. Notwithstanding that testimony, the *Barnes* court found that there was a presumption of correctness attaching to the board's decision not to grant the special zoning permit and found that it would not disturb the decision, unless it was clearly arbitrary or erroneous.

Noise as the foundation of a nuisance citation can be based on the barking of a single dog or many. The standard by which the barking of a dog or dogs would rise to the level of a nuisance is barking that is offensive and inconvenient to a normal person. The timing of the barking, with early morning or night barking being more problematic, may be one factor considered. The amount of barking, such as barking that is excessive or continuous, and whether the dog or dogs have been purposefully incited to bark also is considered in determining whether the noise is deemed sufficient to arise to the level of being a nuisance.

It is important to remember that all the municipal laws that deal with animals must be based on public health, safety or welfare. As seen in recent cases challenging BDL, what the real danger to public health, safety or welfare is from certain breeds of dogs can be highly controversial. The same argument can be made with other municipal laws impacting the ability to have companion animals on a person's property. Certainly there could be better tailored laws to deal with possible nuisance issues than an arbitrary pet limit law. As the relationship between humans and their companion animals change humans could demand changes in municipal laws to reflect the importance of these animals in their lives. Including a dog or cat in a household is not the same as a non-working car sitting on the front lawn. Certainly a time may come in the not too distant future where people will demand more rational and relevant laws relating to companion animals in their municipalities.

FEDERAL LAWS

So far this chapter has discussed the many ways that people may be restricted from having animals in their housing. This section discusses three laws that grant certain individuals the right to have animals in their homes under particular circumstances. The first two laws discussed, grant this right to individuals occupying federally-assisted housing. The third law, the Federal Fair Housing Amendments Act grants persons with qualifying disabilities the right to have service animals with them in almost all forms of housing.

A.　Elderly and Handicapped Housing

The federal provision adopted in 1983 entitled Pet Ownership in Assisted Rental Housing for the Elderly or Handicapped ("POEH") requires that owners and managers of federally assisted housing for the elderly and handicapped cannot prohibit tenants from owning common household pets.[32] The justification provided in the legislative history of POEH for allowing pets in housing for the elderly was the numerous studies that showed the substantial physical and mental benefits that pets can provide to the elderly. In the legislative history for this provision, the Senate found that an absolute no-pets policy had been widely practiced in federally assisted rental projects even though the Department of Housing and Urban Development ("HUD") had not issued regulations governing the keeping of pets. This no-pets policy is not surprising since the same issues that private landlords raise such as the possibility of damage, nuisance and threat of litigation apply equally to federally assisted rental housing. The difference of course is that while there are market forces that may pressure at least some private landlords into allowing animals, providers of federally assisted housing are dealing with a tenant population with few or no housing alternatives.

The regulations developed to implement this provision are extensive.[33] There are mandatory and discretionary rules relating to the keeping of animals. The mandatory rules require that (a) pets must be vaccinated in accordance with state and local laws, (b) sanitary standards must be set governing the disposal of pet waste, and (c) pets must be under the control of a responsible individual and restrained while in common areas.

An additional mandatory rule is that the pet owners must register their pets and update their registration at least annually. One of the pieces of information required for the registration is contact information for a responsible party who will care for the pet if the pet owner is no longer able to do so due to death or disability. The regulations provide that once the owner of federally-assisted housing determines that the health or safety of a pet is threatened by the death or disability of the animal's owner, the responsible party must be contacted to take the animal. If the responsible party cannot be contacted or is unwilling or unable to take care of the pet, the owner of the federally-assisted housing can contact the relevant state or local authority to request removal of the pet. Language in the lease agreement may also provide owners of federally-assisted housing with the right to enter the unit, remove the pet and place it in a facility for a period not exceeding thirty days, at the expense of the pet owner, if the owner is unable to care for the pet.

The discretionary rules allow each housing project to set some of its own standards. These discretionary rules can impact the welfare of the animals. The rules cannot require that a pet's vocal cords be removed (de-barking). The rules may require that dogs and cats be sterilized and may place a limit on the length of time a pet is left unattended in a unit. The discretionary rules also allow the housing project to restrict the number of four-legged, warm-blooded pets to one in each dwelling as well as limit the size, weight and type of animals. A pet deposit may be required but any such deposit is limited to one month's rent or an amount set by HUD annually.

Some states have followed the lead set by the federal government and have adopted similar provisions that will apply to state supported housing. The New Jersey statute provides similar coverage—permitting one domestic animal in senior citizen housing projects.[34] The California provision is more generous allowing persons to keep two pets in their units.[35]

When POEH was passed, there were concerns about potential problems with allowing pets in elderly and handicapped housing. Since the adoption of the provision, individual housing providers have reported that these tenants take excellent care of their pets and the problems that HUD anticipated apparently have not occurred. The lack of problems in federally-assisted housing for the elderly and handicapped was used in the debate over whether to expand the ability to have a companion animal in federally-assisted housing on a broader basis.

B. Public Housing

The more recent adoption of the Pet Ownership in Public Housing ("POPH") provision caused greater controversy.[36] Under POPH, residents of any federally-assisted public housing are allowed to own one or more common household pets subject to the reasonable requirements of the applicable public housing agency. The legislative history for the provision is sparse as the language was included in a significant appropriations bill. Unlike the extensive regulations set forth under POEH, there are relatively few regulations supporting POPH with a great deal of deference given to the rules made by individual public housing authorities.[37] Although the regulations are much less extensive than those provided in POEH, due to the public comment period, there was much more controversy over the provision and regulations themselves. In contrast, when adopting the rules relating to POEH, HUD determined that no public comment period was necessary since the rules, in its opinion, did not affect or establish policy.

Similar to the regulations under POEH, the public housing authority may require pets to be registered and sterilized but cannot require that pets' vocal cords be removed. The reasonable requirements that public housing authorities are allowed to set include (a) the ability to require a pet deposit, (b) limitations on the number of animals in a unit based on unit size and (c) prohibiting animals based on size and weight as well as prohibiting animals classified as dangerous.

The right of public housing authorities to set restrictions or prohibitions based on the size and type of building or project has perhaps impacted the tenants in these developments the most. This restriction has meant that many public housing authorities have prohibited dogs and cats in high-rise or multi family buildings. The rules set by individual public housing authorities implementing POPH took a great deal of time to develop and many of the provisions adopted require significant pet deposits. Another factor decreasing the impact of POPH is the increasing use of Section 8 vouchers and other programs that rely on private housing. Housing provided under these programs is not considered "public housing" thus is exempt from application of POPH.

As with the more extensive regulations under POEH, although regulation may impact the welfare of an animal, such as a ban on debarking, the regulations clearly are weighted towards considering the concerns (whether valid or not) of the owner of federally-assisted housing. An example, is the allowance, and perhaps even the tacit approval of rules that would require a tenant to declaw a cat if it was shown to be necessary to protect the unit. As illustrated by the public comments for POPH and stated policies, the practice of declawing is highly disfavored by almost all animal wefare organizations due to the pain and long term problems such surgery imposes on the cat.

What is the true impact of POEH and POPH? The economic status of tenants of federally-assisted housing will certainly continue to limit the likelihood that many will be able to have companion animals in their housing. More could certainly be done to facilitate the ability of people on limited incomes (whether in federally-assisted housing or not) to have a companion animal in their household. The current efforts in this area, such as the provision of low cost veterinary care, have primarily been local in nature.

These provisions do illustrate the growing recognition that companion animals play an important role in the lives of humans. As with any change in the law, it will take time to determine the impact on the community. With further research it will be possible to confirm whether the impact on the lives of tenants of federally-assisted housing of allowing companion animals in their housing is positive. It is also necessary to take further steps to safeguard the animals (such as prohibiting declawing) while providing this opportunity to a greater number of people in our society.

C. *Federal Fair Housing Amendments Act*

1. Coverage of Federal Fair Housing Amendments Act

Through the application of the Federal Fair Housing Amendments Act ("FHA" or the "Act")[38] a person with a disability may be allowed to keep an animal in housing that ordinarily would ban such an animal. In 1988 the FHA was amended to include persons with disabilities in the classes of persons protected from housing discrimination. (The Act uses the term handicap, this chapter will use the term handicap and disability interchangeably like many of the court decisions covering this issue.) The FHA applies to a broad spectrum of housing providers including single-family homes if a real estate agent or broker is used in the rental or sale of the property. Although cases alleging discrimination by landlords are common, condominium associations also are subject to the Act.

In addition to prohibiting overt discrimination on the basis of a person's handicap, the Act also provides that a person may prove discrimination by showing that the defendant failed to make a reasonable accommodation when such accommodation is necessary to afford the person an equal opportunity to use and enjoy a dwelling. The federal regulations[39] and numerous cases have established that a reasonable accommodation may include waiving or modifying a pet rule to allow for a service animal to be kept in the housing.

The cases analyzing the FHA as it relates to service animals can be divided into three broad categories (a) establishing a nexus between the animal and the disability, (b) determining the status of an animal, and (c) considering the limits of a reasonable accommodation.

2. Necessity to Show a Nexus between the Animal and the Disability

To determine whether there is a nexus between the animal and the disability it is first necessary to determine who will be protected by the Act. Handicap is defined in the Act as "(1) a physical or mental impairment which substantially limits one or more of such person's major life activities, (2) a record of having such an impairment, or (3) being regarded as having such an impairment."[40]

It is important to recognize that the definition includes both physical and mental impairments. The inability to show that a potential plaintiff meets the definition of handicap under the Act will preclude any further consideration of the case. From a practical standpoint, landlords and other potential defendants under the Act generally have been educated enough about their potential liability under state and federal laws that prohibit discrimination, that if someone has a visible physical disability (such as impaired sight or hearing), they will not inquire further into a person's status. If a disability is not obvious, potential defendants under the Act often require some proof of such disability. Cases have found that landlords and other potential defendants under the Act may inquire into or verify an asserted disability as well as the necessity of the reasonable accommodation.

As the FHA states, even if a person has been diagnosed with a physical or mental impairment, that person must show that such impairment must substantially limit a major life activity before the protections of the Act will apply. An example is the *Wells v. State Manufactured Homes, Inc.*[41] case where the plaintiff suffered from Major Depressive Disorder resulting in social anxiety disorder and other symptoms. Since the plaintiff did not establish that her mental impairments and symptoms substantially limited a major life activity, she was not entitled to a summary judgment on liability.

The second part of the nexus requirement is that having the animal in the housing must be necessary for the person to be able to use and enjoy the dwelling. The key to this analysis is that the animal must be medically indicated. Courts generally do not consider whether removal of an animal will cause problems for the person requesting a reasonable accommodation. For example, in *Nason v. Stone Hill Realty Ass'n*,[42] a physician provided a letter for a tenant with multiple sclerosis suggesting "there would be serous negative consequences for her health if she was compelled to remove the cat."[43] The doctor's affidavit listed several specific symptoms including depression, spasticity and fatigue that could increase if the cat was removed. Unlike most courts that do not consider whether other reasonable accommodations are available or whether other therapeutic methods could be used to treat the symptoms, the *Nason* court considered both these issues in denying the motion for a preliminary injunction finding that the record failed to demonstrate the nexus between keeping the cat and the tenant's handicap.

3.   The Animal Must be a Service Animal

In addition to needing the animal on the premises in order to be able to use and enjoy the housing, the status of the animal is key to determining whether the FHA is applicable. If an animal is considered to be only a companion to the person with a disability, rather than a service animal, the FHA does not require a housing provider to make an accommodation allowing the animal to remain. The federal regulations for classification as a service animal only consist of two requirements: (1) the animal must be individually trained and (2) must work for the benefit of the disabled individual.[44] There have been several cases that relate to these requirements.

The training or skill level of the animal is at the core of several cases that focused on whether a housing provider could require some type of certification of the putative service animal's training. An Oregon federal district court found that a housing authority could not require "certification or third party verification of [an] assistance animal's abilities."[45] In contrast, a West Virginia court found that a flexible certification requirement would not run afoul of the FHA.[46] The West Virginia court emphasized that the party with the animal who is requesting a reasonable accommodation has the burden of showing that the animal is properly trained.

A recent case that is being cited frequently in this area deals with the training of an animal to deal with disabilities that are primarily mental in character. In the case of *Prindable v. Ass'n of Apartment Owners of 2987 Kalakaua*,[47] the plaintiff suffered from depression and provided affidavits from physicians stating that diagnosis. The affidavits also stated that the plaintiff would benefit from animal-assisted therapy and that separation from the dog acquired in contravention of a condominium association bylaw would exacerbate his condition. In considering whether the dog was an individually trained service animal, the *Prindable* court rejected plaintiffs' counsel's argument that "canines (as a species) possess the ability to give unconditional love, which simply makes people feel better."[48] The *Prindable* court expressed concern that using that reasoning would permit "no identifiable stopping point" and would change the test from 'individually trained to do work or perform tasks' to 'of some comfort.'[49] The *Prindable* court found that the animal must be "peculiarly suited to ameliorate the unique problems of the mentally disabled"[50] if the primary handicap is mental or emotional in nature. The court, finding that there was nothing in the record that would support a holding that the dog in this case was an individually trained service animal, granted a summary judgment motion in favor of the defendants.

The *Prindable* case as precedent makes it more difficult for attorneys representing clients with mental disabilities to argue that animals used for therapeutic purposes should be excluded from a pet ban. An argument (made by attorneys in the past) that the only requirement for such animal is that the animal is well socialized and able to accompany the person with the disability to public places, will not prevail in courts finding the *Prindable* court's analysis persuasive. Fortunately for plaintiff's attorneys there is some precedent that may be used to support a less onerous standard.

Although interpreting California state law similar to the FHA rather than the FHA itself, *Auburn Woods I Homeowners Ass'n v. Fair Employment Housing Commission*,[51] provides a good example of an alternative theory to determine the status of an animal. The *Auburn Woods* court reiterated that the administrative hearing did not rule that companion animals are always a reasonable accommodation for persons with mental disabilities and found that each case is fact specific. In this case, the parties suffered from severe depression and the court found that it "was the innate qualities of a dog, in particular a dog's friendliness and ability to interact with humans, that made it therapeutic here."[52] In other words, the dog did not need special skills to help ameliorate the effects of the mental disabilities of the condominium owners.

The *Auburn Woods* court used numerous HUD administrative decisions to support its ruling. Recent HUD decisions, demonstrate a clear trend, at the administrative level, to support plaintiffs who request a reasonable accommodation in a pet policy if the plaintiffs are able to show that there is some therapeutic benefit, notwithstanding any evidence of special skills of the animal.

4. The Limits of Reasonable Accommodation

The final broad category of issues that arise under the FHA is determining whether an exemption to a no-pets (or limited pets) rule is unreasonable under the circumstances. Courts have established that is not necessary to do everything humanly possible to accommodate a person with a disability. Both parties needs' will be considered and the cost to the defendant as well as the benefit to the person with a disability will be taken into account when determining whether an accommodation is reasonable.

The *Zapata v. Lowe*[53] case illustrates that it may be possible for a potential defendant under the FHA to limit the breed of dog that is allowed on the property. A tenant suffering from AIDS and long-term clinical depression acquired a dog that was a pit bull terrier or pit bull mix. The landlords were successful in arguing that having a pit bull in the building constituted a nuisance. The *Zapata* court considered analogous United States Supreme Court and Ninth Circuit decisions that indicated "an accommodation need not satisfy the particular preferences of the disabled person in order to be held reasonable."[54] Since the landlords in this case offered to allow the tenant to keep a dog of a different breed (one that they considered safe and gentle) the court found that they had provided a reasonable accommodation to the tenant.

The type of animal is an issue that is sometimes considered in determining whether it is necessary to provide a reasonable accommodation. The *Auburn Woods* case discussed above provides a good example of a court finding that it would be a reasonable accommodation to allow a condominium unit owner to have a dog, rather than a cat. Cats were permitted under the rules of the association but in that case, due to the allergies of the unit owner, having a cat was not feasible.

This chapter has focused on using dogs as service animals but other species of animals are used as well. Cats are commonly used as psychological support animals. Monkeys, miniature horses, potbellied pigs and birds have also been used as service animals. Just as with dogs and cats, the key to determining if a reasonable accommodation must be made allowing a more unusual service animal in housing is whether the animal is necessary for the plaintiff to be able to use and enjoy the premises.

Once an animal is in the housing, the person with the disability may be required to follow reasonable rules or standards regarding that animal. If the health or safety of other residents is put at risk, courts will not require the property owner to allow the animal to stay on the premises. Examples would include the inability to follow rules relating to walking a dog in designated areas, or in a recent case, prohibiting a tenant who had snakes, from carrying the snakes around loosely in common areas and not confining the snakes when maintenance and other property management employees were on the premises.[55]

The final issue relating to the limits of reasonable accommodations relates to financial requirements. It is important to note that under the FHA, the tenant is responsible for any expenses due to modifications within the unit. In practice, it is not worth the risk of a lawsuit for a landlord to require a pet fee or pet deposit relating to a service animal. HUD decisions and consent orders have enjoined landlords from charging a handicapped tenant a deposit for maintaining an auxiliary aid (such as a service dog) in a unit. In addition, state anti-discrimination laws may specifically provide that no pet fee or pet deposit may be required for service animals.[56]

If a landlord wants to take the risk of an administrative action or litigation, there is some precedence that it may not be necessary to make a financial accommodation for a person with a disability under federal law. It is well established by case law that the FHA does not prohibit discrimination based on financial status. The waiver of a fee in general will be judged on the same basis as any other reasonable accommodation. The key is whether the waiver of the fee is necessary to afford a resident the opportunity to use and enjoy the dwelling.

5. Damages Available Under the FHA

A reason for potential defendants to be concerned with complying with the FHA is that substantial damages can be awarded if a violation is found to have occurred. Relief may include actual and punitive damages, injunctions and attorney's fees at the discretion of the court.[57] Damages may include awards for emotional distress.

The FHA and similar state laws provide significant protection for persons with a disability who use a service animal. The requirement that there is a nexus between the animal and disability as well as the (albeit somewhat unsettled) issue that the animal is individually trained, serve to assuage any concerns that the FHA will be used improperly by persons who simply desire to have a companion animal in their housing in violation of a no-pet rule.

CONCLUSION

As illustrated by this chapter, there are significant restrictions on the ability to keep companion animals in housing. It is common for rental housing leases to include a no-pets clause. Even when a person owns his or her unit in a condominium, a no-pets clause may still apply. In single-family dwellings restrictive covenants may limit the number and type of animals. Of course, municipal ordinances providing for similar restrictions apply to all forms of housing in a community. The federal rules allowing for persons to have animals in housing apply only to a small class of persons or particular types of housing.

Housing providers and jurisdictions need to become more thoughtful in their regulation of animals. It is not logical to impose no-pets clauses, pet limit laws or breed specific legislation when it is not clear that there is a benefit to the community or protection for the animals. State or local laws that delineate when a no-pets clause can be enforced or that protect the ability to have companion animals on owned premises indicate that there is a change in how society perceives the value of these animals. Given that the value that humans place on these animals has increased, the law should also be revised to reflect the new status of these animals. Changes can be made now within the current legal system that can significantly impact many human and nonhuman animals' lives.

* Professor of Law, Valparaiso University School of Law. The author thanks Taimie Bryant for her efforts to produce this book and for her comments on earlier drafts of my chapter.

1. The rest of this chapter will use the imprecise, but common term of "animals" when referring to nonhuman animals.

2. For citations to the studies referenced in this chapter on the domestication of animals and further discussion on this topic, see Rebecca J. Huss, *Separation, Custody, and Estate Planning Issues Relating to Companion Animals*, 74 U. Colo. L. Rev. 181, 188–94 (2003).

3. Unless otherwise indicated, all polling and survey data referenced in this chapter can be found in Am. Pet Prods. Mfrs. Ass'n, 2005–2006 APPMA National Pet Owners Survey (2006).

4. For more information about no-pets provisions in leases, see Rebecca J. Huss, *No Pets Allowed: Housing Issues and Companion Animals*, 11 Animal L. 69, 98–110 (2005).

5. N.Y. City, N.Y. Admin. Code § 27–2009.1(b) (2006).

6. 492 A.2d 385 (N.J. Super. Ct. App. Div. 1985).

7. N.J. Rev. Stat. § 2A:18–61.1 (2006).

8. For a discussion of cases that interpret the documents and rules applicable to condominiums, see Huss, *supra* note 4, at 103–08.

9. 878 P.2d 1275 (Cal. 1994).

10. *Id*. at 1278. The restriction permitted residents to keep domestic fish and birds. *Id*.

11. Cal. Civ. Code § 1354(a) (West 2004).

12. *Nahrstedt*, 878 P.2d at 1283.

13. *Id*. at 1292–97.

14. *Id*. at 1295.

15. 679 N.E. 2d 407 (Ill. App. Ct. 1997).

16. 847 So. 2d 1012 (Fla. Dist. Ct. App. 2003).

17. *Id*. at 1013.

18. *Id*. at 1014.

19. Cal. Civ. Code §§ 1360.5, 798.33 (West 2006).

20. 544 S.E.2d 153 (Ga. 2001).

21. *Id*. at 154.

22. 631 N.W.2d 213 (S.D. 2001).

23. *Id*. at 218.

24. 425 N.E.2d 33 (Ill. App. Ct. 1981) (analyzing the validity of Carpentersville, Ill., Village Code § 15–23) (current version at Carpentersville, Ill., Village Code § 6.08.190 (2006)).

25. 510 Ill. Comp. Stat. Ann. 70/2.10 (West 2006).

26. IND. CODE § 6–9–39 (2006). The maximum tax is $5.00 per year for dogs six months or older with special provisions for dogs kept in kennels for breeding, boarding or training purposes.

27. Note that Federal law may also restrict the ability of a person to keep certain types of wild or exotic animals. An example of recent action in this area is the adoption in 2003 of the Captive Wildlife Safety Act, 16 U.S.C. §§ 3371–3378 (2000), that, among other things, prohibits the transportation of certain big cats across state lines. An example of a state that restricts keeping wild animals as pets is New York. *See* N.Y. ENVTL. CONSERV. LAW § 11–0512 (McKinney 2005).

28. 723 So. 2d 1288 (Ala. Civ. App. 1998).

29. 639 A.2d 1296 (Pa. Commw. Ct. 1994).

30. *Id.* at 1300.

31. 987 P.2d 430 (Okla. Civ. App. 1999).

32. 12 U.S.C. § 1701r–1 (2000).

33. *See* 24 C.F.R. §§ 5.300–5.380 (2006).

34. N.J. STAT. ANN. §§ 2A:42–103–2A:42–111 (West 2006).

35. CAL. HEALTH & SAFETY CODE § 19901 (West 2006).

36. 42 U.S.C. § 1437z–3 (2000). The Pet Ownership in Public Housing provision became effective on October 1, 1999 and the rules implementing it were effective on August 9, 2000. *Id.*

37. 24 C.F.R. §§ 960.701–960.707 (2006).

38. 42 U.S.C. §§ 3601–3619 (2000).

39. 24 C.F.R. § 100.204(b) (2006).

40. 42 U.S.C. § 3602(h) (2000).

41. No. 04–169–P–S, 2005 WL 758463 (D. Me. Mar. 11, 2005).

42. No. 961591, 1996 WL 1186942 (Mass. Super. Ct. May 6, 1996).

43. *Id.* at *3.

44. 28 C.F.R. § 36.104 (2006).

45. Green v. Housing Authority of Clackamas County, 994 F.Supp. 1253, 1256 (D. Or. 1998).

46. *In re* Kenna Homes Coop. Corp., 557 S.E.2d 787 (W. Va. 2001).

47. 304 F. Supp. 2d 1245 (D. Haw. 2003), *aff'd sub nom.* Dubois v. Ass'n of Apartment Owners of 2987 Kalakaua, 453 F.3d 1175 (9th Cir. 2006).

48. *Id.* at 1257.

49. *Id.*

50. *Id.* at 1256.

51. 121 Cal. App. 4th 1578 (Cal. Ct. App. 2004).

52. *Id.* at 1596.

53. Order Granting Preliminary Injunction and Requiring Bond, Zapata v. Lowe, No. C 02–02543 (N.D. Cal. Aug. 7, 2002).

54. *Id.* at 12.

55. Assenberg v. Anacortes Hous. Auth., No. C05–1836RSL, 2006 WL 1515603 (W.D. Wash. May 25, 2006).

56.　775 ILL. COMP. STAT. ANN. 5/3–104.1(C) (West 2001).

57.　42 U.S.C. §§ 3612–3613 (2000).

CALIFORNIA CONDOMINIUM PROVISION
CAL. CIV. CODE ANN. § 1360.5 (West 2006).

(a) No governing documents shall prohibit the owner of a separate interest within a common interest development from keeping at least one pet within the common interest development, subject to reasonable rules and regulations of the association. This section may not be construed to affect any other rights provided by law to an owner of a separate interest to keep a pet within the development.

(b) For purposes of this section, "pet" means any domesticated bird, cat, dog, aquatic animal kept within an aquarium, or other animal as agreed to between the association and the homeowner.

(c) If the association implements a rule or regulation restricting the number of pets an owner may keep, the new rule or regulation shall not apply to prohibit an owner from continuing to keep any pet that the owner currently keeps in his or her separate interest if the pet otherwise conforms with the previous rules or regulations relating to pets.

(d) For the purposes of this section, "governing documents" shall include, but are not limited to, the conditions, covenants, and restrictions of the common interest development, and the bylaws, rules, and regulations of the association.

(e) This section shall become operative on January 1, 2001, and shall only apply to governing documents entered into, amended, or otherwise modified on or after that date.

Chapter 6

ESTATE PLANNING TO PROVIDE FOR THE POST-DEATH CARE OF PETS

IN RE ESTATE OF RUSSELL
69 Cal.2d 200, 70 Cal.Rptr. 561, 444 P.2d 353 (Cal. 1968).

SULLIVAN, A.J.

Georgia Nan Russell Hembree appeals from a judgment entered in proceedings for the determination of heirship decreeing inter alia that under the terms of the will of Thelma L. Russell, deceased, all of the residue of her estate should be distributed to Chester H. Quinn.

Thelma L. Russell died testate on September 8, 1965, leaving a validly executed holographic will written on a small card. The front of the card reads:

'Turn the card
March 18–1957

I leave everything
I own Real &
Personal to Chester
H. Quinn & Roxy Russell
Thelma L. Russell'

The reverse side reads:

'My ($10.) Ten dollar gold
Piece & diamonds I leave to Georgia Nan Russell.
Alverata, Geogia (sic).'

Chester H. Quinn was a close friend and companion of testatrix, who for over 25 years prior to her death had resided in one of the living units on her property and had stood in a relation of personal trust and confidence toward here. Roxy Russell was testatrix' pet dog which was alive on the date of the execution of testatrix' will but predeceased her.[2] Plaintiff is testatrix' niece and her only heir-at-law.

2. Actually the record indicates the existence of two Roxy Russells. The original Roxy was an Airedale dog which testatrix owned at the time she made her will, but which, according to Quinn, died after having had a fox tail removed from its nose, and which, according to the testimony of one Arthur Turner, owner of a pet cemetery, was buried on June 9, 1958. Roxy was replaced with another dog (breed not indi-

In her petition for determination of heirship plaintiff alleges, inter alia, that 'Roxy Russell is an Airedale dog'; that section 27 enumerates those entitled to take by will; that 'Dogs are not included among those listed in * * * Section 27. Not even Airedale dogs'; that the gift of one-half of the residue of testatrix' estate to Roxy Russell is invalid and void; and that plaintiff was entitled to such one-half as testatrix' sole heir-at-law.

At the hearing on the petition, plaintiff introduced without objection extrinsic evidence establishing that Roxy Russell was testatrix' Airedale dog which died on June 9, 1958. To this end plaintiff, in addition to an independent witness, called defendant. * * * Upon redirect examination, counsel for Quinn then sought to introduce evidence of the latter's relationship with testatrix 'in the event that your Honor feels that there is any necessity for further ascertainment of the intent above and beyond the document.' Plaintiff's objections on the ground that it was inadmissible under the statute of wills and the parol evidence rule 'because there is no ambiguity.' * * * Over plaintiff's objection, counsel for Quinn also introduced certain documentary evidence consisting of testatrix' address book and a certain quitclaim deed 'for the purpose of demonstrating the intention on the part of the deceased that she not die intestate.' Of all this extrinsic evidence only the following infinitesimal portion of Quinn's testimony relates to care of the dog: 'Q (Counsel for Quinn) Prior to the first Roxy's death did you ever discuss with Miss Russell taking care of Roxy if anything should ever happen to her? A Yes.' * * *

The trial court found, so far as is here material, that it was the intention of testatrix 'that CHESTER H. QUINN was to receive her entire estate, excepting the gold coin and diamonds bequeathed to' plaintiff and that Quinn 'was to care for the dog, ROXY RUSSELL, in the event of Testatrix's death. The language contained in the Will concerning the dog, ROXY RUSSELL, was precatory in nature only, and merely indicative of the wish, desire and concern of Testatrix that CHESTER H. QUINN was to care for the dog, ROXY RUSSELL, subsequent to Testatrix's death.' The court concluded that testatrix intended to and did make an absolute and outright gift to Mr. Quinn of all the residue of her estate, adding: 'There occurred no lapse as to any portion of the residuary gift to CHESTER H. QUINN by reason of the language contained in the Will concerning the dog, ROXY RUSSELL, such language not having the effect of being an attempted outright gift or gift in trust to the dog. The effect of such language is merely to indicate the intention of Testatrix that CHESTER H. QUINN was to take the entire residuary estate and to use whatever portion thereof as might be necessary to care for and maintain the dog, ROXY RUSSELL.' Judgment was entered accordingly. This appeal followed.

* * *

First, as we have said many times: 'The paramount rule in the construction of wills, to which all other rules must yield, is that a will is

cated in the record before us) which, although it answered to the name Roxy, was, according to the record, in fact registered with the American Kennel Club as 'Russel's [sic] Royal Kick Roxy.'

to be construed according to the intention of the testator as expressed therein, and this intention must be given effect as far as possible.' (*Estate of Wilson* (1920) 184 Cal. 63, 66–67.) [Citations omitted.] The rule is imbedded in [section 101 of] the Probate Code. * * *

When the language of a will is ambiguous or uncertain resort may be had to extrinsic evidence in order to ascertain the intention of the testator. * * *

* * *

Examining testatrix' will in the light of the foregoing rules, we arrive at the following conclusions: Extrinsic evidence offered by plaintiff was admitted without objection and indeed would have been properly admitted over objection to raise and resolve the latent ambiguity as to Roxy Russell and ultimately to establish that Roxy Russell was a dog. Extrinsic evidence of the surrounding circumstances[20] was properly considered in order to ascertain what testatrix meant by the words of the will, including the words: 'I leave everything I own Real & Personal to Chester H. Quinn & Roxy Russell' or as those words can now be read 'to Chester H. Quinn and my dog Roxy Russell.'

However, viewing the will in the light of the surrounding circumstances as are disclosed by the record, we conclude that the will cannot reasonably be construed as urged by Quinn and determined by the trial court as providing that testatrix intended to make an absolute and outright gift of the entire residue of her estate to Quinn who was 'to use whatever portion thereof as might be necessary to care for and maintain the dog.' No words of the will give the entire residuum to Quinn, much less indicate that the provisions for the dog is merely precatory in nature. Such an interpretation is not consistent with a disposition which by its language leaves the residuum in equal shares to Quinn and the dog. A disposition in equal shares to two beneficiaries cannot be equated with a disposition of the whole to one of them who may use 'whatever portion thereof as might be necessary' on behalf of the other. (See [Probate Code §] 104; cf. *Estate of Kearns* (1950) 36 Cal.2d 531, 534–536.) Neither can the bare language of a gift of one-half of the residue to the dog be so expanded as to mean a gift to Quinn in trust for the care of the dog, there being no words indicating an enforceable duty upon Quinn to do so or indicating to whom the trust property is to go upon termination of the trust. 'While no particular form of expression is necessary for the creation of a trust, nevertheless some expression of intent to that end is requisite.' (*Estate of Doane* (1923) 190 Cal. 412, 415; [Probate Code §] 104 [remaining citations omitted].)

Accordingly, since in the light of the extrinsic evidence introduced below, the terms of the will are not reasonably susceptible of the meaning claimed by Quinn to have been intended by testatrix, the extrinsic evidence offered to show such an intention should have been excluded by the trial court. Upon an independent examination of the will we conclude that the trial court's interpretation of the terms thereof was

---

20. Excluding however the oral declarations of testatrix as to her intentions. * * * It is to be noted that no such declarations are herein involved.

erroneous. Interpreting the provisions relating to testatrix' residuary estate in accordance with the only meaning to which they are reasonably susceptible, we conclude that testatrix intended to make a disposition of all of the residue of the estate to Quinn and the dog in equal shares; therefore, as tenants in common. As a dog cannot be the beneficiary under a will the attempted gift to Roxy Russell is void.[22]

There remains only the necessity of determining the effect of the void gift to the dog upon the disposition of the residuary estate. That portion of any residuary estate that is the subject of a lapsed gift to one of the residuary beneficiaries remains undisposed of by the will and passes to the heirs. * * * We conclude that the residue of testatrix' estate should be distributed in equal shares to Chester H. Quinn and Georgia Nan Russell Hembree, testatrix' niece.

The judgment is reversed. * * *

CHIEF JUSTICE TRAYNOR, and JUSTICES PETERS, TOBRINER, MOSK, and BURKE, concur.

* * *

22. As a consequence, the fact that Roxy Russell predeceased the testatrix is of no legal import. As appears, we have disposed of the issue raised by plaintiff's frontal attack on the eligibility of the dog to take a testamentary gift and therefore need not concern ourselves with the novel question as to whether the death of the dog during the lifetime of the testatrix resulted in a lapsed gift.

IN RE SEARIGHT'S ESTATE
87 Ohio App. 417, 95 N.E.2d 779 (1950).

HUNSICKER, JUDGE.

George P. Searight, a resident of Wayne county, Ohio, died testate on November 27, 1948. Item "third" of his will provided:

I give and bequeath my dog, Trixie, to Florence Hand of Wooster, Ohio, and I direct my executor to deposit in the Peoples Federal Savings and Loan Association, Wooster, Ohio, the sum of $1000.00 to be used by him to pay Florence Hand at the rate of 75 cents per day for the keep and care of my dog as long as it shall live. If my dog shall die before the said $1000.00 and the interest accruing therefrom shall have been used up, I give and bequeath whatever remains of said $1000.00 to be divided equally among those of the following persons who are living at that time, to wit: Bessie Immler, Florence Hand, Reed Searight, Fern Olson and Willis Horn.

At the time of his death, all of the persons, and his dog, Trixie, named in such item third, were living.

Florence Hand accepted the bequest of Trixie, and the executor paid to her from the $1000 fund, 75 cents a day for the keep and care of the dog. The value of Trixie was agreed to be $5.

The Probate Court made a determination of inheritance tax due from the estate of George P. Searight, deceased, the pertinent part of this judgment reading as follows:

The court further finds that the value of the dog Trixie is taxable as a succession to Florence Hand; that the said dog inherits the sum of $1000.00 with power to consume both the interest and principal at a limited rate; that the state of Ohio, Sec. 5332, levying a tax on successions to property does not levy a tax upon the succession to any property passing to an animal; that the $1000.00 bequest to said dog is therefore not taxable; that the remainder of the $1000.00, if any, remaining after the death of said dog is taxable in the hands of the remaindermen * * *

The Department of Taxation of Ohio appeals to this court from such judgment....

The questions presented by this appeal on questions of law are:

1. Is the testamentary bequest for the care of Trixie (a dog) valid in Ohio—(a) as a proper subject of a so-called 'honorary trust'? (b) as not being in violation of the rule against perpetuities?

2. Is the bequest set forth in item third of testator's will subject to the inheritance tax laws of Ohio?

* * *

[1(a).]

In 1 Scott on the Law of Trusts, Section 124, the author says:

There are certain classes of cases similar to those discussed in the preceding section in that there is no one who as beneficiary can enforce the purpose of the testator, but different in one respect, namely, that the purpose is definite. Such, for example, are bequests for the erection or maintenance of tombstones or monuments or for the care of graves, and bequests for the support of specific animals. It has been held in a number of cases that such bequests as these do not necessarily fail. It is true that the legatee cannot be compelled to carry out the intended purpose, since there is no one to whom he owes a duty to carry out the purpose.

Even though the legatee cannot be compelled to apply the property to the designated purpose, the courts have very generally held that he can properly do so, and that no resulting trust arises so long as he is ready and willing to carry it out. The legatee will not, however, be permitted to retain the property for his own benefit; and if he refuses or neglects to carry out the purpose, a resulting trust will arise in favor of the testator's residuary legatee or next of kin.

* * *

The object and purpose sought to be accomplished by the testator in the instant case is not capricious or illegal. He sought to effect a worthy purpose—the care of his pet dog.

Whether we designate the gift in this case as an 'honorary trust' or a gift with a power which is valid when exercised is not important, for we do know that the one to whom the dog was given accepted the gift and indicated her willingness to care for such dog, and the executor proceeded to carry out the wishes of the testator.

* * * [T]he transferee has power to apply the property to the designated purpose, unless he is authorized by the terms of the intended trust so to apply the property beyond the period of the rule against perpetuities, or the purpose is capricious.' I Restatement of the Law of Trusts, Section 124.

* * *

[1(b).]

Restatement of the Law of Property, Section 374 states the maximum period allowed by the rule against perpetuities as:

(a) lives of persons who are

(i) in being at the commencement of such period, and

(ii) neither so numerous nor so situated that evidence of their deaths is likely to be unreasonably difficult to obtain; and

(b) twenty-one years. * * *

This same text, with reference to the application of such rule to 'honorary trusts,' says, at Section 379:

A limitation of property on an intended trust is invalid when * * *

(a) the conveyee is to administer the property for the accomplishment of a specific noncharitable purpose and there is no definite or definitely ascertainable beneficiary designated; and

(b) such administration can continue for longer than the maximum period described in Section 374 * * *

The lives, in being, which are the measure of the period set out in the rule against perpetuities, must be determined from the creating instrument.

If we then examine item third of testator's will, we discover that, although the bequest for his dog is for 'as long as it shall live,' the money given for this purpose is $1000 payable at the rate of 75c a day. By simple mathematical computation, this sum of money, expended at the rate determined by the testator, will be fully exhausted in three years and 238–1/3 days. If we assume that this $1000 is deposited in a bank so that interest at the high rate of 6% per annum were earned thereon, the time needed to consume both principal and interest thereon (based on semi-annual computation of such interest on the average unused balance during such six month period) would be four years, 57 1/2 days.

It is thus very apparent that the testator provided a time limit for the exercise of the power given his executor, and that such time limit is much less than the maximum period allowed under the rule against perpetuities.

* * *

We therefore conclude that the bequest in the instant case for the care of the dog, Trixie, does not, by the terms of the creating instrument, violate the rule against perpetuities.

[2.]

We next consider the problem of the inheritance tax, if any, to be levied on the bequest contained in item third of testator's will.

Section 5332, General Code, says, in part:

A tax is hereby levied upon the succession to any property passing, in trust or otherwise, to or for the use of a person, institution or corporation * * *

* * *

This statute determines that a tax shall be levied upon succession to all property passing to a person, institution or corporation. Certainly, a dog is neither an institution nor a corporation. Can it be successfully contended that a dog is a person? A "person" is defined as "3. A human being." Webster's New International Dictionary, Second Edition.

We have hereinabove indicated that the bequest for the dog, Trixie, comes within the designation of an "honorary trust," and, as such, is proper in the instant case. A tax based on the amount expended for the care of the dog cannot lawfully be levied against the monies so expended, since it is not property passing for the use of a "person, institution or corporation."

* * *

We therefore conclude that no succession tax may be levied against such funds as are expended by the executor in carrying out the power granted to him by item third of testator's will.

The judgment of the Probate Court is affirmed.

ESTATE PLANNING TO PROVIDE FOR THE POST-DEATH CARE OF PETS

William A. Reppy, Jr.*

INTRODUCTION

The law of trusts and wills in the main is consistent with other areas of the law in viewing a living, breathing animal as just another piece of personal property subject to ownership and disposition, like a chair, book, or television set. This is generally the case even though the animal at issue has been for its whole life a beloved pet, considered by its owner as a dear friend or a member of the owner's family.

One exception to this approach is found in a string of trial court decisions—beginning in the 1960's—invalidating as against public policy a will provision calling for the decedent's executor to have surviving pets put to death. In sparing these animals' lives, the judges in these cases have recognized that a dog or cat or horse is a unique kind of property, not the same as an inanimate table or automobile. This development is discussed in detail in this chapter.

Compared to will directives to end pets' lives when their owners die, there clearly are more instances in which owners seek to keep their pets alive by the provision of funds for their pets' care after the owner dies. However, owners' efforts to set up trusts for their pets have met with resistance from probate judges unwilling to validate such trusts. Much of this chapter describes those judicially created obstacles and attorneys' and legislatures' responses to those obstacles. Due to those obstacles, attempting to assist clients who wish to establish pet trusts requires considerable effort and attention to arcane features of trust law. Indeed, the two cases excerpted at the outset of this chapter reveal that even a seemingly simple desire to provide for the future care of a pet involves highly complex legal concepts such as "perpetuities," "lapsed legacies," and the kind of "extrinsic evidence" that can be examined in interpreting a will provision dealing with pets. The text below will address this complex material, but we begin with some basic considerations: for instance, is there a public policy recognized by the law that precludes the use of wills to order the deaths of pets that survive their owners? What would be the source of such a public policy? Would it arise from the anticruelty statutes that have been enacted in all the American states? If not, may judges create a judicially-enforced public policy that gives more protection to animals than such anticruelty statutes would give? Through an examination of extant case law concerning the will directives of pet owners, we shall see that the cases to date create law very favorable to pets.

We shall also see, however, that animals fare poorly when courts consider attempts to create trusts for their benefit, even if the failure of such a trust would increase the risk that an animal will be put to death when the animal's owner dies. Under the common law a court would not enforce a will attempting to create a true trust to care for animals.

Where a non-mandatory "trust" has been set out in a will to a pet, the courts applied a standard rule for limiting the perpetual burdening of property—the infamously complex common law Rule Against Perpetuities—in a way that prevented such trusts from being valid, even though such decisions were not compelled by precedent. The common law Rule Against Perpetuities required that, to be valid at all, we must be able to predict with certainty that future interests in property will vest or fail within 21 years of the death of some life in being at the time the future interest was created. Only humans who were alive at the time a future interest was created could be "measuring" lives for purposes of testing the validity of a future interest. If it could be shown that a future interest might vest outside that "perpetuities period" of 21 years past the death of a "life in being at the time of the conveyance," then the future interest was immediately invalidated; no future interest was created because of the possibility that it *might* not vest or fail "in time." In the case of unenforceable trusts to benefit animals,—called honorary trusts—the duration of the trust had to be measured by reference to the life span of human individuals alive when the instrument under which payments were to be made to benefit animals became effective, plus an additional 21 years. Courts applying this duration limit seemed to understand that the animals to be benefited were living creatures that had life expectancies. Yet the courts forbade measuring the duration of the honorary trust for their benefit by the animals' own life spans. Only human lives could be used in determining the permissible duration of honorary trusts for animals. It is true that an honorary trust for a parrot might last, if measured by the bird's life, longer than it could if human lives were used to fix the duration. But the cases barring use of animal lives to measure duration dealt not with long-lived creatures like parrots and tortoises, but with pets like dogs whose life spans are shorter than the average for humans.

Having held that the benefited pets cannot supply the measuring lives for measuring honorary trust duration, the courts should have fixed the maximum duration as the life-span of the human being appointed by the will to apply funds for care of the pets. Inexplicably, however, some decisions ignored the fact that the human being named in the will as "trustee" had a life expectancy that, under the Rule Against Perpetuities, could be used to measure the duration of the honorary trust. The courts might also have allowed the trusts to run for 21 years after the death of the testator who created the interest for his or her pet. However, courts declined to follow either course. Consequently, there were *no* measuring lives to be used to apply the Rule Against Perpetuities. These attempted trusts failed, and the animals sought to be benefited were the losers.

In sum, the common law of trusts and wills has in large measure developed—unnecessarily—in ways that are not hospitable to animals. There have been some changes in trust law that allow owners to provide for the care of their pets under some circumstances, but trust law has not developed sufficiently to allow owners to insure the future care of their pets. It is the lawyer's duty to effectuate the intent of the client within the bounds of law. Lawyers interested in helping animals, as well as clients who care for animals, must work within relatively narrow limits when it comes to creating trusts. This chapter will first consider positive legal developments for animals in the form of invalidating owners' requests that their animals be euthanized upon the owners' deaths. The chapter next considers, by contrast, the limitations on owners who seek the opposite—to provide for their pets after the owners' deaths. Finally, the chapter will conclude with an examination of several mechanisms available today to provide for the care of pets both before and after the deaths of their owners.

WILL DIRECTIVES PROVIDING FOR THE EUTHANASIA OF PETS UPON THE DEATH OF THEIR OWNERS: LEGAL DEVELOPMENTS AND ETHICAL CONSIDERATIONS

On occasion the owner of one or more pets wishes to provide that, upon the owner's death, the animals will be euthanized. The reasons an owner includes this kind of a death-sentence provision in estate planning documents vary. The owner may believe that, after her death, the person appointed as her personal representative would be unable to find a new adoptive home where the decedent's pets would receive the same level of care that the decedent had provided. Or she may believe that a good home for her pets can be found after her death yet fear that circumstances could change, resulting in her animals being subjected to ill-treatment. The new owner could die leaving an heir who does not like pets and takes them to a "shelter," which in turn sells the client's beloved pets to a laboratory to be used in painful experiments. Or the owner may fear that a person who appears to be an excellent caretaker might not be or might undergo a change of personality due, perhaps, to mental illness, drug addiction, or falling into poverty, with the result that proper care is no longer provided to the animals.

Is a clause in a will void as against public policy when it directs that, upon the death of the owner, pets are not to be adopted out but instead promptly euthanized? Probably not in the case of a pet who is terminally ill. Less clear is the case of a pet that is healthy but very old. Let us focus on the most difficult case: the directive to kill a pet that is not only healthy but comparatively young.

Consistent with the common law, section 3–703 of the Uniform Probate Code (enacted in about half the states) provides that an executor "is under a duty to settle ... the estate of the decedent in accordance with the terms of any probated and effective will ... as expeditiously and efficiently as is consistent with the best interests of the estate."[1] But this kind of statute obviously assumes a lawful directive in the will. The executor surely may disregard a command in the decedent's will that he sell into slavery the decedent's young son. Similarly, a directive in the will that the executor take Fido, the dog, out into the countryside and abandon him there would also be illegal, as violative of criminal statutes against abandoning animals. What about a will directive to euthanize a healthy, young pet?

A. *State of the Case Law*

There is no precedent case—no reported appellate court decision—dealing with the public policy question raised by a directive to the executor to euthanize an adoptable pet. A few trial courts have decided that a directive in a will that a healthy pet be euthanized is void as against public policy.[2]

Whether the trial court decisions saving the decedent's pets from immediate death are legally—or even morally—correct should begin with an inquiry into whether any rule of law, such as the anticruelty statute enacted in each American state, prohibits the living, mentally healthy (that is, competent) owner of a pet from humanely killing the animal himself or having a veterinarian humanely destroy the animal without any good reason for its destruction. Again, there seems to be no precedent directly on point. In North Carolina, the anticruelty statute[3] criminalizes the "unjustifiable" killing of an animal, and the state's Supreme Court has stated in dictum that needless killing of chickens without torture would be a violation.[4]

But that dictum is unique. For most purposes the law treats a pet as inanimate personal property. One who owns such an inanimate object can legally destroy it—for example, burn it, or pound it into pieces—so long as the resulting debris is lawfully disposed of.

Here's what one treatise written for veterinarians has to say on the issue of euthanizing a healthy pet:

> Clients will sometimes ask veterinarians to euthanize a perfectly healthy animal. This may be morally repulsive to many veterinarians, but animals are legally classified as property. Therefore, the owner, under current law, still has the right to humanely bring about the death of that property.[5]

Of course, unlike a chair or automobile, a dog or cat or horse is animate property, property protected by the anticruelty statute. Many of these statutes, like North Carolina's, criminalize the "unjustifiable" killing of an animal,[6] or killing the animal "unnecessarily,"[7] with courts usually construing the latter term as meaning much the same as "unjustifiably." Suppose Mary Smith, owner of dog Rover (age 5 and healthy), is hospitalized with a terminal illness, unable personally to care for Rover any longer, although she has the funds to hire someone else to do so. Would you expect a court to hold that Mary's having Rover euthanized was a criminal act because the death was "unjustified"?[8] If so, would it not follow that the same public policy barring Mary from having the dog killed when she was dying in a hospital would bar her from having her executor do the killing immediately after her death?

Let's assume, however, that there may be situations where the state's anticruelty statute is not violated by a pet owner's decision to have the animal euthanized, although a new adoptive home could have been found for the animal. The trial court in a 1999 case from Vermont[9] assumed that the living owner of a horse could lawfully have the animal euthanized but held that some things a person can do himself while alive he cannot have done after death by directives in his will.[10] The Vermont judge cited a Missouri case in support of this holding, but that case does not clearly support the distinction drawn by the Vermont judge.[11] The will at issue in the Missouri case ordered the razing of a residence in good condition in a neighborhood that had been declared a historic landmark, with the court's opinion suggesting that because of this fact, destruction could have been enjoined if the owner had planned to do the razing while alive. The destruction of pets is not like the razing of buildings. Accordingly, this case does not support the conclusion that what a pet owner could do during life (kill his pet) may be different than what his will could direct his executor to do (kill his pet).

Does not the scope of a state's anticruelty statute lay out the state's public policy concerning the killing of animals? If the pet owner could, during the owner's life, euthanize his adoptable pet without violating any state or local anticruelty statute, would it not necessarily follow that the executor could euthanize the owner's adoptable pet if the owner so directed in his will? What is the best counter-argument to this argument?

Consider the language of California Penal code section 599e, enacted in 1905 and amended in 1963, which provides as follows:

> Every animal which is unfit, by reason of its physical condition, for the purpose for which such animals are usually employed, and when there is no reasonable probability of such animal ever becoming fit for the purpose of which it is usually employed, shall be by the owner or lawful possessor of the same, deprived of life within 12 hours after being notified by any peace officer, officer of said [humane] society, or employee of a pound or animal regulation department of a public agency who is a veterinarian, to kill the same ... ; provided, that this shall not apply to such owner keeping any old or diseased animal belonging to him on his own premises with proper care.[12]

Violation of California Penal Code section 599e is a misdemeanor. Does this provide any evidence of the public policy in California concerning the euthanasia of an unwanted animal? It is likely most judges would hold that it does, but the statute may be unconstitutional, at least in part. Suppose Joe, who lives in a city apartment, owns a horse, Dobbin, whom he has boarded for years on a friend's farm in the country. Dobbin is now so feeble he cannot be ridden, although the horse is not in pain when not being ridden. A policeman tells Joe to kill Dobbin. As a matter of substantive due process of law, can Joe be convicted of a crime and jailed for refusing to kill the horse and instead providing the aging Dobbin the very best care so that the horse can live the rest of his life in dignity? The law would seem to apply to Joe because he is not keeping Dobbin "on his own premises," but such an application of the California statute seems totally irrational.

It is more likely that a California court would look to California Penal Code section 599d to interpret Penal Code section 599e. Penal Code section 599d provides in pertinent part:

> (a) It is the policy of the state that no adoptable animal should be euthanized if it can be adopted into a suitable home ...

> (b) It is the policy of the state that no treatable animal should be euthanized. A treatable animal shall include any animal that is not adoptable but that could become adoptable with reasonable efforts. ....[13]

There are cases from Pennsylvania and California in which trial courts did not enforce will directives to euthanize healthy pets.[14] In these cases, the trial judges relied on the terminology of the state statute creating the right to make a will, not just the state's anticruelty statutes. In both cases, the applicable statute referred to the power to "dispose of" property by will. As stated by the California trial judge: "The word 'dispose' cannot be interpreted to mean that of destroying, damaging."[15] Did the court so hold as a matter of interpreting the word "dispose" as a general matter or because of the context of the case—"disposal" of a healthy pet?

Suppose John Jones wrote a will leaving all his property to his only close relative, a niece, Nancy, a very religious and conservative young woman. John had a collection of soft-core (hence legal) pornography. His will directed his executor to burn the pornography. It is hard to imagine a court holding that the word "dispose" in the jurisdiction's wills statute means this directive is illegal because burning is not an allowable type of "disposing" within the statute. The result of such a holding would be that if John wanted Nancy not to have the pornography distributed to her following his death, he would have to direct his executor to sell the collection rather than burn it or dump it in a landfill, to be destroyed there.

In the case from Pennsylvania[16] the directive in the decedent's will held to be invalid directed the executor to euthanize "any dog which I may own at the time of my death,"[17] rather than a specifically named or described pet. Such a clause seems even more unreasonable than one that refers to a specific animal, living at the time the owner was writing her will, along with a statement of reasons given by the testatrix as to why she doubts a good home can be found for that specific pet after her death. Directing the death of *any* pet the testatrix *might own* before her death seems contrary to public policy because it would apply to an animal whose adoptability the testatrix could not have assessed.

An attorney wishing to carry out the client's request to provide in the client's will for euthanizing an unhealthy or unadoptable pet would be well advised to state in the will the client's reasons for the decision. Such will directives may seal the demise of impacted pets, because even if it could be proved in court after the pet owner's death that her stated belief that the pet was "unadoptable" was wrong, judicial relief for the pet on that basis is very unlikely. Apparently, a provision in a will making a bequest or other testamentary deposition has never been held invalid on a "mistake of fact" theory.

If a court holds invalid as against public policy a clause in the will of Tess Testatrix directing her executrix to have her 10–year-old but healthy dog Snoopy—who had lived outdoors—euthanized, what happens to Snoopy? Suppose the will, after providing for the killing of the dog, went on to state: "I leave to my sister Sue my home at 123 Ledge Lane and the personal property located therein, and the rest and residue of my estate to my alma mater ABC University." Should the court give an artificial interpretation of the bequest of the personal property inside the home to include Snoopy so that Sue gets the dog? Or should the university get him? What is ABC University likely to do with Snoopy?

In the case from Pennsylvania,[18] after holding invalid the directive in the decedent's will to have two Irish setters killed, the trial court ordered the adoption of the two dogs. The identity of the residuary legatee is not specifically stated in the court's opinion, although there is some hint it was a humane organization. Could such an order be made without the approval of the residuary legatee (or heir, if there is no residuary clause in the will)? In the case of Snoopy, ABC University probably would consent to an adoption order, but may not if a researcher at the school thought the dog well-suited for a scientific experiment in his classroom laboratory.

In the California case of a death-sentence-by-will for a specific pet,[19] the state Legislature passed a special bill[20] interpreting the decedent's will, contrary to its plain language, as not calling for destruction of the dog if an excellent adoptive home could be found for it. Surely such a statute is unconstitutional under any view of the state constitution's provisions for separation of powers between the legislative and judicial branches. Interpreting a will is obviously a judicial and not a legislative function. A generally applicable law invalidating all pet-kill clauses in wills in situations where an adoptive home could be found for the animal at issue would not invade the judicial function of courts. Moreover, it is very likely that it could apply retroactively to the wills of decedents who died before the new statute was passed, because the United States Supreme Court has been extremely liberal in permitting legislatures to enact statutes that apply retroactively.[21]

B.   *Ethical Considerations for Attorney–Drafters*

Consider the ethical implications of the following hypothetical estate planning strategy. Attorney Ann Adams is told by Client to draft a will directing the executor to euthanize Client's cat Tabby and dog Fido, upon Client's death. Ann asks Client to find out if Client's veterinarian, Vic Vernon, is willing to euthanize the animals if asked to do so, and Client reports that he is. Ann now proposes that the will not reveal on its face the decedent's intent to have her pets destroyed upon her death but instead just bequeath them to Vic, who will have been paid in advance by Client the fee for euthanizing the animals and has agreed to do so (in his capacity as new owner). Ann explains to Client that if the will on its face provided for the killing of the pets, an attack on it might be made in court, and estate funds would be consumed in paying legal fees to defend the will provision. Ann's plan seeks to avoid such expenditure. First, is this a workable plan? What facts might cause it to fail? Second, is it ethical?

Rule 1.2(d) of the American Bar Association's Model Rules of Professional Conduct prohibits a lawyer from assisting in conduct that is "fraudulent," a term broadly defined in comment 5 to this rule to include in some situations of "withholding information from a court."[22] An annotation to Rule 8.4(c) states that a lawyer's "[d]eceiving third parties"[23]—that could include deceiving humane activists who would seek to enjoin the euthanizing of a healthy pet—can be an ethics violation. But comment 6 to Rule 1.2(d) also makes clear there is no fraud if the lawyer acts based on his or her "making a good faith determination"[24] that the law authorizes the activity. Apparently, then, Ann could not be guilty of an ethics violation if she drafted the bequest of the pets to Vic after having concluded in good faith, based on precedent in the state, that Client could lawfully have Tabby and Fido euthanized while Client was alive and that the trial court decisions concerning euthanasia directives in a will erred in holding the pet owner could not achieve the same end through her will.

Is it a violation of legal ethics rules for Ann—despite her good faith belief—to try to hide from concerned persons and from the probate court judge a plan of action that has been enjoined by several trial courts as contrary to public policy? Does it matter whether Ann is practicing in Pennsylvania, Vermont, or another state where such trial court decisions have been rendered? Keep in mind; trial court decisions are not binding precedent.

If the will contains a directive to euthanize the decedent's pets, who has standing to seek a court order declaring the clause invalid as against public policy? In the Vermont case,[25] the public policy issue was raised by an intervener, an unincorporated association entitled Coalition to Save Brand's Horses. Members of the Coalition included the state's primary humane organizations and an individual who was a prior owner of one of the horses to be killed. If you have studied the issue of standing to enforce statutes enacted to protect animals, this grant of standing may seem surprising. However, standing to intervene in the probate of wills is controlled by state rules that differ from rules about standing under state criminal anticruelty statutes or federal animal protection laws.

If an ethical standard needs to be formulated to restrict the power of a decedent by will to direct that his or her surviving pets be euthanized, are not veterinarians best suited for the job? The American Veterinary Medical Association ("AVMA"), the veterinarian's equivalent to the American Bar Association, has not yet taken a firm position, and as a result an executor directed by a will to have pets killed can find a veterinarian willing to do it.

As of March 2007, the AVMA's official website did no more than discourage unnecessary euthanasia:

> Economic, emotional, and space limitations or changes in life-style ... may force an owner to consider euthanasia of a pet, but it is better to find another solution or an alternative home for these pets. Euthanasia should be considered only when another alternative is not available.[26]

On the same website, which is directed to practicing veterinarians, the AVMA's "policy statement" on the issue of *Euthanasia of Unwanted Animals* declares that

> [t]he AVMA is not opposed to the euthanasia of unwanted animals when appropriate, by properly trained personnel, using acceptable humane methods.[27]

Suppose a state regulatory agency adopted the "when appropriate" test in a rule found in official regulations governing unprofessional conduct by veterinarians, violations of which could result in loss of one's state license to practice veterinary medicine. Veterinarian Velma euthanizes healthy, 4–year-old cat Muffin brought to Velma's clinic by the executor of the will of Muffin's recently deceased owner, after the executor shows Velma that the probated will directs the euthanasia of Muffin. Would a court of law uphold or set aside an order of the state regulatory agency stripping Velma of her veterinarian's license based on a finding that euthanasia of Muffin was not "appropriate" due to the cat's age and health? Velma could argue that the "when appropriate" standard is far too vague to provide her the notice of what she is not to do, as required by the due process clause of the Fourteenth Amendment to the U.S. Constitution and maybe the constitution of her state as well. Unless before Velma acted there existed published rulings by the administrative body that enforced the rules concerning unprofessional conduct by veterinarians that provided guidance as to what the vague term "when appropriate" meant, Velma is likely to prevail.

Pet Trusts

Just as one would expect, the reported cases indicate more pet owners seek to provide for their pets than to kill them. Far more common than a will provision calling for the killing of a pet is one that seeks to set up a bequest of money or other assets to care for pets after the death of the testator. Such clauses raise many difficult legal issues, but we begin with a rather basic one dealing with the process by which a court determines the intent of the decedent as to how the assets at issue are to be handled. The text below considers, in part, whether *Estate of Russell*,[28] the California case excerpted above, requires more clarity in expression in providing by will for care of pets than would be demanded if the bequest sought to care for an infant or a severely disabled adult human.

A.   Obstacles to Drafting and Construction of Express Pet Trusts

   1.   How to Show Intent

   "I leave everything I own to my friend Chester and my dog Roxy."
This clause is similar to what testatrix Thelma Russell wrote in her
holographic will. It suggests Thelma wanted to do something for her dog,
yes? Amazingly, the trial court found that the language in the will
mentioning Roxy was only "precatory" (from the Latin verb *precar*, to
pray). According to the court, it merely showed Thelma's "wish, desire"
that Chester apply some of the money to the care of the dog; it did not
create a legal duty that Chester take care of Roxy. In other words, if the
language were merely precatory, Chester could spend all of Thelma's
property on himself alone while Roxy starved to death. Chester might
thereby violate the state's anticruelty statute, but he would not be
violating the terms of Thelma's will. Such usage would not cause Chester
to be divested of any part of the bequest to him of the entire estate. The
California Supreme Court quite properly reversed this part of the trial
judge's rulings.

   Since the language about Roxy was not precatory, Thelma's statement must be construed as intending to create some mandatory benefit
for her dog. The California Supreme Court held that the only possible
interpretation was the literal interpretation that Thelma intended Roxy
to be the actual owner of half her property. Is that not just as unrealistic
as a finding that Thelma's language was only precatory? Was Thelma
expecting Roxy to take the cash down to a local bank and open an
account with it? Surely Thelma was no fool who might think a dog could
own an interest in her house. She was educated enough to know that the
law classified property into "Real and Personal" categories. Why not
construe her will this way: "I want half my estate to benefit my dog, and
the court should proceed to do this in the manner approved by law"?
The device for doing so, we shall see, is called an "honorary trust." It is
not a real trust because no enforceable duties are created. Instead, it
creates a "power" to act to benefit an animal. If the holder of the power
chooses not to apply the funds for the care of the pet, a court will take
the property from him or her and distribute it to the person who would
get it upon the death of the pet. In *Russell*, that person was Thelma's
niece Georgia Nan, although in other situations it would be the residuary legatee under the will.

   The California Supreme Court stressed that Thelma's language did
not equate to "a gift to Quinn [Chester] in trust for the care of the dog,
there being no words indicating an *enforceable duty* upon Quinn to do
so."[29] California did not in 1968—and still does not today—recognize a
trust to benefit a pet that a court will enforce by appropriate orders. So
Thelma would have been just as legally wrong in writing words that
literally asked for an enforceable trust as she was in writing words that
literally sought to vest full ownership of a half interest in her property in
the dog. Apparently, the California Supreme Court is saying this: if
Thelma had written out *the language* of an enforceable trust for her dog,
even though there is no such thing in law, we *might* have come to her
rescue by recognizing a power in Chester to apply the funds for Roxy's

benefit. But we will not do that when her mistake of law is to try literally to constitute Chester and Roxy as co-owners.

We emphasize the word "might" because the court might have found it reasonable to convert Chester from a would-be trustee of an unenforceable trust to the holder of an enforceable power to use funds for the dog, although it would not vest such power in him when the mistake was that Chester was named tenant in common, or co-owner with Roxy. But if Chester and Roxy could have been deemed tenants in common of Thelma's property, Chester would have had a right of possession over all of the property. Converting an ineffective attempt to create an enforceable trust into a power would not be that much different from turning possession of all and not half of property into a power over the unowned half.

The California Supreme Court accordingly was needlessly strict in interpreting Thelma's will such that the dog got no benefit from it. Roxy I, had she survived Thelma, would have been disadvantaged as a result. If the will can be construed as intended to benefit Roxy II (more on that below) the animal would have suffered because of the court's lack of creativity and flexibility in construing the will. The court's attitude in rejecting an interpretation of the will that would have benefited a dog contrasts starkly with what courts routinely do to carry out a bequest to an infant human or an adult human so disabled that he or she cannot deal with property.

Suppose Chester Quinn survived the testatrix but after the will was written began to suffer from Alzheimer's disease and, at the time of Thelma's death, was totally disabled and living in a charity-operated home for Alzheimer's patients. It is true that because the will does not even hint at the need for a third party to manage assets for a disabled Chester, no full-blown private trust would be created for Chester's benefit by the probate court supervising Thelma's estate. But distribution of estate assets would be made for the incompetent Chester to a conservator for Chester, appointed by an appropriate court, so that the intended gift for Chester's benefit would not fail. This would be done even without any extrinsic evidence that the testatrix knew before she died that Chester had become disabled.

Is there any rational basis for the law's willingness to effectuate a gift to an incompetent Chester by the appointment of a conservator while being unwilling to validate the intent to care for Roxy the dog because Thelma failed to designate Roxy's intended caretaker as the holder of a power to apply funds for Roxy's benefit? The Supreme Court of California declared in *Russell* that the decedent's "intention must be given effect as far as possible." That rule may apply in California to a perceived testamentary intention to benefit a human being. Why should it not apply in the same way when the intent is to benefit a beloved pet?

2.   Who Owns the Benefited Animals When an Honorary Trust is Created?

Consider this will:

I leave my home to my sister Sal and my beach cottage to brother Bob. I leave $10,000 to ABC Church. I leave $25,000 to my friend Frieda to be applied to the care of my dogs Dusty and Rusty for the rest of their lives, or until Frieda dies. The rest and residue of my estate I leave to my alma mater, XYZ University.

Since the will does not expressly provide for the ownership of Dusty and Rusty, does it make sense to construe this will as vesting title to the dogs in Sal, if it is proved that the dogs lived at the home devised to Sal? Surely not. Is it possible to construe the will as bequeathing the two dogs to Frieda? Can Frieda be awarded ownership of Dusty and Rusty in California if there is testimony from third parties who overheard the testator telling Frieda how happy he was his dogs would live with her after he died? (The flexibility of California's version of the parol evidence rule, which deals with the admissibility of extrinsic evidence to clarify the terms of a writing, is discussed below.)

If extrinsic evidence is not sufficient to permit a construction of the will that vests title to the dogs in Frieda along with her power to apply $25,000 for their benefit, the dogs are part of the "rest and residue" of the decedent's estate that pass to the university. As owner of the dogs, University can take Dusty and Rusty to a research lab on the campus where they could be used in experiments. At the same time University could demand that Frieda pay for the food and veterinary care the dogs needed. The decedent could not possibly have intended this to happen, but the will is so badly drafted that such a result is the most likely.

3.   How to Save a Pet Trust with Creative Interpretation of the Will

The final footnote in *Russell* says that since the provision in the will to benefit the first dog named Roxy was void, the issue whether that dog's death resulted in a "lapse" was moot. A lapse occurs where a bequest is valid when written but the donee under the bequest dies before the testator and no provision in the will or any statute provides what happens to the property. In such a situation the property subject to the lapsed bequest would go to the residuary legatee under the will or to the decedent's heir. If the will had been construed as intending to create an honorary trust to benefit "Roxy Russell," when Roxy I predeceased Thelma a lapse could be avoided by construing the will as, in effect, providing the beneficiary was "any dog named Roxy that I own at my death." On the face of the will, such an argument would probably fail. But with extrinsic evidence useful to Roxy II, maybe not.

Russell is considered a seminal case in California that substantially liberalized the application of the parol evidence rule. Prior to *Russell*, the rule was viewed as barring admission of extrinsic evidence to interpret a testamentary document unless an ambiguity appeared on the face of it. A portion of the opinion not reproduced above holds that extrinsic evidence should be admitted even though the document's wording on its face seems unambiguous if, in light of such evidence, an ambiguity becomes apparent.[30]

Consider a provision in Thelma Russell's will stating: "I leave $10,000 to Chester Quinn to care for my dog Roxy." This seems unambiguous, and evidence that the dog named Roxy, alive when the will was executed, predeceased the testatrix would result in a lapse of the disposition of the $10,000. But extrinsic evidence showing that, after the original Roxy died, Thelma soon bought a new dog also named Roxy and often reminded her friend Chester that he had volunteered to take care of the new Roxy when Thelma died would arguably create an ambiguity: the possibility that "my dog Roxy" was intended to refer to any dog of that name the testatrix owned at her death. Thelma's having verbally reminded Chester that she intended for Chester to take care of Roxy II, also seems not the kind of extrinsic evidence about Thelma's intention in drafting her will that the *Russell* opinion makes inadmissible. Rather, a statement Thelma might have made as to how she interpreted her will— that is, that mention of a dog named Roxy was intended to include *any* dog named Roxy, even one acquired after the will was written—seems to be the kind of evidence the *Russell* court would have excluded.[31]

This problem could have been avoided. A lesson of *Russell* is that if a client asks for preparation of a will that provides funds to care for a specific, named living pet, counsel should inquire whether the client wants a similar provision made for a pet acquired after the will is executed. Very likely the answer will be "Yes." If so, there really is no need to mention the existing pet by name. "All pets I own at my death" would be a sufficient description of the beneficiaries of the honorary trust to be created under the client's will. Note, too, the size of the corpus can be made flexible: e.g., "$10,000 for each pet I own at my death."

B. Honorary Pet Trusts

At common law, a "trust" for an animal cannot be a true trust; it can only be an "honorary trust," which is a common law device that recognizes that a specified person has been given a power over certain property. The power-holder is not held to the fiduciary duties of a trustee. In refusing to recognize an enforceable trust to benefit an animal, courts often reason that the intended beneficiary of a pet trust (the pet) cannot go to court to prove that trust duties have not been carried out. There are some chimpanzees and birds that have been trained to communicate at about the level of a three or four year-old human child, but even these animals and their caretakers lack standing to seek judicial relief based on a breach of a trust established for their benefit.

Suppose Thelma's will provided: "I bequeath $500,000 to Chester H Quinn, as trustee, for the benefit of my dog Roxy," and went on to describe the kind of investments the trustee could make and the list of trustee's powers—those normally included in a will naming a trustee for a human beneficiary who is not a good manager of wealth. The intent to create a true trust would be clear, but at common law that intent would be defeated by order of the court supervising the administration of the decedent's estate. The stated reason would be that Roxy is unable to bring Chester to court should he fail to use the trust assets appropriately.

The differences between an honorary trust for a pet[32] and a private express trust for the benefit of a human are many, with the animal beneficiary coming out on the short end every time:

1.   If the will names no trustee for a pet trust, the court will not appoint one—not so for the private express trust. If the will names Testator's brother, Bob, as the honorary trustee for Testator's dogs and Bob dies before the testator does but Testator's sister, Sue, files a motion with the probate court asking that she be appointed the power-holder in lieu of Bob, the motion will be denied. This is true even if Sue is quite capable of managing the funds earmarked in the will for post-death care of the dogs. However, if the trust created by the will were to benefit a human and not an animal, Bob's death before the testator would not cause the trust to fail. The court would name someone like Sue as substitute trustee.

Note that the lack of a beneficiary to enforce a pet trust does not explain why the court cannot appoint a substitute to carry out, voluntarily, an "honorary" trust for animals. It is hard to find any basis in public policy to support the rule requiring rejection of Sue as a substitute "trustee" (power-holder). Perhaps some of the law of common law honorary trusts that we have today stems from lack of concern for animals on the part of judges that long ago wrote the decisions carrying precedential value in this area of law.

2.   If the named honorary trustee of a pet trust accepts the power but becomes incompetent, no substitute will be named; not so with a "real" trust to benefit humans. A bit of drafting advice here: make sure if creating a common law honorary trust for pets to name one or more substitute "trustees" (i.e., power-holders) to apply the funds for the benefit of the animals should the first, second or even third choice for trustee not be able to serve. The common law of powers of appointment under which a holder of a power can determine which human being or charity will receive the benefit of distributed wealth permits the designation of "an alternative donee" of the power to exercise it if the first named donee of the power cannot.[33] There is no reason why this rule of law should not also apply to powers to apply funds for the care of pets.

The will may name a successor "trustee" for this situation, but it is unclear how that party will learn that the original "trustee" has ceased doing his job. Where there is only one "trustee" named, the party who will take the property upon termination of the honorary trust—often a residuary legatee under the will or the decedent's heir[34]—may, especially if substantial funds are at stake, keep an eye on the "trustee" and seek a court order to obtain possession of the property if misuse of "trust" assets can be proved. Where the will names B as successor trustee should A default, however, B has far less incentive to watch how A is using the honorary trust assets because the removal of A as trustee would shift all the responsibility to manage the trust to B. Providing in the will a fair fee for B, should A be removed for misuse of the assets, may give B an incentive to keep watch on how A performs.

3.   Unlike the case of a trustee charged with managing funds for humans' benefit, if the named honorary trustee of a $100,000 fund "invests" it in a savings account paying 2/10 of one percent interest when the same bank offers certificates of deposit at five percent interest, apparently no court can surcharge the honorary "trustee" for such a foolish investment decision. That party has not used any funds for himself, and a court would have no basis for stripping him of the power given him by the will upon request of the heir or residuary legatee who will take when the honorary trust ends. The result might be different if the will creating the power included investment directions with a substitute power-holder named to take over if the directions were not followed, but apparently the common law does not imply into an honorary trust a duty to invest funds prudently.

4.   If the court supervising the decedent's estate decides the corpus of the honorary trust is larger than the benefited animals need, a "cut-down order" will be entered.[35] For example, the will says that $1 million of stocks and bonds should fund an honorary trust to benefit decedent's six horses, but the probate judges makes an order that $400,000 is adequate (with the "unnecessary" $600,000 distributed to beneficiaries named in the residuary clause of the will). The judge may guess wrong in making the cut-down order such that at some point in the future the "trust" lacks the assets to pay for surgery necessary to save the life of one of the benefited pets. The size of the corpus of a trust for the benefit of a human, by contrast, would never be cut down by a court on the ground it was too generous.

With respect to enforceable charitable trusts, the cut-down rule operates quite differently. Suppose a case where the decedent's will left $10 million to trustees to apply the income for the care of stray dogs in decedent's home county. The object of the charitable trust is valid: stray animals are a permissible object for a charitable trust to be enforced by the attorney general's office even though the decedent's own animals are not a permissible object for a charitable trust. Even if the number of strays in the county was rather small and a court might hold $10 million was too large a corpus for the trust as laid out by the testator, it is unlikely that excess corpus would be diverted to residuary legatees under the will. Probably a cy pres order would be made by a court to broaden the scope of animal beneficiaries so that the corpus would then not be unreasonably large, such as by including homeless dogs other than strays (e.g., pets surrendered to the county animal shelter by their owners, puppies born at the shelter, etc).[36]

Counsel should be able to draft an honorary trust for animals to preclude a cut-down order by a court. Example: "I leave $200,000 to Chester Quinn to care for my cats, Ruby and Trixie, so long as they live. Each month Quinn shall pay to the ABC Humane Society income from the corpus not required for the care of the cats." This prevents the appearance of providing for excessive expenditures for pets. The rights of the Society as a bona fide charity surely cannot be cut back by reducing the corpus to be managed by Chester, even if the judge considers the total sum of trust assets to be far more than needed to produce income for care of the two cats. The corpus will always be available in case some unforeseen and expensive medical procedure is required. However, since it seems clear that regular payments will be made to a named charity, this trust likely would be treated by the court as partly an express charitable trust, imposing investment duties on Chester to be enforced by the charitable trust division of the state attorney general's office. Apparently, if Chester failed his trust duties to the Humane Society but not to the cats, a court would then split the corpus into a smaller part to be the basis of an honorary trust for the cats managed by Chester and a larger component to be a charitable trust for the benefit of ABC Humane Society. A court would have the power to name a new trustee for the part of the trust that benefits the ABC Humane Society.

An attorney asked to draft a pet trust needs to discuss with the client whether the trustee (i.e., power holder) is the same party the client wishes to have possession of the animals and to have control over what veterinary care the animal will receive. A fervid dog-lover may be a terrific owner of the pets after the testator dies but not want to manage the investments producing funds for their care. The manager of the money need not be the same person who is managing the pets.

C. *Misapplication of the Rule Against Perpetuities*

As originally developed by courts, the Rule Against Perpetuities invalidated certain types of future interests that might not, under the terms of the instrument creating them, vest within 21 years after the deaths of identifiable persons alive when the instrument creating the future interests became effective. Subsequently, some but by no means all American states applied the rule period—lives in being plus 21 years—to measure the permissible duration of private express trusts for human beneficiaries.[37]

So far all courts that have considered whether the Rule period also applies to limit the duration of an honorary trust for animals have held that it does,[38] often invalidating the attempt to create such an honorary trust due to a violation of the "trust duration prong" of the Rule Against Perpetuities. The influential Restatement (Second) of Trusts, section 124,[39] would limit the duration of a pet trust to the Rule Against Perpetuities period. The courts are directed to borrow the period of time used in vesting-of-interest cases to measure the permissible duration of an honorary trust. In one case of an honorary trust for care of a graveyard—like an pet trust, it must be at common law merely honorary and is not enforceable because there is no human being as beneficiary— the will satisfied the Rule Against Perpetuities issue by measuring the duration of the trust by the lives of eight named individuals, most of them blood relatives of the testatrix.[40] The few cases to consider the matter do not require that the lives in being used to satisfy the Rule be those of persons related to the testator or testatrix. By statute in Kentucky the persons whose lives are used to satisfy the Rule Against Perpetuities must have "a causal connection to the vesting or failure of the interest."[41] In enacting this statute, the legislature obviously had in mind only the matter of the vesting of future interests subject to the Rule Against Perpetuities and not the specific application of the Rule period to limit the duration of honorary trusts. A Kentucky court might draw on the statute, however, to hold that the human lives referred to in a will to measure the maximum duration of an honorary trust for animals had to be family members of the testator or, perhaps, persons who had cared for the animals, such as a trainer or groomer.

Except in Kentucky and in other states where, as discussed below, a court could hold that statutes dealing with honorary trusts have superseded the common law, it seems a draftsman could create an honorary trust for animals and their offspring and their offspring, etc., that would last until 21 years after the death of the last to die of 10 healthy babies recently born to families known for their longevity. Use of this means of "measuring" the perpetuities period could create almost certainly a trust that would last for more than 100 years. (The document should name the babies and their parents and provide as much contact information about them as possible to assist a court at some time in the future in determining if it should hold the honorary trust has terminated.) The named lives cannot exceed "a reasonable number."[42] When using the ten-healthy-babies device to obtain an honorary trust for animals of long duration, it is essential that the honorary trustee (or at least the substitute honorary trustee to fill in when the first, a human, cannot serve) be a corporation, such as an animal protection society. That is so because the court will not appoint a replacement trustee when the named trustee of an honorary trust dies. Only a corporation, a juristic entity, can serve as trustee until 21 years after the death of the named healthy babies.

Since the courts imposing the trust duration rule borrow the permissible period from cases involving the time of vesting of future interests, it should follow that the draftsman of an honorary trust can also borrow an alternative "period in gross"[43] found in statutes in many states that reform the common law Rule as applied to vesting of future interests. For example, California Probate Code section 21205, based on the Uniform Statutory Rule Against Perpetuities,[44] provides:

> A non-vested property interest is invalid unless one of the following conditions is satisfied:
>
> (a) When the interest is created, it is certain to vest or terminate no later than 21 years after the death of an individual then alive.
>
> (b) The interest either vests or terminates within 90 years after its creation.[45]

Although such a statute does not deal with the trust duration issue, courts almost certainly will hold that if the jurisdiction enacting a 90–year rule for vesting issues recognizes common law honorary trusts for animals, the will creating one can specify that the trust shall endure for 90 years, absent a specific statute dealing with the duration of trusts for animals.

There are some states, such as Wisconsin,[46] that do not apply the Rule period to restrict the duration of private express trusts to benefit humans. These states apparently have yet to decide whether the same leniency will be employed for honorary trusts. Example:

> I leave Acme Manor to Z Church in fee simple, subject to a power in X Bank to apply so much of the net rentals from Acme Manor as are necessary to provide care for the dogs I may own at my death *and any lineal descendants (offspring) of any of such dogs.*

When this testator died he owned an apartment building with 20 rental units called Acme Manor and also owned five intact dogs, including three females capable of having puppies. Since Bank is a corporation with an infinite "life" and the offspring of the benefited dogs could themselves produce offspring indefinitely, the will provision seeks an honorary trust that could last forever. Will a court allow this by borrowing the jurisdiction's rule that the Rule Against Perpetuities has no application to private express trusts for human beneficiaries? The amount of wealth tied up in dog-care is relatively small. Z Church can sell the apartment building to a buyer willing to discount the purchase price due to the obligation to remit to Bank what Bank says it needs for the dogs. So long as the flow of money to benefit the dogs is not interrupted it seems that the owner of the property can raze the apartment house and build in its place a multi-story rental office building, subject to the Bank's power to collect rents to carry out the honorary trust. Whatever policy analysis caused Wisconsin and some other states to provide that the Rule Against Perpetuities does not limit the duration of a private express trust funded by an apartment building would seem to apply to honorary trusts for animals as well. The argument is not as strong where the corpus of the honorary trust is cash because the "trustee" of such a trust is not required, under court supervision, to invest the corpus wisely, unlike trustees of private express trusts that benefit humans.

Even when an honorary trust provides for only a modest amount of assets dedicated to the benefit of beneficiaries of private express trusts or honorary trusts, the Rule Against Perpetuities is still applied. Notwithstanding the widely applied legal maxim *de minimus non curat lex*[47] it seems that a "trifles" exception has not been applied to prevent the Rule Against Perpetuities' application to trusts of any kind—private express or honorary. Note the *Searight* court felt obliged to apply the Rule to an honorary trust producing only 75 cents a day for a dog from a fund of only $1,000.

Several courts have invalidated will provisions seeking to appoint a human being as honorary trustee to provide for specified animals so long as the animals live. It is true that the common law does not allow the use of animal lives in applying the Rule Against Perpetuities, but the courts invalidating these attempts to create a pet trust forget that under the basic principals of honorary trust law, only the named honorary "trustee" can hold the position of honorary trustee. If the trustee is a human being, that person's death will terminate the honorary trust despite the directive in the will that it continue until all the animals to be benefited are dead. In the *Searight* case the executor is referred to at the end of the opinion as "him," a human. It is certainly true, that if a named executor of a will dies, a successor will be appointed, but it by no means follows that the successor personal representative will acquire the power to provide funds for a dog, a power recognized only under the law of honorary trusts. Consequently, there really was no need to "cheat" in *Searight,* as the court did with respect to settled law concerning how the Rule Against Perpetuities is to be applied.[48] The court should have announced that the trust for the dog did not violate the Rule Against Perpetuities because the trust could not have a duration that extended beyond the Rule Against Perpetuities period; it would end when the named executor, a human being, died.

In *Searight*, suppose the named executor of the will was a corporation, which cannot supply a measuring life for the life of the honorary trust. Should the court in that situation consider whether Florence Hand, who was to spend the 75 cents a day on Trixie the dog (whom she now owned) could be the "measuring life" to satisfy the Rule Against Perpetuities as applied to limit the duration of honorary trusts?

One expert on the law of trusts and estates opines that a human being as trustee of an honorary trust "is not a validating life" under the Rule Against Perpetuities because his or her "power ... is usually not deemed personal but assignable."[49] That may be true in the sense that if the will directs Ms. X to invest $200,000 to earn an annual income for four named horses, she can assign to an investment advisor the decision which stocks and bonds to buy with the money. It hardly follows from this that the investment advisor, on death of the named trustee, can continue implementing the trust for the horses, not having been named in the will as a substitute honorary trustee. Moreover, the honorary trustee appointed by the will is very often the same person designated by the will to provide care to the benefited animals—the person who will decide how the money will be spent on the animals, such as what veterinary care is proper. The testator has placed his trust in the judgment of such a person, and his or her power to expend the funds for the animal at issue should be viewed as personal to him or her and not assignable to a third party. It is just wrong, then, to assert that a human being named as trustee of an honorary trust cannot be considered as the measuring life that validates the trust thereby assuring a duration of it that cannot exceed the Rule Against Perpetuities period.[50]

One state has by statute altered the Rule Against Perpetuities as it applies to pet trusts. California Probate Code section 15212 provides:

> A trust for the care of a designated domestic or pet animal *may* be performed by the trustee for the life of the animal, whether or not there is a beneficiary who can seek enforcement or termination of the trust and whether or not the terms of the trust contemplate a longer duration.[51]

Although an official comment to the statute says it "is drawn from section 2–907(b) of the Uniform Probate Code—which, we shall soon see, makes pet trusts enforceable and not honorary"—the use of the word "may" indicates California animal "trusts" remain only honorary.

Consider a case where a California attorney is asked by his client to draft a will that sets up a fund for care of the client's cats and the offspring of those cats for as long as the law permits. The client does not care about other needy cats in his city, so use of a charitable trust to avoid the problem posed by the trust-duration prong of the Rule Against Perpetuities is not available.

Recall that the California statute dealing generally with perpetuities issues[52] seems to permit drafting the trust to continue taking care of generation after generation of cats by providing for the termination of the trust either 90 years after the testator dies or 21 years after the death of ten healthy babies named in the instrument. But the last clause (the "whether or not" proviso) of section 15212 may forbid the draftsman from employing the general perpetuities statute to extend the trust longer than the death of the cats living when the testator died. Why would the legislature want to restrict pet trusts in a way that the common law did not?

Another official comment to section 15212 says: "On the death of the designated animal, *the trust permitted by section 15212 terminates.*"[53] Do the emphasized words imply that honorary trusts for animals also may be "permitted" by common law in California? Can a client choose to create a pet trust for the cats at common law without invoking the benefits and limitations of section 15212? Keep in mind the maxim of construction that if two statutes appear to be in conflict, the more specific statute (surely, here, that is section 15212, dealing only with the duration of honorary trusts for animals) prevails over the general statute.

If counsel is worried that section 15212 will not be construed to allow a drafter, in effect, to opt out of section 15212 and instead employ human lives rather than animal lives to measure the duration of a California pet trust, counsel could suggest that testator acquire a couple of young tortoises or parrots with a life expectancy of over 80 to 100 years and add these animals to the list of pets to be benefited by the trust. This raises the issue whether the California statute intends to ban use of trust funds to benefit offspring of animals alive when the trust commences even when original animals are still living on the theory that offspring cannot be "designated" animals. A California court is required to give some meaning to "designated" so that it is not mere surplusage in the statute. It may be relevant in answering this question that California chose not to follow a restriction in the pet-trust proviso of the Uniform Trust Act (section 408), enacted in several states,[54] that says the enforceable trust may "provide for the care of an animal alive during the settlor's lifetime."

D. Modern Statutes that Make Pet Trusts Enforceable

More than half the American jurisdictions have enacted statutes that make some, but not all, trusts to benefit animals enforceable and not just "honorary."[55] Key enforcement provisions state that if the will reveals an intent to create a pet trust but no trustee is named or the named trustee cannot serve, a court will appoint a trustee. If a trustee becomes unable to continue to do the job, the court will appoint a substitute, even if the will makes no mention of a possible substitute.

1. Vagueness on the Issues of Eligible Beneficiaries and Duration of Statutorily Authorized Enforceable Trusts

Adopting the language of section 2–907(b) of the Uniform Probate Code (UPC), most of the statutes confine beneficiary status to "designated domestic or pet animals."[56] Colorado adds to the class of permitted beneficiaries " 'the animals' offspring in gestation" when the trust commences.[57] Washington restricts the beneficiary to an "animal with vertebrae."[58]

If the will says the trust is for "any dog or cat I own at my death," does this language "designate" a pet as the UPC requires? If so, what does the word "designated" add to the statute? A maxim of construction requires a court, if possible, to give meaning to every word in a statute and not interpret it as mere surplusage. If the trust is for ten named horses "and the offspring born to any of the above mares while the trust is enforceable," have the offspring been "designated" as the statute requires?

If the testatrix is a research scientist owning four chimpanzees she uses in experiments in her laboratory, it is unlikely that she could make a testamentary trust for their benefit because a chimpanzee that lives in a laboratory cage is not a "domestic or pet animal" under a statute employing the UPC language. Alternatively, can the testatrix avoid the restrictions of the statute creating enforceable pet trusts by creating a common law honorary trust for the four chimpanzees? The question—an important one—is whether by enactment of a statute making some but not all pet trusts enforceable, the legislature impliedly intended to abolish common law honorary trusts for animals. It is highly unlikely that any legislative history of the several statutes providing for enforceable pet trusts bears on the question. Nevertheless, it seems probable that appellate courts in many of the states with these modern statutes will hold that they give pet owners a choice: use the statute or use the pre-statutory common law. Therefore, the testatrix in this example may well be able to establish an honorary trust under the common law for her chimpanzees, even if she could not establish an enforceable trust enacted by her state legislature on the basis of UPC language.

In a number of states it is clear that an enforceable trust for chimpanzees can be created by will. These states, following the Uniform Trust Act model, have enacted statutes providing for enforcement of a trust for "an animal alive during the settlor's lifetime."[59] A chimp surely is "an animal" under such a statute, but what about other creatures? For instance, if a trust in Texas, which enacted this statute,[60] were drafted by a testator for "all my animals," would a court there hold a goldfish owned by the testator at his death was "an animal" under the statute?

Courts hold that the scope and meaning of "animal" in a statute vary according to the purpose and context of each statute at issue.[61] Thus, one cannot be at all certain that a court will use the definition of "animal" previously employed in implementing the state's criminal statutes barring animal cruelty in defining the scope of "animal" as used in a person's will or in a statute providing for enforceable trusts for "animals."

With respect to trust duration, the great majority of statutes follows the text of the 1993 version of Uniform Probate Code section 2–907(b) providing that an enforceable trust terminates when all benefited animals alive at the trust's commencement are dead. Unfortunately for some owners of horses, parrots, tortoises, and long-lived cats, New York, New Jersey, Missouri and Tennessee still have a duration rule on the books drawn from the pre–1993 UPC, which requires termination of the trust after 21 years even though benefited animals are still alive and in need of care.[62] No one knows if judges in these states will hold that the statutes impliedly abrogate the common law of honorary trusts for animals, under which a non-enforceable "trust" for horses and parrots could last for the longest life of ten healthy human babies plus 21 years under a carefully drafted perpetuities savings clause.

2.   Naming a Pet Trust "Enforcer" Under the Modern Statutes

Most of the statutes changing the common law to provide for court supervision of trusts for pets recognize the position of "enforcer" of the pet trust. Uniform Probate Code ("UPC") section 2–907(c)(4) states: "The intended use of the principal or income can be enforced by an individual designated for that purpose in the trust instrument or, if none, by a court upon application to it by an individual." Many states have enacted this language. "Individual" is not a defined term in the UPC, but section 1–201(34) provides that " 'person' means an individual or an organization." The drafters of the UPC section on pet trusts may or may not have deliberately chosen not to provide that a "person" could be named the enforcer because "person" would include an organization. If the choice was deliberate, courts could and probably would hold that a humane society is ineligible to be an enforcer of a pet trust under the UPC model. It is hard to imagine, however, any reason for excluding such an organization as enforcer.

Suppose Testator names his sister, Sue, trustee of a trust for his dogs and Sarah Smith, president of the local humane society, as enforcer. Without compensation, how likely is it that Sarah will check on whether Sue is properly using trust funds? In such a case, neither Sarah nor her organization benefits if Sarah goes to court to get Sue removed as trustee for having spent trust income for her own use. However, nothing in the modern trust statutes precludes a provision that if the named enforcer successfully brings about a change in administration of the trust, the new trustee must pay the enforcer a specified sum of money from the trust corpus. How big do you think such a reward would have to be to get the named enforcer to be substantially more observant of the actions of the first trustee than he or she would be without the reward? Would the fact that the humane society's nonprofit status is based on a mission to protect animals make a difference in your estimate?

3. Determining the Formalities of Administration Applied Under the Modern Statutes to Express Pet Trusts

In order to be valid, a trust of any kind must be established in accordance with legal formalities of administration. Eleven states (Alaska, Arizona, Colorado, Hawaii, Illinois, Michigan, Montana, North Carolina, Texas, Rhode Island, and Utah) follow the Uniform Probate Code's section 2–907(c)(5), which states: "Except as ordered by the court or required by the trust instrument, no filing, report, registration, periodic accounting, separate maintenance of funds, appointment or fee is required by reason of the existence of the fiduciary relationship of the trustee." Does this authorize the trustee to commingle trust funds with his own investments? Colorado Revised Statute section 15–11–901(e) states: "All trusts created under this section shall be registered and all trustees shall be subject to the laws of this state applying to trusts and trustees." Thus, pet trusts in Colorado subject the trustee to the same administrative requirements as private express trusts for humans.

Which approach is more sensible? In Colorado, the trustee would have to earmark trust funds, refrain from commingling trust properties with his own, invest trust assets prudently, and keep records. If the corpus of a Colorado pet trust were rather small, the general requirement that trust investments be diversified would likely be relaxed to take into account the small amount of funds on hand. In states like Colorado, the will might usefully provide that the trustee is authorized to invest the corpus in mutual funds, to eliminate any possible claim that such an investment involves a delegation to the mutual fund manager of the trustee's own duty—statutorily borrowed from the law applied to private express trusts—to invest wisely. Counsel may want to discuss with the client a specific provision relaxing the statutory command that all the rules of administration of private express trusts apply to trusts for pets. Most likely a court would uphold reasonable departures from the statutory provision. In states other than Colorado with modern pet trust statutes, counsel should discuss with the client drafting into the trust the rules of administration that seem appropriate for the type of trust involved and the amount of corpus involved.[63]

4.   Can Statutory Cut Down Provisions be Finessed?

Most of the modern pet trust statutes, following the UPC, codify the common law rule for honorary trusts that a court may cut down the size of the trust corpus if, as stated in a typical statute, the "court determines that the value of the trust property exceeds the amount required for the intended use."[64] It was suggested above that a court probably would not cut down the corpus of an honorary trust for pets if the will directed that income not needed in any year by the animal beneficiaries be paid to a humane charity.

In that discussion above it was noted that such a provision makes the trust a hybrid: partly honorary and partly a charitable trust subject to enforcement by the office of the attorney general of the state of administration.[65] That creates a problem under statutes that provide that the trustee of a pet trust is not subject to the fiduciary responsibility rules applicable to private express trusts. An attempt to draft provisions in a true charitable trust (not a hybrid) relieving the trustee of all the rules creating fiduciary duties could well be invalid as contrary to mandatory law. The hybrid trust probably should impose on the trustee the most fundamental of the standard fiduciary duties, such as that against self-dealing.

E.   *Getting the Most for the Pet*

1.   Using the Statute from a State Other than the Pet Owner's Domicile

Choice of law clauses may be employed to make applicable law concerning pet trusts more favorable than that of the testator's domicile at death. The client seeking estate-planning assistance for a pet trust will likely seek out an attorney in the client's state of domicile, and the attorney will likely prepare an estate plan on the assumption that the client will die a domiciliary of the state where he or she now lives. Absent a valid choice of law clause in the pet trust, courts will test the validity of the trust and interpret its provisions under the law of the decedent's domicile at death (assuming the corpus does not include any out-of-state land).

If that domicile state has not enacted a modern pet trust statute, counsel will assume that the common law[66] of honorary trusts applies even if there is no reported case in the state involving honorary trusts for animals. If the client, advised of the non-enforceability of honorary trusts, tells counsel that he or she wants the pet trust to be enforceable in the courts of his or her domicile if that is legally possible, counsel may seek to achieve this goal by inserting a choice of law clause in the trust. The Colorado pet trust statute seems to be one of the best. Thus, counsel in another state might prepare a will to direct that the law of Colorado concerning trusts for animals applies to the client's will. With respect to most legal issues about the trust that might arise, such a clause should be valid and cause the courts of the decedent's domicile to apply the Colorado statute even though Colorado has nothing whatsoever to do with the trust.

The widely respected Restatement (Second) of Conflict of Laws provides in section 271:

> The administration of a trust in movables [i.e. land is not involved] created by will is governed as to matters which can be controlled by the terms of the trust (a) by the local law of the state designated by the testator to govern the administration of the trust.[67]

Comment *a* to the section says that "matters of administration ... include the removal of the trustee and the appointment of successor trustees ... [and] the terminability of the trust." Comment *b* states that as to such matters, the will may select the law of "a state which has no relation to the trust." Removal of a trustee lies at the heart of enforceability of a pet trust, and hence the Restatement, at least arguably, treats the creation of an enforceable trust as a matter of administration and not of validity.

On the other hand, the courts of the decedent's domicile might hold that whether they have jurisdiction to enforce a pet trust has to be determined by the common law and statutes of that state and is not a "matter[] which can be controlled by the terms of the trust," the test employed in section 271 of the Restatement, quoted above. If so, counsel may want to create some connection of the trust to Colorado, a strategy discussed below.

2.   When Connection to the State is Required

On some issues, the choice of law clause will be ineffective unless the trust has some connection to the state whose law is specified for application. For instance, the courts of the decedent's domicile at death very likely will hold that section 271 does not apply to the *duration* of a pet trust, because application of the Rule Against Perpetuities is not a matter that "can be controlled by the terms of the trust." One solution to this problem is to provide that the trust shall terminate at the earlier of the death of all the benefited animals (consistent with Colorado law) *or* 21 years after the death of the last of ten named healthy babies, using the perpetuities law of the domicile state (which allows such a duration for an honorary trust) to prevent Colorado law from continuing the trust for a period longer than domicile law allows. The Restatement clearly envisions application of different laws (*depeçage*) to the issues of trust administration and trust validity.

If counsel worries that courts of the domicile will hold that enforceability is not a matter subject to section 271 of the Second Restatement, to make Colorado law on that issue applicable in the courts of the domicile state it will be necessary to create some connection to Colorado for the trust, while convincing the courts of the domicile that the choice of law clause is not being used to evade an important public policy of the domicile state. To that policy issue we turn first.

Where the corpus of the trust is personal property (e.g., stocks and bonds and not land), the Restatement employs a two-part test to determine the enforceability of a choice of law clause as applied to a validity issue. The first test is whether the law of decedent's domicile, which would be evaded by the choice of law clause in the pet trust, reflects "a strong public policy" of the domicile state.[68] Since a majority of American states now provide for enforceable pet trusts, it is highly unlikely that courts in a state where pet trusts are honorary rather than enforceable would hold that enforceability violates any public policy of that state, let alone a strong public policy. If it is perceived that a difference between honorary and enforceable pet trusts is that the former do not generate litigation but that the latter do, perhaps there would there be a public policy argument that animals are unimportant to the law when the courts are already overloaded with litigation.

The second test for enforceability of the choice of law clause that seeks to displace domicile law that would invalidate the desired trust is whether the state chosen for its favorable law "has a substantial relation to the trust."[69] Comment *f* to this section states that the place of administration of the trust has the required "substantial relationship" and that the test is satisfied if the chosen state is the location of the place of business of a trustee of the trust. In addition the comment recognizes that "[t]here may be other contacts or groupings of contacts which will likewise suffice." If Colorado is the chosen state, directions to have the trust corpus invested via a brokerage house in Denver probably creates the required connection, and it could be bolstered by naming a Colorado resident as an alternate trustee.[70] Yet another connection to Colorado could be created by having the client pet-owner go to Colorado to execute the will containing the pet trust. To avoid a court decision in the state of the client's domicile invalidating the pet trust as structured in the will, that document should provide a savings clause. That clause should state that if the choice of law clause to Colorado is held ineffective despite the connections created to that state, the pet trust is to be governed by the common law (that is, honorary trust law) of the domicile state.

3.   Benefiting from Statutes that Allow Honorary Pet Trusts

A trust clause making applicable the law of a state other than that of the decedent's domicile may be useful to a client living in a state with one of the modern statutes limiting the duration of an enforceable trust to the lives of animals living when the decedent dies. The client may wish to include offspring of such living animals as trust beneficiaries and want the trust to continue for as many generations of offspring as the law permits. Pet owners in New Jersey and New York, where the statutes limit enforceable pet trusts to 21 years' duration, have reason to seek a more favorable law governing trusts for their horses, parrots, and cats, even if they do not wish to include offspring as beneficiaries. Counsel should caution a client who wants a pet trust that lasts longer than those statutes permit. The courts in those states could possibly hold that the pet trust statutes have displaced the common law of honorary trusts in those jurisdictions so that it is not an option under local law to employ the common law device applied to honorary trusts of measuring the duration by the longest life of ten healthy babies plus 21 years.

Counsel may propose a choice of law clause adopting the honorary trust law of Pennsylvania, which has not enacted a pet trust statute and has a handful of reported cases laying out the common law of honorary trusts for pets.[71] As was noted above, the courts of the state of domicile of the deceased pet owner will probably treat the duration issue as one of validity of the trust and require the choice of law clause to satisfy both tests laid out in section 269 of the Second Restatement. The ways to create the required connection of the trust to Pennsylvania are similar to those discussed above concerning Colorado.

Likewise, public policy of the domicile state should not present a problem. The statutory provision restricting the duration of the enforceable pet trust to 21 years or to the lives of animals living when the decedent dies do not reflect a "strong" public policy of the domicile state. For instance, that jurisdiction almost certainly will permit common law honorary trusts for the care of tombstones that continue for the lives of ten healthy babies and 21 years. Thus, far more wealth than would be made the corpus of any pet trust can, under the perpetuities law of the domicile state, be tied up for such lives in being plus 21 years. Moreover, the domicile state might be one of those that does not apply the rule against perpetuities to limit the duration of private express trusts. These possible applications of trust duration law in the domicile state where animals are not beneficiaries should be seen as the source of the public policy of the state at issue. They will be the means through which to test the validity of the trust clause choosing the common law of Pennsylvania in order to obtain a trust lasting longer than the pet trust statute of the domicile state would permit.

F.   Taxation of Honorary Pet Trusts

Many states impose an inheritance tax on the succession to property of a decedent.[72] The holding of *Estate of Searight*, that no inheritance tax is owed on property passing to an honorary trust for a pet, is unsound and should not be relied on outside Ohio. The "logic" of *Searight* would apply to an enforceable pet trust created under the modern Ohio statute. Indeed, for that reason Ohio appellate courts may ultimately reconsider *Searight*. Also likely to be reexamined is the current approach of the Internal Revenue Service in imposing federal income tax liability on the income of honorary trusts for pets, which seems to be in error. Future rulings more favorable to taxpayers should be sought.

First, we examine the inheritance tax issue. The *Searight* will begins, "I give and bequeath my dog, Trixie, to Florence Hand." Why did the Ohio appellate court hold that the $1,000 did not constitute "property passing for the use of a 'person'" so that no inheritance tax was owing? Did the court decide that this was not a gift for the benefit of a "person," despite the fact that Florence would be benefited to the extent she received funds with which to care for Trixie? Discussing honorary trusts, a respected treatise states:

After the creation of the trust for their benefit, some one must remain or become the owner of the horse, dog, [etc.].... To feed and care for the animal ... will naturally relieve such owner of burdens under which he would otherwise rest.[73]

Is not "relief" from the "burden" of buying dog food for Trixie of "use" to Florence? Would an inheritance tax have been owed on the $1,000 if the inheritance tax statute of Ohio imposed the tax not on property passing for the "use" of a person but for the "benefit" of a person? Is the basis for the holding in *Searight* that Florence did not "use" the dog food bought with the 75 cents per day paid to her on behalf of Trixie because she herself did not eat it? It would seem there is no substantial difference between the concepts of making "use" of the money and getting a "benefit" from it. *Searight* is just wrongly decided.

For federal income tax purposes, the Internal Revenue Service has seized on the "logic" of *Searight* to rule that the income from an honorary trust for a pet is not taxable income to the owner of the animal (that is, Florence in the *Searight* situation). Rather, the honorary trust itself must pay the income tax under the rate schedules for "real" trusts. Unlike the result in *Searight*, this ends up in most instances with more income tax owing than would be the case if the payments for upkeep of the pet were taxed to the owner of the pet. For a single person, the first $6,000 of income is not subject to federal personal income tax at all (first $12,000 for married persons filing jointly is not taxed), and the initial tax rate is 10 percent. All income of a private express trust is taxed, and the lowest rate is 15 percent.[74]

If a trust created to benefit a human distributes income to the human beneficiary, the trust can deduct that income from the sums it owes taxes on (and the beneficiary must include the income in her tax return). The IRS specifically disallows such a deduction for distributions from an honorary trust to pay for the upkeep of the decedent's animals on the theory that the current owner of the animals is not a "beneficiary" of the trust.[75]

The IRS rules fail to consider the realities of honorary trusts. An honorary trust is not an "entity" under the law of any state. State law conceives of the device as actually the granting to a person a power to apply property as directed by the will. Unlike a human, a corporation, or an enforceable trust, which is viewed as an "entity" under the law, a 'power' cannot owe taxes. Thus, the entire IRS scheme of taxing the income of an honorary trust ought to collapse once it is tested in an appropriate federal court before an intelligent judge. In the meanwhile counsel drafting a pet trust should consider stating in the document creating it that its purpose is to benefit both the specified animals and the person owning the animals (who often will be the honorary trustee).

OTHER MECHANISMS AVAILABLE TO PROVIDE FOR THE CARE OF
PETS WHEN OWNERS CANNOT CARE FOR THEIR PETS

A.   *When the Owner is Temporarily Incompetent: The Durable Power of Attorney*

Thus far, this chapter has considered problems associated with pet owners creating trusts to provide for the care of their pets when the owners die. However, pet owners can become unable to care for their pets even while the owners are still alive. As previously discussed, pets are considered the personal property of their owners. Every American state has by statute authorized a person to execute what is called a durable power of attorney, appointing an agent to deal with property of the person making the appointment even though that person has become incompetent or comatose due to illness or injury. At common law, the incompetence of the property owner annulled an agent's powers to act on behalf of that owner (the principal). The term "durable" in the statutes signifies that the common law is being changed so that the power of the agent survives the incompetence of the principal—the property owner. Indeed, it is common for the agent's—attorney in fact's—power under a durable power of attorney to lie dormant *until* incompetency is established.

The person that an estate planning client wants to be his or her attorney in fact under a durable power to manage business affairs and investments is often not the same person the client would want to manage and protect the client's personal property pets, upon the client's becoming incompetent. Counsel should discuss with the client the execution of two different durable-power documents so that an appropriate attorney in fact will deal with the owner's pets while another attorney in fact may deal with other types of property.

The courts should find valid the language in a durable power of attorney dealing with pets that directs the appointed agent with regard to the amount of life-saving veterinary care the animals should receive. The durable power of attorney should also include the circumstances under which the attorney in fact may terminate such care and instead have the injured or ill animal euthanized. Such provisions for the cat or dog are the equivalent of those contained in what is called a "Living Will" for a human—a directive stating when extraordinary life-saving medical care should be terminated so that death of the human can take its course.

Suppose client Carla is driving with her dog Dooby through a state far from their home when their car is in a wreck. Carla is seriously injured and taken to a hospital in a coma. Dooby, too, is badly injured and taken to a veterinarian. How will the vet know what level of care Carla is willing to pay for to save the life of her dog and under what circumstances—that is, the animal would, if treated, survive but with serious disabilities—Carla would want veterinary care withheld? One possibility: Dooby is carrying a rabies tag with the telephone number of his regular veterinarian back home, with whom Carla has entrusted a copy of the pet-care durable power of attorney she executed. Likely the veterinarian who has taken custody of Dooby will telephone the dog's regular veterinarian, who in turn can alert the holder of the power of attorney to deal with Carla's pets to contact the veterinarian who has possession of the dog with pertinent instructions. If the company that keeps microchip records of a pet could provide to a veterinarian taking possession of a pet—who has scanned the animal and found its micro-chip—contact information for not only the animal's owner but also the holder of the durable power of attorney relating to pet care, an equally useful route to finding the person who can authorize (or restrict) life-saving measures for the animal will have been established.

B.   *Immediate Pet Care After the Owner's Death*

When a pet owner dies, it will usually take several days—maybe even weeks—to find the owner's will, file it with the appropriate court, obtain orders probating the will (based on a finding it is proper in form), and obtain authorization for the appropriate party to deal with the decedent's property, including her pets. In the meantime, the decedent's animals must be fed, sheltered, given needed medicines and the like.

Since death of the principal (the pet owner, in this case) terminates the powers of the holder of a durable power of attorney, a concerned pet owner should have a separate document, a caretaker's contract, entitling the named caretaker to enter premises owned by her before she died and either take possession of the pets or care for them on the premises where they are found. The right to be on such premises is no more than a contractual license that the decedent's heir very likely can cancel, just as the owner of real property can cancel any license to be on his or her land granted while the owner is alive. To avoid any difficulties with heirs, the contract should specifically authorize removal of the pets that the caretaker has agreed to provide for immediately after the death of their owner.

As a general matter, a contract to provide personal services is often terminated by the death of the party who has promised to perform the services. But in this case of an owner creating a contract by which the owner will pay for caretaking services, the death of the owner should not result in termination of the obligation of the decedent in the caretaker contract to provide funds to the caretaker. Nor should the owner's death terminate the contract's provision that the caretaker take possession of personal property pets. Death of a party (the pet owner) having made a promise to perform in these ways (provide funds and possession of the pets) will not terminate the contract.[76] The appointed caretaker can display the contract to the decedent's heir or other relatives who may object to the removal of the animals; an attorney will advise a potential objector that the contract is valid.

The contract should, of course, detail the care needed by the pets and should also state that the contract terminates only when a personal representative for the decedent, such as an executor, has been appointed and is able to take over care of the animals. The executor very likely will employ the caretaker that the decedent trusted to continue providing the care the animals need, and the will could direct the executor to do so.

The caretaker arrangement should be fully discussed in advance with the named caretaker and a substitute caretaker, also to be named in the contract, who will perform if the first-named caretaker cannot do so for any reason. The contract should provide for a fee for services, if agreed on, and it should direct the personal representative to reimburse the caretaker for costs of upkeep, including veterinary care. It is likely that the contractually-appointed caretaker can bind the executor to pay necessary veterinary bills incurred by the caretaker before appointment of the executor to the extent the veterinarian is willing to extend credit.

The pet owner may want to post in her home—for example, affixed to the door of her refrigerator—a visible card stating something like CARE OF MY PETS in big type, with contact information for the holder of the durable pet-care power of attorney and the post-death caretakers' contract. After her death, the first person to enter her residence will, it is hoped, see the posting and make the requested contact.

Some states have statutes that address this issue. One state, Oregon, deals with this issue by statute, which provides:

> Any animal of a value less than $2,500 that belonged to the decedent and that was kept by the decedent as a pet need not be listed on the inventory of the estate. Any family member of the decedent, friend of the decedent or animal shelter may take custody of the animal immediately upon the death of the decedent. A family member, friend, or animal shelter that takes custody of an animal under this subsection is entitled to payment from the estate for the cost of caring for the animal. A family member, friend or animal shelter that takes custody of an animal under this subsection shall deliver the animal to the personal representative for the decedent, or to any heir or devisee entitled to possession of the animal, upon request of the personal representative, heir or devisee.[77]

Does this statute obviate the need for a written immediate-care contract? Despite the statute, are there not many matters upon which an Oregon attorney could advise a pet owner when contemplating a pet's immediate-care needs and who will best take care of those needs?

C.   *Defeasible Transfers of Pets*

If the estate planning client has a friend or relative who is fond of the client's pets and can be trusted to make adequate plans for the animals in the event of his or her own death, an outright (that is, not in trust) bequest of the client's animals to such a person makes sense. No trust is needed. A cash bequest, in addition, may be appropriate to recognize that the legatee will have added expenses in caring for her new pets.

If the potential caretaker needs some substantial encouragement to care for the pets, and a watchdog—so to speak—might increase the chances that such a person would indeed provide the desired care, an outright bequest of a property of some value subject to a defeasance clause is an approach worth considering. Example:

> I leave my dogs and $200,000 worth of shares of ABC Inc [which pays good dividends] to my friend Fred and his heirs, who shall

enjoy the income therefrom so long as any of my dogs are alive. Should Fred fail to provide proper care to any of my dogs, his estate in this bequest—the dogs and the stock—shall terminate, and title shall vest in the XYZ Humane Society. This defeasing condition shall become inoperative upon the earlier of the death of all my dogs or the death of Fred, at which time Fred, if alive, or the XYZ Humane Society shall own the dogs and stock in fee simple absolute.

The future interest in the Humane Society is an executory interest, and the common law Rule Against Perpetuities requires that it vest in possession within the Rule period, which it will, as Fred is a valid measuring life. The estate in the XYZ Humane Society could be made defeasible on the same care-of-dogs condition, with a future interest in ABC Animal Rescue, Inc. and a perpetuities savings clause.

The Rule Against Perpetuities does not apply to conveyances in which the grantor retains the future interest associated with the present interest given to the caretaker. For example, if Vicki transfers her dogs to Fred and his heirs with the explicit proviso that the dogs will return to her or her heirs if Fred does not provide proper care, that future interest held by Vicki and her heirs is not subject to the Rule Against Perpetuities. The requirement that Fred and his heirs look after the dogs could last indefinitely. Immediately after creating that future interest, Vicki could—in the great majority of states—transfer her future interest to the organization she would like to have as the enforcer of Fred's obligation. Although that future interest in the third party enforcer would violate the Rule Against Perpetuities if Vicki created it directly, Vicki's having created a future interest in herself (which is immune to the Rule) and then transferring it to the chosen enforcer circumvents the application of the Rule.

This scheme works if the bequest has enough value to make Fred want not to be divested—that is, it is the "carrot" that motivates him to continue providing excellent care for the dogs as long as necessary. The "carrot" should also be big enough to cause the enforcer organization to keep an eye on how the dogs are being cared for so it can bring a lawsuit seeking to "divest" Fred (or his heir, Fred, Jr.) and take over the care of the dogs because Fred (or Fred, Jr.) has broken the condition of providing care.

A potential problem is that a court might hold that "failure to provide proper care" is too subjective a test for defeasance to be judicially enforced. A provision that a licensed veterinarian make that determination may solve that potential problem. The bequest could be drafted so that Fred loses ownership of the dogs if a licensed veterinarian executes under oath a declaration stating that, in the bona fide judgment of the veterinarian, Fred has failed to provide proper care for one or more of the dogs. Of course, it could happen that the veterinarian conspires with the holder of the future interest (such as a humane society) to strip Fred of the property fraudulently. However, the question of whether the veterinarian's decision was made in good faith or fraudulently is the kind of fact question courts answer frequently.

Rather than using the device of a defeasible fee, the client may prefer another nontrust alternative: a contract with a well respected organization such as a humane society or the veterinary school of a state university, under which the organization agrees for a fee to provide the best possible care for specified pets until they die. For instance, the website of the veterinary school of Purdue University states that it will provide such care for a dog or cat for $25,000.[78] The client's will could charge the executor with the obligation of enforcing such a contract until estate administration is closed and the executor is discharged. At that point, this contractual approach to providing post-death care for pets mainly depends on the good faith of the institution to keep its promises plus its interest in maintaining its good reputation in the community.

Conclusion

The law—statutory and judge-made—relating to estate planning for pets is at present quite satisfactory in many areas, such as the recognition of pet-care durable powers of attorney. In other areas, law reform is badly needed. The common law should imply that the decedent wants a caretaker to manage funds designated for post-death pet care as readily as the law implies the need for a conservator for an infant or disabled human legatee. Where the courts apply the common law Rule Against Perpetuities to limit the duration of a pet trust, judges should use as measuring lives the lives of the (human) honorary trustee or of the legatee becoming owner of the benefited animals so that the trust does not fail due to lack of an express perpetuities savings clause.

In addition to necessary common law refinements, most of the pet trust statutes also need amendments to improve pet owners' ability to provide for their pets. For instance, no conceivable reasons exist for limiting pet trusts to 21 years, as four state statutes do. Many modern statutes are ambiguous as to whether human lives can be designated to measure the duration of the trust by the testator's opting out of the statute and using the common law honorary trust device instead. An amendment easily could resolve this uncertainty.

Finally, many of the pet-trust statutes are also ambiguous as to which animals can be made beneficiaries of these trusts. The solution is an amendment approving the trust for "any animal." Such amendments might also provide expressly that such trusts could apply to the offspring of animals the pet owner owns at the time of death, subject to the Rule Against Perpetuities.

* Charles L.B. Lowndes Emeritus Professor of Law, Duke Law School. A.B. 1963, J.D. 1966, Stanford University.

1. Unif. Probate Code § 3–703, 8 U.L.A. 138–40 (1998 & Supp. 2005).

2. One is reported, *In re* Capers' Estate, 34 Pa. D. & C.2d 121 (Pa. Orphan's Ct. 1964). A 1999 trial court decision from Vermont, *In re* Estate of Howard H. Brand, No. 28473 (Vt. Prob. Ct., Chittenden County, Mar. 17, 1999), is reprinted in Sonia Waisman et al., Animal

LAW: CASES & MATERIALS 592 (3d ed. 2006), and a 1980 decision by a California trial court in San Francisco, Smith v. Avanzino, No. 225698 (Cal. Super. Ct., S.F. County, June 17, 1980) (holding such a euthanasia directive in a will void as against public policy), *discussed in* Frances Carlisle, *The* Sido *Case and Beyond: Destruction of Pets by Will Provision*, 16 REAL PROP. & TR. J. 894 (1981), and *quoted in* WAISMAN ET AL., *supra*. Two other trial court decisions reaching the same result come from Florida, *In re* Estate of India F. Webster (Fla. County Ct., Pinellas County, 1942), *discussed in Capers' Estate*, 34 D. & C.2d at 134, and New York, *In re* Reed, No. 206602 (N.Y. Sur. Ct., Nassau County, Mar. 12, 1981), *discussed in* Abigail J. Sykas, Note, *Waste Not, Want Not: Can the Public Policy Doctrine Prohibit the Destruction of Property by Testamentary Directive?*, 25 VT. L. REV. 911 (2001). A trial court decision holding the death sentence clause valid has not been located but may well exist.

3. N.C. GEN. STAT. ANN. § 14–360(c) (West 2005).

4. State v. Neal, 27 S.E. 81, 84 (N.C. 1897).

5. JAMES F. WILSON ET AL., LAW AND ETHICS OF THE VETERINARY PROFESSION 4 (1988).

6. *E.g.*, NEV. REV. STAT. ANN. § 574.100 (West 2004).

7. *E.g.*, FLA. STAT. ANN. § 828.12(1) (West 2006).

8. *See* Darian M. Ibrahim, *The Anticruelty Statute: A Study in Animal Welfare*, 1 J. ANIMAL L. & ETHICS 175 (2006).

9. *In re* Estate of Howard H. Brand, No. 28473 (Vt. Prob. Ct., Chittenden County, Mar. 17, 1999), *reprinted in* WAISMAN ET AL., *supra* note 2.

10. *See* WAISMAN ET AL., *supra* note 2, at 593.

11. The Vermont Probate Court held that "There is a distinction between what a person may do himself and what he may cause another to do on his behalf. This distinction between the rights of a testator and of an executor has roots in early common law." *Id.* The court then relied on Eyerman v. Mercantile Trust Co., 524 S.W.2d 210 (Mo. Ct. App. 1975), and quoted the following passage from *Eyerman*: "The owner of an estate may do many things which he could not (by a condition) compel his successor to do." *Id.* at 215 (quoting Egerton v. Brownlow, (1853) 10 Eng. Rep. 359, 417 (H.L.)).

12. CAL. PENAL CODE § 599e (West 1999).

13. *Id.* § 599d.

14. *In re* Capers' Estate, 34 Pa. D. & C.2d 121 (Pa. Orphan's Ct. 1964); Smith v. Avanzino, No. 225698 (Cal. Super. Ct., S.F. County, June 17, 1980), *discussed in* Carlisle, *supra* note 2.

15. *Smith*, No. 225698, *quoted in* WAISMAN ET AL., *supra* note 2, at 597 n.1.

16. *Capers' Estate*, 34 Pa. D. & C.2d 121.

17. *Id.* at 122.

18. *Id.*

19. *Smith*, No. 225698, *discussed in* Carlisle, *supra* note 2.

20. S.B. 2059, 1979–1980 Reg. Sess. (Cal. 1980).

21. Pension Benefits Guar. Corp. v. R. A. Gray & Co., 467 U.S. 717, 729–30 (1984) ("[O]ur cases are clear that legislation readjusting rights and burdens is not unlawful solely because it upsets otherwise settled expectations.... This is true even though the effect of the legislation is to impose a new duty or liability based on past acts."); *accord* Usery v. Turner Elkhorn Mining Co., 428 U.S. 1 (1976).

22. MODEL RULES OF PROF'L CONDUCT R. 1.2(d) (2002).

23. ANN. MODEL RULES OF PROF'L CONDUCT R. 8.4(c) annots. at 611–12 (2003).

24. MODEL RULES OF PROF'L CONDUCT R. 1.2(d) cmt. 6.

25. *In re* Estate of Howard H. Brand, No. 28473 (Vt. Prob. Ct., Chittenden County, Mar. 17, 1999), *reprinted in* WAISMAN ET AL., *supra* note 2.

26. AVMA, Making the Decision, What If the Animal is Healthy? (2007), http://www.vma.org/careforanimals/animatedjourneys/goodbye friend/goodbye.asp.

27. AVMA, Policy Statement: Euthanasia of Unwanted Animals (2005), http://www.avma.org/issues/policy/animal_welfare/euthanasia.asp.

28. 444 P.2d 353 (Cal. 1968).

29. *Id.* at 363 (emphasis added).

30. The California Supreme Court initially expanded the parol evidence rule in a case dealing with a contractual indemnity provision that was susceptible to multiple interpretations. *See* Pac. Gas & Elec. Co. v. G.W. Thomas Drayage & Rigging Co., 442 P.2d 641 (Cal. 1968). The case was decided only a few months before *Russell* and is cited several times by the *Russell* court.

31. *Russell*, 444 P.2d at 362 n.20, quoted at p. 212, *supra*.

32. A brief summary of the law concerning honorary trusts appears in the *Searight* case excerpted at the beginning of this chapter.

33. Lewis Simes & Allan Smith, Future Interests § 943 (2d ed. 1956); *accord* Restatement (Second) of Property § 11.2 cmt. B (1984). Example: I leave Blackacre to my wife Wilma for life, remainder as appointed by deed by my son Seth, but if Seth dies or is declared incompetent by a court before exercising this power, the appointment may be made by my granddaughter Dora.

34. The will, of course, can name a specific taker of the honorary trust corpus upon the termination of the trust. Example: " . . . and upon termination of this honorary trust for the benefit of my dogs for any reason, funds remaining on hand shall be paid to the Smith County Humane Society."

35. *See, e.g., In re* Lyon's Estate, 67 Pa. D & C.2d 474 (Pa. Orphan's. Ct. 1974).

36. The cy pres doctrine, applicable to all kinds of charitable trusts, is discussed in Iva Austin Wakeman Scott & William Franklin Fratcher, The Law of Trusts § 400 (4th ed. 1989) (dealing with cases of surplus income).

37. *See* George G. Bogert et al., The Law of Trusts and Trustees § 165 (2d rev. ed. 1992).

38. *Id.* at 313 & n.23.

39. Restatement (Second) of Trusts § 124 (1957).

40. Angus v. Noble, 46 A. 278, 280 (Conn. 1900).

41. Ky. Rev. Stat. Ann. § 381.216 (West 2002).

42. Restatement (Second) of Property: Donative Transfers § 1.3(1) (1983).

43. "Period in gross" is a legal term of art meaning one measured numerically, usually in years, as opposed to a period of uncertain duration, such as "until the death of Mary Jones."

44. Unif. Statutory Rule Against Perpetuities (1990).

45. Cal. Prob. Code § 21205 (West Supp. 2007).

46. W. Barton Leach, *Perpetuities: The Nutshell Revisited*, 78 Harv. L. Rev. 973, 974–75 (1965) (discussing *In re* Walker's Will, 45 N.W.2d 94 (Wis. 1950)).

47. A query of Westlaw's "ALLCASES" database using the phrase "*de minimus non curat lex*" on Nov. 14, 2007 yielded 1,866 state and federal cases in which the maxim was used.

48. The aspect of the Rule the *Searight* court failed to apply is called the all possibilities test, which requires a court to imagine extremely improbable (if not impossible) facts occurring that might cause a violation of the Rule. An example is the classroom favorite case of the "unborn widow." *See* Dickerson v. Union Nat'l Bank, 595 S.W.2d 677, 680 (Ark. 1980). Consider a will in which Mother dies at age 95, devising land to unmarried and gay Son, age 75 at her death, for life, remainder to his surviving widow for life, remainder to Son's heirs who survive the widow. The final interest is a contingent remainder subject to the Rule Against Perpetuities, and it is void because it is *possible* that Son at age 95 would marry a 19–year-old girl who was not a life in being when the will took effect, and the contingent remainder would not vest until her subsequent death. It is no more preposterous to assume that the executor in *Searight* could make a deal with People's Federal Savings and Loan to pay 27.375 percent interest on the deposit of the $1,000, which would assure the production of 75 cents per day income indefinitely.

49. Jesse Dukeminier, *Perpetuities: The Measuring Lives*, 85 Colum. L. Rev. 1648, 1704 (1985).

50. Whether Professor Dukeminier's reason for disqualifying the trustee of an honorary trust as a measuring life under the Rule Against Perpetuities is sound when applied to trusts for maintaining grave sites is debatable; it seems flat wrong when applied to the typical animal honorary trust.

51. Cal. Prob. Code § 15212 (West Supp. 2007) (emphasis added).

52. *Id.* § 21205.

53. *Id.* § 15212 (emphasis added).

54. *See, e.g.*, NEB. REV. STAT. § 30–3834(a) (Supp. 2006).

55. These states are: Alaska, Arkansas, Colorado, Delaware, District of Columbia, Florida, Hawaii, Illinois, Indiana, Iowa, Kansas, Maine, Michigan, Missouri, Montana, Nebraska, Nevada, New Hampshire, New Jersey, New Mexico, New York, North Carolina, Ohio, Oregon, Rhode Island, South Carolina, South Dakota, Tennessee, Texas, Utah, Virginia and Washington.

56. *E.g.*, N.C. GEN. STAT. § 36C–4–408(a) (2005).

57. COLO. REV. STAT. ANN. § 15–11–901(2) (2006).

58. WASH. REV. CODE ANN. § 11.118.010 (West 2006).

59. *See, e.g.*, TEX. PROP. CODE ANN. § 112.037(a) (Vernon 2007).

60. *Id.*

61. *See* PAMELA D. FRASCH, ET AL., ANIMAL LAW 22–43 (1st ed. 2000).

62. *See, e.g.*, TENN. CODE ANN. § 35–15–408(a) (2005).

63. *See* UNIF. TRUST CODE § 110(b) (2003), which holds trustees accountable and allows persons not identified in the trust to petition the court to evaluate the trustee's management. Section 110 provides in pertinent part: "[A] person appointed to enforce a trust created for the care of an animal or another noncharitable purpose as provided in Section 408 [Trust for Care of Animal] or 409 [Noncharitable Trust without Ascertainable Beneficiary] has the rights of a qualified beneficiary under this [Code]."

64. D.C. CODE § 19–1304.08(c) (2004).

65. If the excess income were to be paid not to a charity but to a person, such as a relative of the settlor, the trust would be a hybrid of statutory pet trust enforced in court by the named enforcer and of a private express trust enforced in court by the human beneficiary.

66. Such an assumption would not be appropriate in Louisiana, which is a civil law and not a common law jurisdiction.

67. RESTATEMENT (SECOND) OF CONFLICT OF LAWS § 271 (1971).

68. *Id.* § 269(b)(i).

69. *Id.* § 269(b)(ii).

70. *See* Wilmington Tr. Co. v. Wilmington Tr. Co., 24 A.2d 309 (Del. Ch. 1942) (directive to remove corpus of inter vivos trust from domicile state to Delaware authorized choice of Delaware law on validity issues).

71. *See, e.g.*, *In re* Renner's Estate, 57 A. 2d 836 (Pa. 1948); *In re* Lyon's Estate, 67 Pa. D. & C.2d 474 (Pa. Orphan's Ct. 1974).

72. The state inheritance statutes typically create classes of legatees/beneficiaries. The closest relatives are taxed at the lowest rate; unrelated friends of the decedent who succeed to some property are taxed at the highest rate.

73. BOGERT ET AL., *supra* note 37, § 165, at 162.

74. 26 U.S.C. § 1(e) (2000).

75. REV. RUL. 76–486 1976–2 C.B. 192.

76. *See* 14 JAMES P. NEHF, CORBIN ON CONTRACTS–IMPOSSIBILITY § 75.1 (Joseph M. Perillo ed., rev. ed. 2001).

77. OR. REV. STAT. § 114.215 (2005).

78. *Golden Retriever Owner Ensures 'Peace of Mind': Nearly $5 Million in Gifts Help Purdue Vet School Care for Animals*, PURDUE NEWS, Sept. 25, 2002, http://www.purdue.edu/UNS/html3month/020925.Rebar.vetgifts.html.

Chapter 7

FALSE CONFLICTS BETWEEN ANIMAL SPECIES

VIVA! INT'L VOICE FOR ANIMALS v. ADIDAS PROMOTIONAL RETAIL OPERATIONS, INC.

41 Cal.4th 929, 63 Cal.Rptr.3d 50, 162 P.3d 569 (Cal. 2007).

WERDEGAR, J.

State law prohibits the importation into or sale within California of products made from kangaroo. (Pen. Code, § 653*o*.) Defendant Adidas Promotional Retail Operations, Inc., concedes it imports into and sells in California athletic shoes made from kangaroo hide, but argues Penal Code section 653*o* is preempted because it conflicts with federal policies intended to influence Australian kangaroo management practices. As section 653*o* poses no obstacle to any current federal policy, we conclude it is not preempted, and we reverse the Court of Appeal's contrary judgment.

FACTUAL AND PROCEDURAL BACKGROUND

The material facts are undisputed. Defendants Adidas Promotional Retail Operations, Inc., Sport Chalet, and Offside Soccer (collectively Adidas) are California retailers that sell athletic shoes made from kangaroo leather imported from Australia. Specifically, Adidas sells athletic shoes made from the hides of three kangaroo species: the red kangaroo * * *, the eastern grey kangaroo * * *, and the western grey kangaroo * * *. Kangaroos are indigenous to Australia and New Guinea; the three species at issue here exist only in Australia.

Plaintiff Viva! International Voice for Animals is an international nonprofit organization devoted to protecting animals. * * * Plaintiffs (collectively Viva) sued Adidas for engaging in an unlawful business practice by importing and selling athletic shoes made from kangaroo leather. Viva alleged the importation and sale of Adidas's shoes violated

254 FALSE CONFLICTS Ch. 7

Penal Code section 653o, which regulates trade in various animal species, including kangaroos.

* * * [T]he trial court ... granted Adidas's motion [for summary judgment]. It agreed with Adidas that Penal Code section 653o was preempted by the Endangered Species Act of 1973 because it undermined federal actions taken under the act to influence the Australian state and federal governments to preserve threatened kangaroo species.

The Court of Appeal affirmed. While acknowledging the preemption question was close, it agreed with the trial court that the "statute as applied to defendants in this case conflicts with federal law and with substantial federal objectives of persuading Australian federal and state governments to impose kangaroo population management programs, in exchange for allowing the importation of kangaroo products."

We granted review to resolve this important preemption question.

DISCUSSION

We begin by noting what we are not called upon to decide. The Commonwealth of Australia is free to manage its indigenous wildlife populations in any manner it sees fit, subject to international treaty obligations. Likewise, California is free to regulate within its own borders unless federal law or the United States Constitution requires otherwise. It is not our role to judge the wisdom of Australia's wildlife management practices, which Adidas and amicus curiae the Government of the Commonwealth of Australia defend and Viva and amicus curiae the Animal Legal Defense Fund criticize, nor the wisdom of California's wildlife rules or the federal government's statutes and regulations. The only question before us is whether California's rules can coexist with federal law.

I. PREEMPTION PRINCIPLES

The supremacy clause of the United States Constitution establishes a constitutional choice-of-law rule, makes federal law paramount, and vests Congress with the power to preempt state law. * * *

First, express preemption arises when Congress "define[s] explicitly the extent to which its enactments pre-empt state law. Pre-emption fundamentally is a question of congressional intent, and when Congress has made its intent known through explicit statutory language, the courts' task is any [sic] easy one." (*English v. General Electric Co.* [1990] 496 U.S. [72,] 78–79.) Second, conflict preemption will be found when simultaneous compliance with both state and federal directives is impossible. Third, obstacle preemption arises when " 'under the circumstances of [a] particular case, [the challenged state law] stands as an obstacle to the accomplishment and execution of the full purposes and objectives of Congress.' " (*Crosby v. National Foreign Trade Council* [2000] 530 U.S. [363,] 373, quoting *Hines v. Davidowitz* (1941) 312 U.S. 52, 67.) Finally, field preemption, i.e., "Congress' intent to pre-empt all state law in a particular area," applies "where the scheme of federal regulation is sufficiently comprehensive to make reasonable the inference that Congress 'left no room' for supplementary state regulation." (*Hillsborough County* [*v. Automated Medical Labs* (1985) 471 U.S. 707,] 713, quoting *Rice v. Santa Fe Elevator Corp.* (1947) 331 U.S. 218, 230.)

"'[C]ourts are reluctant to infer preemption, and it is the burden of the party claiming that Congress intended to preempt state law to prove it.'" (*Olszewski v. Scripps Health* [(2003) 30 Cal.4th 798,] 815, quoting *Elsworth v. Beech Aircraft Corp.* (1984) 37 Cal.3d 540, 548.)

II. Penal Code Section 653o and Preemption Presumptions

Penal Code section 653o was enacted in 1970 and expanded to include kangaroos in 1971. Subdivision (a) of section 653o provides in relevant part: "It is unlawful to import into this state for commercial purposes, to possess with intent to sell, or to sell within the state, the dead body, or any part or product thereof, of any polar bear, leopard, ocelot, tiger, cheetah, jaguar, sable antelope, wolf (Canis lupus), zebra, whale, cobra, python, sea turtle, colobus monkey, *kangaroo*, vicuna, sea otter, free-roaming feral horse, dolphin or porpoise (Delphinidae), Spanish lynx, or elephant." (Italics added.) Section 653o was passed to prevent the extinction of species the Legislature deemed threatened.

In the trial court and Court of Appeal, Adidas argued unsuccessfully that Penal Code section 653o should be construed as applying only to those species currently *federally* listed as endangered. Each court concluded section 653o's plain language dictated a contrary result, as the statute applies to "any . . . kangaroo" product, without qualification for federal endangered species status. Instead, the statute rests on a legislative judgment that the species listed merit special state concern, without regard to their federal status. Like the Court of Appeal, we agree the plain language of the statute extends its scope to all kangaroos and does not depend on the vicissitudes of federal protection.

Penal Code section 653o addresses an area typically regulated by, and historically within the traditional police powers of, the states— wildlife management. Notwithstanding Adidas's contrary argument, the scope of this power has long been recognized as extending even to regulation of foreign species: "[A] state may constitutionally conserve wildlife elsewhere by refusing to accept local complicity in its destruction. The states' authority to establish local prohibitions with respect to out-of-state wildlife has, since the late nineteenth-century, been recognized by the courts." (*Cresenzi Bird Importers, Inc. v. State of N.Y.* (S.D.N.Y. 1987) 658 F.Supp. 1441, 1447.) This broad power is justified in part by an increased understanding of the deep interconnectedness of the global ecosystem, because "'[i]t is now generally recognized that the destruction or disturbance of vital life cycles or of the balance of a species of wildlife, even though initiated in one part of the world, may have a profound effect upon the health and welfare of people in other distant parts.'" (*People v. K. Sakai Co.* [(1976)] 56 Cal.App.3d [531,]

535–536, quoting *Palladio, Inc. v. Diamond* (S.D.N.Y. 1970) 321 F.Supp. 630, 631, aff'd (2d Cir. 1971) 440 F.2d 1319.)

There is a presumption against federal preemption in those areas traditionally regulated by the states: "[W]e start with the assumption that the historic police powers of the States were not to be superseded by the Federal Act unless that was the clear and manifest purpose of Congress." (*Rice v. Santa Fe Elevator Corp.*, *supra*, 331 U.S. at p. 230.)

However, Penal Code section 653*o* and the Endangered Species Act of 1973 also touch on matters implicating foreign affairs. As previously noted, the entire wild kangaroo population is confined to the Commonwealth of Australia and Papua New Guinea, and the three species at issue here exist only in Australia. Additionally, * * * the act itself was passed in part to ensure the United States could meet its international conservation treaty obligations.

In *Crosby v. National Foreign Trade Council, supra*, the United States Supreme Court addressed an exercise of a state's traditional powers (its spending power) in a manner that touched on foreign affairs. It concluded Massachusetts's policy of not purchasing goods and services from persons doing business with Myanmar (Burma) was preempted by a federal act imposing its own sanctions on Burma. In doing so, the high court elected to "leave for another day a consideration in this context of a presumption against preemption." * * * *Crosby* thus left open the possibility that either no presumption, or a substantially weakened presumption, should apply in such instances.

In *American Ins. Assn. v. Garamendi* (2003) 539 U.S. 396, the United States Supreme Court returned to foreign affairs preemption, this time in the context of a putative conflict between executive agreements reached with various foreign nations and a California law regulating insurers who had issued Holocaust-era insurance policies. The court concluded that under either a field or obstacle preemption analysis the law was preempted. In the course of its preemption analysis, it neither referenced nor applied any presumptions, instead concluding under neutral analytical principles there was a "clear conflict" between state law and federal policy.

Taking the most conservative course, we read *Crosby* and *American Ins. Assn.* as implying that, where a traditional state exercise of the police power implicates foreign affairs concerns, no particular presumption applies. Instead, we turn to the language of the Endangered Species Act of 1973 and allow the statute's text to guide us under ordinary principles of interpretation.

In every preemption analysis, congressional intent is the "'ultimate touchstone'" and the statutory text the best indicator of that intent. * * *

III. THE ENDANGERED SPECIES ACT OF 1973

Responding to rising national and international concern over the impact of humans on other species, Congress passed the Endangered

Species Act of 1973 (16 U.S.C. § 1531 et seq.) (Act), at the time "the most comprehensive legislation for the preservation of endangered species ever enacted by any nation." (*TVA v. Hill* (1978) 437 U.S. 153, 180.) Congress found that various species of fish, wildlife, and plants in the United States had been rendered extinct or threatened with extinction. It identified as the purposes of the Act "to provide a means whereby the ecosystems upon which endangered species and threatened species depend may be conserved, to provide a program for the conservation of such endangered species and threatened species," and to effectuate various international conservation treaties and conventions. (16 U.S.C. § 1531(b).) "The plain intent of Congress in enacting [the Act] was to halt and reverse the trend toward species extinction, whatever the cost." (*TVA*, at p. 184.)

States were to play an essential role in species preservation. Congress declared that "encouraging the States ... through Federal financial assistance and a system of incentives, to develop and maintain conservation programs which meet national and international standards is a key to meeting the Nation's international commitments and to better safeguarding, for the benefit of all citizens, the Nation's heritage in fish, wildlife, and plants." (16 U.S.C. § 1531(a)(5).) * * *

The Act's legislative history confirms this vision of a joint cooperative state-federal approach to wildlife preservation. * * *

With that background in mind, we turn to the Act's key provision for our purposes, section 6(f) of the Act * * *, which expressly spells out the intended preemptive scope of the Act: "Any State law or regulation which applies with respect to the importation or exportation of, or interstate or foreign commerce in, endangered species or threatened species is void to the extent that it may effectively (1) *permit what is prohibited* by this chapter or by any regulation which implements this chapter, or (2) *prohibit what is authorized* pursuant to an exemption or permit provided for in this chapter or in any regulation which implements this chapter." The second half of section 6(f) is a savings clause: "This chapter shall not otherwise be construed to void any State law or regulation which is intended to conserve migratory, resident, or introduced fish or wildlife, or to permit or prohibit sale of such fish or wildlife. Any State law or regulation respecting the taking of an endangered species or threatened species may be more restrictive than the exemptions or permits provided for in this chapter or in any regulation which implements this chapter but not less restrictive than the prohibitions so defined."

Various aspects of the express preemption clause and savings clause are significant. First, these provisions continue the cooperative framework established elsewhere in the Act, under which federal and state regulation should be allowed to coexist to the extent practicable. Where Congress establishes a regime of dual state-federal regulation, "conflict-pre-emption analysis must be applied sensitively ... so as to prevent the diminution of the role Congress reserved to the States while at the same time preserving the federal role." (*Northwest Cent. Pipeline v. Kan. Corp. Comm'n* (1989) 489 U.S. 493, 515.)

Second, section 6(f) demonstrates a congressional intent to preempt only narrowly. While federal law establishes a regulatory floor for listed (i.e., endangered or threatened) species, "[a]ny State law or regulation respecting the taking of an endangered species or threatened species may be *more restrictive* than the exemptions or permits provided for in this chapter or in any regulation which implements this chapter." (§ 6(f), italics added.)

Third, with respect to unlisted species, section 6(f) leaves undisturbed the states' broad traditional regulatory authority. The text of the section's savings clause preserves state power to enact more stringent regulations even with respect to threatened and endangered species, those species for which federal concern is greatest. Neither section 6(f)'s preemption clause nor its savings clause mentions any impact on state power over unlisted species; by inference, that power is at least as great or greater than over federally regulated endangered or threatened species.

The legislative history confirms as much. * * *

The federal courts that have interpreted the Act agree. Thus, in *H.J. Justin & Sons, Inc. v. Deukmejian* (9th Cir. 1983) 702 F.2d 758, a boot manufacturer sought preemption of Penal Code section 653o with respect to two unlisted species, including the wallaby kangaroo, and one listed species. The Ninth Circuit found no preemption of section 653o as it applied to unlisted species; because the species were neither endangered nor threatened, "section 6(f) of the Act has no application to state regulations restricting or prohibiting trade in those species."

The only exception to this preservation of state power is for activities specifically authorized by a federal exemption or permit.

Section 6(f) does not expressly preempt Penal Code section 653o; the Act does not occupy the field of kangaroo import and sales regulation; and there is no conflict preemption, as simultaneous compliance with both federal law, which as a floor matter allows kangaroo trade, and state law, which imposes a higher standard and prohibits it, is not a " 'physical impossibility'." Thus, we consider the interplay of section 6(f) and the Act's implementing regulations with Penal Code section 653o solely in the context of an assertion of obstacle preemption.

IV. OBSTACLE PREEMPTION

A. *The Role of an Express Preemption Provision in Implied Preemption Analysis*

We begin with a point overlooked by the Court of Appeal: the central role of the Act's express preemption provision even in implied preemption analysis.

A majority of the United States Supreme Court once suggested that where Congress had enacted an express preemption provision, that provision was the exclusive and final statement of congressional preemptive intent and thus obviated *any* consideration of implied preemption doctrines.

A slightly more tempered view of the force of express preemption provisions has since prevailed. In *Freightliner Corp. v. Myrick* (1995) 514 U.S. 280, the court clarified the relation between express preemption clauses and implied preemption doctrines, explaining that "an express definition of the pre-emptive reach of a statute 'implies'—*i.e.*, supports a reasonable inference—that Congress did not intend to pre-empt other matters," but the express clause does not "entirely foreclose[] any possibility of implied pre-emption." (*Id.* at p. 288–89.) * * *

The *Freightliner* inference applies here. Congress has expressly identified the scope of the state law it intends to preempt; hence, we infer Congress intended to preempt no more than that absent sound contrary evidence. * * * Adidas's evidence is insufficient to contradict the inference under any standard.

B.   *Preemption by Nonregulation*

Here, Adidas asserts preemption by nonregulation. In the absence of any positive statutory provision or regulation governing kangaroos, Adidas relies on the history of the federal government's involvement with Australian kangaroo management practices.

The United States Supreme Court has recognized that even the absence of federal regulation may give rise to implied preemption. However, preemption in such circumstances is confined to situations " 'where failure of . . . federal officials affirmatively to exercise their full authority takes on the character of a ruling that no such regulation is appropriate or approved pursuant to the policy of the statute.' " (*Ray v. Atlantic Richfield Co.* (1978) 425 U.S. 151, 178, quoting *Bethlehem Co. State Board* (1947) 330 U.S. 767, 774.) In essence, Congress or federal authorities may preempt without regulating, but only by affirmatively deciding no state regulation is permitted.

Congress certainly has not done so. Instead, Adidas argues, and the Court of Appeal agreed, that the United States Fish and Wildlife Service's (Fish and Wildlife) historical treatment of red, eastern grey, and western grey kangaroos demonstrates an affirmative intent to create, with respect to these three species, a zone free from state regulation. According to Adidas, that history shows Fish and Wildlife has adopted a "carrot and stick" approach, offering the threat of a ban on imports as a stick and access to United States markets as a carrot to induce Australian state and federal governments to conserve kangaroos. Thus, Adidas reasons, Penal Code section 653*o*'s ban stands as an obstacle to federal policy by diminishing the size of the carrot Fish and Wildlife can offer.

We examine the regulatory history mindful of the fact this is an area where Congress expressly contemplated a cooperative system of state and federal regulation, and where preemption analysis must remain sensitive to preserving the respective state and federal roles. As well, we are especially reluctant to infer obstacle preemption based on agency actions as opposed to statute. Thus, Adidas must show in the history it relies on an " 'authoritative' message of a federal policy against" state regulation and "clear evidence of a conflict" between state and federal goals.

C. *Federal Regulation—and Deregulation—of Kangaroos*

The parties do not dispute the outline of Fish and Wildlife's treatment of kangaroos as recited by the Court of Appeal and reflected in the Federal Register. * * *

In the 20th century, a commercial market developed in Australia for kangaroo hides and meat. By the early 1970's, the kangaroo population had dropped to the point that the Australian state and federal governments instituted protective measures such as a ban on exports and species-specific quotas on the killing of kangaroos for commercial use.

In April 1974, Fish and Wildlife proposed listing the red, eastern grey, and western grey kangaroo as endangered species under the Act. In December 1974, after receiving public input and further considering the Act's criteria, Fish and Wildlife instead listed these three species as threatened. * * * Fish and Wildlife thereafter formally banned commercial importation of the three species, as well as their body parts and products made from the bodies of the species. The ban was to remain in place until those Australian states commercially harvesting the three species "could assure the United States that they had effective management plans for the kangaroos, and that taking would not be detrimental to the survival of kangaroos." (60 Fed.Reg. 12905 (Mar. 9, 1995).)

In 1979, * * * Fish and Wildlife revisited the listing of these kangaroo species. It found all three remained threatened "because of the susceptibility of these animals to overexploitation and because of the difficulty in predicting the severity and damage that might be caused by natural or man-made factors affecting them" (46 Fed.Reg. 23929 (Apr. 29, 1981)), but concluded the four states commercially harvesting kangaroo—Queensland, New South Wales, South Australia, and Western Australia—had adopted effective management plans and commercial killing within the limits the plans established would "not be detrimental to the survival of the species." (*Ibid.*) On that basis, in April 1981 Fish and Wildlife issued a special final rule, subject to reevaluation after two years, lifting the ban on commercial importation into the United States of products made from the red, eastern grey, and western grey kangaroo.

In 1983, Fish and Wildlife reviewed the situation and elected to continue allowing commercial importation. It also proposed delisting the three kangaroo species. Subsequently, however, new data from the Australian government showed the severe drought of the summer of 1982–1983 had significantly depleted kangaroo populations. As a result, Fish and Wildlife withdrew its proposal to delist the species.

* * *

* * * [In January 1993,] Fish and Wildlife published a proposed rule delisting the three kangaroo species. Fish and Wildlife found the four Australian states "had developed and implemented adequate and effective conservation programs that ensured the protection of these species, ... kangaroo populations were high[,] ... the three species were protected by appropriate legislation, [they] had their populations regularly monitored by direct and indirect procedures, and [they] were managed by a complex licensing system which regulated the extent of the legal harvest." (60 Fed.Reg. 12888 (Mar. 9, 1995).)

In March 1995, Fish and Wildlife removed the three kangaroo species from the Act's list of endangered or threatened species. It "delist[ed] these three species of kangaroos on the basis of their successful recovery because the best scientific and commercial information available indicates the species are now not likely to become an endangered species in the foreseeable future throughout all or a significant part of [their] range." (60 Fed.Reg. 12888 (Mar. 9, 1995).) * * * It characterized the red, eastern grey, and western grey populations as "abundant." As required by the Act, Fish and Wildlife also indicated it would monitor species populations for at least five years.

Today, the Australian government permits the commercial use of kangaroos and the exportation of kangaroo leather and meat, subject to quotas and other government regulation. According to amicus curiae the Government of the Commonwealth of Australia, the 2005 population of red, eastern grey, and western grey kangaroos was just under 25 million. The Australian government still considers some species threatened or endangered, but not the species at issue here.

The parties agree that since the three species have been delisted under the Act, their importation into the United States is not prohibited by federal law.

D. *Analysis*

This history does not establish any "authoritative" policy against state regulation. Fish and Wildlife listed the red, eastern grey, and western grey kangaroo in 1974 based solely on the ecological considerations contained in the Act. It thereafter reconsidered and retained that listed status, again based solely on the ecological considerations in the Act. Finally, it delisted these species in 1995, not as a "carrot" for Australia, in Adidas's and the Court of Appeal's carrot-and-stick metaphor, but because the three species had, in Fish and Wildlife's eyes, recovered. In short, these species of kangaroos were delisted because they received a clean bill of health.

Nor is there authoritative evidence that there exists *today* a federal kangaroo policy implemented by Fish and Wildlife to which Penal Code section 653*o* would stand as an obstacle. Delisting brought to an end federal regulation; Fish and Wildlife rescinded the special rule governing importation. There is no current federal concern. So long as kangaroo populations remain healthy, Fish and Wildlife possesses neither carrots nor sticks, because it cannot regulate species that do not meet the Act's ecological requirements for threatened or endangered status. But the termination of regulation, because *federal* goals have been met, does not preempt further state efforts; instead, it leaves the field open for states to act as they individually see fit.

The Court of Appeal found significant Fish and Wildlife's 1974 imposition of an import ban on kangaroo products, subject to development of Australian species management plans, and its 1981 decision to lift the import ban, as reflective of a then extant policy to persuade the Australian federal and state governments to change their kangaroo management practices. Fish and Wildlife's actions may well have reflected such a policy, and were we presented with this preemption question 20 years ago, we might have found these actions similarly significant.[15] Today, however, they have no relevance. Species management plans have been adopted; the three species have recovered; the special rule allowing imports has been rescinded; the species are no longer the subject of ongoing federal regulation; and the Government of the Commonwealth of Australia professes to have, and Fish and Wildlife believes it sincerely has, an independent, strong, ongoing interest in species conservation and in preservation of a national symbol. Fish and Wildlife's actions in 1974 and 1981 do not demonstrate any *current* policy that states must be excluded from regulating.

The Court of Appeal also found it significant that after delisting, Fish and Wildlife would continue to monitor the three kangaroo species' status and could invoke emergency listing procedures if necessary. However, these are simply inherent features of the Act; monitoring is mandatory for all delisted species, and the emergency listing procedures apply to all unlisted species, period. They do not imply a policy that states must refrain from regulating such species. Moreover, a reading of these provisions as implying any such policy would be at odds with section 6(f), which in describing the scope of the Act's intended preemptive effect left undisturbed the states' broad regulatory authority over unlisted species, and would effectively create field preemption for delisted or unlisted species, in contravention of the narrow preemption Congress intended. To the contrary, such species are outside significant present federal concern and, so long as they remain unlisted, are left exclusively to state regulation.

In the end, Adidas's preemption argument rests on the assertion that Penal Code section 653*o* is an obstacle to federal law because the current state of federal law allows kangaroo trade. Not so. The key here is the meaning of the word "authorized" in section 6(f). The trial court and Court of Appeal viewed a "failure to prohibit" as equivalent to "authorization." But if that were so, there would be no room for state regulation, despite an evident federal intention that there be significant room for such regulation. Either an action would be prohibited by federal law, in which case state regulation would be superfluous, or it would not be prohibited by federal law, in which case state regulation

---

15. Or not. Even in 1983, when Fish and Wildlife extended the lifting of the import ban, it recognized "[t]he U.S. market has been small (less than 5 percent of total exported), and has had no effect on kanga- roo populations or kill quotas." (48 Fed. Reg. 34757 (Aug. 1, 1983).) Thus, even then one state's import ban may have posed no obstacle to Fish and Wildlife's overall conservation goals.

would be preempted (in these courts' views). The express language and legislative history of section 6(f) preclude this reading. Instead, every action falls within one of three possible federal categories. An action may be prohibited, it may be authorized, or it may be neither prohibited nor authorized. Within this last gray category of actions—a category that at present includes the import of products made from these three kangaroo species—section 6(f) grants states free room to regulate.

This case is analogous to *Bronco Wine Co. v. Jolly* [(2004)] 33 Cal.4th 943. There, as here, the party arguing preemption contended that state law prohibited what federal law authorized and was therefore preempted. As we explained in rejecting this argument, " '[t]here is a difference between (1) not making an activity unlawful, and (2) making that activity lawful.' In our view it is more accurate to characterize the state statute as prohibiting ... what the federal [regulation] *does not prohibit*." (*Ibid.* quoting *Cel Tech Communications, Inc. v. Los Angeles Cellular Telephone Co.* (1999) 20 Cal.4th 163, 183.) So too here: federal law does not prohibit importation of kangaroo products, while state law does. That arrangement poses no obstacle to current federal policy.

DISPOSITION

The Court of Appeal's judgment is reversed, and this case is remanded to allow the Court of Appeal to address Adidas's remaining claims.

CHIEF JUSTICE GEORGE, and JUSTICES KENNARD, BAXTER, CHIN, MORENO, CORRIGAN, concur.

FALSE CONFLICTS BETWEEN ANIMAL SPECIES

Taimie L. Bryant*

Kangaroos are native only to Australia and Papua New Guinea where many different kangaroo species co-evolved over thousands of years with native vegetation and with other native animal species. Revered in aboriginal mythology, they remain symbols of Australia both internationally and in their home country.

> Aussie kids curl up to stories of kangaroos at night while cuddling their soft toy kangaroos. They dress up as kangaroos for birthday parties and recite 'kangaroo facts' at school. Kangaroos are part of [Australia's] national identity . . .

> [Yet,] ask an average Australian why the Kangaroo is killed. The answer will be simply because they are a 'pest.' This term justifies the annual slaughter of millions of kangaroos [even as] esteemed scientists and animal advocates argue that the kangaroo is not in fact a pest. If this is indeed the case [that kangaroos are not pests], how then will we Australians continue to justify their slaughter? Perhaps we will simply transfer the kangaroo from the category of 'pest' to that of 'food.'[1]

Those are the words of Ondine Sherman, director and co-founder of Voiceless, an animal protection organization in Australia. Her words summarize the ease with which kangaroos have become subject to intensive slaughter, despite the fact that some species have been threatened with extinction. For reasons explored in this chapter, kangaroos are killed in great numbers now because they are deemed to be "pests." However, as Sherman points out, in the future they may be killed in even greater numbers. A market for the "byproducts" of killing "pest" kangaroos has already developed in Australia, and kangaroos' vulnerability will increase if global markets develop beyond the point of utilizing mere "byproducts" of nuisance-based killing. Kangaroos will then be ranched specifically for the production of consumer goods. This is one reason several animal protection organizations in Australia are seeking to stop the domestic and international sale of kangaroo-based products.

The case of *Viva! International Voice for Animals v. Adidas Promotional Retail Operations, Inc.* (*"Viva! v. Adidas"*)[2] represents one such attempt to stop the sale of kangaroo-based products. In *Viva! v. Adidas*, Viva! sought to enforce California Penal Code section 653o, which prohibited the importation and sale of kangaroo parts in California.[3] Viva! sued Adidas, Sport Chalet, and Offside Soccer (referred to collectively as "Adidas") because those entities import and sell in California soccer shoes partially made of kangaroos' skin. Adidas argued that section 653o is preempted by federal policy, which allows the importation of kangaroo parts into the United States in exchange for the Commonwealth of Australia's maintaining a kangaroo population management plan. According to Adidas, such a plan is necessary to avoid dangerously low population levels while also avoiding "unacceptably" high population levels that result in the intensive slaughter of kangaroos.[4] Intensive killing in the past had led to the federal listing of three kangaroo species as "threatened with extinction" in 1973. Although the kangaroo species were "delisted" in 1995, Adidas contended that a management plan that includes sustainable "harvesting" of kangaroos would best preserve kangaroo species from endangerment.

In its response to Adidas, Viva! made two arguments. First, California is legally allowed to provide more protection to kangaroo species than is provided under federal law. When enacting the Endangered Species Act,[5] Congress explicitly anticipated a role for the states in assessing the need for species protection. The only limitation under the Act is that a state cannot permit what is prohibited under the Act or prohibit what is permitted under the Act.[6] In this case, the federal government did not formally establish any kind of permitting or other authorization scheme for the importation of kangaroo parts when it delisted kangaroo species from their previous status as "threatened with extinction." Because the federal government failed to establish such a regulatory scheme for the importation of kangaroo parts into the United States, California retains the authority to protect wildlife to a greater extent than is currently provided by federal law.

Viva! made a second, related argument. States have traditionally held the legal authority to regulate wildlife species, and in areas of law traditionally "occupied" by the states, there is a legal presumption against federal preemption. In other words, the U. S. Fish and Wildlife Service bears a heavy burden of justification before it can impinge on California's authority to regulate wildlife. Viva! contended that in this case the U.S. Fish and Wildlife Service did not meet that burden; there is no explicit or sufficiently strong federal policy to override California's ban on the importation and sale of kangaroo parts. Any deal between Australia and the United States to allow importation was too informal to constitute federal action sufficient to preempt state authority. Moreover, since Australia stated for the litigation record that it would manage kangaroo populations regardless, Viva! argued that there was no meaningful deal between the United States and Australia. Accordingly, there is no justification for the United States government to force states to provide commercial outlets for Australia's kangaroo-based products.

This lawsuit reached the California Supreme Court on appeal by Viva! after both the trial and appellate courts agreed with Adidas that upholding California's ban on the sale of kangaroo-based products would impermissibly conflict with federal law and policy. The Supreme Court decided that those courts did not correctly apply the doctrine of federal preemption and that federal law does not preempt California's ban on the import and sale of kangaroo products.[7]

Although *Viva! v. Adidas* is framed in terms of legal arguments about federal preemption, standing, and interstate commerce, this chapter is not about any of those technical legal doctrines. The purpose of this chapter is to explore issues that motivated the lawsuit but which could not be addressed directly in the lawsuit. Viva! cares about the treatment of kangaroos, but the legal system and the requirements of legal argument squeeze the frame of legal relevance so tightly that Viva!'s primary interests cannot be considered. For instance, concern about the suffering of kangaroos when they are killed surfaced only by way of amicus briefs filed by the Animal Legal Defense Fund and the Humane Society of the United States ("HSUS"). Both of these animal protection organizations claimed that the cruelty inherent in kangaroo slaughter in Australia justifies California's right to exclude the products of such cruelty.

Australia responded with its own amicus brief, which was dedicated to a defense of methods of killing that cause kangaroos to suffer. Australia argued as follows: although kangaroos undoubtedly suffer, if the means used to kill them are the ones that cause the *least* suffering, then those means cannot be said to be cruel.[8] Although Viva! may have contended that kangaroos are killed for no better purpose than to make soccer shoes, Australia contended in response that the killing of kangaroos serves the noble goal of responsibly managing kangaroo populations; turning the kangaroos' skin into commercial products is simply making use of a byproduct of responsible, humane kangaroo population management.

In its reply to Australia's amicus brief, Viva! described in great detail why current kangaroo killing practices are properly characterized as cruel, though it recognized that this was something of a detour. Viva! acknowledged, and the California Supreme Court agreed, that the *legal* issues in this lawsuit related only to state versus federal authority to regulate wildlife, plaintiff's right to bring the lawsuit, and whether the Commerce Clause prohibits California from banning the sales of kangaroo products. Predictably, the California Supreme Court did not take any more judicial notice of kangaroos' suffering than did the lower courts. Yet, the suffering inherent in kangaroo slaughter provided moral momentum to the argument that California *ought* to be able to exclude kangaroo-skin products.

There can be no doubt that kangaroos suffer horrible deaths at the hands of kangaroo shooters. Wild animals who cannot be forcibly marshaled to walk down slaughterhouse chutes to orchestrated deaths, kangaroos are shot at night by shooters in moving vehicles who blind the kangaroos with bright spotlights.[9] Kangaroos targeted in these hunts live in open country with no places to hide, and, blinded by spotlights, they do not run. As David Nicholls, an ex-kangaroo shooter has noted, delivering a fatal headshot to a kangaroo is virtually impossible because their heads are so small and the shooting process is fast-moving.[10] Accordingly, many kangaroos die slow deaths. Australian law requires that in-pouch infants of their incapacitated or dead mothers be killed immediately by decapitation with a sharp implement, by bludgeoning to destroy the brain or by gunshot.[11] No such provision is made for juveniles who are still dependent on their mothers but not in-pouch when their mothers are killed; these juveniles subsequently die of starvation or predation. Although Australia requires hunters to be licensed and trained in humane killing, these measures cannot make up for technological limitations in humanely killing kangaroos or individual variation among hunters as to accuracy or concern about the suffering of their targets.

Although the issue of kangaroos' suffering in the context of population management did surface explicitly in the legal discourse, in the form of amicus briefs, at least two additional animal advocacy issues remain in the background. One is that there are limitations on what a plaintiff can ask the court to do. Viva! cannot ask the Court to order Adidas to sell shoes made only of synthetic materials; it can only ask the Court to stop Adidas from selling kangaroo-based products in violation of Penal Code section 653*o*. If barred from using kangaroos' skin, Adidas may legally use cows' skin instead. By reducing one kind of animal suffering (killing kangaroos in horrible ways), have advocates accomplished anything besides increasing another (killing cows in horrible ways)? Is it sufficient justification to proceed with kangaroo-protective litigation simply because one can (thanks to a law prohibiting the import and sale of kangaroo parts)? Or, is there—or should there be—an ethical imperative to consider the other-animal impacts of advocacy for a particular species?

Another background issue presented by the Viva! case is the extent to which lethal animal population management is or is not (a) necessary or (b) an animal-respectful activity. Some argue that it is important *for animals* to engage in consistent, lethal management of populations to prevent population peaks that result in intensive killing intended to reduce "overgrown" populations rapidly. Not only is such mass killing likely to result in the horrible suffering of even more animals, it could also result in the threat of extinction. This is especially true if an intensive killing campaign happens to fall before a natural event, such as a drought, that further reduces the population.

It is also argued that some animals are so destructive of other animals or of their own or others' habitats that it is necessary to manage their population sizes as rapidly as possible. Lethal methods seem fast and effective, so they are presented as good for animals generally even though some members of a population are "sacrificed" in order to most rapidly reduce the harms caused by the population as a whole.

Others argue that it is all too easy to find "necessity" for regulating a population by lethal means, leading to over-reliance on lethal methods rather than developing real solutions to ecosystem imbalance. Nonlethal methods usually already exist, and if one can consistently use lethal methods one can just as consistently and more productively use nonlethal methods. Also, it is difficult to develop humane lethal methods of population management. What may seem "humane" in the abstract may be impossible to realize. For example, a single fatal headshot to a kangaroo might be a relatively painless way for the kangaroo to die, but even the highest legal standard requiring the use of single fatal headshots cannot insure that most kangaroos will die quickly from single fatal headshots. Ultimately—and most importantly to many advocates—a lethal management approach is wrong because it implies that animals deserve to die for causing problems for which humans are actually responsible.

The problems of other-animal impacts and the justification for lethal management of animal populations are interwoven, but both raise independently difficult questions about ethical means of protecting animals. Part I of this chapter examines issues of other-animal impacts. Lethal methods are generally justified with the claim that some animals must be killed to protect other animals, but these are often false conflicts. When all relevant facts are considered, it is most often the case that animals are killed primarily to benefit humans rather than other animals. It is also most often the case that humans have created the circumstances under which animal populations grow to the point that humans decide to manage them with lethal means. Part II contrasts arguments in support of lethal and nonlethal means of managing populations. Once an animal population is categorized as a nuisance, there are few impediments to the use of lethal methods of elimination or management. However, depending on the species and the location in which population control is undertaken, lethal methods have been resisted on ethical and pragmatic grounds in favor of nonlethal methods.

OTHER-ANIMAL IMPACTS: PROTECTING ONE GROUP OF ANIMALS AT THE EXPENSE OF ANOTHER GROUP OF ANIMALS

A. *Viva! v. Adidas as an Example of the Difficulty of Making Other–Animal Impact Assessments*

Reading the accounts of kangaroo killing that appear in amicus briefs submitted to the *Viva!* Court is disquieting. There is ample evidence of ongoing practices that undoubtedly cause kangaroos to suffer. Australia has been criticized from within and without its boundaries for its role in facilitating that suffering by commercializing a national symbol of Australia and by legally endorsing practices that cause obvious, horrific suffering. It is no wonder that Australia dedicated its entire amicus brief to contesting claims of cruelty. Nor is it any wonder that Viva! is doing everything it can legally to stop the causes of kangaroos' suffering, such as the commercialization of their body parts.

As important as it is to address the suffering of wild animals such as kangaroos and to challenge the ideology of lethal population management, several questions arise from close consideration of a litigation record that does not allow ready access to the issues and ideas about which animals' advocates care most. If, as Australia claimed and Viva! acknowledged, Australia would engage in lethal kangaroo population management no matter what U.S. federal or state governments do, why was it important for Viva! to engage in this litigation in California? If Viva! were to win this lawsuit such that Adidas (or any other shoe manufacturer) would be prohibited from selling kangaroo-skin soccer shoes in California, would there be any significant difference in the way kangaroos are treated in Australia? If Adidas were prohibited from selling kangaroo-skin shoes in California, a large market for Adidas, would that not simply result in more cow-skin shoes being sold instead? None of these questions has a simple answer.

Viva! recognized that cows suffer, too, in the production of cow-skin products such as leather jackets and shoes. Viva!'s legal pleadings explicitly refer to the fact that Adidas could sell shoes made from synthetic materials instead of kangaroos' skin. The problem is, Viva! was limited in what it could ask the court to order Adidas to do. Penal Code section 653o does not prohibit the sale of cow parts, and no other law adequately addresses the suffering of cows as they are turned into human consumption products. Due to the limits of what can be accomplished through any one lawsuit, cows may be disadvantaged by advocacy that forecloses the use of kangaroos' skin.

Advocates concerned about other-animal impacts might have tried to make a decision—to sue Adidas or not to sue Adidas—based on information about the sourcing of cows' skin for consumer products. It is widely assumed that cow skin is a byproduct of the meat and dairy industries from which there is sufficient surplus skin to cover an increase in cow-skin consumer goods, like Adidas shoes, if kangaroo-skin products are banned. Unfortunately, information about the sourcing of cows' skin for consumer goods is not straightforward enough to answer that question definitively.[12] The question is also complicated by the fact that Adidas's success in this lawsuit would result in legal sales of *all* kangaroo-based products, not just skin, and greater sales of kangaroo-based products as a whole might reduce the killing of cows.

Instead of focusing on whether demand for cow-based products would increase, advocates concerned about other-animal impacts might have made a decision about suing Adidas based on estimates of the relative suffering of kangaroos and cows prior to their deaths. If kangaroos lead *relatively cruelty-free lives* as wild animals before their horrible deaths, while cows lead *relatively cruelty-filled lives* as factory-farmed animals before their horrible deaths, then it might be preferable to avoid any potential for increasing the use of cow-based products because cows are doubly burdened with cruelty-filled lives *and* deaths. An advocate concerned about other-animal impacts who is persuaded by this comparison might refrain from suing Adidas even if doing so means foregoing the opportunity to stop the suffering of kangaroos killed for the production of kangaroo-based products.

On the other hand, the decision could be influenced by estimates of the suffering of cows killed under *relatively controlled slaughter* in slaughterhouses as compared to estimates of the suffering of kangaroos killed during *relatively uncontrolled slaughter* in open country. Unlike the previous reasoning, which would privilege cows, this reasoning would militate in favor of pursuing the Adidas litigation if such litigation would reduce kangaroo killing and the advocate believes that kangaroos suffer more in the process of dying than do cows.

Another line of other-animal impact reasoning rests on distinctions between the categories of "wild" and "domesticated" animals. The decision to sue Adidas may be easy for some, even if it were to result in more consumption of cows' skin, because, they reason, cows have been "designed" through domestication to be consumed while kangaroos have not been domesticated and raised for consumption purposes. Along this line of reasoning, a potentially compelling argument in favor of pursuing kangaroo protection by suing Adidas is that, if enough commercial outlets for kangaroo-based products can be shut down, then kangaroos will be less likely to be *turned into* domesticated animals. If American (and other countries') consumers were to become accustomed to kangaroo-based products, demand could rise sufficiently that there would be profit incentives to ranch kangaroos.

In fact, the Kangaroo Industry Trade Association in Australia already promotes the consumption of kangaroo-based products, not just skin, and the ranching of kangaroos is already starting to develop in Australia in anticipation of a global market in those products.[13] Ranchers are unlikely to want to deal with wild kangaroos for long, however. Through bioengineering and selective breeding of the most docile kangaroos, ranchers will be able to raise kangaroos with fewer concerns for the ranchers' safety. In the process they will be changing the very nature of kangaroos into an archetypical—probably "meatier"—species of kangaroo most valued for commercial purposes. Those kangaroos could then be factory-farmed with intensive confinement methods. In the end, why would it be necessary to protect wild species of kangaroos, who use land humans want to use and who don't particularly care to get along with humans? Perhaps some would be relegated to zoos, but that is most often a very poor substitute for life in the wild and may result in insufficient genetic diversity to sustain the many currently existing species of kangaroos.

In short, what may really be at stake in Viva!'s litigation is protection of kangaroos' wildness. Suffering is certainly a predominant concern, but it is the suffering inflicted on domesticated animals that may be informing the decision just as much as the suffering of kangaroos as wild animals. Even if Australia continues to manage kangaroo populations in ways that cause tremendous suffering, the unavailability of world markets would at least reduce incentives to develop those means by which kangaroos become subject to the tremendous suffering experienced by domesticated animals raised for human consumption.

Unfortunately, to understand the need to prevent domestication and factory-farming for commercial exploitation, it is necessary to comprehend either (a) the extent to which factory-farming of animals results in extreme animal suffering, or (b) the extent to which factory-farming results in severe environmental degradation. However, most consumers of animal-flesh-based products reject as unreliable information which, if taken seriously, would necessitate changes in their consumption of animals. Therefore, advocates have difficulty persuading consumers that domestication of animals is bad and that yet another species, kangaroos, should not be domesticated.

The *Viva! v. Adidas* litigation suggests that, even without the intent to protect one species at the expense of another, litigation on behalf of one species can adversely affect other species. Much of the discussion thus far has considered different criteria by which advocates could have decided to pursue or to forego the Adidas litigation based on other-animal impacts, but there is an even more basic question than *which* criteria are relevant. That question is *whether* considering other-animal impacts is an ethical prerequisite to taking legal action on behalf of a particular species. Is addressing harm (such as kangaroos' suffering or loss of "wildness") where there is some—albeit limited—means of re-dress (using a specific law to stop the sale of kangaroo-skin products) sufficient in and of itself as an ethical prerequisite to taking action? Is more inclusive consideration of the impact on other animals legally possible, even if it is ethically preferable?

In a legal system in which disputes are framed and resolved by advocates who zealously pursue the interests of their respective clients, it seems natural and sufficient for legal advocates for animals to ap-proach litigation with the same perspective. It seems that it should be enough—or perhaps all that is possible—to represent kangaroos or a specific kangaroo. Some would argue that the only solution in such a system of zealous adversarial representation is for cows to get their own zealous advocate. Even those who consider themselves advocates for all animals must, if they are legal advocates, engage in litigation within a system that is based on a single, definable client or client-group. For instance, it takes only a quick glance at Viva!'s website to know that Viva! is dedicated to protecting all animals, including cows. However, when it comes right down to litigation under a specific law to address a specific harm, other-animal interests may have to be ignored because of the way the legal system operates, despite advocates' preferences.

B. *Audubon v. Davis as an Example of "Single–Animal" Advocacy*

A clear example of zealous "single-animal" advocacy is the case of *National Audubon Society v. Gray Davis ("Audubon v. Davis").*[14] In *Audubon v. Davis*, the National Audubon Society ("Audubon") sued to invalidate that part of a California law that bans the use of steel-jawed leghold traps.[15] In 1998, California voters decided to ban steel-jawed leghold traps because animals caught in the traps die horribly slow and painful deaths if they are not found and killed immediately after entrap-ment. Steel-jawed leghold traps snap closed on whatever part of an animal happens to trigger the mechanism, the steel teeth of the jaws often breaking bones as well as tearing skin and muscle. Trapped animals often remain caught for long periods, and animals' futile at-tempts to free themselves results in even more severe injury and suffering. Although Audubon was not oblivious to the suffering of animals trapped by steel-jawed leghold traps, it argued on behalf of bird species that the ban on these particular traps caused birds to be more subject to predation because more bird predators would be killed if steel-jawed leghold traps continued to be used.

That cows may be disadvantaged by advocacy that benefits kangaroos was not immediately obvious in the case of *Viva! v. Adidas*, and any disadvantage to cows would ultimately be only an indirect result of advocacy for kangaroos. By contrast, in *Audubon v. Davis* the plaintiffs' chosen means of protecting one type of animal (birds) would directly result in subjecting another (mammals) to terrible suffering and death. Judge Fletcher, writing for the Ninth Circuit Court of Appeals, began the Court's opinion with the observation that "[t]his case pits bird-lovers, seeking to protect endangered and threatened species, against fox-lovers, seeking to protect predators from inhumane traps."[16] Actually, the groups that defended the ban on steel-jawed leghold traps did so on behalf of all ground-dwelling animals, including domesticated animals such as cats and dogs, who are vulnerable to being caught in the traps. And, even if Audubon intended to protect only endangered and threatened bird species, removing the ban would benefit all birds, not just birds threatened with extinction.

The court held that the federal Endangered Species Act preempted the California law that banned the use of steel-jawed leghold traps. It invoked the implicit hierarchy of animal species created by the Endangered Species Act in which animal species threatened with extinction (endangered or threatened birds) must be privileged over non-threatened animal species (non-endangered or threatened ground-dwelling species). Stated differently, even severe other-animal impacts may not overwhelm endangered species protection. The appellate court agreed with the district court that California law could not prevent federal agencies from issuing permits for the use of steel-jawed leghold traps to protect endangered species.

Although the Court noted that "federal authorities believe that leghold traps are uniquely effective,"[17] the question of whether such traps *are* uniquely effective was not before the Court. As in the previous case of *Viva! v. Adidas*, it was not possible to ask the Court to address all of the issues that advocates for animals would want a court to decide. As in *Viva! v. Adidas*, the legal question was only federal preemption, and the Court decided that federal agencies' decision to use the traps would preempt California's ban, as long as the agencies' decision was based on federal law, such as the Endangered Species Act.

C. *Other–Animal Impacts When Both Animals Are Protected*

What if a group representing endangered ground-dwelling animals had defended against Audubon's lawsuit to reinstate the lawful use of steel-jawed leghold traps? In that case, the court would have had to decide a much harder question of protecting one endangered species of animal at the cost of harming another endangered species. Under those circumstances, the court may have required more proof of the indispensability of steel-jawed leghold traps and evidence that nonlethal methods had been unsuccessful. Or, perhaps if the traps resulted in too many deaths of endangered predators of endangered birds, the court might have severely restricted the use of the traps.

An illustrative dispute in which both animals are protected exists at the Bonneville Dam in Oregon where sea lions, protected under the federal Marine Mammal Protection Act,[18] are eating chinook salmon, protected under the federal Endangered Species Act.[19] Washington and Oregon wildlife agencies claim that sea lion consumption of salmon is so problematic that they should be able to kill sea lions to protect the salmon, even though sea lions are protected.[20] The wildlife agencies claim that they have made unavailing use of nonlethal methods such as placing bars on the entrances of the ladders fish use to navigate the dam, shooting sea lions with rubber bullets, broadcasting sounds made by whales who eat sea lions, and transporting sea lions to other Pacific coastal locations. The agencies are now beginning a lengthy process of securing permits to kill those sea lions who seem to be particularly adept salmon predators in order to "teach" other sea lions to stay away. Meanwhile, representatives to Congress from Washington and Oregon are sponsoring legislation that would amend the Marine Mammal Protection Act so that lethal management methods could be used more quickly in the future.

There are at least two ways of understanding this approach to resolving the perceived problem of sea lions' eating salmon. One is that humans, competitors with sea lions for the same fish, intend to win in the contest for the fish. Humans control the rules of the contest, of course, and they can create a significant advantage for themselves by amending the Marine Mammal Protection Act to insure speedier recourse to lethal methods of preserving fish for human consumption. From this perspective, the key difference between sea lions and salmon is that salmon have significantly more commercial value than do sea lions.

Or, killing sea lions could be viewed exclusively from the perspective of protecting chinook salmon. Although it is true that both sea lions and chinook salmon are legally protected, sea lions are currently perceived to be plentiful while salmon population sizes are plummeting. The argument that killing is a painful necessity is easy to adopt when the situation seems so dire. According to its executive director, the Oregon Humane Society would be reluctant to oppose the killings of sea lions if it were likely that "we could end up with no salmon while we discuss the issue to death."[21]

A problem with both perspectives on lethal management of sea lions is that we might well lose chinook salmon *even if* we kill sea lions. Sea lion predation is but one of the factors associated with a decline in the number of chinook salmon. In fact, HSUS cites predation by birds, commercial takes by Canadian and U.S. fishermen, and disruptive human forestry and agricultural practices as the real reasons for salmon population decline.[22] HSUS argues that even though sea lions eat salmon, they eat predators of salmon, such as lamprey, in even greater numbers.[23] In recognition of those factors, HSUS opposes the killing of the sea lions.

By expanding the frame of relevant information, HSUS calls into question the motives and predicted success of killing sea lions to protect chinook salmon. Taking the facts HSUS cites as a whole, it is clear that little can be gained from killing sea lions. Nevertheless, if sea lions' lives are not valued by humans, then *any* help afforded to the chinook salmon population by killing sea lions, no matter how minimal, will be considered sufficient justification for killing them. Even completely accurate quantification of the numerous deadly human sources of harm to salmon versus the relatively insignificant sea lion sources of harm would not stave off efforts to kill sea lions. Once they are labeled a "pest," it doesn't matter how much of a pest they are; it is easy to justify killing them.

This fact is illustrated by the Court's reasoning in a lawsuit filed in 1996 by three animal protection organizations seeking to protect sea lions at the Ballard Locks in Washington State.[24] The controversy about killing sea lions at Ballard Locks is similar in all respects to the current controversy over sea lions at Bonneville Dam, except that the Ballard Locks sea lions were accused of preying on a different salmonid species: steelhead trout. Then, as now, the Marine Mammal Protection Act required the use of nonlethal means to deter sea lions from eating the trout, so Washington's Department of Fish and Wildlife tried scaring sea lions with firecrackers, installing barrier nets, changing water flow through the Locks, shooting sea lions with rubber-tipped arrows, stocking the water with foul-tasting (to sea lions) fish, and transporting sea lions to California. Also, as in the case of the Bonneville Dam sea lions, some individual sea lions were identified as better at killing fish than other sea lions. Excelling at what sea lions do—killing and eating fish—made them specific targets for "lethal management."

By 1994 the Marine Mammal Protection Act had been amended to allow for the targeted killing of specific sea lions known to be killing steelhead trout, if procedural requirements of environmental review had been fulfilled. For that purpose, Washington's Department of Fish and Wildlife documented declining steelhead trout passage through the Locks, despite the Department's use of nonlethal means of controlling sea lion predation and temporary removal (during steelhead trout runs) of sea lions who had been identified as preying on steelhead trout. On the basis of that documentation, the National Marine Fisheries Service issued provisional permits to kill five particular sea lions. Shortly thereafter, in 1996, the Humane Society of the United States, Earth Island Institute, and The Progressive Animal Welfare Society filed suit to prevent the killing of the sea lions.[25] Plaintiffs argued that Washington's Department of Fish and Wildlife and the National Marine Fisheries Service failed to inform themselves sufficiently to avoid arbitrary and capricious decisions, as required by such laws as the Administrative

Procedure Act and the National Environmental Protection Act. In deciding against the plaintiffs, the Court characterized their position as

> object[ing] to the modest scope of the proposal submitted by the State, believing that lethal removal of sea lions is a futile gesture unless the State simultaneously addresses other systemic problems at the Locks.... Plaintiffs attack the wisdom of the proposal because sea lion predation is one of many factors presently contributing to the steelhead's decline."[26]

The Court did not reject plaintiffs' claim that killing sea lions would do little to address trout population decline, but it disagreed with plaintiffs about the legal significance of their contention. "[The] National Environmental Protection Act prohibits uninformed rather than unwise agency action."[27] Having informed themselves of various factors, the agencies had the authority to reach conclusions with which others, including the plaintiffs, might disagree.

Although the Court ultimately decided against the plaintiffs in the Ballard Locks case, no sea lions were killed because sea lion predation had dropped so significantly by the time the Court ruled in April of 1999.[28] In fact, by May 1999, near the end of the trouts' spawning run for the year, the National Marine Fisheries Service reported zero steelhead trout take by sea lions at the Ballard Locks.[29] What accounted for the decrease? The National Marine Fisheries Services attributed the decrease to the permanent relocation of three of the most predatory sea lions to Sea World in Orlando, Florida.[30] But, in confirmation of HSUS's position that removing sea lions will not save a fish population from decline, the National Marine Fisheries Service predicted that the 1999 steelhead trout run would be smaller than the 1998 figure, despite its prediction that sea lions would take no steelhead trout that year.[31] At most, removal of the sea lions only slightly slowed the decline in the fish population. That lethal removal of sea lions is now suggested for the Bonneville Dam sea lions, even after the Ballard Locks experience, suggests that *any* predicted reduction in killing of fish attributable to sea lions—even if it does not meaningfully stop the decline of fish populations—can be used to justify lethal methods.

D. Other–Animal Impacts When Neither Animal Enjoys Particular Legal Protection

Thus far, discussion of other-animal impacts has concerned situations in which one or both of the animal species is protected under federal law. There are other situations in which a preference for one species or another is embedded in state or federal law. For instance, in the *Viva! v. Adidas* litigation, Adidas argued that California has relatively less authority to regulate wildlife that is not native to California. Adidas made a common distinction: animals native to a state are generally preferred over non-native animals, which have been intentionally or unintentionally introduced to places where they did not co-evolve with other species. It would be a reach to argue that California does not have sufficient interest in or legal right to protect its native plant and animal populations from *invasive* non-native animals, so Adidas must have meant that California should have less authority than the federal government when it comes to the importation of *dead* non-native wildlife. But Adidas was on weak ground with that argument, too; a California appellate court previously decided that California does have the authority to regulate the importation of dead non-native wildlife because of the recognized relationship between commercialization of animals and those animals' continued viability as species. In *People v. K. Sakai Co.*,[32] the Court held that California had the authority under Penal Code section 653o to ban the sale of canned whale meat, including the sale of canned whale meat that had been imported before section 653o was enacted. In doing so, the Court stated the following:

> It is now generally recognized that the destruction or distur-
> bance of vital life cycles or of the balance of a species of wildlife,
> even though initiated in one part of the world, may have a
> profound effect upon the health and welfare of people in other
> distant parts. We have come to appreciate the interdependence
> of different forms of life. We realize that by killing certain
> species in one area we may sound our own death knell. For
> these reasons ecology has become everyone's business. Like
> pollution it does not cease to be of vital concern merely because
> the problem is created at a distant point.[33]

The Penal Code section at issue in *Sakai* was the same Penal Code section at issue in *Viva! v. Adidas*. So how could two lower courts have agreed with Adidas that it should be able to import kangaroo-based products, despite section 653o's ban on such importation? The lower courts in *Viva! v. Adidas* focused on evidence of federal negotiation of a deal with Australia to enable importation of kangaroo-based products into the United States in return for Australia's engaging in kangaroo population management; there was no argument of federal preemption in the *Sakai* case. In addition, in the case of kangaroos, the lower *Viva! v. Adidas* courts were persuaded that commercialization as a part of management of kangaroos would preserve kangaroos, whereas the *Sakai* court was persuaded that commercialization of whales would endanger whales. The dividing line is the context in which commercialization and killing takes place, which is why it is important to consider in Part II various contextual issues related to lethal management of animal populations.

The distinction drawn by Adidas regarding non-native/native species is a common distinction used to justify lethal management of non-native wild animal populations. The definition of a "native" prey species in this context is a species that has co-evolved with predators and with the environment over enough time for the natural selection of adaptive characteristics, thereby enabling a sufficiently genetically diverse population to survive despite the presence of predators. Non-native predator species that adapt readily in the new environment can wipe out native prey species before the process of natural selection can confer survival potential to those native prey species. For example, non-native mongooses have been known to kill large numbers of native birds in addition to the rats they were introduced to kill.[34] Does the defense of native species justify slaughter of non-native species? Surely nonlethal methods would seem preferable, but what if those methods do not work as quickly or effectively?

There are other types of negative impact besides members of non-native species directly killing members of native species of animals. In some cases of non-native competition with native species, members of the non-native species take over habitat occupied by native species or alter habitat upon which native species depend. For instance, rabbits introduced to Laysan Island in the Hawaiian Islands have been blamed—correctly or incorrectly—for altering the habitat so much that 26 species of plants and 3 species of birds have been eliminated.[35] Is slaughter of non-native animals justified for the sake of preserving the environment on which other animals depend? Is the source of ecosystem imbalance relevant? Some argue that humans should not use lethal methods against species they themselves have introduced, while others argue that the most expedient means should be used because redressing ecosystem imbalance is conceptually separable from the blameworthiness of humans for causing that imbalance.

It is not always the case that the native animal species wins, however. Kangaroos are native to Australia, but sheep and cattle, which are non-native, are given preference to kangaroos when kangaroos are perceived to be occupying land upon which sheep or cattle could be grazed. Sheep and cattle are preferred even though their hooves destroy the viability of the ground upon which native species of vegetation depend, vegetation with which kangaroos co-evolved.[36] When sheep and cattle are valued more than kangaroos, kangaroos will be the ones deemed a "nuisance" and killed when they interfere with the land, water, and other resource requirements of cattle and sheep producers. Commercializing kangaroos would make them more valued by humans, but it is no "elevation" to achieve the status of domestic commercial animals exploited for their flesh and skin. Such animals are subjected to terrible conditions for the purpose of keeping consumer prices as low as possible.

When both animals are native and not specially protected, the "nuisance" designation can turn on more subtle features of context. An example of this is native free-roaming cats and native songbirds living in the same urban environment. When bird populations decline, it is easy to blame free-roaming cats regardless of whether the cats are actually preying on birds. Cats are opportunistic hunters who will eat whatever is easiest to obtain by hunting. It is rarely easy for a cat to catch a bird or to raid tree-dwelling birds' nests; cats are better able to catch insects and ground-dwelling animals such as mice, rats, and lizards.[37] In reality, free-roaming cats are labeled "nuisance" animals, even if their food is wholly supplied by humans.

For some, the desire to eliminate free-roaming cats may have more to do with concerns about cats' defecating in flower beds but it can seem nobler to defend birds than to defend flower beds. For others the concern really is songbird population decline. However, when specific bird populations decline the reasons could be as various as changes in vegetation, changes in climate, changes in the presence of other competitor bird species, and changes in the prevalence of windows that result in deadly window-strikes because birds cannot see glass. The National Audubon Society states that habitat loss and alteration are primary causes of the nationwide decline in bird populations,[38] but it still recommends lethal management of free-roaming cats.[39]

The occasional bird-killing by a cat may be only the tip of the iceberg, just as the sea lions' killing of fish accounts for only a very small percentage of the fish population decline. But, no matter how small the taking of birds or fish, that source of harm is perceived to be addressable by killing "culprit" cats and sea lions. Indeed, killing animals ostensibly to save other animals or habitats gives the erroneous impression that problems have been solved. By contrast, fully recognizing human responsibility for the underlying sources of problems would require more significant adjustments on the part of humans than simply killing animals.

ANIMAL POPULATION MANAGEMENT AS AN ANIMAL-RESPECTING ACTIVITY

A. *Lethal Animal Population Management*

The legal posture of the dispute in *Viva! v. Adidas* did not easily reveal the extent to which other animals' interests are affected by the commercialization of kangaroos. Viva!'s lawsuit could not reveal the extent to which cows' interests may be compromised if kangaroo skin cannot be imported for sale. Nor was the interplay between commercialization of kangaroos and existing commercialized exploitation of Australian sheep and cattle on the legal radar screen.

The legal posture of the *Viva! v. Adidas* case also did not easily allow for examination of the argument that it is good for kangaroos that humans manage their population sizes. The legal question before the Court was whether federal policy regarding kangaroo population management preempts state law, not whether it is good policy. The position of the United States government, as described by Adidas, is: if kangaroo populations are not controlled to prevent sharp peaks and valleys in population size, kangaroos could become extinct. Viva!'s position is subject to more interpretation. By seeking a ban on sales in California, Viva! may be completely rejecting the ideology of lethal population management. Or, Viva! could be seeking to hinder the application of lethal management ideology that, coupled with commercialization, would result in creating a consumer market sufficient to justify the ranching and ultimate domestication of kangaroos as livestock animals.

Animals' advocates are appropriately skeptical of claims that lethal management of wild animal populations benefits those wild animals, such as when it is claimed that deer hunting reduces the incidence of more painful deaths from starvation, illness, and predation. Though humans cause deer populations to increase by the way hunting seasons are structured or by removing environmental pressures on deer living in parks and reserves, deer are blamed for over-reproduction, destruction of their own (and other animal species') habitats by over-grazing, and invading neighboring private property. Then, intensive hunting to reduce a deer population's size is proclaimed necessary for the environment, deer, and other animals.

Philosopher Gary E. Varner calls this "therapeutic hunting" of an "obligatory management species." An "obligatory management species" is a species that "has a fairly regular tendency to overshoot the carrying capacity of its range, to the detriment of future generations of it and other species."[40] Varner contends that animal rights activists should agree that such therapeutic hunting is ethically justified, and he raises several important considerations. At the outset, however, the appearance of a double standard for non-human animal species and human animal species is troubling to those who seek to avoid "speciesism."[41]

It seems quite clear that human beings meet the definition of an "obligatory management species," but no one openly supports the idea that hunting humans would be ethical, even if it would be "therapeutic" by Varner's terms. Varner argues that the reason it is not ethical to hunt humans, even if they are "obligatory management species," is that humans, unlike other animals, can choose to regulate themselves knowing that over-reproduction is harmful. Varner may be correct that humans could theoretically choose to limit their population and destructive impact on environments, but they rarely do so. In contrast, wild animals co-existing in ecosystems tend to remain in relative ecosystem balance, regardless of whether they intelligently decide to do so.

Varner seems to take as his starting point situations in which an ecosystem has been severely constrained or altered, without considering the role of humans in creating the severe ecosystem imbalance that humans then seek to cure by killing animals. Most causes of permanent ecosystem alteration that results in "overabundance" of some wild animals and obliteration of others can be traced to humans' introduction of non-native species, humans' usurpation of or damage to animals' habitat, and humans' restriction of animals to ecologically imbalanced parks and reserves.

Another problem with ready acceptance of Varner's thesis is that, while some massive deer hunts are engineered to address large populations of deer, the most common type of deer hunting takes place in accordance with hunting seasons that do not seem to be structured primarily to correct for deer overpopulation or to prevent starvation of deer. Deer hunting regulations, such as which deer can be killed and during what period of time, reveal that hunting seasons are designed primarily to insure that there will be deer to hunt every year. For instance, Vermont hunting regulations explicitly aim to provide hunters with a more satisfying hunting experience by restricting the age and size of animals that can be killed.[42]

The same argument of ethical "therapeutic hunting" or "culling" has been used to justify killing of kangaroos for population management. Australia defends the practice of lethal management by arguing that maintaining consistent kangaroo population sizes prevents intensive killing campaigns during which many more kangaroos are killed. The reason given for managing kangaroos at all is that kangaroos are "obligatory management species" that destroy their habitat when they over-reproduce. However, research does not support this claim. Biologist Daniel Ramp reports that "many of Australia's leading plant ecologists have validated the idea that plant communities in Australia have evolved with various levels of grazing pressure and are adapted to it."[43] On the basis of research conducted at two locations where kangaroos grazed extensively, Ramp concluded that native vegetation recovers even from extensive grazing by kangaroos because kangaroos do not damage the ecological infrastructure needed for vegetation recovery. Zoologist Juliet Gellatley confirms this when she writes that

> A primary school kid could demolish this [argument for killing kangaroos]. [Kangaroos are u]nique animals with long, soft feet [that] flit over the delicate scrub—an environment with which they have evolved over millions of years and are an essential part of. Their toe nails make small holes in the ground—holes into which salt bush seeds are washed to germinate and be protected. They are animals which nibble at vegetation rather than tug at it … and are finely attuned to the native vegetation.

> [By contrast, t]here are two alien animals … which do none of these things and which are inexorably turning the outback into desert—160 million sheep and cattle.[44]

Another claim that has been contested is the claim that kangaroos reproduce at such a high rate that they must be killed. Australians who want to kill kangaroos claim that it is necessary because dingoes and aboriginal Australians no longer keep kangaroo population sizes low. However, critics of that claim assert that neither dingoes not aborigines were likely to have killed enough kangaroos to significantly impact kangaroo populations.[45] Early European settlers noted an abundance of kangaroos during their early explorations of the continent, and the hunting methods employed by aborigines, though sufficient to meet their need for sustenance, were inefficient and energy-consuming.

It is difficult to know the size of kangaroo populations at different points in history. It is difficult to know the size of populations even now. Estimates are derived from aerial counting and the use of statistical models, and they vary considerably depending on the circumstances of a particular count and the specific statistical model that is used. The federal governments of the U.S. and Australia claim that no kangaroo species is at risk of extinction, and Australia has established quotas for the lawful killing of kangaroos. However, the National Kangaroo Protection Coalition in Australia reports that in spite of crashing kangaroo numbers in every State, the quotas for 2004, 2005, and 2006 were set at the same percentage of the estimated reduced population,[46] and the Wildlife Protection Association of Australia reported that in 2003, the quota was "overshot" by thousands of kangaroos.[47]

The problem is all the more complicated because "ecosystem balance" does not mean an unchanging configuration of animals and plants; kangaroo populations rise and fall in relation to available habitat, drought cycles, and the population cycles of various predators. An ecosystem can appear to be out of balance when, in fact, it is not. Nevertheless, it is clearly to the advantage of landowners and farmers (who want to use native land used by kangaroos) to claim that kangaroos are so numerous that lethal management is warranted, regardless of whether a particular population is merely at the high end of a natural fluctuation.

There is no denying that humans can induce kangaroo population increases that overwhelm a particular ecosystem. For example, both of Ramp's research sites were national reserves at which ecological pressures on kangaroos were reduced by excluding or restricting predators in environments that held abundant sources of water and vegetation preferred by kangaroos. Kangaroos could reproduce in numbers beyond those that would result in ecosystems that naturally fluctuate within the parameters of relatively balanced numbers of predators and native vegetation that sustains a variety of species. When the number of kangaroos rose to the point that neighboring farmers protested kangaroo "invasions" of their fields or reserve managers worried about public safety, culling programs were instituted.[48]

Obviously, killing kangaroos only temporarily reduces their population size if the conditions that led to large populations remain unchanged. Long-term management of kangaroo populations really means restoration of native ecosystems of sufficient size to allow natural checks and balances to occur. Ramp points out that farmers could reserve perimeter native ecosystem land or that reserves could be planted with native vegetation of different types that support an internally balancing native ecosystem.[49] He contends that the technical knowledge to do so exists but that the will to do so lags. After all, it is most expedient to simply kill off kangaroos, and, if a market is readily available for their flesh, all the more justification exists for reliance on culling. The cost of reliance on culling is high levels of kangaroo suffering and unaddressed harm to native ecosystems, which is indicated—not caused—by the high number of kangaroos. But, to date, those costs have not been sufficient to outweigh perceived benefits of culling.

These two examples of deer and kangaroos reveal a significant obstacle to acceptance of Varner's argument that it is ethically responsible to lethally manage populations of "obligatory management species." Once it has been decided that "therapeutic hunting" is ethical, it is simply too easy to decide that an animal is an "obligatory management species." In the case of deer, sport hunters and landowners seeking to use what was once deer habitat are given control over the definition of the term "too numerous." In the case of kangaroos, farmers and ranchers are powerful enough to dictate when kangaroo populations have reached "plague proportions."

In both cases, concentrations of animal species occur primarily in areas that have been designated as reserves, including national or state parks, but which are not large enough or designed specifically to sustain internally balancing ecosystems of predator and prey animals. In both cases, ecosystem pressures that would have checked the growth of the deer or kangaroo populations have been removed, thereby creating the conditions that lead to "overabundance" of animals. In both cases, having created conditions of "overabundance," humans resort to killing in order to bring population numbers down quickly. To the extent that "therapeutic hunting" supports this cycle of creating overabundance and then slaughtering animals by whatever expedient means possible, it cannot be an ethical practice.

Varner's thesis is noteworthy for his effort to account for values shared by advocates for animals: (a) that suffering of animals should be minimized; and (b) that individual lives matter. He contends that even if individual animals suffer as a result of therapeutic hunting, such hunting is ethical. He thinks that hunts well-managed to cause less suffering than animals would experience in nature are currently more effective than nonlethal means of responding to overabundance. According to Varner, it isn't that individual lives do not matter, it is that some individuals will die in any event, and our only real choice lies in limiting those deaths to as few as possible by well-executed therapeutic hunts.

Some people find Varner's notion of therapeutic culling of animals to be concordant with their values, at least in theory. His perspective is shared by those who accept the argument that consistent kangaroo or deer hunting is necessary to avoid population peaks which result in intensive hunting that causes extreme suffering. Using lethal methods before large populations develop is thought to be humane and ethical because the goal of population stability is reached with fewer deaths overall. Varner's perspective is also shared by those who genuinely believe that death in nature results in more suffering for animals than death by hunting. One frequently hears that deaths caused by natural processes are far worse than those caused by a well-placed bullet or arrow.

Varner's view of therapeutic hunting is also espoused by those who think that their primary responsibility is to protect the particular animals for whom they advocate and that lethal methods are the best we can do under the circumstances; killing a few sea lions may be regrettable but necessary in order to protect fish. But, many disagree with this philosophy of "it is the best we can do in an imperfect world." This philosophy is not shared by those who hold firm to the belief that killing undermines efforts to find and address the real reasons for the cyclic, apparent need for more killing. It is also not shared by those who believe that violent methods should never be prioritized in any context, those who pay close attention to the role of humans in setting up the conditions whereby therapeutic hunting is perceived as necessary, and those who believe that ready acceptance of an ideology of "ethical killing" deters efforts to find good nonlethal solutions.

As we have seen, many of these controversies about therapeutic hunting are at work in consideration of lethal management of kangaroos, deer, and sea lions. All involve deciding which animals are expendable for the good of the species as a whole or for the good of other animals. But such decisions are not limited to animals we rarely see, such as kangaroos, deer, and sea lions. The prevalence of pest control services indicates that these decisions are made every day by people who have decided for one reason or another that a particular animal or animal population is a nuisance that must be controlled in the quickest possible manner. Sometimes the targeted animal is considered a pest because of preference for another animal, as when pest control services are hired to eliminate free-roaming cats with the goal of saving songbirds. Other times, an animal is identified as a pest because the animal species itself is despised or feared (for example, rats) or because the animal population has grown too large for the comfort and convenience of landowners in a particular area (for example, rabbits or squirrels).

Nonlethal methods usually exist. For example, rat populations can be humanely controlled by gradually excluding them from the places they nest and reducing their sources of food. A growing number of internet-based information sources are promoting nonlethal methods of rat and mouse control. One actually claims that we should use humane mouse population control methods because laboratory mice have contributed to advances in human health![50] However, if speedy reduction of the nuisance animal population is the primary value, killing as many individual members of that animal population as quickly as possible will be the preferred route. There are nonlethal rat traps that work as quickly as lethal rat traps, but they require the additional step of relocating the rats. Few people will bother with such methods if they have not experienced the stench of a decaying rat who crawled into an inaccessible area to die from consuming poison or who was left in a trap long after his or her death.

While one rarely hears complaints about the suffering of rats killed in whatever way is deemed most expedient by "rodent control" companies, one does occasionally hear complaints about such killing when other animal populations are involved, such as skunks, raccoons, possums, squirrels, or free-roaming cats. While the decision to reduce animal populations may not be challenged, the means by which animals are eliminated may receive scrutiny. A particular population of squirrels or peacocks or cats may be spared lethal management when enough neighbors intervene in live-trap and kill ("trap-and-kill") plans. Indeed, because nonlethal means are rarely considered when a decision is first made to limit a "nuisance" animal population, public complaint about lethal methods and insistence on nonlethal methods is usually necessary to stimulate the use of nonlethal methods.

An illustrative example is the public outcry that led to the use of contraception to control a squirrel population in Palisades Park in Santa Monica, California. According to news reports, Los Angeles County cited the City five times for having too many squirrels, which the County claims are aggressive and carry diseases.[51] In 2005 and 2006, Santa Monica attempted to poison the squirrels. Following protests, the City hired a pest control operator to trap-and-kill the squirrels with carbon dioxide. That method, too, was obstructed by protesters who, among other things, reportedly destroyed traps and stole trapping supplies from the operator's truck. Finally, Santa Monica decided to use a nonlethal method, an immuno-contraceptive proven safe for use in squirrels. A Santa Monica resident was quoted as saying, "only in a city like Santa Monica would you expect this behavior. Even our squirrels are living on the progressive edge."[52]

That resident is probably correct; most people do not appear to trouble themselves at all with the ethics of killing pest animals. Outside of specific locales, where certain animal species may be protected from lethal management by people who take a particular interest in them, most "pest" species have not yet garnered the kind of respect that would lead to the systematic use of nonlethal means of population control. Seldom do we actually know what happens to these animals. People are increasingly relying on "nuisance wildlife control" companies to eradicate wild animals such as opossums, skunks, raccoons, badgers, and weasels, in addition to smaller mammals such as rats, mice, moles, and gophers.[53] Kieran J. Lindsey, who has researched the size and regulatory environment of nuisance wildlife control companies, reports that "one need only look at the number of [nuisance wildlife control] businesses in the U.S. and the amount of sales revenue the industry generates to realize that removal of wild animals from established territories is happening on a very large scale."[54] The large scale of this activity suggests that, just as factory farms are interposed between consumers and animals to shield consumers from dealing with the reality and ethical considerations of their choice to eat animals, nuisance wildlife control companies are easily interposed between consumers and animals to shield consumers from dealing with the reality and ethical considerations inherent in their choice to eradicate animals they consider to be pests.

Lindsey reports that an increasing number of states regulate nuisance wildlife control companies with licensing requirements that include humane care and euthanasia provisions.[55] The number of states requiring specific humane treatment standards be met is still small, however. Only 4 states have such requirements, although as many as 25 states now mention humane treatment without establishing standards for what "humane" treatment is.[56] There has been an even larger increase in the number of states that require animals to be killed in accordance with American Veterinary Medical Association ("AVMA") standards. In 1997, only 3 states had such a requirement, but that number increased to 20 by 2007.[57]

Requiring an AVMA-approved method of euthanasia does not necessarily mean that an animal's suffering will be minimal. The AVMA states explicitly that its standards cannot always be followed in the field, that it prioritizes human safety concerns over minimizing animal suffering, and that killing wildlife creates exceptional challenges.[58] The AVMA's acknowledgement of such factors probably opens the door to the use of many otherwise unacceptable methods. Moreover, the AVMA can be criticized for continuing to approve many methods of killing animals that cause suffering, such as the use of gas for killing cats and dogs in shelters, the use of microwave irradiation for rats and mice, the bludgeoning of young pigs, and the use of carbon dioxide to kill birds (which causes them to die by suffocation).[59] That said, however, at least the AVMA does not approve some methods currently in use, such as burning animals alive, injecting them with acetone, strangling them, drowning them, and grinding animals in wood chippers (as was done to thousands of unwanted chickens in 2003).[60]

Lindsey's research reveals that most states do not yet have regulations that require for-profit nuisance wildlife control operators to provide humane treatment and euthanasia to nuisance wildlife. Moreover, property owners can kill nuisance wildlife without any regulatory oversight, and trappers that do not charge a fee for the service are also free from state regulation. Thus, most "nuisance wildlife" can be killed by any method the trapper finds most expedient, including drowning, stabbing, shooting, or starving animals in traps.

One might think that such methods would be prohibited by state anticruelty statutes, but state laws offer little, if any, protection. Forty-seven states explicitly state that statutes prohibiting cruel acts against animals do not apply to wildlife or "pest control" activities.[61] Even in the three states where anticruelty statutes do not explicitly exclude wildlife or pest control activities, it would be difficult to prosecute those who are causing great suffering to wild animals in accordance with common practices of "nuisance wildlife management."[62] Anticruelty statutes are designed to address individual acts of senseless harm to individual animals rather than to address common practices in businesses that kill animals for human benefit, including medical research, food production, and pest control.

Even if, as Lindsey's research indicates, more states are requiring licensing and humane treatment, the impetus behind such legislation may not necessarily be due solely to increasing respect for wildlife. For instance, recently proposed legislation in California was introduced primarily because of a desire to stop inhumane methods of nuisance wildlife population control but also because of constituents' complaints that their companion animals were disappearing after traps for skunks, raccoons, or other relatively large mammals had been used in the area.[63] Such concerns are reminiscent of the arguments made by respondents in *Audubon v. Davis* about the ease with which non-target animals are caught in steel-jawed leghold traps. Banning certain kinds of traps and regulating trappers may have as much, or more, to do with protecting companion animals as it does with protecting wildlife.

In reality, "pest" animals have few advocates. Since there are few legally required standards for how nuisance wildlife are killed, and few consumers ask for details about how "pest" animals are killed, "nuisance" wild animals are literally at the mercy of the operators who trap them. Only in isolated instances (such as the case of squirrels in Santa Monica) is there serious opposition to lethal methods of nuisance wildlife control and advocacy for nonlethal means of reducing particular populations of animals. For instance, egg replacement protocols have been developed to reduce populations of Canada geese humanely, immuno-contraceptives have been used for humane deer population control, and wary coexistence with coyotes is increasingly recommended as an alternative to killing them. Coexistence does not mean habituating wildlife to people. People living within known coyote ranges are advised, among other things, to keep garbage, fallen fruit, and rodent habitat from accumulating in their yards. Coyote behavior is explained, and ways of avoiding coyote contact are suggested.

This trend does not necessarily indicate increasing respect for wildlife, however. Squirrels, Canada geese, deer, and coyotes are difficult to manage by lethal means. For instance, coyotes' ranges are large, they are intelligent enough to avoid many traps, and they can live in a wide variety of environments. To some extent increasing use of nonlethal methods and suggested coexistence with wildlife may reflect only the realization that lethal methods do not actually eliminate very many animals in the long run.

There may also be changed circumstances that make lethal management impractical or impossible. George Reiger, Conservation Editor Emeritus for *Field and Stream*, bemoans the fact that it is illegal to discharge firearms in an increasing number of places where deer live in great numbers.[64] Reiger is not simply objecting to the loss of hunting opportunities; he believes that the inability to shoot deer and local residents' preferences for relatively expensive deer relocation and contraceptive methods leads to cost-ineffective use of limited conservation-dedicated funds. However, residents impacted by deer population increases may be factoring in costs of lethal management that Reiger excludes, namely, the lack of lasting results and the suffering of deer caused by inefficient lethal management programs those residents have witnessed in the past.

Reiger is not alone in lamenting what he considers to be irrational resistance to killing nuisance wildlife. The term "Bambi syndrome" was coined to refer to people whose resistance to killing deer lies in their attributing to deer the same thoughts and feelings that humans experience.[65] The claim of inappropriately anthropomorphizing animals has been used generally to demean those who protest the killing or exploitation of animals. But, not all protectors of deer—or other animals—are irrational or protest lethal population management methods because they believe that animals suffer the way humans do when they or their family members are shot. In fact, people may be concerned about the suffering that animals experience, even if the suffering of animals differs from that of humans. They may dislike violence as a general matter or be guided by a sense of the unfairness of killing animals to address population "excesses" created by human activity. These concerns could lead to the rational selection of nonlethal methods even when those methods exceed the financial cost of lethal methods.

B.   *Nonlethal Animal Population Management: The Case of Feral Cats*

All of these concerns—the suffering of animals, the violence of lethal methods, placing unfair blame on target animals for population problems caused by humans—are at play in controversies about lethal methods of controlling feral cats. Feral cats live in many different ecosystems all over the world where they are frequently blamed for decimating other animal species. They have been blamed, correctly or incorrectly, for more extinctions of native animals worldwide than any other single animal species (other than humans).[66] Accordingly, wherever feral cats live there are calls for their eradication by lethal methods. Nevertheless, strong resistance to those methods also exists. For that reason, they represent an interesting case study of issues related to the development of nonlethal methods of "nuisance wildlife" management. Unlike the sporadic and occasional use of nonlethal methods to control particular populations (such as the squirrel population in a particular park in a particular city), nonlethal feral cat colony management is being adopted in many places, at least in the United States. Moreover, the case of feral cat colony management involves many of the themes of this chapter: the extent to which animals are falsely pitted against each other, the degree of human responsibility for "overabundance," and the ease with which lethal methods are initiated.

Although the word "feral" is used variously, in this context "feral" refers to cats who share the same genotype as domestic cats but who are human-avoidant. Where feral cats are non-native to an area, they were most often introduced as domesticated cats, but, because cats were domesticated only relatively recently in human history, some cats revert to a wild or semi-wild state soon after escape or abandonment. Also, kittens born to completely tame cats can be feral if they do not receive sufficient socialization by humans within the first two months of life. Since cats can reproduce at young ages and can have multiple litters in a single year, it is easy for feral colonies to develop wherever there are domestic cats.

Individual cats may have greater or lesser ability to manage without human assistance, but feral cats in general can readily adapt to many environments. The Kerguelen Islands, located midway between Antarctica, Australia, and Africa have a harsh climate with rain and snow most days of the year, but cats have survived by living in rabbit or native sea bird burrows, by developing thick fur and layers of fat, and by eating many native species of animals, including ground-nesting sea birds and their eggs.[67] The Galapagos Islands offer a totally different environment where cats have survived in even the most arid regions by finding shelter in remnant lava folds and by eating many different species of native wildlife.[68]

Between these two extreme types of environments are many other environments in the world, rural and urban, where feral cats have adapted to local sources of food, water, and shelter. For instance, "tens of millions" of feral cats are reported to roam Australia, where "the National Parks and Wildlife Service claims that a wild cat can kill as many as 1000 animals and birds per year."[69] Feral cats have been blamed for the extinction or near extinction of 39 species of native Australian wildlife.[70] There are also places in the United States, such as the Florida Keys, where feral cats are said to further imperil already endangered species of wildlife.[71]

Feral cats are adaptable in large part because they can subsist on many different kinds of prey. Populations of native prey species are easily impacted because they have not evolved in response to feral cat predation pressure. Non-native predators like feral cats, who are efficient at killing and at reproduction, can wipe out native prey species before the process of natural selection results in protective adaptation. This can result in local extinction or near extinction of native prey animals, and it is one of the most potent rallying cries for the eradication of non-native feral cats.

Attempts to eradicate feral cats in the Galapagos Islands present a case in point. According to the Charles Darwin Research Station, feral cat populations developed from cats who entered the Islands originally on cargo ships or as the pets of settlers.[72] Because the Galapagos Islands are known throughout the world as a "hot spot" of biodiversity one might expect consensus on the desirability of prompt eradication of feral cats, who are blamed for threatening many native Galapagos species with extinction. That has not been the case, however. Feral cats on Baltra Island have been eradicated with lethal methods, but lethal programs have not been successful on the other Galapagos Islands of Isabela, San Cristobal, Santa Cruz, and Floreana, which are more heavily populated by humans than is Baltra Island. The Charles Darwin Research Station reports that "the perception of cats as pets rather than as ruthless killers makes it difficult to gain acceptance for the control of cats in Galapagos."[73]

Disputes about feral cats are no less controversial when feral cats are considered to be native species. Throughout the United States native feral and free-roaming cats are blamed for killing off native songbird populations. And, everywhere there is conflict between feral cats and other species—be they native, endangered, or simply preferred—lethal management programs are used to limit feral cat populations. The most common lethal method is trap-and-kill, although shooting and poisoning are also used. In theory, trap-and-kill programs should work. They did work on Baltra Island where the introduction of new cats could be controlled and few humans populate the Island. But Baltra Island is an exception, even among the Galapagos Islands. As a general matter, trap-and-kill eradication programs fail because it is too labor-intensive, expensive, and time-consuming to trap consistently enough to kill all individuals capable of reproducing. Moreover, as the Charles Darwin Research Station reports, sufficiently aggressive trapping is difficult where opposition to lethal methods is strenuous.

Opposition to lethal methods is always strenuous because free-roaming cats subject to trapping may be people's free-roaming companion cats and also because feral cats look like companion cats even when they are not. In 2005, when members of the Wisconsin Conservation Congress, a public advisory group, proposed to legalize the shooting of feral cats to protect songbirds, Governor Jim Doyle, among others, rejected the idea on grounds that Wisconsin should not "become known as a state where we shoot cats"[74] and opponents argued that such a move "sort of crosses the line from wildlife management to people's pets."[75]

In fact, in many cases where feral cats live near humans, it is difficult to draw the line between cats as "pets" and cats as "wildlife" because there is a spectrum of temperament and dependency on humans from free-roaming, totally tame pet cats to totally human-avoidant cats. Even when feral cats have the temperament of wild animals, their resemblance to pet cats results in people providing food and defending them vigorously when others seek to eradicate the cat population. Whenever lethal population management is proposed, cat defenders protest verbally or by sabotaging trap-and-kill programs. Some cat defenders feed cats so that they will not be tempted by traps, release trapped cats, or steal traps or disable traps. The programs become too expensive to continue, and, of course, they do not address the underlying reasons for cat population build-ups.

Trap-and-kill methods have been used for decades to little avail. Usually they are initiated when a feral cat colony has grown noticeably large. Trapping continues until enough cat detractors are sufficiently satisfied or cat defenders have created too many obstacles for trapping to continue. Cats who elude the traps continue to reproduce, and newcomer cats join them. The end result is another population build-up until the numbers get so high that there is a perceived need to take action as quickly as possible.

Consistently applied cat sterilization programs are the only known means of breaking free from the cycle of feral cat population peaks and valleys created by sporadic use of lethal methods. The theory of "trap-neuter-return" ("TNR") is that feral cat populations can be controlled by consistently sterilizing cats because colonies will naturally decline as individuals fall victim to accident, injury, disease, and predation as long as individuals who die are not replaced by newcomer cats. In most TNR situations, food, water, and shelter are provided by feral cat colony managers. This is not only for the sake of the sterilized cats; it is for the purpose of identifying and removing newcomer tame cats before they "go feral," thereby increasing the size of the colony.

In theory, the lethal method of trap-and-kill and the nonlethal method of trap-neuter-return should be equally effective in reducing a feral cat population. But, for either method to work there must be consistency, since cats reproduce at prodigious rates. Consistency is a function of two things: (a) community support sufficient to allow the program to proceed without hindrance, and (b) resources allocated to the program. Trap-and-kill methods generally provoke so much controversy that they cannot be applied consistently over time. By contrast, trap-neuter-return programs tend to provoke less controversy once they are implemented because the method does not involve killing cats. Traps are not usually sabotaged or stolen when they are used as part of a trap-neuter-return program, and it is easier to attract volunteers to assist with a nonlethal program. However, when it comes to the second requirement of consistency—resources allocated to the program—trap-neuter-return programs are severely disadvantaged as compared to trap-and-kill methods.

Both trap-and-kill and trap-neuter-return programs involve costs of trapping, but trap-and-kill programs involve the additional costs of killing while trap-neuter-return programs involve the additional costs of sterilization. At the moment, trap-and-kill programs receive considerable public funding in the form of taxpayer support of animal shelters where feral cats are taken to be killed.[76] The vast majority of cats who enter animal shelters are killed there, and a large percentage of the cats who enter shelters are free-roaming or feral.[77]

Trap-neuter-return programs are not comparably funded in the form of subsidies for sterilization, despite evidence that rates of killing cats at shelters drop in an apparent direct relationship to the availability of low-cost spay and neuter. For instance, New Jersey, home to one of the longest running subsidized spay/neuter programs, saw a 41% drop in shelter kills over the course of fifteen years.[78] New Hampshire achieved a 75% drop in euthanasia over the course of nine years.[79] Without financial assistance it is difficult for most feral cat colony managers to sterilize feral cats consistently enough to reduce colony sizes. Unlike pest control companies, feral cat colony managers are typically volunteers who do not receive payment for the work they do and the costs they incur, such as sterilization, to reduce feral cat populations. Therefore, before nonlethal programs can be fairly condemned as ineffective, there would have to be a trial of subsidized (nonlethal) trap-neuter-return programs to compare with the already observed results of consistently subsidized (lethal) trap-and-kill programs.

The controversial nature of trap-neuter-return methods is reflected in the law. Although Connecticut does have a statute that enables local governments to adopt ordinances requiring the registration of feral cat "keepers,"[80] most laws pertaining to feral cats are municipal ordinances because feral cat disputes are largely matters of local, rather than state, concern. Municipal laws reflect differing views on the best way to handle "nuisance" feral cats. For instance, in 2004, the City of Glendale, California, enacted ordinances analogous to those allowed under Connecticut state law for the registration and regulation of feral cat colonies.[81] Two years prior, the City of Akron, Ohio went in the opposite direction. In 2002, the City of Akron enacted ordinances that created a new criminal offense for permitting a cat to "run at large" and allow animal control agents to seize and immediately euthanize cats who are difficult to handle.[82] Most trapped cats are fractious, so the authority to immediately euthanize them could result in the deaths of many tame as well as feral cats. The ordinances also allow animal control to issue traps to individuals who want to trap cats they consider nuisances. Although there are rules for the humane trapping of cats, there is no way of enforcing those rules.

In 2003, cat owners filed suit against the City, alleging deprivation of rights associated with the seizure and killing of their cats, but the trial and appellate courts held that the ordinances only minimally interfered with cat owners' rights.[83] The court explicitly held that the damage cats can cause to property, such as spraying on windows or defecating in flower beds, is a sufficiently rational basis for the City to enact ordinances that would allow for immediate euthanasia of fractious free-roaming cats.[84] In other words, the court decided that it is within the authority of the City to decide that those cats' lives are worth less than the cost of cleaning a window.

A third approach to feral cat disputes is illustrated by an ordinance enacted in West Hollywood, California, in 1997. Instead of establishing rules that support trap-neuter-return (as did the City of Glendale) or rules that support trap-and-kill (as did the City of Akron), West Hollywood established a procedure whereby all interested parties can propose strategies for resolving a dispute about a particular population of feral cats.[85] If a complaint about feral cats is filed with the City Manager and the complaint is not found to be frivolous, the City Manager is directed to call a public hearing at which evidence and proposed solutions can be offered. Following that public hearing the City Manager can order conditions specific to the management of the particular feral cat colony in return for allowing the colony to remain in place. On the other hand, the dispute could end in the cats' being trapped and removed, although the ordinance does provide that the cats be relocated rather than killed if at all possible.

Feral cat population management controversies exemplify several themes of this chapter. The most typical presentation of a controversy is the pitting of birds' interests against cats' interests. Bird defenders argue that birds must live outside but that cats need not live outside. Cat defenders respond that truly feral cats must live outside, too, and that other causes account for most of the decline in songbird populations. They also argue that humans' role in cat abandonment means that humans owe cats the least destructive means of resolving problems that arise from large feral cat populations.

Bird defenders can show that cats can kill birds, but they cannot show that such kills are the primary cause of bird population decline. Nevertheless, just as sea lions are killed regardless of how small an impact they have on declining fish populations, bird defenders argue that cats should be killed regardless of how small a role they may play in the decline of songbird populations. In their view, any method that leaves a cat alive with the potential to eat a bird is not an effective method. Bird defenders agree that humans are to blame for putting cats outside, but, ultimately, their interest lies in the fastest means by which songbird population decline can be arrested. Despite lack of evidence that lethal methods actually produce faster or more efficient results than nonlethal methods, bird defenders continue to promote lethal methods because it seems intuitively correct that killing cats is the most efficient means of solving problems attributed to cats. After all, it is standard procedure to kill "pest" animals.

Some bird defenders backstop their arguments with claims that lethal management is a kindness to feral cats for the same reason that lethal management of other targeted wild animals is sometimes claimed to be good for those animals: deaths in nature are portrayed as causing more suffering than deaths by well-executed hunting or trap-and-kill programs. At least one major animal protection organization agrees with that perspective when it comes to feral cats. People for the Ethical Treatment of Animals ("PETA") has taken the position that "having witnessed firsthand the gruesome things that can happen to feral cats and to the animals they prey on, PETA cannot in good conscience oppose euthanasia as a humane alternative to dealing with cat overpopulation."[86] Once one adopts the position that lethal population control is ethical, it becomes easier to find "necessity" to kill, and the focus shifts from *whether* there is a need to kill to *how* to kill humanely. If inhumane methods of killing, such as drowning cats in traps or injecting trapped cats with acetone, could be outlawed and requirements of humane methods, such as relatively painless injections of sedative and euthanizing agents, could be enforced, human-induced deaths *might* be more quick and less painful than some, but not all, natural deaths. But even if all human-induced deaths involved less suffering than natural deaths, the fact of taking a healthy animal's life would remain troubling.

A premise of the argument that humane human-caused death of a currently healthy animal is preferable to "letting nature takes its course" is that some lives are not worth living because of the high risk of suffering those individuals will have to endure in nature if they are allowed to live out their lives. Because animals are so vulnerable to humans, the potential is great for humans to act out on animals beliefs about whether their *own* human lives are worth living and about whether, from a human's perspective, *animals'* lives are worth living. Animals might well make different judgments about the value of life, pain and suffering notwithstanding. Surely animals would prefer that humans reduce the human-caused suffering animals endure rather than kill animals to prevent suffering.

From the perspective of people who care deeply about double standards for different kinds of animals, it is troubling to recommend humane killing of healthy feral cats when their lives may not be substantially different from the lives of other wildlife, such as raccoons, possums, and squirrels. Would PETA recommend the wholesale euthanasia of such creatures because of the difficulties and suffering they will experience in the future? Perhaps. But, it is also possible that feral cats are seen as different from those other species of wildlife because many feral cats in the United States are dependent on human sources of food in ways that those other species are not. The image is not one of self-sufficient cats on Kerguelen Island; the image is one of urban feral cats waiting for human caretakers to arrive at a feeding site. The position that healthy feral cats are better off humanely killed may reflect a judgment about the likelihood that human caretakers will betray feral cats dependent on them for food, water, and shelter. In other words, this position may be a statement about the nature of humans rather than a statement about the nature of wildlife.

There is another way in which the recommendation of humane killing as good for healthy feral cats troubles those who care about double standards. To some, it is as wrong to kill wild animals whose prospects for experiencing pain and suffering are great as it is to kill people who, by reason of poverty or illness or temperament or homelessness, are likely to experience much more pain and suffering than other people. The ideal for humans is to reduce the potential for suffering and to accept the suffering we cannot prevent, rather than to use the potential for future suffering as justification for a speedy and early death. Why should that not be the ideal for animals as well?

CONCLUSION

This chapter explored two related issues masked by legal argumentation about federal preemption in the case of *Viva! v. Adidas*: other-animal impacts as a result of advocacy and as justification for lethal management of animal populations. Those matters are not unique to the situation of kangaroos and advocacy on their behalf. Rather, similar themes emerge when one considers the rationales for lethal management of species as diverse as kangaroos, sea lions, deer, and cats. A common feature is that lethal management is often undertaken in the name of other animal species. Kangaroos and deer are blamed for the destruction of habitat used by other species; cats kill songbirds and sea lions eat fish. Another common feature is the ease with which lethal methods are used. These two aspects come together when lethal methods are praised as the fastest and most effective means by which some animals can be protected from other animals. Yet, lethal methods are rarely effective for any period of time because they do not address underlying problems.

Nonlethal methods are usually available, but they are slow to gain traction when animals are not generally valued. We kill readily, especially when individual animal lives are not valued. Typically, we stop to consider nonlethal methods only when forced to do so and only in a few situations. One such situation arises when two animal species are similarly protected by law, such as sea lions and endangered fish. Another occurs when two species are similarly valued but by different members of society, such as cats and songbirds. Yet another situation is that of particular local populations of animals for whom there is a vociferous protective group of humans willing to champion their cause, such as the squirrels in Santa Monica. But, as the pest control operator pointed out in the Santa Monica case, "I understand squirrels are cute, 'Ayres [said]', but if they were rats or cockroaches, would they get the same treatment?"[87]

Ayres' question implies another: why *shouldn't* rats or cockroaches receive the same treatment? One set of answers to that question lies in understanding the value of life to those animals and respect for life generally. Another set of answers to that question lies in the fact that protecting *all* animals from killing lies in breaking the conceptual linkage between the lowliest of them all ("pests") and killing as a "natural" way of dealing with them. Rats and cockroaches are emblematic "pests," and, as such, they give content to the term "pest." Indeed, because of low regard for those animals "pest" and "lethal management" are conceptually tightly bound. Kangaroos, deer, and cats are not generally considered to be pests, but once kangaroos, deer, or cats are designated as "pests," they become "rats." They become candidates for eradication, without consideration of nonlethal methods, because the categories of "pest" and "lethal methods" are coterminous. Only the most strenuous advocacy can forestall the use of lethal methods once animals are deemed to be pests. Thus, it is extremely important to break the close conceptual linkage of "pest" and "lethal methodology" by shifting how we deal with even the most unpopular of animals.

* Professor of Law, UCLA School of Law. The author thanks David Cassuto for his comments on a draft of the manuscript and Matthew Moore and Inna Stepanenko for their research assistance. Special thanks to Vicki Steiner for her thoughtful comments on several drafts in addition to her meticulous supervision of various aspects of the research and final production of this chapter. The research for this chapter was funded by Mr. Bob Barker's generous endowment of UCLA Law School for teaching and scholarship dedicated to animal protection law.

1. Ondine Sherman, *Introduction* to KANGAROOS: MYTHS AND REALITIES 7, 7 (Maryland Wilson & David B. Croft eds., Austl. Wildlife Prot. Council Inc. 2005) (1992).

2. 36 Cal. Rptr. 3d 19 (Cal. Ct. App. 2005), *rev'd*, 162 P.3d 569 (Cal. 2007).

3. CAL. PENAL CODE § 653o (West Supp. 2007). After the California Supreme Court issued its decision in *Viva! v. Adidas*, the California Legislature passed, and California Governor Arnold Schwarzenegger signed into law, a bill that amended Penal Code section 653o to make sales of kangaroo parts and products legal. *See* S. B. 880, 2007–2008 Reg. Sess. (Cal. 2007).

4. Brief of Defendants–Respondents at 6, Viva! Int'l Voice for Animals v. Adidas Promotional Retail Operations, Inc., 36 Cal. Rptr. 3d 19 (Cal. Ct. App. 2005) (No. S140064).

5. 16 U.S.C. § 1535(f) (2000).

6. *Id.*

7. Although Viva! won as to the matter of federal preemption, the lawsuit was rendered moot by the fact that California's Legislature and Governor enacted Adidas-sponsored legislation to amend Penal Code section 653*o* to legalize the sale of kangaroo products in California. *See supra* note 3.

8. Amicus Curiae Brief of the Gov't of the Commonwealth of Austl. at 24, Viva! Int'l Voice for Animals v. Adidas Promotional Retail Operations, Inc., 162 P.3d 569 (Cal. 2007) (No. S140064).

9. *Id.* at 19.

10. David Nicholls, *Kangaroos Falsely Maligned by Tradition, in* KANGAROOS *supra* note 1, at 33, 38.

11. Amicus Curiae Brief of the Gov't of the Commonwealth of Austl., *supra* note 8, at 20 n. 7.

12. *See* U.S. CENSUS BUREAU, LEATHER AND HIDE TANNING AND FISHING: 2002 (Jan. 2005), *available at* http://www.census.gov/prod/ec02/ec0231i316110.pdf; Bureau of Economic Analysis, Gross–Domestic–Product-by-Industry Accounts (Apr. 24, 2007), http://www.bea.gov/industry/gpotables/default.cfm (click "Value Added by Industry"); TradeStats Express— National Trade Data, 2006 Imports of HS 4101, Raw Hides and Skins of Bovine or Equine Animals (2006), http://tse.export.gov/NTDHome.aspx (click "Global Patterns of U.S. Merchandise Trade," in "Product" field, change "Exports" to "Imports," change "Item" to "Raw Hides and Skins of Bovine or Equine Animals," click "Update," click "Go").

13. Nicholls, *supra* note 10, at 38.

14. 307 F.3d 835, 842 (9th Cir. 2002).

15. CAL. FISH & GAME CODE § 3003.1(c) (West Supp. 2007).

16. *Nat'l Audubon*, 307 F.3d at 842.

17. *Id.* at 844.

18. 16 U.S.C. § 1362(6) (2000).

19. *Id.* § 1532.

20. John Ritter, *Sea Lions Show Salmon What it Really Means to be Endangered*, USA TODAY, Apr. 17, 2007, at 11A.

21. *Id.*

22. Press Release, Humane Society of the United States, The Humane Society of the United States Opposes Bill to Kill Sea Lions (Apr. 5, 2007), *available at* http://www.hsus.org/press_and_publications/press_releases/oppose_bill_kill_sea_lions.html.

23. *Id.*

24. Mem. Op. at 9, Humane Soc'y of the U.S. v. U.S. Dep't of Commerce, No. 96–0623 (filed Apr. 12, 1999) (complaint filed Mar. 28, 1996).

25. *Id.*

26. *Id.* at 11.

27. *Id.* at 9.

28. Press Release, National Oceanic and Atmospheric Administration, NOAA 99–R128, Steelhead Eating Sea Lions All But Gone from Seattle's Ballard Locks (May 26, 1999), *available at* http://www.public affairs.noaa.gov/releases99/may99/noaa99r128.html.

29. *Id.*

30. *Id.*

31. *Id.*

32. 128 Cal. Rptr. 3d 531 (Cal. Ct. App. 1976).

33. *Id.* at 539 (quoting with approval from Palladio, Inc. v. Diamond, 321 F. Supp. 630, 631 (1970), *aff'd* 440 F.2d 1319 (2d Cir. 1971)).

34. Franck Courchamp et al., *Mammal Invaders on Islands: Impact, Control and Control Impact*, 78 BIOLOGICAL REVS. 347, 367 (2003).

35. Franck Courchamp et al., *Control of Rabbits to Protect Island Birds From Cat Predation*, 89 BIOLOGICAL CONSERVATION 219 (1999).

36. Nicholls, *supra* note 10, at 33.

37. NATHAN J. WINOGRAD, REDEMPTION: THE MYTH OF PET OVERPOPULATION AND THE NO KILL REVOLUTION IN AMERICA 78 (2007); *see also* Maryann Mott, *U.S. Faces Growing Feral Cat Problem*, NAT'L GEOGRAPHIC NEWS, Sept. 7, 2004, http://news.nationalgeographic.com/news/2004/51f09/0907_040907_feralcats.html.

38. Alison Williams, *Number of Birds in State Declining: Study Shows That Several California Species Have Declined by 75% to 96%*, L.A. TIMES, June 15, 2007, at B1.

39. Susan Roney Drennan, *Cats*, 3 NAT'L AUDUBON SOC'Y (Mar. 1998), http://www.audubon.org/local/cn/98march/cats.html.

40. Gary E. Varner, *Can Animal Rights Activists be Environmentalists?*, *in* ENVIRONMENTAL PHILOSOPHY & ENVIRONMENTAL ACTIVISM 169 (Donald Marietta & Lester Embree eds., 1995).

41. RICHARD D. RYDER, ANIMAL REVOLUTION: CHANGING ATTITUDES TOWARDS SPECIESISM (2000).

42. Press Release, Vermont Fish and Wildlife Department, Deer Hunting Results Are on Track (Dec. 1, 2005), *available at* http://www.vtfishandwildlife.com/Detail.CFM?Agency_ID=932.

43. Daniel Ramp, *Is Control of Kangaroo Populations Really Necessary?*, *in* KANGAROOS *supra* note 1, at 208, 212.

44. Juliet Gellatley, *Killing for Kicks*, *in* KANGAROOS *supra* note 1, at 50, 54.

45. John Auty, *Red Plague Grey Plague: The Kangaroo Myths and Legends*, *in* KANGAROOS *supra* note 1, at 56–62.

46. National Kangaroo Protection Coalition, Facts About the Kangaroo Industry, http://www.kangaroo-protection-coalition.com/kangaroo-facts.html (last visited June 27, 2007).

47. Assemb. Water, Parks & Wildlife Comm. Bill Analysis, Assemb. B. 734, 2005–2006 Reg. Sess. (Cal. Feb. 17, 2005), *available at* http://info.sen.ca.gov/pub/05–06/bill/asm/ab_0701–0750/ab_734_cfa_20050422_144526_asm_comm.html.

48. Ramp, *supra* note 43, at 208, 210.

49. *Id.*

50. IPM of Alaska, The Problem: House Mice (2007), http://www.ipmofalaska.com/files/housemouse.html.

51. Francisco Vara–Orta, *For Squirrels Gone Wild, City Plans a Turnoff*, L.A. TIMES, Mar. 06, 2007, at A2.

52. *Id.*

53. Kieran J. Lindsey, Privatization and Regulatory Oversight of Commercial Nuisance Wildlife Control in the United States (Aug. 2007) (unpublished Ph.D. dissertation, Texas A & M Univ., on file with author).

54. *Id.* at 66.

55. Despite overwhelming support by the Legislature, Governeror Schwarzenegger vetoed both A.B. 1477 and A.B. 449 in October 2007. Governor Arnold Scwarzenegger, Veto Message for A.B. 1477 (Oct. 10, 2007), *available at* http://www.leginfo.ca.gov/pub/07–08/bill/asm/ab_1451–1500/ab_1477_vt_20071010.html. Governor Arnold Schwarzenegger, Veto Message for A.B. 449 (Oct. 13, 2007), *available at* http://www.leginfo.ca.gov/pub/07–08/bill/asm/ab_0401–0450/ab_449_vt_20071013.html.

56. Lindsey, *supra* note 53, at 49.

57. *Id.* at 44.

58. *2000 Report of the AVMA Panel on Euthanasia*, 218 J. AM. VETERINARY MED. ASS'N 669, 682 (2001).

59. *Id.* at 677–83.

60. Elizabeth Fitzsimons, *No Cruelty Charges in Chicken Killings*, SIGNONSANDIEGO. COM, Apr. 11, 2003, http://www.signonsandiego.com/news/northcounty/20030411–9999_1mi11chip.html.

61. Pamela D. Frasch et al., *State Animal Anti–Cruelty Statutes: An Overview*, 5 ANIMAL L. 69, 79 (1999).

62. In those states that do not provide exemptions, the courts write them in according to the principles of statutory interpretation. *See* Darian M. Ibrahim, *The Anticruelty Statute: A Study in Animal Welfare*, 1 J. ANIMAL L. & ETHICS 175, 193 (2006).

63. Assemb. B. 1477, 2007–2008 Reg. Sess. (Cal. 2007) (requiring nuisance wildlife control operators to inform consumers of nonlethal methods before relying on lethal methods); Assemb. B. 449, 2007–08 Reg. Sess. (Cal. 2007) (requiring the use of AVMA procedures when lethal methods are used and certification of nuisance wildlife operators in humane and nonlethal methods as a condition of licensure); Assemb. Water, Parks & Wildlife Comm. Bill Analysis, Assemb. B. 449, 2007–2008 Reg. Sess. (Cal. Apr. 23, 2007), *available at* http://www.leginfo.ca.gov/pub/07–08/bill/asm/ab_0401–0450/ab_449_cfa_20070423_111603_asm_comm.html.

64. George Reiger, *Wishful Wildlife Management*, 99 FIELD & STREAM 12 (1994).

65. Matt Cartmill, *The Bambi Syndrome*, 102 NAT. HIST. 6 (1993).

66. Drennan, *supra* note 39.

67. Franck Courchamp & George Sugihara, *Modeling the Biological Control of an Alien Predator to Protect Island Species from Extinction*, 9 ECOLOGICAL APPLICATIONS 112, 112 (1999).

68. Charles Darwin Foundation for the Galapagos Islands, Charles Darwin Research Station Fact Sheet: The Impact of Cats on Galapagos (2006), *available at* http://www.darwinfoundation.org/files/species/pdf/cats-en.pdf.

69. MICHAEL P. MOULTON & JAMES SANDERSON, *Examples of Wildlife Issues*, in WILDLIFE ISSUES IN A CHANGING WORLD 69, 98 (2d ed. 1999).

70. *Id.*

71. Charles A. Drost & Gary M. Fellers, *Non-Native Animals on Public Lands*, in OUR LIVING RESOURCES 440 (Edward T. LaRoe et al. eds, U.S. Dep't of the Interior 1995).

72. Auty, *supra* note 45.

73. CHARLES DARWIN FOUNDATION FOR THE GALAPAGOS ISLANDS, *supra* note 68.

74. Ryan J. Foley, *Cat-Kill Bill 'Not Going Anywhere'*, CBS NEWS, Apr. 13, 2005, http://www.cbsnews.com/stories/2005/04/13/national/printable687961.shtml.

75. Dean Schabner, *Wisconsin Voters Back Plan to Hunt Cats*, ABC NEWS, Apr. 12, 2005, http://abcnews.go.com/print?id=662272.

76. WINOGRAD, *supra* note 37, at 1–2.

77. Kris Rerecich, *Advocating for Feral Cats*, 6 FERAL CAT ACTIVIST 1, 5 (May 2007), *available at* http://www.alleycat.org/pdf/fca_spring07.pdf.

78. Gregory Farrar & Cynthia Farrar, Escambia County Pet Overpopulation Report: Prevention and Initiative (2006), *available at* http://www.jury-duty.org/files/Escambia_County_Assessment.doc.index.cfm/fuseaction/main.assessments/index.cfm.

79. *Id.*

80. CONN. GEN. STAT. ANN. § 22–339d(a) (West 2007).

81. GLENDALE, CAL., MUN. CODE §§ 6.03.010, 6.03.020, 6.03.030, 6.04.130B (2004).

82. AKRON, OHIO, CITY CODE §§ 92.01, 92.13, 92.15 (2002) (amended by Ordinance Nos. 132–2002, 332–2002).

83. City of Akron *ex rel.* Christman–Resch v. City of Akron, 825 N.E.2d 189 (Ohio Ct. App. 2005).

84. *Id.* at 196–97.

85. WEST HOLLYWOOD, CAL., MUN. CODE § 9.48.070 (1997).

86. PETA Media Center, Trap, Neuter, Return, and Monitor Programs for Feral Cats: Doing it Right, http://www.peta.org/mc/factsheet_display.asp?ID=120 (last visited June 27, 2007).

87. David Page, *Damn Cute Menace*, L.A. TIMES, June 3, 2007, West Mag., at 20.

*